IMPROVISING
SABOR

Cuban Dance Music in New York

SUE MILLER

UNIVERSITY PRESS OF MISSISSIPPI /JACKSON

The University Press of Mississippi is the scholarly publishing agency of
the Mississippi Institutions of Higher Learning: Alcorn State University,
Delta State University, Jackson State University, Mississippi State University,
Mississippi University for Women, Mississippi Valley State University,
University of Mississippi, and University of Southern Mississippi.

www.upress.state.ms.us

The University Press of Mississippi is a member
of the Association of University Presses.

Copyright © 2021 by University Press of Mississippi
All rights reserved

First printing 2021
∞

Library of Congress Control Number: 2020947852
Hardback: 978-1-4968-3215-3
Trade paperback: 978-1-4968-3216-0
E-pub single: 978-1-4968-3217-7
E-pub institutional: 978-1-4968-3218-4
PDF single: 978-1-4968-3219-1
PDF institutional: 978-1-4968-3220-7

British Library Cataloging-in-Publication Data available

CONTENTS

Notes and Abbreviations IX
Foreword by Professor David Garcia XI
Preface XIII
Acknowledgments XIX
Introduction 3

1 Spaces and Places 27

2 *Los Tres Grandes*: Redefining the Mambo Genre 54

3 *La Mecha*: Belisario López, José Fajardo, and Rolando Lozano 77

4 Exile and Adaptation: Eddy Zervigón and Orquesta Broadway 91

5 Charanga or Pachanga? 125

6 Charanga *Embalao*: Charlie Palmieri and Johnny Pacheco 144

7 *Charangueaʼo en Típico*: Eddie Palmieri's La Perfecta 169

8 "I Don't Like It Like That": The Latin *Bugalú* 189

9 La Charanga Moderna and the Modern Charanga 207

Conclusion: Defining New York *Sabor* 221

Glossary 233
Notes 246
Bibliography 269
Discography 281
Index 292

This book is dedicated to Eddy Zervigón, charanga flute player and bandleader of Orquesta Broadway since 1962.

Eddy Zervigón, Manhattan Bridge, June 16, 2018. Copyright Sue Miller.

NOTES AND ABBREVIATIONS

All scores of annotated transcriptions within the text are those of the author. All translations from Spanish to English are by the author. Explanations of Cuban and Latin terms are to be found within the text and/or in the glossary at the end. To avoid confusion with Western art orchestras, the charanga orchestra or band will, in the main, be referred to as *charanga orquesta*. When citing interviews, the initials of the interviewee and interviewer are used. For example:

SM   Sue Miller
EZ   Eddy Zervigón
MW   Mark Weinstein
WR   Willie Rodríguez
DP   David Pérez
CG   Connie Grossman
KJ   Karen Joseph

A full list of all recordings cited and analyzed in the book is given in the discography. An accompanying set of recordings by Charanga del Norte of repertoire analyzed is available on the websites www.charangadelnorte.co.uk and www.charangasue.com.

FOREWORD

Besides being colleagues in the academic study of music, Sue Miller and I direct charanga groups—hers in Leeds, Yorkshire, mine in North Carolina. Surely we came to devote our musical activities to leading charangas because of its fascinating mix of European-derived and Afro-Cuban instruments and performance aesthetics. Or did we want to distinguish our ensembles from the much more familiar—in both academic and popular dance music worlds—salsa and Latin jazz repertories? In any event, Dr. Miller's specialization in charanga music, performance aesthetics, and history transcends her work with Charanga del Norte, and after many years of research, writing, and publishing, she offers her second book on charanga music, this one focused on the music's transplanted history in New York City. Indeed, Miller is the first academic to publish research on charanga music of both Cuba and the United States. As a student of Richard Egües and with Eddy Zervigón as her primary collaborator, Miller's *Improvising Sabor: Cuban Dance Music in New York* provides much-needed musicological insight into the important place charanga musicians, music, and performance aesthetics have in the history of Latin music in the United States. Whereas many US-based academics—whether in social and cultural studies or history and ethnomusicology—have researched the historical and performance aesthetic significances of big band mambo and salsa music, Miller stands alone in the musicological and ethnomusicological scholarship on charanga.

At the crux of the matter of charanga performance aesthetics are the concepts *sabor* and *cubanía*, into which Miller dives with the combined sensibilities of musician and academic in order to unravel the nuanced complexities of these concepts and make them legible for novices and experts alike. In other words, she is masterful in analyzing the aural literacy codified by generations of Cuban musicians—dating to those of the *orquesta típicas* of the nineteenth century—and at translating this knowledge from the aural to the written language. Indeed, Miller writes against the conventional understanding of New York salsa dura's debt to Cuban conjunto and jazz music by revealing salsa dura's equally important debt to charanga's distinct improvisational dialects of *sabor* and *cubanía*.

The following pages demonstrate an expert interlacing of historical documentation, ethnographic exploration, and musical analysis that brings the past of charanga music performance throughout Manhattan and the Bronx into the combined present of its performance today. Miller begins our journey with New York charanga's first generation of Cuban flautists Rolando Lozano, José Fajardo, and Belisario López, who transplanted the music to the dancehalls and clubs of New York in the 1950s. The journey continues with more New York–based charanga flautists, beginning with Eddy Zervigón and eventually non-Cuban charanga flautists and bandleaders Charlie Palmieri, Johnny Pacheco, Eddie Palmieri, Dave Valentín, and Ray Barretto. Miller's annotated transcriptions are exceptional in their detail and clarity, as are her reproductions of Zervigón's equally insightful graphs of fingerings on the Cuban wooden flute. In a word, these graphs are gold! I'm also intrigued by Miller's explanation of the significance of the charanga aesthetic in the performance practices of New York–based percussionists such as timbalero Manny Oquendo, as well as her discussion of lesser-known but equally important charanga musicians Rod Lewis Sánchez, George Castro, and José Canoura.

As a fan and student of charanga music and history, I am thrilled with the publication of Miller's second volume for all of these reasons. I suppose a foreword would not be complete, however, without mentioning some unanswered questions such as the heavily male-dominated presence of charanga musicians, flautists in particular, which Miller dutifully mentions in the conclusion. It is only within the last several decades that women musicians such as Andrea Brachfeld, Connie Grossman, Karen Joseph, and Sue Miller herself have emerged as important contributors to the music in the United States and the United Kingdom. Why? And who are the women charanga musicians of the past and present in Cuba? Perhaps a third volume will follow. Until then, *Improvising Sabor: Cuban Dance Music in New York* is a must-read for all students, musicians, dancers, and fans of Latin music performance and history. Indeed, it will be required reading for my charanga students for the foreseeable future. ¡Gracias, Sue, por *su trabajo y erudición*!

—David F. Garcia, professor of music
University of North Carolina at Chapel Hill

PREFACE

EL MAMONCILLO

In the preface to *Cuban Flute Style: Interpretation and Improvisation*,[1] I document how I discovered charanga music in the Casa Latina nightclub in Leeds, England, in the late 1990s. Named after the famous East Harlem record shop (see figure P.2), Casa Latina was started by the DJs Lubomir "Lubi" Jovanovic and Chris "Chico Malo" Murphy, both fanatical salsa aficionados who regularly played the music of Eddie Palmieri, Mongo Santamaría, Ray Barretto, and the Fania All Stars in their DJ sets. Live Cuban music and salsa bands from the UK, USA, and Cuba featured regularly every Thursday night. In addition to UK salsa bands, Cuban bands such as Son 14, Maraca Valle y Otra Vision, and Sierra Maestra performed at the Casa Latina following the success of *Buena Vista Social Club* in 1999. Although fewer US bands performed there at this time, Eddie Palmieri's band was booked in 1999 for the Casa Latina Summer Ball in the larger venue of the Town and Country Club situated above the Underground Club (which hosted the Casa Latina nights).[2]

Figure P.1 Sue Miller and Eddy Zervigón at El Mamoncillo Festival, New Jersey, July 15, 2007. Copyright Sue Miller.

Figure P.2 The New York Casa Latina. Copyright Sue Miller.

Inspired by the music I heard at the club, I set up my group Charanga del Norte in 1998, and made arrangements of both Cuba-based and US-based charanga, including the Mongo Santamaría songs "Olga Pachanga"[3] and "Que Maravilloso"[4] and Ray Barretto's "Esa Es La del Solar" ("Bilongo").[5] At this time Charanga del Norte's debut single "Violin Pachanguero" featured on a salsa compilation *Everybody Salsa*.[6] This captured the interest of DJ Al Angeloro, the manager of New York–based Charanga Soleil, and he subsequently interviewed me live by telephone for his show on WBAI in 1999.[7] The very early days of my group reflected this balance between Cuba- and US-based charanga music. As I researched Cuban charanga more, however, I gravitated toward the Cuban charangas of the 1950s, studying with Richard Egües in 2000 and 2001, as documented in my doctoral practice research (2010) and book *Cuban Flute Style* (2014).[8] At this time I mainly studied the improvisations of Richard Egües, José Fajardo, and other veteran Cuban players such as Melquiades Fundora from Orquesta Sublime. My interest in US-based charanga was reignited in 2006 when I received a phone call out of the blue from Eddy Zervigón inviting me to New York to play with his Orquesta Broadway at the Mamoncillo Festival in New York.[9] He had watched me perform with my own band Charanga del Norte and with charanga orquestas in Havana on YouTube videos; he was intrigued by the fact that I played traditional charanga flute despite being a "non-Latino" from the UK. We subsequently spoke regularly by phone and corresponded via email about the charanga flute style, sharing our enthusiasm for the virtuosic soloing styles of Richard Egües and José Fajardo. As I had studied with Richard Egües in Havana, much of our conversation focused on Richard and his family. It turned out that in his teenage years Eddy knew Richard's children Ricardito, Gladys, and Rembert and had often heard Richard Egües practicing his flute when he was at their family home studying music (solfège) with Richard's father Eduardo Egües, a renowned music educator in the province of Las Villas.[10] Zervigón later became a colleague and friend of José Fajardo in New York. It was a unique opportunity to link up to charanga flute history on either side of the 1959 Cuban Revolution divide, and without hesitation I accepted Eddy's invitation to perform as a guest with Orquesta Broadway.

Armed with a photograph of Eddy from a 1970s newspaper article that he sent so that I would recognize him, I arrived at JFK airport in July 2007, flute in hand and a little nervous about performing with one of North America's most accomplished charanga orquestas. I need not have worried. Eddy and his wife Nancy met me at the airport and, along with their dog Snoopy, made me feel right at home in their house in the quiet suburb of Maspeth in Queens. Chatting to Eddy about how he left Cuba in 1962 and how Orquesta Broadway was formed, my fascination with US-based Cuban charanga was rekindled. Eddy showed me Belisario López's five-key flute that was gifted to him, and holding it I felt instantly connected to this wonderful Cuban tradition brought over from Havana to New York by the likes of López and Fajardo in the early sixties.[11] Of course Cuban music had been a feature of New York's music scene long before their arrival—Cuban classical flute player Alberto Socarrás arrived in New York in 1927 and is said to have recorded the first jazz flute solo in 1929, for example;[12] and the 1950s *mambo* bands of Tito Puente, Machito, and Tito Rodríguez, among others, utilized the charanga flute from time to time, particularly with the popularity of the *chachachá* in the mid-1950s.[13] Cuban musician Gilberto Valdés set up the first charanga orquesta in New York in 1952 and players from this seminal group (such as Mongo Santamaría and Johnny Pacheco) went on to perform in and direct charangas of their own.[14]

The first chapters of this book delve into the history of Cuban music in New York from the *rhumba* bands of the 1930s and '40s to the 1950s *mambo* bands, *conjuntos*, and *charangas* of the Palladium era. After the 1959 Cuban Revolution, more Cuban musicians came to Miami and New York; but as Christina Abreu's research on Cuban musicians in New York and Miami (between 1940 and 1960) has shown, it is important to challenge the

Figure P.3 Poster for the 2007 Mamoncillo Festival in New Jersey. Author's copy. Public domain.

"exile model" and acknowledge the influence of earlier Cuban migrations on musical developments. Abreu also notes that it is important to critique assumptions made regarding the relationship between population size and musical influence when analyzing Cuban and Puerto Rican musical cultures.[15] Individual musicians can be highly influential, causing sparks of interest and scene-specific creativity; the relationship between musicians, their local cultures, and their audiences are complex, and lines of influence follow a variety of tributaries within this transnational performance

Figure P.4 Eddy Zervigón, Manhattan Bridge, New York, June 16, 2016. Copyright Sue Miller.

tradition. Following the mambo's popularity, the chachachá was on the wane toward the end of the 1950s but was rejuvenated by visiting charangas such as Fajardo y sus Estrellas and Orquesta Aragón, and then by the new wave of immigration in the early sixties. Charanga orquestas became popular at this time, performing in the Palladium on Broadway and at other Latin music venues in New York such as the Caborrojeño, Casa Blanca, the Bronx Casino, and the Club Cubano Interamericano. Arriving in 1962, Eddy Zervigón found work in these clubs almost immediately.[16] Performing with his own band Orquesta Broadway since its inception, Eddy also performed with Eddie Palmieri's ensembles and Conjunto Libre. I performed with Orquesta Broadway at the Mamoncillo Festival that July, and also had the opportunity to hear Charanga América and Manny Oquendo's Conjunto Libre, in which Eddy Zervigón's virtuosic *clave*-driven flute solos soared above a four-strong trombone section. Having spent several years in Havana on research, I now found myself amongst a different "pan-Latino" community with performers connected to pre-revolutionary Cuban charanga and *son* on the one hand, and to US-based charanga, *mambo*, and *conjunto* culture on the other. The Cuban five-key wooden flute and charanga violins of La Broadway rubbed shoulders with Oquendo's fizzing trombone section, reflecting aspects of *cubanía*, *sabor cubano*, and a distinctive New York *sabor*.

Intrigued by this new grassroots charanga/*trombanga*[17] environment, I returned to New York in 2012 for further fieldwork research. On my visits, Eddy drove me around New York, pointing out where Latin music venues such as the Palladium used to be in the 1960s. He recounted fascinating anecdotes as we passed various landmarks, including one where a riotous gig with Tito Puente on a boat resulted in a piano being tossed into the Hudson River by the revelers onboard! Thus the seeds for this second part of the charanga flute story were sown, and I knew I would be returning to New York once the first book on Cuban charanga was complete.[18] This is the second part of the journey—one in which Cuban dance music in the USA is explored, and where musical changes in the Cuban flute style of improvisation are further examined to evaluate those changes and their wider relevance to Latin music performance aesthetics. Through this work I hope to document the enormous contribution of performers of Cuban dance music in New York and to demonstrate the improvisational creativity and vitality of the charanga flute soloists in these groups.

This book is therefore dedicated to Eddy Zervigón in honor of his immense contribution to both the Cuban flute style and to popular Cuban dance music in New York and internationally over the last fifty-eight years.

ACKNOWLEDGMENTS

I would most like to thank Eddy Zervigón for inspiring this current work; without his support and generosity this book would not have been written. I would also particularly like to thank the musicians from Charanga Del Norte, Orquesta Broadway, Charanga Soleil, and Charansalsa. I would especially like to thank the following people in New York and Miami for their invaluable help: Joe de Jesus, Al Angeloro, Nestor Torres, Mark Weinstein, Willie Rodríguez, David A. Pérez and family, Connie Grossman, Karen Joseph, John Berdeguer, Andrea Brachfeld, Ben Lapidus, Jessica Valiente, John Berdeguer, Jesse Herrero, Eduardo Aguirre, Gustavo Cruz, Rene Lorente, Andy Harlow/Kahn, Robert Heredia, and Manny Rivera. I would like to thank Latin American Music Journal for their kind permission to reproduce material from my article 'Pacheco and Charanga: Imitation, Innovation and Cultural Appropriation in the Típico Tradition of New York City' (Latin American Music Review, Spring 2020) in chapters 5 and 6 of this book. I would like to thank Latin American Music Journal for their kind permission to reproduce material from my article 'Pacheco and Charanga: Imitation, Innovation and Cultural Appropriation in the Típico Tradition of New York City' (Latin American Music Review, Spring 2020) in chapters 5 and 6 of this book. A big thank-you to Dr. George Kennaway (University of Huddersfield) for his helpful and timely proofreading; thanks also to Dr. John Cowley for advice on the presentation of the discography, and to Nigel Humphries for the clear technical drawing of the five-key flute fingerings in chapter 9. A huge thank-you also to Barkley McKay, Michael Ward, and Dr. Paul Thompson (Leeds Beckett University) for their expertise in recording, mixing, and mastering Charanga del Norte's *Charanga Time* and *Pachanga Time* albums created especially to accompany this book. Thanks also to Leeds Beckett University for funding a twelve-week sabbatical in 2017 and a four-week fieldwork trip to New York and Miami in 2016. *Music and Letters* have funded several other short research trips to New York in 2012 and 2015, for which I am very grateful. Finally a very special thanks goes to Dr. Nick Williams, my partner, for his support throughout.

IMPROVISING SABOR

INTRODUCTION

Chupa la caña, nena,
Tiene sabor, sabor, sabor . . . y nada más

There are many versions of the song "Tiene Sabor," including those by Cuban groups Abelardo Barosso (*Cha Cha Chá with Orquesta Sensacíon*) and later Omara Portuondo (Buena Vista Social Club's *Lost and Found*), and also by New York's Típica Novel (*Se Colo La Novel*) and Charlie Palmieri (*Salsa Na' Ma'*).[1] *Sabor* is evoked through the song's lyrics using signifiers of *cubanía* (Cubanness)—a river through palm groves, the sea, the province of Matanzas, a fishing boat, the Havana suburb of Callo Hueso, the railroad, sugarcane, the machete, the national flag, and a rifle—all emblematic of Cuba's history of slavery, colonialism, plantation culture, and revolutionary struggle. Here the concept of *sabor* is linked intimately to the Cuban experience, symbolized by the taste of sugarcane with its recurrent *coro* "*chupa la caña, nena, tiene sabor, sabor, sabor . . . y nada más*" [suck the sugar cane, girl, it has flavor and nothing more]. The use of the term is, however, much wider; Berríos-Miranda, Dudley, and Habell-Pallán, for example, in their book *American Sabor*, describe *sabor* as an essential quality of Latin music that "evokes the delights of music and of food" and "makes our bodies want to move."[2] Janice Mahinka has discussed the difficulties of translating the term *sabor* and rejects the common translation of "flavor," putting forward instead the optional (and non-encompassing) term "savor."[3] This term fits well with the idea of savoring the taste of the sugarcane in the context of the song's lyrics.

When asked in an interview with Israel Sánchez-Coll about what made a good charanga flute player, Eddy Zervigón, bandleader of New York–based Orquesta Broadway, emphasized sabor as the most important aspect of Cuban flute improvisation: "Un sonido limpio, ideas para desarrollar frases melódicas, algo importante, que le pongan sabor, no es la velocidad de 8,000 notas por minuto, es el sabor" [a clean sound, ideas that generate melodic phrases, which, importantly, are given sabor, not 8,000 notes a minute, it's sabor].[4] Zervigón did not reference food associations in this interview with

Sánchez-Coll, but he has talked at length about the dance imperative of Cuban popular forms, a quality also emphasized above by Berríos-Miranda et al. For Zervigón, sabor is about natural talent, creativity, cultural background (for example, having a deep knowledge of the danzón repertoire) and rhythmic placement. He cites the flute player Joseíto Valdés in Orquesta Ideal as having more sabor than Antonio Arcaño (while acknowledging Arcaño's importance as an innovator) due to Valdés's ability to play four well-placed notes—"he could do a solo full of sabor on one note only."[5]

So what does sabor signify to Cuban musicians, who, like Zervigón, were later based in the United States, such as Cuban trumpet player Alfredo "Chocolate" Armenteros and charanga flute players José Fajardo, Rolando Lozano, or Belisario López? And is sabor understood in relation to nostalgia for a "lost" homeland and/or cubanía? Max Salazar certainly wrote about Zervigón in terms of nostalgia for a pre-revolutionary Cuba: "For Cubans, his music evokes pleasant memories of the swank cocktail lounge at the Hotel Nacional, the saltwater aroma of El Malecón, the palm trees on the gray sandy beaches of La Concha and Varadero, danzón and *guajira* music floating from the cantinas along El Paseo del Prado, and the flickering neon lights of the Havana skyline."[6] In relation to Cuban flute improvisation and charanga performance, Zervigón referred to *clave* feel, rhythmic placement, and interaction with the ensemble, and was certainly being less poetic than Salazar.[7] Instead, Zervigón prefers to talk about melody, repertoire, and rhythm and does not talk about his own playing in Salazar's evocative yet romanticized terms. The context for Cuban charanga performance in New York was and is related to, but different from, that of Havana. Even though the source of the music is acknowledged as Cuban by the musicians I interviewed, they described the Cuban sound as more laid back, confident, or tropical, and the New York sound as being more aggressive, urban, and gritty (although few were able to give specific musical details to describe this different feel). These somewhat essentialized explanations are interrogated throughout this book using music analysis and comparative transcription to gain further clarity on the music's development. Sabor in the context of Cuban music performance in New York may draw upon or subsume aspects of cubanía, particularly as many influential Cuban musicians were on the scene, but the terms are different and, as will be demonstrated in later chapters, one may have sabor without necessarily having much cubanía. Sabor might have connoted nostalgia for the homeland for those Puerto Rican musicians in New York in the 1930s and '40s such as Noro and Esy Morales and Rafael Hernández, where similar experiences of migration and homesickness formed part of the performance context. But sabor may have a different meaning for those Puerto Rican musicians born and brought up in the Big Apple, the so-called "Nuyoricans" like Tito Puente, Charlie and Eddie Palmieri, and Ray Barretto. Aside from evocations of homeland (for example, the islands of Cuba and Puerto Rico) or references to the barrios of New York, sabor must also, as Zervigón implies, be seen to relate to a Latin performance aesthetic that includes a dance imperative, melodic call and response–styled improvised *inspiraciones*, and a clave feel—performance aspects intrinsically linked to the music's historical development. Sabor is a multifaceted concept that cannot, however, be explained purely in terms of flavor, nostalgia for the homeland, or clave adherence. This book, then, seeks to explore and define what it means to have sabor in the context of Cuban dance music performance in New York.

TAXONOMIES: LATIN MUSIC, AFRO-CUBAN/CUBAN DANCE MUSIC, TÍPICO, OR SALSA?

The naming of this music is problematic and there have been a considerable number of debates about the term *salsa* among musicians and scholars alike.[8] The music industries have always had an influence on the naming of musical idioms, with styles such as rumba/rhumba, mambo, and *pachanga* also raising similar controversies and disputes over definition and ownership (see chapters 2 and 5). The term *salsa* has come to stand for a particular standardized set of performance practices, and the dominant narrative of its origins has tended to oversimplify Latin music history in the USA. This book seeks to document an understudied period of Latin music history across the divide of the Cuban Revolution of 1959 to demonstrate a plurality of narratives including the history of the influential charanga orquestas of 1960s New York.

Performers interviewed for this book were asked how they wanted to name the music they played, and many stated a preference for "Cuban" or "Afro-Cuban" music and rejected "salsa." Some New York Puerto Ricans interviewed prefer to call the music "Afro-Cuban" to acknowledge its Cuban origins and the debt to Africa.[9] The term "Latin music" was on the whole disliked for being too general, as was the term "salsa." It is well known that Palladium musicians like Tito Puente and Frank Grillo (aka Machito) never accepted the term "salsa" and that Puente preferred the "Cuban" or "Afro-Cuban" music descriptors.[10] Most of the musicians interviewed, however, still used the "Latin music" term when talking more generally about their music in conversation, but very rarely employed the term "salsa." UK-based rumba[11] specialist and ethnomusicologist Christian Weaver critiques the "Afro" prefix when writing about Cuban music on the island, but affirms that the use of either "Cuban" and "Afro-Cuban" terms is acceptable when used with the knowledge of their inherent historical meanings:

> If the island's culture has, for some considerable time, been seen as a combination of the "Afro-Cuban" and the "Hispano-Cuban" we can surely say that by now the Cuban has arrived. Furthermore, we can say that the idea of Cuban is contained within, or in some cases encapsulated by certain practices, ideas and activities that arose as a result of its formation. . . . I maintain that we can talk of the Afro-Cuban and the Cuban. This is not to try to imply that Cuban culture is built from a European basis and "the African" is something extra to this; it is to distinguish between those manifestations that most likely existed, albeit in other forms, outside of Cuba and those that arose within it. The use of the term Afro-Cuban however still brings with it a suggestion of otherness that I find problematic in some instances.[12]

I perceive a difference in meaning of the term "Afro-Cuban" in the New York context, as many musicians use it to refer to *son*, mambo, chachachá, and pachanga styles as performed by mambo big bands, son bands, charangas, and conjuntos. This is a legacy of Machito and also of the later political and cultural movements of the 1970s in the USA. Mario Bauzá's deliberate choice to call the band he cofounded in 1940 "Machito and his Afro-Cubans" lay in his pan-African perspective, inspired by the Harlem Renaissance and his experiences in the swing bands of Noble Sissle, Chick Webb, and Cab Calloway. Paul Austerlitz documents this perspective, showing how, while forced to work with the exoticization of Cuban music, Mario Bauzá and Frank Grillo also subverted it with black pride:

> Stereotyped Afro-Cuban culture had become popular among white Cubans. The Machito band rode the wave of these stereotypes, taking advantage of the aperture that they afforded into the limelight. They used this window of opportunity to display open pride in real Afro-Cuban culture: Machito and Bauzá determined to call the band Machito and his Afro-Cubans. Bauzá later said that some "people didn't want that title; the people say, why the 'Afro?' I said because the music we represent come[s] from Africa, and we come from Africa."[13] Machito and Bauzá were articulating an overt ideology of pan-Africanism.[14]

This philosophy took root in New York City given the central role of the Machito band in Latin music history there and also due to the advent of Pan-African and civil rights movements in the late 1960s and 1970s among Puerto Ricans and African Americans. In the Cuban context the term "Afro-Cuban" is applied more frequently to rumba, and Afro-Cuban religious music and dance forms such as Santería and Palo Monte.[15] I use the term "Cuban" following Weaver's perspective and to avoid confusion between Cuban popular dance styles with Cuban rumba and religious forms. I employ the "Cuban dance music" descriptor in the book's title because the term "Cuban" should subsume both the African and Hispanic aspects of the music. I also use the term "Latin," despite its lack of specificity, particularly when I want to include a wide range of clave-based musical practices, and to be inclusive when specific detail is not at issue. I refer to "salsa" when discussing the music of those who identify themselves as salsa musicians or dancers; I will not be examining the rise of the Fania All Stars in the 1970s in detail, as this has been documented and critiqued elsewhere.[16] Many of the musicians profiled and analyzed in this book have nevertheless been part of the Fania story (for example, Ray Barretto and Johnny Pacheco have played major roles), and the history of this music is tied up with the history of the record industry in New York, where the Alegre, Fania, and Tico record labels, in particular, played a fundamental part in the music's dissemination.

CUBANIDAD, HISPANIDAD, OR LATINIDAD?

Christina Abreu has documented the history of two of the more well-known social clubs in New York, El Club Cubano Inter-Americano and the Ateneo Cubano de Nueva York, and also the Círculo Cubano and Juventud Cubana social clubs of Miami in her book *Rhythms of Race*, where she examines the terms *Cubanidad*, *Hispanidad*, and *Latinidad* in order to explain how Latin, Cuban, and Afro-Cuban identities were formed through Cuban music performance and social dancing.[17] She also shows how the press and later film and television played a part in disseminating ideas (and stereotypes) of "Latin" identity in the USA. How Cubans, Puerto Ricans, and other Latin communities interacted culturally with these stereotyped portrayals of Latinidad and Cubanidad are important to consider in the context of emerging styles and in the historical accounts of the careers of individual musicians. David Garcia, for example, documents the problems Arsenio Rodríguez had in New York due to not fitting the media perception of Latinidad.[18] Issues of race, gender, age, disability, and physical appearance are therefore also key when looking at the promotion of Cuban dance music in New York. As I show in chapter 1, the Palladium was praised for its racial inclusiveness but was, in reality, less racially mixed than reported. What became clear to me during my research in New York was that there was still a grassroots Latin community bound by a long tradition of Cuban dance music performance across the city. These roots continually feed the more commercial side of Cuban dance music/salsa in New York, although the nature of these support structures has been changing for some time, particularly since the 1980s when the Dominican presence and the popularity of *merengue* displaced Cuban music from its central role.[19] Certainly at the Foley Square performance in Lower Manhattan I was able to observe dancing to Puerto Rican bands playing a variety of Cuban dance music interspersed with a merengue or two; the Dominican style of dancing of one couple was clearly different from the son steps of the majority of that audience. Similarly, the music I heard on the streets of Bushwick (a working-class area of Brooklyn) on Puerto Rican Day was an eclectic mix of international salsa, son, merengue, and *bachata* mixed with Latin pop (including a Latin version of Barry White's "All Around the World").

THE AESTHETICS OF TÍPICO PLAYING IN NEW YORK

It was the típicas that were the movers of change, you know. Yeah, they played danzones but they played everything else. They sounded like Dixieland jazz bands. I played clarinet in one. Coño! It was hard to be heard. These guys blasted away on the horns while the timbalero hit the danzón beat, sometimes on the skins, and sometimes on the cowbell that usually hung on the side. The trumpet and cornet players used to cut the shafts so they could sound louder—louder was better. Coño! This is where it all started. Later the son came along and the white people said that it was the real Cuban music. Shit! The same thing happened in New Orleans. Ahí es donde el jazz toma vigor con las típicas de Dixieland [That's where jazz came into force, with the típica Dixieland bands]. The big band grew from the American típicas.[20]

Referring to the wind bands in New Orleans and Havana, Mario Bauzá, cofounder of Machito and his Afro-Cubans, is in conversation above with the pianist and bandleader Charlie Palmieri, promoter Federico Pagani, timbale player and bandleader Tito Puente, and singer Miguelito Valdés. In this informal discussion on charangas and orquesta típicas, Bauzá makes a very important point about how mainstream narratives of music history are formed. Bauzá claims here that the origins of jazz are to be found in the orquesta típicas in the Americas, and that favoring jazz over other African American music and dance forms is not that different from the privileging of Cuban son over other Cuban styles that were played in the larger típica band formations, with their obvious connections to European military and civic wind band music.

The meaning of the word *típico* in New York is not quite the same as its Cuban counterpart term, which has its roots in the orquestas típicas, *bandas municipales*, and *danzón orquestas* mentioned by Bauzá (although they are intrinsically tied up with the history of Latin music). In Cuba the term has a slightly different meaning in that historically it was used by two different ensemble types. The Cuban nineteenth-century orquesta típica (a wind-band-type ensemble comprising two clarinets, two violins, a cornet, timpani, *güiro*, ophicleide, double bass, valve trombone, and tuba) is more generally referred to as an orquesta típica in Cuba, as opposed to the later *charanga francesa* or *charanga orquesta*. Nonetheless, *charanga típica* is also used to denote the lineup and performance aesthetics of violin and flute charanga dance bands such as Arcaño y sus Maravillas and Orquesta Aragón. Cuban son forms are more commonly described as *música tradicional* (as distinct from other traditional Afro-Cuban forms of secular rumba), and Afro-Cuban religious forms of music and dance are referred to as *música folklórico*.[21]

Musicologist Roberta Singer clarifies the use of *típico* in New York as applying to "island" rather than New York–based music styles and that "some contemporary performers in New York define *típico* as 'source music': the non-commercial traditional and popular styles from which contemporary commercial styles are derived and reinterpreted."[22] For New York musicians, típico thus reflects a migrant perspective, one that values authenticity and an adherence to a particular style of playing. Many Latin musicians in New York see their music in terms of fidelity to their island roots with a need to assert their cultural identity, whether that be in *típico* performance or in more hybridized/modernized form. In New York *típico* is a term most often used to describe traditional charanga or conjunto performance, which confuses these earlier distinctions to some degree. Típico is an important concept for New York players. For example, an adherence to the charanga sound exemplified by bands such as Havana-based Orquesta Aragón and New York's Orquesta Broadway is very much valued among practitioners and their audiences. The term is applied to Cuban son performance as popularized in conjunto format by Arsenio Rodríguez and his Cuba-based and later New

York-based *son conjunto* (in Cuba, the son conjunto is not generally referred to in típico terms). This does not mean that the charanga or son traditions in New York are all about preservation and revival, however; the popularity of the charanga in New York evolved from previous waves of Cuban dance music performance practice in the city with charanga musicians present from at least the late 1920s. Cuban flute player Alberto Socarrás arrived in New York in 1927 and the influential Cuban pianist Anselmo Sacasas arrived in New York in 1940 from the charanga Orquesta Tata Pereira[23] and Cuban "jazz" band Casino de La Playa.[24] Visiting bands from Cuba like Orquesta Aragón and Fajardo y sus Estrellas also popularized the form, as did the many commercial recordings of Cuban music disseminated widely by companies such as RCA Victor.

A MI GENTE

The phrase *A Mi Gente* ("for my people") is ubiquitous in grassroots performances of Cuban dance music in the city. As historian Christina Abreu has documented, Cuban social clubs have had a major role in developing a "Latino/a" identity through Cuban musical performance at social dances in both New York and Miami.[25] New York–born Puerto Rican David A. Pérez remarked about his own cultural background:

DP: From early youth, the music was always in the house. This was a neighborhood where you would know which was Puerto Rican and Cuban, and our friends were both Puerto Rican and Cuban, so we used to go and listen to music. The music that they usually played was the Orquesta Aragón, Orquesta Almendra, the old Cuban danzones, and, in those days, we were just starting out with the chachachá. The big bands were the Mambo, with the Machito.

SM: **So, we're talking 1950s, yes?**

DP: Right, 1950s, the Machito, Tito Rodríguez, and Tito Puente. Those were the big orchestras—there were a lot of those. New York was a very busy city in terms of its growth of Latin American people. The Puerto Ricans were starting to come from the island and settling here. My parents had come way before in the twenties. They were here in the 1920s.

SM: **Did they go to rhumba dances?**

DP: My mother and father met in what they used to call *civicas* social clubs, *civicas*. The one that they met was—where the heck was it—

Figure I.1 Puerto Rican dancer wrapping herself in the Puerto Rican flag, Festival of San Bautista, the patron saint of Puerto Rico, New York, June 26, 2016. Copyright Sue Miller.

it was in Brooklyn? It was a very leftist, socialist type, intellectual, where you'd talk about independence for Puerto Rico and the Cubans were talking about how things were all screwed up in Cuba. They were all trying to figure out what the best route politically was and that's where my mother and father met. However, what they did mostly is they brought bands in and people danced and they socialized and that's how my mother and father met. . . . So, we had this New York—we're New Yorkers. We're New Yorkers, whereas I like to tell everybody "I'm a New York–born Puerto Rican."

There are still many local performances of Cuban music in New York, from street festivals and fundraisers to church-led or social-club events in honor of patron saints (see figure I.1). The resurgence of mambo big bands (professional and amateur) in the city in recent years (for example, the Mambo Legends, the Bronx Conexión, and the Spanish Harlem Orchestra) also demonstrates that there is continuing support for Cuban dance music from the Latino/a community and more widely, albeit perhaps on a smaller scale than in the past (although I suspect many performances are not well paid). Many of the new mambo big bands have an educational remit to keep the Cuban musical traditions alive. For example, musician and educator Bobby Sanabria directs his Afro-Cuban Jazz Orchestras at the New School and the Manhattan School of Music, Dr. Willie Rodríguez's work at the Lehman Center as educator and performer has also been important, and Victor Rendón directs the Bronx Conexión big band, all of them providing training for the next generation of Latin players. The Boy's Harbor Conservatory used to fulfill this function on a grassroots level,[26] as did the Johnny Colón School of Music and City College (where Charlie Palmieri directed a Latin band). As Pérez mentions, the influence of the Big Three (Tito Puente, Tito Rodríguez, and the Machito orchestra) at the Palladium ballroom cannot be overstated when discussing the role of Cuban music in the making of Latin New York. The influence of jazz (particularly swing) on these Palladium bands also constitutes an important ingredient in the development of Cuban dance music in the city.

LATIN PERFORMANCE AESTHETICS—*CUBANÍA* AND *SABOR*

A Latin performance aesthetic comprises several factors tied to the concepts of *cubanía* and *sabor*, terms which are related but not synonymous. Characteristic rhythmic phrasing forms part of this aesthetic, as does adherence to clave as an organizational principle. A knowledge of the repertoire is also essential along with the ability to improvise and quote melodies from son, charanga, and other related idioms. Other factors are less tangible, however, and social and cultural factors play an immense part. As a cultural outsider and performer of Cuban/Latin music myself, I have to accept that the cubanía of the Cuban players I admire so much, such as Richard Egües and José Fajardo, comes from their lived experience as Cuban musicians and as products of their own respective generation, sociocultural background, and musical environment. As Ry Cooder remarked on the original Buena Vista Social Club musicians: "they were dramatic personalities and they're now nearly all gone. There's nobody left like that anymore."[27] Their lives shaped their musical development and performance style in an era where live performance was thriving. This is not to say that Cuban dance music should remain the preserve of only those from Cuba (non-Cuban New York players are a case in point), but the lived part of cubanía cannot easily be replicated. Instead, one can learn the more tangible aspects of the style (drawing on Cuban cultural elements) and work at understanding the culture(s) that gave rise to the music; as New York Latin players would say, one needs to be respectful of the "source music." Pianist Willie Rodríguez (Pete El Conde Rodríguez, Charanga América, Machito, Orquesta Broadway) underlines the importance of respect for the Cuban music forms that inspire US-based Cuban music, also stressing how important it is to acknowledge the significant contribution of Puerto Rican performers to the history of Latin music in the USA:

> WR: I think it's important for people to know that I always found that whether they [the US charanga bands] were playing that music or copying the name or wanting to have some sort of—all the musicians and all of the bands always had a tremendous respect for playing it right, for this is the way it goes, this is the true . . .
> **SM: That's the clave feel as well?**
> WR: The clave feel, the presentation of the group, how it looks, that kind of thing—I think one of the things I learned quickly was that Cuban music was respected. Then of course New York City particularly had all these Puerto Rican musicians who were keeping that alive by playing in the orchestras. That's true in jazz—more limited, but true in jazz as well—is how they influenced all these bands and kept that music alive.[28]

Crediting Puerto Rican musicians for keeping Cuban music alive (particularly after the 1959 revolution) is a common theme often expressed by Puerto Rican musicians on the Latin music scene in New York today. The contribution of Puerto Rican musicians to both jazz and Cuban dance music since the 1920s has been immense. In New York, a rich musical culture has been created by Cuban, Puerto Rican, Dominican, Panamanian, Mexican, New York Italian and Jewish musicians, among others.

The típico aesthetic is an important one in New York and the combination of charanga and conjunto stylings has given rise to a plurality of ensemble types, each with a distinctive sabor and varying degrees of cubanía. The musical developments in New York, particularly in the Latin American/Caribbean communities, created a different type of sabor from the cubanía-infused sabor of Havana, although it is important to recognize that the cubanía of the US-based Cuban musicians was ever-present and influential.

Some of the characteristic stylistic elements that form part of the Cuban charanga improvisational style are listed in Table I.1 to demonstrate aspects of cubanía. These rhythms, breaks, embellishments, and characteristic melodic movements are not exclusive to the flute but are also found in Latin trumpet, clarinet, saxophone, trombone, and piano improvisational styles,

Stylistic Feature	Musical Examples Taken From Cuban Charanga Flute Improvisations
i. Amphibrach/ Cakewalk	*[notation example showing amphibrach and cakewalk]*
ii. Habanera/ Tango	*[notation example, m. 76, showing habanera rhythm, E⁷]*
iii. Cinquillo	*[notation example, m. 47]*
iv Cascara	*[notation example, m. 164, timbales 2–3 cascara pattern, D⁷]*
v. Danzón Otra	*[notation example, C⁶, characteristic of percussion break]*
vi. Ponce Break	*[notation example, C⁶, double ponce]*
vii. Mordents and Turns	*[notation example, m. 43, mordent, mordent, mordent, turn]*
viii. Acciaccatura	*[notation example, m. 94, D⁷, G]*
ix. Octave Leap Mambitos	*[notation example, m. 61]*
x. '3 in a grid of 4'	*[notation example, Cross-rhythms: 3 eighth notes in a grid of 4, G, D⁷]*
xi. Rising phrases from a 5th degree axis note	*[notation example, m. 120, B⁷, Em, sequence using b2 as an axis note for ascending chord notes, B⁷]*

Table I.1 The Stylistic Features of *Cubania* in Charanga Flute Improvisation

Stylistic Feature	Musical Examples Taken From Cuban Charanga Flute Improvisations
xii. Ascending sequences within a third to fourth octave tessitura between dominant notes.	
xiii. sextuplets	*sextuplets with "cheat" fingerings*
xiv. Movement in thirds	
xv. Movement in sixths	

Table I.1 Stylistic vocabulary characteristic of the Cuban flute style of improvisation.

as they developed in the orquesta típicas and charangas through danzón performance. This shared musical inheritance in the town *bandas* and típicas produced many of New York's most influential players, including Mario Bauzá (clarinet, cornet, trumpet), José Fajardo (five-key flute), and Alfredo "Chocolate" Armenteros (trumpet). Many of the elements shown draw upon the stylistic components of the danzón, mambo, son/*guaracha*, and son montuno in terms of rhythms played by the percussion section, particularly by the timbales, although bass line patterns (*tumbaos*) are also present (in *tresillo* and *habanera* patterns, for example). The *florear* approach to improvisation was followed by wind, brass and piano players and there are many shared characteristics in their respective improvisational styles.

The links between flute and trumpet improvisational styles are demonstrated in example I.1, an annotated transcription of a solo by Cuban trumpet player Alfredo "Chocolate" Armenteros on "Bilongo" by Eddie Palmieri's 1968 New York–based band. Here Armenteros employs sextuplets (xiii, Table I.1), "3 in a grid of 4" repeated motifs (x), mordents and turns (xii), appoggiaturas, and acciaccaturas (viii). Armenteros, like Eddy Zervigón, was taught music by Richard Egües's father, Eduardo Egües, a well-known music educator in the province;[29] Armenteros grew up with Richard Egües in the same hometown of Ranchuelo in Santa Clara, demonstrating direct links between both of these influential players. Armenteros had a highly successful professional career in Cuba and the USA and first performed in New York on tour with José Fajardo and his charanga in 1959 before moving there permanently in 1960 to perform with the Machito Orchestra.[30] He therefore has conjunto, charanga, and mambo big band experience and was influenced himself by the *septeto* and *bandas municipales* traditions (he was particularly inspired by the trumpet player Enrique "Florecita" Velazco).[31] In the solo transcription in example I.1, aspects of the Cuban improvisational style are clearly in evidence and reflect the style's history in terms of a *florear* approach to melody (motif 1 development), a *rubatiando* approach common in Cuban danzón interpretation, and a one-octave tessitura in terms of melodic direction (see the bugle motif mm. 29 to 34, tessitura of d^2 to d^3 rising from tonic to the dominant note in the key of G minor (concert pitch)).

Bilongo

from Eddie Palmieri and His Orchestra, Tico T-574, 1968, Vinyl USA.
(at Concert Pitch)

trumpet solo - Alfredo 'Chocolate' Armenteros, transcribed Sue Miller.

Example I.1 Trumpet solo by Alfredo "Chocolate" Armenteros on the 1968 recording of "Bilongo" by Eddie Palmieri and His Orchestra.

Armenteros uses a high register (reaching d³ as the apex note) and a wide tessitura, has considerable *clave* feel, a melodic call-and-response approach with motivic material derived from the arrangement and the wider repertoire, triplet quarter-note phrases linking to rumba performance (the *diana* opening phrase is drawn on here), a bugle call (*llamada*), axis note breaks (*efectos* or *mambitos*), and classically phrased runs and sequences typical of the Cuban improvisation style that also has roots in Western art music. The solo is shot through with cubanía—clave sensibility, melodic call and response and references to the Cuban repertoire and Afro-Cuban culture (rumba). It also has sabor in that his *rubatiando* approach and textural variety produce a solo where notes and sequences are developed creatively, where rhythmic placement is intricately related to clave direction. The flute and trumpet styles of improvisation ultimately developed from Cuban danzón performance practice in the orquesta típicas, the charangas, and the bandas municipales with their *florear* approach to improvisation.[33] As demonstrated, a solo can have both cubanía and sabor, where sabor is reflected in the creative development of melo-rhythmic material played in dialogue with the ensemble.

One aspect of cubanía is quotation and manipulation of melodic material culled from a large repertoire of pieces mostly from the Cuban son and charanga traditions, ranging from danzón and son melodies to well-known guarachas, guajiras, and oft-cited foreign melodies from the American songbook, films, and light classical repertoire.[34] In example I.1 melodic material from the arrangement (verse and rumba introduction) are drawn upon alongside the bugle call quotation. The use of rubato to embellish composed material is also in evidence in this solo. Eddy Zervigón, in conversation, emphasized the importance of the danzón, stating that unless you know how to play danzón you can never be a true *charanguero*; a florear approach, which can involve rubato, is part of the foundational danzón performance practice in both orquesta típicas and charangas.[35] Stylistic vocabulary and generative processes linked to the style can be learned; but without knowledge of the wider Cuban music repertoire and its relationship to Cuban culture, performance can be superficial even when virtuosic. A knowledge of the Cuban popular repertoire is therefore an integral part of cubanía and is one element of sabor. This then leads to a consideration of clave feel or sensibility; how musicians engage creatively with this underlying timeline ultimately decides whether a solo or an ensemble performance has sabor.

The assertion by Joe Conzo and David Pérez that "it sounded Cuban and felt New York"[36] in relation to the Palladium bands of the 1950s is interesting in terms of how one describes the New York sabor, which is related to cubanía but somehow a little different from the source (even with the presence of Cuban musicians in many of the bands). In the following analyses of arrangements and charanga flute solos, I investigate whether cubanía and sabor (*sabor cubano* and/or New York sabor) are apparent in the ensemble playing and in the improvisational style of key charanga (and trombanga) bands and flute players based in New York, tracing lines of influence between players.

WHY *IMPROVISING SABOR*?

Central to this research is an examination of "Latin" performance aesthetics using the Cuban charanga format (flute, violins, timbales, congas, güiro, piano, bass, and vocals), as the main case study. Here the concept of sabor in performance is explored and interrogated and the book's main themes are therefore sabor, cubanía, and Cuban dance music performance aesthetics in the context of New York. The foundations of this music are undoubtedly Cuban, but this music has taken on new characteristics in its many US guises and these differences are interesting both from a musical as well as a cultural perspective; in fact, the two are intertwined. Innovation is often credited to those musicians who undertake obvious fusions (particularly those most malleable for music industry promotion purposes), but the smaller, quieter innovations within the típico approach demand closer attention.

While studies in jazz improvisation are numerous, it is time to turn attention to the study of improvisational creativity in the domain of transnational Cuban dance music, drawing on Latin music performance aesthetics as a frame of reference for music analysis. The title *Improvising Sabor* was coined with the intention of communicating the vitality of Cuban dance music in New York, demonstrating how these clave-based improvisations are integral to the movements of dancers in the clubs, streets, cafés, and dancehalls of the city. The focus, in terms of improvisation, is on charanga performance in the 1950s and 1960s with perspectives from musicians both past and present given throughout. Analysis attempts to define New York sabor as related to but different from Cuban sabor and to evaluate how the improvisational style changed (radically or incrementally) from the mid-century Cuba-based tradition pioneered by Richard Egües and José Fajardo. In *Cuban Flute Style* the development of improvisation in the danzón through the mambo, son, and chachachá was analyzed, showcasing the contributions of Cuban soloists and founders of the charanga flute style from Tata Pereira (1874–1933) and Miguel "El Moro" Vázquez Tuero (1889–1925) to *Nuevo Ritmo* players such as Antonio Arcaño (1911–1994) and José Antonio Díaz (b. 1908) to Francisco

Delabart (b. 1903) in Orquesta Antonio María Romeu and then the later mid-twentieth-century virtuoso players José Fajardo (1919–2001) and Richard Egües (1923–2006). All analyses of charanga flute players in the USA (whether Cuban, Puerto Rican, or of other nationalities) relate in various ways to this foundational style. Although not a prerequisite to understanding this current work, readers interested in Latin forms of improvisation are encouraged to read the earlier book to gain a broader understanding of the style's development.[37]

The concept of sabor is evaluated within a variety of formats, including the conjunto with its trumpet- or trombone-led son, the charanga, and the mambo big band. Sabor as a performance concept will be examined in order to explain how cubanía, sabor cubano, and the related but distinct New York sabor coexist or combine, giving ethnographic and musical detail to illustrate findings.[38] I examine Latin performance aesthetics through the analysis of recordings, annotated transcription, performances, and through the voices of musicians, promoters, writers, and DJs based in New York and Miami. Some of the music analyzed here has been recorded by my UK-based orquesta Charanga del Norte on the accompanying album *Pachanga Time*, and these recordings can be accessed via the band websites www.charangadelnorte.co.uk and www.charangasue.com. The original recordings are listed in the discography, as are all the songs and albums referred to in the book; timecode is also given so that those who do not read music can consult specific parts of the recordings to understand the notated analyses.

The focus of the research is on the New York–based charanga orquestas and their flute soloists, who have been consistently left out of mainstream Latin music history. Some readers may be surprised by the centrality of the charanga when previous accounts of Latin music history have traditionally focused on the mambo big bands, the Latin jazz experiments of Dizzy Gillespie and Chano Pozo, Eddie Palmieri and/or the later 1970s Fania-label salsa bands, and their successors.[39] The conjunto and charanga traditions are often eclipsed in these narratives and their legacy in New York needs to be more greatly acknowledged. Indeed, David Garcia, in his article "Contesting that Damned Mambo," has argued for the centrality of Arsenio Rodríguez y su Conjunto de Estrellas in the history, not only of the mambo but also of the wider development of Cuban dance music in the city. Rodríguez's music has often been sidelined in the history of the Palladium, despite the fact that his US conjunto performed there, as well as in the Bronx social clubs and other music venues such as the Park Plaza. Garcia points out that the conjunto and charanga were the bands of choice in the Cuban social clubs and other venues in the Bronx but were largely ignored by the mainstream American press.[40] In the article, Garcia cites Cuban Melba Alvarado, a longtime member of the Club Cubano Inter-Americano in the Bronx, who comments that the three *típicas* of bolero, son, and danzón were performed there and that mambo was not a feature of the club's music. Similarly another club veteran, Puerto Rican Sara Martínez Baro, comments that these típico forms made her nostalgic for her homeland and made her want to dance both Cuban and Puerto Rican styles.[41] It is therefore time to reconsider the relevance of the charanga orquesta, often omitted from traditional accounts of Latin music history, and the place of the Cuban flute style within Latin improvisation aesthetics more widely.

The study of the Cuban flute improvisational style, from the late nineteenth century to contemporary times, offers a window into broader issues of Latin music performance practice and the creative process itself. Leading Puerto Rican and Dominican musicians in New York such as Eddie and Charlie Palmieri, Manny Oquendo, Johnny Pacheco (himself a charanga flute player), and Ray Barretto, for example, were inspired by both the charanga and the conjunto/*sonora* bands of Sonora Matancera, Arsenio Rodríguez y sus Estrellas, Arcaño y sus Maravillas, Fajardo y sus Estrellas, and Orquesta Aragón.[42] The five-key charanga flute is seen by many as emblematic of cubanía with its roots in the Cuban danzón. The trajectory of the Cuban trumpet style from the *contradanza* to the Cuban son is equally representative of Latin performance aesthetics, documented to some extent by Rick Davies in his book *Trompeta*, and there are many stylistic convergences between the Cuban flute and trumpet improvisation style as demonstrated in example I.1.[43] The influence of charanga and conjunto form the backbone of what is generally known today as salsa; the big band mambo style forms part of this history (as chapters 1 and 2 demonstrate), but it is not the sole foundation for later developments as is frequently stated. Indeed, it is interesting to investigate just how the grassroots musical influence from the Bronx social club performances fed into the more well-known downtown Latin music scene.

Musical developments after the 1959 Cuban Revolution are relevant in terms of the charanga's popularity in early 1960s New York, but in order to understand later forms it is also important to acknowledge the development of Cuban music in the USA in the first part of the twentieth century. Without the earlier work of lesser-known bandleaders such as Gilberto Valdés and Alberto Socarrás, the pervasive presence of Arsenio Rodríguez y sus Estrellas, or the influence of the rhumba orchestras of the 1920s–1940s (such as Vicente Sigler in the 1920s, Don Azpiazu in the 1930s, and Xavier Cugat, Marcelino Guerra, and Noro Morales in the 1940s), and the Palladium mambo big bands of the mid-1940s and 1950s (Machito, Tito Rodríguez, and Tito Puente), the ground would not have been prepared for the emergence of charanga groups, such as those led by José Fajardo, Lou Pérez, Eddy Zervigón, Charlie Palmieri, or Johnny Pacheco, and of the trombone-infused conjuntos of Eddie Palmieri's La Perfecta and Manny Oquendo's Orquesta/Conjunto Libre in the 1960s.[44] Throughout this book the interconnections between the Palladium big bands, the conjunto of Arsenio Rodríguez, and the midcentury charanga bands are explored in order to underline the importance of the charanga and conjunto formats and their associated styles, and to reveal how all these types of musical formation (and the musicians within them) have contributed to the development of what is commonly termed salsa (or Latin music) today.

New York in the 1960s was fertile territory for the charanga orquesta, a scene that included Alfredito Valdés y su Orquesta, Orquesta Broadway, Charles Fox's Charanga, Charlie Palmieri's La Duboney, Johnny Pacheco y su Charanga, Orquesta Belisario López, the Lou Pérez Orchestra, Mongo Santamaría's La Sabrosa, Orquesta Novel, Orquesta Nuevo Ritmo de Cuba,[45] Pete Terrace and his Orchestra, Rafael Seijo y su Orquesta, Ray Barretto's Charanga Moderna, Rosendo Ruiz Jr. and his Latino Charanga, Tito Rodríguez and his Orchestra, and Fajardo y sus Estrellas.[46] This book profiles some of these groups and their soloists, many of whom have had a major influence on the development of Latin music in New York. The Fania-driven salsa narrative is only one perspective and this research seeks to expand on the work by John Storm Roberts and Juan Flores in order to dispel the idea of an inevitable "salsa" endpoint for "Latin music" history.[47] The charanga lineup gave rise to the mambo, chachachá, and pachanga ("styles" that took on a different performance aesthetic in New York), and I therefore reinscribe the Cuban charanga into this story because the lineup forms an important part of Cuban dance music history in Cuba, the USA, and Latin America, not least in terms of its influence. Similarly Christine Abreu's ethnographic research into Cuban Inter-Americano social clubs between 1940 and 1960 has widened the perspectives on "the making of Latino New York City and Miami."[48] Rather than "salsa rising," in Flores's terms, I believe a further reappraisal of the manifestations of Cuban dance music in New York is now due, where influence is traced through detailed musical analysis combined with perspectives from performers. The aim is to broaden the context for a more nuanced view of Cuban dance music history in New York, taking into consideration the interactions between musicians from the charangas, conjuntos, and mambo big bands. Stylistic change has been forged, I argue, by the actions of many creative individual musicians from these performance contexts, who, in turn, have sparked new points of departure and influence.

CHAPTER OUTLINE

Some chapters in this book provide historical and ethnographic detail and a focus on musical arrangement, style, and performance aesthetics; others draw on these contextual and stylistic matters to inform more detailed musical analysis of improvised solos. When examining improvisational style, the US-based charanga style of flute improvisation is explored by looking at the charanga orquestas Nuevo Ritmo de Cuba, Belisario López y su Charanga, Mongo Santamaría's La Sabrosa, Fajardo's All Stars, Orquesta Broadway, Pacheco y su Charanga, Charlie Palmieri's La Duboney, Eddie Palmieri's La Perfecta, and Ray Barretto's Charanga Moderna. Other influential musicians and groups are considered with those selected for detailed study having played a significant part in Latin music's development in the USA. Through analysis of recordings, live performances, and social dance contexts, individual style is examined in order to demonstrate a Latin aesthetic in performance practice specific to the New York context.

Chapter 1, "Spaces and Places," provides a summary of the most important venues in New York where musicians have performed danzón, rhumba/son, mambo, chachachá, and pachanga. Aside the Palladium, other venues operating in the 1950s and '60s are examined in terms of the types of Latin music played in them, documenting the experiences of performers of Cuban dance music in the Bronx, Spanish Harlem, downtown Manhattan, Brooklyn, and the Catskills resort venues.[49] The usual narrative of the Palladium as "home of the mambo" is not negated, but the narrative is expanded so that the relationships between the various performance scenes can be more fully evaluated. In the latter part of this chapter the history of the dance hall from 1947 to 1966 is examined in terms of the mambo big bands, conjuntos, and charanga bands that performed there, drawing on the perspectives of musicians who experienced live performances there.

Chapter 2, "*Los Tres Grandes*: Redefining the Mambo Genre," examines the different manifestations of mambo in Havana and New York to demonstrate the musical connections between the big bands, son conjuntos, and charangas across three decades of regular Cuban dance music performance. The Palladium, in addition to the music venues in the Bronx, provided various opportunities for New York–based musicians to create their own versions of Cuban dance music. Recordings by mambo big bands are analyzed alongside Arsenio Rodríguez's mambo diablos and Antonio Arcaño's charanga composition "Mambo" to outline the historic connections between these formats.

Chapter 3, "*La Mecha* [The Fuse]: Belisario López, José Fajardo, and Rolando Lozano," seeks to understand the context for the popularity of Cuban charanga in the early 1960s in New York through the work of renowned Cuban flute players Rolando Lozano (Orquesta Aragón, Orquesta América), Belisario López, and José Fajardo. Lozano was a member of Orquesta Nuevo Ritmo de Cuba, a Chicago-based charanga formed by conga player Armando Sánchez in 1956; their album *Heart of Cuba: Pachangas & Charangas* (New York, 1959) is said by Orquesta Broadway bandleader Eddy Zervigón to have ignited the interest in Cuban charanga in New York.[50] Lozano later played in Mongo Santamaría's charanga, the George Shearing Quintet, and with West Coast vibraphonist Cal Tjader, and his soloing style is evaluated here. The work of two other established Cuban flute players, Belisario López and José Fajardo, are examined in the light of their exile in the USA after the 1959 Cuban Revolution, testing the hypothesis that their improvisation styles did not alter much but that their repertoire sometimes did, as they performed with US-based musicians and worked within new performance and recording environments. An evaluation of all three players' work (in both Cuba and the USA) provides a more complete evaluation of their contribution to the style and to Cuban music internationally.

In chapter 4, "Exile and Adaptation: Eddy Zervigón and Orquesta Broadway," Zervigón's improvisation style is analyzed in depth. Analyses of his recorded solos are combined with interviews with Zervigón, providing his own perspectives on performing Cuban charanga in New York and internationally, from 1961 to the present day.

In chapter 5, "Charanga or Pachanga?," the issue of Cuban models and cultural appropriation is tackled and then is evaluated further in chapter 6 in relation to innovation within the típico style. To this day, in New York there remains some confusion between charanga (the name for the lineup of flute, violins, piano, bass, timbales, congas, güiro, and singers) and pachanga (a contested musical style and dance), a confusion with its origins in this early 1960s period. Often this confusion is compounded by discussion of the charanga feel (referred to as "charanga style" or "*ritmo*") which has then been mistaken for a genre-based style rather than a style of playing. There are also contradictory accounts of the pachanga dance, and the origins of the New York–specific pachanga dance are examined here.

Chapter 6, "Charanga *Embalao*: Charlie Palmieri and Johnny Pacheco," features the work of charanga flute player Johnny Pacheco in New York before he became known as the creator of the Fania All Stars, and also the work of pianist Charlie Palmieri and his Charanga La Duboney. The Puerto Rican brothers Eddie and Charlie Palmieri have been highly influential in the development of Latin music in the United States. While Eddie Palmieri's La Perfecta utilized the charanga flute of George Castro, Charlie Palmieri's charanga (one of the first to play the Palladium), featured flautists Johnny Pacheco and Rod Lewis Sánchez. Flute solos by Pacheco and Sánchez on the Charanga Duboney recordings of "Bronx Pachanga" and "Mack the Knife" are analyzed here to ascertain whether a distinctive New York sabor is present.

Much has been written on the creation of the "salsa" marketing term coined by Dominican-born Johnny Pacheco when he and his lawyer Jerry Masucci created the Fania record label. While his work as a bandleader and shrewd businessman are well known, not much has been written analytically about Pacheco's early recordings as a charanga flute player. Here his solos are analyzed with a view to exploring his influences. Pacheco has stated his initial inspiration came from the Havana-based charangas Orquesta Aragón and Arcaño y sus Maravillas and the son group Sonora Matancera.[51] Critiqued by some such as Juan Flores as a "traditionalist" or Storm Roberts as a "revivalist," I demonstrate here, through analysis of these recordings, how Pacheco's soloing style illustrates an innovative New York *típico* sound with a fast, percussive *embalao* style distinct from his Cuban role models.[52]

Chapter 7, "*Charangueaó en Típico*: Eddie Palmieri's La Perfecta," looks at flute player George Castro's improvisational style in this "trombanga" [trombones and flute] lineup. This combines charanga and conjunto elements, providing the template for the New York *salsa dura* [hard salsa] sound later developed by the likes of Willie Colón. Here Castro's típico five-key soloing style is compared to La Perfecta II's twenty-first-century versions by Eddy Zervigón and Dave Valentín to further explore manifestations of cubanía, sabor, Latinidad, jazz inflection, and freer forms of extemporization. The legacy of Eddie Palmieri's experimental approach is also evaluated here.

Chapter 8, "'I Don't Like It Like That': The Latin Bugalú," reflects on two different approaches to the Latin boogaloo/*bugalú* style from its origins in the Bronx and downtown Manhattan clubs through direct interaction with African American dancers to other more commercial fusions in the wake of the successful *bugalú conjuntos* of Pete Rodríguez, Ricardo Ray, and Joe Cuba.

Chapter 9, "La Charanga Moderna and the Modern Charanga," profiles the work of another key figure in Cuban dance music in New York: Puerto Rican conga player, bandleader, and arranger Ray Barretto. Like Eddie Palmieri, Barretto embraced charanga and conjunto aesthetics, combining Cuban forms with jazz, soul, and blues inflection. Flute player José/Joe Canoura's soloing style with Barretto's Charanga Moderna is examined here.

An evaluation of the US-based charangas and their respective flute soloists is then undertaken by looking at the various current manifestations of the típico charanga sound in New York. The voices of female musicians are more in evidence here, although the professional field remains male-dominated.[53]

Charanga flute players active on the New York scene today such as Karen Joseph, Joe de Jesus, and Connie Grossman contribute their perspectives on charanga performance past and present in the city.

In the Conclusion, "Defining New York *Sabor*," research findings are summarized, defining a variety of distinctive New York performance aesthetics and sounds that go beyond the usual description of New York–based Latin music as being simply loud, gritty, and aggressive. Conclusions are drawn here that have implications for future studies on the history of clave-based Latin dance music, performance aesthetics, and improvisational creativity.

- 1 -

SPACES AND PLACES

The old landmarks may have disappeared from the New York scene, but they will live forever in our memory. We shall never forget such places as the Park Plaza, the Club Caborrojeño, The Tropicana Club and the Palladium Ballroom. On their dance floors, our parents and grandparents and, in some cases, even we, danced away many an evening. The new generations have seen new landmarks rise. In due time, they shall become as venerable as the ones mentioned above. We can be certain that all those landmarks that we have remembered over the years shall help us to unlock the precious musical memories we keep in our hearts.[1]

Drawing on the memories of musicians who played in these "landmark" places, this chapter looks at the importance and continuing legacy of mid-twentieth-century venues for Cuban dance music in New York, examining

Figure 1.1 Fiesta de San Juan Bautista, Foley Square, New York, June 26, 2016. Copyright Sue Miller.

Figure 1.2 Joe de Jesus with his band Charansalsa, Foley Square, New York, June 26, 2016. Copyright Sue Miller.

how a sense of place and identity was formed through collective music-making and dancing in the ballrooms and clubs of New York and its barrios. Throughout these first few chapters, the adoption and adaptation of Cuban music by a majority–Puerto Rican community (in collaboration with Cuban musicians, other Latin Americans, and Anglo-Americans) is explored through the words of musicians themselves and in dialogue with numerous academic and popular works on the subject. Later I will be exploring musical style and Latin music performance aesthetics in the light of this ethnographic work, but first I give an outline of these landmark venues with particular focus on the Palladium era.

The event in Foley Square in Lower Manhattan (see figures 1.1 and 1.2) took place on a sunny June afternoon in 2016 in Thomas Paine Park, for the Fiesta de San Juan Bautista, the patron saint of Puerto Rico. Two bands were featured, Los Cachimbos de Hoy and Charansalsa, the latter led by trombonist and five-key flute player Joe de Jesus. The event was organized by the Comité de la Fiesta de San Juan Bautista and supported by New York's Parks and Recreation Commission. In many ways Charansalsa demonstrates the complexity of Cuban dance music history in New York by showcasing elements from the charanga format (five-key flute, cello, and violin), the conjunto format (bongos), and the musical influence of the Latin big band (trombone) and later US salsa forms (also demonstrating elements of Cuban *timba* in Charansalsa's arrangements).[2] Jewish American Lewis Kahn, a violinist and trombone player (a longtime member of the Fania All Stars and Larry Harlow's conjunto) performed here on violin, and African American John Henry Robinson III played cello in the vein of Tomás Valdes of Orquesta Aragón. US-born Puerto Rican Joe de Jesus performed on both the Cuban five-key wooden flute (the quintessential sound of the Cuban charanga) and the trombone (the emblematic instrument of US-based Cuban dance music) and has performed and recorded with Tito Puente, Ray Barretto, Celia Cruz, and David Byrne's Latin Band. On bongos that afternoon was Luis Mangual Jr., the grandson of the famous José Luis Mangual who performed with Tito Rodríguez and Tito Puente at the Palladium in the 1940s. The conga player Pito Castillo studied Latin percussion at the Boys Harbor School (this grassroots endeavor produced some of the finest Latin musicians on the New York scene) and he subsequently worked with Charlie Palmieri's and Joe Quijano's bands. Eddie Rivera, Charansalsa's timbales player, has also performed with Hector Lavoe's famous salsa group.[3]

This traditional festival organized by a Puerto Rican church group mirrors that of the annual New York Mamoncillo Festival organized by the Club Cubano Interamericano. These Puerto Rican and Cuban community-led events have sustained the employment of the Latin music community during times of plenty and times of famine, as Christina Abreu documents in detail.[4] With the focus on the music industry and commercial recordings in many accounts of Latin music history, these grassroots networks are often left out of the narrative, but they are essential for any understanding of socially-rooted musical development. As Eddy Zervigón states, the Club Cubano held the best dances and provided rehearsal space for bands:

SM: Una pregunta sobre los clubes sociales, el Club Cubano Interamericano...

EZ: En esos tiempos el Club Cubano era uno de los mejores bailes, no era un lugar bonito, ni nada de eso. Era un lugar viejo, mantenido por unos cubanos que llevaban mucho tiempo en los Estados Unidos. ... Lo que pasa es que en ese tiempo si tú querías gozar de verdad, el Club Cubano. Ahí se daban unos bailes y ahí se metían 600 personas. Era en Broadway, 669 de Prospect Avenue. Y allí ensayamos muchos de nosotros. Había otra cosa que era el Club Cubano de la 125, en Harlem. Allí yo toqué. Ese Club Cubano de la 125 estaba en contra del Club Cubano este.[5]

[SM: Just a question about the social clubs, the Club Cubano Interamericano...

EZ: At that time the Club Cubano was one of the best dances around, it wasn't a pretty place, nothing like that. It was an old place, maintained by a few Cubans who had lived a long time in the United States.... What happened was that at that time if you really wanted to have fun then the Club Cubano was the place. They put on several dances there which accommodated 600 people. It was on Broadway, 669 Prospect Avenue. And many of us rehearsed there too. There was another club which was the Club Cubano of 125th Street in Harlem. I played there. This Club Cubano from 125th Street was against the East-Side Club Cubano].

Abreu also notes that the Club Cubano Interamericano put on many successful popular dances and events and that there was some rivalry between different Cuban social clubs. Zervigón could well be referring to the Ateneo Cubano Social Club. (Abreu locates this at 2824 Broadway between 109th and 110th Streets, but Zervigón gives the location of the other Cuban club as higher up in Harlem on 125th Street, so this may have been a different club.) Through her detailed archival research into both the Club Cubano Interamericano and the Ateneo Cubano, Abreu concludes that El Ateneo Cubano was less racially inclusive and a "much more closed organization than El Club Cubano," and she documents several clashes of interest.[6] Solidarity amongst New York's *colonia cubana* was often broken through disagreements on race and politics amongst the different associations.[7] The Club Cubano Interamericano with its more inclusive agenda outlasted the Ateneo and had a major influence on the development of Latin music and dance in New York. Abreu shows how Cuban dance music became emblematic of Latin identity as a whole in New York (1940–60), concluding that "Cuban migrants did in fact create an identifiable *colonia cubana* for themselves, one with a considerable amount of symbolic and cultural capital that became an undeniable presence in New York city in the 1940s and 1950s, particularly in the realm of popular culture."[8] She refutes the argument often put forward that Cuban popular culture had less influence due to its smaller population size in relation to the Puerto Rican community, and demonstrates how Cuban popular music and dance were central to the development of a New York Latin identity for both communities. Cuban music was undoubtedly the most prominent genre due to its promotion by record companies such as RCA Victor, Puchito, Panart, Kubaney, and Gema.[9]

THE LATIN MUSIC AND DANCE COMMUNITY

Flute player Connie Grossman from New York charanga band SonSublime talks about the Latin music scene as being like one big family, mentioning the camaraderie of a community of musicians who not only guest or "sub" for each other but who also invite each other to social and family events. Speaking about the various lineups and styles of Latin music in New York in comparison to the Cuba-based models that inspired them, she says: "I just think in New York it's kind of like a mecca where it all comes together and you have these roots, but just like a tree, the roots grow a trunk and then they have so many different branches. Then the branches have branches, and then the branches have leaves." Grossman also discusses the idea of a New York sound and emphasizes place over ethnicity in the formation of that sound. She points out that some charangas and conjuntos were more influenced by bugalú and jazz than others, and that other US bands, in contrast, strive for a more típico Cuban 1950s sound as represented by famous groups such as Orquesta Aragón or Sonora Matancera. She attributes the sabor of New York to the places where Latin music is played, referring to the sound as "the geographical signature of New York."[10] And this sonic signature is of the Bronx and Spanish Harlem in particular, with many of the key figures in the history of Cuban music coming from these locations.

Roberta Singer and Elena Martínez paint a vivid picture of grassroots musical development in the South Bronx, where many mostly Puerto Rican musicians formed groups in the same streets, schools, and social clubs and where they hung out in stickball teams or in the "mambo" candy stores and ice cream parlors of the 1950s. Eddie and Charlie Palmieri's father, for example, ran a candy store with a juke box in it, as did Tito Puente's uncle; and these hangouts, in addition to social clubs, local theaters, and clubs, were to be the crucible for US-based Cuban dance music in the mid-twentieth century.[11] As far back as the 1920s local stores sold records and even made recordings such as Victoria Hernández's Almacenes Hernández (opened in 1927) and Tatay's Spanish Music Center, run by Puerto Rican Gabriel Oller (opened in 1934). Also foundational were pool halls such as El Billar de Los Músicos (Musicians' Poolroom) on 113th Street and Madison Avenue in Spanish Harlem, which acted as an informal musician employment agency.[12]

In June 2016 I persuaded author David A. Pérez[13] to drive me around New York visiting all the locations where the main music venues stood in the 1950s and '60s, such as El Campoamor, Broadway Casino, El Caborrojeño, the Caravana Club, the Triton, and the Taft Hotel. He kindly agreed to this slightly impractical scheme and, accompanied and assisted by his actress daughter Rachel and artist son David, we drove up and down New York, stopping to take photographs of the key locations "where it all happened." What follows is an exploration of Cuban dance music's history in mid-twentieth-century New York through some of the places and the people who have contributed to this rich seam of musical culture.

THE VENUES

Some venues where Cuban dance music was performed remained in the same location throughout the 1940s, '50s, and '60s but changed their names under new management or to accord with changing demographics and tastes. The Caravana Club (formerly the Tara Ballroom)[14] later became known as the Bronx Casino; the East Harlem Mack Morris Theater became the Hispano and then the Campoamor dance hall. Singer and Martínez emphasize the importance of the South Bronx and its key role as a center for Latin music in the USA, pointing out that patterns of Puerto Rican migration in the city have privileged Spanish Harlem (El Barrio) over other communities in the Bronx such as Hunts Point, Longwood, and Mott Haven: "In large part historical narratives about Puerto Ricans in the Bronx, most especially but not solely by outsiders to the area and the culture, take a temporal leap into the fires of the Bronx in the 1970s, overlooking three decades of vital, thriving, rich community life with an infrastructure to support a stable community."[15]

These three decades of rich musical development continue to influence the development of Latin music forms today, and more knowledge about these times is therefore crucial to an understanding of later musical developments. Accounts such as those by Brooklyn-based journalist Ed Morales and Venezuelan journalist, author, and radio and television producer César Miguel Rondón, while rich in detail in many respects, imply that musical styles played from the 1940s to the mid-1960s simply crystallized into what is now known as salsa.[16] Many histories of salsa follow the Fania narrative favored by Rondón and Morales, where the focus is on the internationalization of Latin music, through the label's success connecting with marginalized Latinos in New York and disaffected Latin American youth in the *barrios* of other countries such as Peru, Colombia, and Venezuela. In terms of the development of Cuban dance music in New York, however, it is important to acknowledge the decades preceding the difficult times of the 1970s and not to fall into a simplistic view of salsa emerging from the *barrios* in the late 1960s and '70s as something entirely new. This music had been forged by the rich community life documented by Singer and Martínez over a much longer period of time. Certainly the history of Cuban charanga in New York has been eclipsed by this more mainstream narrative and the late 1950s through the '60s needs to be studied afresh to more completely understand the intergenerational changes between the rhumba, mambo, and pachanga generations before, during, and after the 1959 Cuban Revolution and the ensuing political embargo.

"ESOS MUY HERMOSOS E INOLVIDABLES TIEMPOS EN NEW YORK"

Eddy Zervigón describes his experiences performing in these venues in the 1960s as "the most beautiful and unforgettable time of his life" and many of the venues listed are ones he performed in with his Orquesta Broadway.[17] Mid-twentieth-century venues for Cuban music important to the music's history and development include Park Plaza, El Campoamor, the Broadway Casino, the Caborrojeño, the Caravana Club, the Bronx Triton Social Club, Hunts Point Palace, Club La Conga, the Bronx Tropicana, the Havana San Juan (previously the Monte Carlo), the Roseland Ballroom, the Taft Hotel, and the Waldorf Astoria in Manhattan, as well as social clubs like the Club Cubano Interamericano and theaters like the Teatro Puerto Rico in the South Bronx. Church dances were also organized in many clubs and theaters in Brooklyn and Queens.

Venues for Latin music in downtown Manhattan were much sought after by musicians, as they paid well and augmented the prestige of the band. Lou Pérez mentions performing in the 1960s at the Roseland Ballroom (West 52nd Street near the Local 802 Musicians Union Hall), the Waldorf Astoria (301 Park Avenue), the Manhattan Center (at 34th Street and 7th Avenue), the Chateau Madrid (known previously as the Havana Madrid), the Palladium, the Copacabana (10 East 60th Street, which opened in 1940),[18] and the China Doll (which opened in 1946 at 52nd Street and Broadway). The China Doll was previously known as Club London and before that as Club La Conga (where Puerto Rican pianist Noro Morales directed the house rhumba band).[19] Zervigón also mentions the Casa Blanca Club in the Hotel Riverside:

> El más popular de todos fue El Casa Blanca, que empeso en la calle 73 entre Broadway y Amsterdam avenida. Después se mudo para la calle 52 y Broadway en los finales de los 1970 y 1980 y fue el club más popular de New York.

[The most popular [club] of all was the Casa Blanca, which started out on 73rd Street between Broadway and Amsterdam Avenue, then moved to 52nd Street and Broadway at the end of the 1970s and 1980s, and was the most popular club in New York.][20]

Another Bronx venue mentioned by Zervigón was the Casa Galicia on Basin Street East, where he performed on Sundays in the 1960s.[21] He also mentioned the Happy Hill Casino on 157th Street between Broadway and Amsterdam Avenue, owned by a Puerto Rican promoter named Alvarito, and El Hipocampo in the Bronx.[22] He also listed clubs from both the 1960s and '70s including El Casino 14 on 14th Street, Club 80 at 95th and Broadway opposite Club Broadway, and El Corso at 86th Street and 2nd Avenue.[23] Alongside the Palladium, many of these clubs formed part of the mambo era scene, popular once the rhumba bands and orchestras were declining in popularity in the early 1940s (although the musical styles of rhumba and mambo are not as distinct as often implied, with son/rhumba elements combined in the mambo big bands of the 1940s and '50s).[24] Zervigón has frequently told me in conversation that once you had your band's name up outside the Palladium you were in business (Orquesta Broadway was booked there in late 1962); the Palladium will be examined later in this chapter due to its crucial role in the development of Cuban dance music from the late 1940s until 1966.

Time frames may appear fixed when pinned to openings and closings of venues but are not static in terms of musical development, and many musicians who played in the 1960s obviously continued performing; a few are still on the scene today, some having changed with the times and others remain more típico but do not necessarily lack creativity or innovation. Processes of cultural change and exchange are subtle and difficult to define. Processes of *musical* change are also complex, necessitating a close reading of how the music sounds, how it works, how it is produced, and how it is received within these contexts. Musical analysis demonstrating creative process is therefore central to an understanding of New York's adoption and transformation (whether small-scale or more revolutionary) of Cuban dance music. Just as in pre-revolutionary Havana, 1960s New York offered a huge array of diverse performance opportunities for musicians, with a large Latin demographic to support the various forms of Cuban dance music performed in the city. These performance opportunities created favorable conditions for a rich and creative musical environment. Profiled below are grassroots clubs such as the Bronx Tropicana, the Triton, the Caborrojeño, the Campoamor and upscale downtown locations such as the Taft Hotel and the Waldorf Astoria. Here I privilege the venues that performers from various New York charangas,

Figure 1.3 Site of the old Bronx Tropicana. Copyright Sue Miller.

Afro-Cuban big bands, and conjuntos have mentioned as being fundamental to their lives and careers.

In terms of architecture, many of the key venues for Cuban dance music in the Bronx were housed in late nineteenth-century or early twentieth-century commercial buildings. Theaters such as the Spooner and the Manhattan have a paneled look with stripped-down classicism and Art Deco design. The Campoamor has a neoclassical façade of the big theater/cinema box typical of cinemas and theaters in the early twentieth century up until the 1940s. The downtown Manhattan venues, in contrast, were larger and more elaborate, designed to attract a wealthier clientèle.[25] The Waldorf Astoria, for example, with its two towers and bronze cupolas, is designed in the Art Deco style and was the inspiration for Fritz Lang's film *Metropolis*, as Will Jones remarks: "From the tips of its twin towers to the décor on its elevator doors, the hotel oozes architectural and artistic glamour, and as such it is one of the most famous hotels in the world."[26]

THE BRONX TROPICANA BALLROOM

The Bronx Tropicana Ballroom on Westchester Avenue and 163rd Street was opened in 1945 by two Cuban brothers, Manolo and Tony Alfaro, and they hired the earliest known US-based charanga band, directed by Cuban

Figure 1.4 The Opera House Hotel, formerly the Caravana Club. Copyright Sue Miller.

flute player and bandleader Gilberto Valdés, to perform there in 1952. The ballroom was inspired by the Havana Tropicana and featured top bands from Cuba (for example, Conjunto Casino in 1953) alongside US-based Latin bands. Hunts Point Palace was located nearby on Southern Boulevard and 163rd Street. In 1957, according to Ed Morales, Johnny Pacheco performed as a percussionist with Valdés's charanga here (although no longer under Valdés's leadership), taking over from Mongo Santamaría. After a stint with Charlie Palmieri's Charanga La Duboney, Pacheco formed his own charanga group in the early 1960s, performing regularly at the nearby Triton and Caravana Clubs.[27]

THE TRITON CLUB

The Triton Club was situated in the same area of the Bronx as the Tropicana, at 961 Southern Boulevard, and was built on the second floor of the former Spooner Theater, next door to the Hunts Point Palace Ballroom at 963 Southern Boulevard.[28] Here the charanga bands of Charlie Palmieri and Johnny Pacheco performed in the "hottest after-hours club" of the early

1960s.²⁹ The Alegre All Stars began life here as part of a *descarga* jam session set up by promoter Al Santiago, who later created the Alegre record label.³⁰ The Alegre All Stars and label paved the way for the Fania All Stars and label a decade later.

THE CARAVANA CLUB/BRONX CASINO/EL CERROMAR

Situated on 149th Street between 3rd Avenue and Brook Avenue, the Caravana was an important venue for musicians such as Charlie Palmieri, who recorded his album *Live at the Caravana Club* there in 1962.³¹ The Caravana Club used to be next door to the Bronx Opera House building, and the club's location is now taken by The Opera House Hotel (see figure 1.4). According to Singer and Martínez, the Caravana Club closed in 1962 and reopened in 1963 renamed the Bronx Casino, which stayed open until 1973. Eddy Zervigón states that the Bronx Casino was owned by two Cubans, one of whom was named José Maceda. It then opened in 1975 as El Cerromar, offering Latin music until the early 1980s.

EL CABORROJEÑO

This popular dance hall was situated on 145th Street and Broadway, a few blocks down from the Caravana. The Caborrojeño Club was housed in the building pictured in figure 1.5. With typical neoclassical ornamentation on its façade of "egg and darts" (see figure 1.8) and draped acanthus leaves (see figure 1.6), this building features second storey windows that show where the long dance floor would have been. Named after the owner of the dance hall who came from a town in Puerto Rico called Caborrojeño, there is now a club next door called El Morocco (see figure 1.7).³²

El Morocco, originally a speakeasy at 154 East 54th Street, which later moved across 54th to 307, was also a venue for Latin music in the 1950s and the 145th Street El Morocco (not the original) is inspired by the old East 54th Street club, which had a reputation for American and Latin bands and celebrity clientèle.³³ As Conzo and Pérez note, zebra-striped seats were part of the distinctive décor of the club, a design now featured in today's Morocco Club advertisement board.³⁴ These Manhattan venues had dress code policies; according to Zervigón, men had to wear a suit and tie at the Caborrojeño and the owner Ruperto Roberto had strict house rules on dress and gender roles:

Figure 1.5 El Caborrojeña's location. Copyright Sue Miller.

Figure 1.6 Neoclassical acanthus leaves. Copyright Sue Miller.

Figure 1.7 El Morocco. Copyright Sue Miller.

Figure 1.8 Neoclassical egg and darts. Copyright Sue Miller.

El Caborrojeño era propiedad de un señor Puertorriqueño llamado Ruperto Roberto y quedaba en la 145 calle y la avenida Broadway. Este era un lugar muy estricto pues habia que ir con traje y corbata y si no tenias corbata Ruperto Roberto te las alquilaba por 2$ y no dejaba a dos mujeres bailar.

[The Caborrojeño was owned by a Puerto Rican gentleman named Ruperto Roberto and was situated on 145th Street and Broadway. It was a place with strict rules where you had to wear a suit and a tie—if you did not have a tie Ruperto Roberto would hire you out one for $2 and he would also not allow two women to dance together.][35]

David Garcia describes racial discrimination at the Caborrojeño during the 1950s, and although racially discriminatory practices seem to have not been continued by the new owner in 1960, other "strict rules" mentioned by Eddy Zervigón may well have built on this past reputation.[36]

THE MONTE CARLO/HAVANA SAN JUAN

The Monte Carlo/Havana San Juan club was situated on 137th Street and Broadway. When Eddy Zervigón arrived in New York from Miami in the summer of 1962, he performed as a guest at the Monte Carlo club with the charangas of Lou Pérez (later recording on Lou Pérez's LP *Pa' Fricarse los Pollos*, in 1964),[37] with Alfredo Valdés Senior's charanga, and with Arsenio Rodriguez's conjunto.[38] Salazar and Zervigón both state that this club was located at 137th Street and Broadway.[39] According to Zervigón the Monte Carlo later became the Havana San Juan. Max Salazar gives a different location, as does Figueroa, for the earlier Monte Carlo Cabaret, 102nd Street and Madison Avenue. If the two are connected, then this earlier cabaret may perhaps have moved location by the 1960s.[40]

En la esquina de la calle 137 y avenida Broadway lo que estaba al principio cuando yo llegue a New York era El Monte Carlo que era propiedad de un señor Ingles creo que se llamaba Mr. John. Después lo compraron dos Cubanos y un Puertorriqueño y le pusieron el Habana San Juan, que fue muy popular.[41]

[On the corner of 137th Street and Broadway the main club when I arrived in New York was the Monte Carlo, which was owned by an

Figure 1.9 Site of the Campoamor, now the J.C. Christ of the Apostle Church. Copyright Sue Miller.

Englishman who was called Mr. John. Then two Cubans and a Puerto Rican bought it and gave it the name Havana San Juan, which was very popular.]

Max Salazar and Juan Flores both mention that pianist Charlie Palmieri first met Johnny Pacheco in the Monte Carlo in 1958 and that Pacheco then joined Palmieri's group firstly as a timbales player and then as a flute soloist.[42]

EL CAMPOAMOR

El Campoamor was situated on 116th Street and 5th Avenue. This venue is now the Church of the Lord Jesus Christ of the Apostolic Faith (see figure 1.9). According to Figueroa, this was a theater where musicians were hired to accompany silent film in the early part of the twentieth century.[43] The club was formerly the Mount Morris Theater and was renamed El Campoamor by Puerto Rican promoter Marcial Flores in 1934 when he booked Carlos Gardel to appear alongside his film showing of *Cuesta Abajo*. He later booked Cuban flute player Alberto Socarrás's rhumba band to back the stage shows presented there in the 1930s.[44]

Marcial Flores also ran the Club Cubanacán and opened it in the same year as the Campoamor, 1934.[45] Socarrás also performed at the Cubanacán, situated at 114th Street and Lenox Avenue (Malcolm X Boulevard). According to Abreu, Alberto Socarrás held a residency there for four years.[46]

PARK PLAZA AND PARK PALACE

The Park Plaza dance hall was situated on 110th Street and 5th Avenue in Spanish Harlem. Machito, Tito Puente, and Tito Rodríguez all played here in the 1940s through the early 1950s. Duke Ellington is commemorated in a statue standing next to his piano on a plinth here. Although there has yet to be a statue raised to honor Machito, Tito Puente, or Tito Rodríguez, East 110th Street is also honorarily titled Tito Puente Way. Both the Park Palace Ballroom and Park Plaza venues on the northwest corner of the two streets hosted Cuban dance music. The Park Palace was originally a Jewish caterer's hall which was hired out for Saturday night dances and was smaller than the Park Plaza club which was located above it.[47]

MANHATTAN'S DOWNTOWN LATIN VENUES

THE TAFT HOTEL

The famous Taft Hotel on 51st Street and 7th Avenue is where Cuban flute player Belisario López's charanga performed regularly as the house band in the 1960s.[48]

Concerts at the Taft Hotel were well paid. Eddy Zervigón said they paid $32 per musician in the 1960s and that he also danced there, stating a preference for the romantic *boleros* (it was where he met his first wife):

SM: ¿Has también bailado en el Taft Hotel o solamente tocado?
EZ: He bailado también.
SM: ¿Y **cómo fue eso**?
EZ: ¿Buscando muchachas? Sí, seguro. Yo era soltero cuando habré ido y
    en el Hotel Taft fue donde conocí a la mamá de los hijos míos, Ivan
    y Eddy, sí, en un baile del Hotel Taft. Que eran los sábados. El Club
    Coronel, de los hermanos Cámara, eran los que daban los bailes ahí
    en el Hotel Taft. Iba mucha gente americana.
SM: ¿Has **bailado chachachá, mambo, pachanga, guaracha**?

Figure 1.10 The Taft Hotel. Copyright Sue Miller.

Figure 1.11 The Taft Hotel. Copyright Sue Miller.

EZ: Sí, de todo. Pero más el *bolero*.

SM: ¿Un **público mezclado de americanos y latinos en el Taft?**

EZ: Sí, muchos italianos. Y también iba un cómico mexicano muy famoso en ese tiempo que se llamaba Tin Tan, era fantástico, iba casi todos los sábados.

[SM: **Did you also dance at the Taft Hotel as well as play?**

EZ: I danced too.

SM: **And what was that like?**

EZ: Looking for girls for sure. I was single when I came (to New York) and it was at the Taft Hotel where I met the mother of my two children Ivan and Eddy, at a dance at the Taft, which were on Saturdays. The Coronel Club was run by the Cámara brothers, who were the ones who put on those dances there at the Taft Hotel. Lots of Americans came to it.

SM: **Did you dance the chachachá, mambo, pachanga, guaracha?**

EZ: Yes everything. But I danced bolero the most.

SM: **Was the audience a mix of Americans and Latinos at the Taft?**

EZ: Yes there were a lot of Italians. Also a very famous Mexican comedian called Tin Tan was there. He was fantastic and was there nearly every Saturday.]⁴⁹

WALDORF ASTORIA

A New York institution, the Waldorf Astoria on 301 Park Avenue in Manhattan was a high-class venue much sought after by musicians. In 1926 the Vicente Sigler orchestra was the first Latin band to perform there, according

Figure 1.12 Waldorf Astoria's Starlight Roof. Copyright Sue Miller.

Figure 1.13 Ballroom ceiling, Waldorf Astoria. Copyright Sue Miller.

to Salazar, this event was advertised as for *gallegos* (white Spanish) only. A whole host of mixed-race Latin musicians performed in Sigler's orquesta, however, including Cuban clarinetist, saxophonist, and trumpet player Mario Bauzá; Cuban flute player and bandleader Alberto Socarrás; Puerto Rican trumpeter/bandleader Augusto Coen; and Cuban violinist/arranger Alberto Iznaga.[50] Xavier Cugat's band became the house band here in the 1940s.[51]

THE ROSELAND BALLROOM

Don Azpiazu's band was the house band at the Roseland Ballroom when Eddy Zervigón arrived in New York in 1962. According to Zervigón, by then these dances were aimed at an older audience:

> El Roseland era otra cosa. Roseland ahí estaba la orquesta de Azpiazu. Ahí habia no más una orquesta Latina para los viejos, por elderly.

> [Roseland was something else. Roseland then was where Azpiazu's band played. There was only one Latin band there to play for old people, for the elderly].[52]

Also located in the ballroom was the Local 802, the musicians' union hall on West 52nd Street.[53] Don Azpiazu's band, featuring the singer Antonio Machín, performed "El Manisero" ("The Peanut Vendor") at the RKO Theater in 1930. Following its recording on May 13, 1930, and its use in the movie *Cuban Love*

Song in 1931 (performed by Ernesto Lecuona and the Palau Brothers' Cuban Orchestra), Don Azpiazu and Machín became the catalysts for the "rhumba craze."[54] This appetite for commercialized Cuban son known as rhumba was on the wane in the 1940s when the mambo became the more prominent music and dance form. When Eddy Zervigón arrived, the Latin big bands were still performing but the charangas and conjuntos were beginning to take over in popularity—particularly once the Palladium lost its liquor license. The musicians' union had two pay scales, for Class A and Class B venues, and according to vocalist Willie Torres, it also depended on which night of the week you played as to which class you were assigned. The Roseland Ballroom commanded the higher Class A wage on the weekend, whereas its "Latin Tuesdays" commanded a lower Class B fee despite always attracting a full house.[55]

The Roseland Ballroom was demolished in 2015, having fallen into disrepair, and it is most regrettable that such an important cultural institution was not renovated as part of New York's heritage. These venues have been central to the history of Cuban music and dance in the city, and for more biographical detail of the musicians and venues mentioned, readers are encouraged to refer to the contextually rich profiles given by Max Salazar.[56] Other informative works on Latin music history include Juan Flores, *Salsa Rising*; David Garcia, *Arsenio Rodríguez and the Transnational Flows of Latin Popular Music*; and John Storm Roberts's pioneering works, *The Latin Tinge* and *Latin Jazz: The First of the Fusions*. The City Lore project "Place Matters" is also ethnographically rich.[57]

The next section examines the creative interplay between the various types of Cuban dance bands in the Palladium era, examining how the mambo of Israel and Orestes López, the charanga of Arcaño y Sus Maravillas, the *diablos* of Arsenio Rodríguez's conjunto-styled son, and the big band mambos of Benny Moré and Pérez Prado combined in the swing-influenced big bands of Machito, Tito Puente, and Tito Rodríguez. The commonly stated idea that the Palladium was "the home of the mambo" in New York is also interrogated, situating the music played there from 1947 to 1966 within a wider network of grassroots music and dance.

THE PALLADIUM—HOME OF THE MAMBO?

I watched Tito's band and like I said, I would get goosebumps listening to that band . . . he was really playing, this guy, it was incredible! And how they locked in, how the percussionists locked in . . . like a clock, like a heart beating.[58]

The Palladium Ballroom, situated on the corner of 53rd Street and Broadway, hosted live Latin music performances from 1947 or '48 until 1966.[59] Previously known as the Dreamland Dancing Academy and Alma Dance Studios, the Palladium no longer exists as a Latin music and dance venue; in its place now stands a Sheraton hotel. Famous for its regular Latin music nights from the big bands of Machito, Tito Rodríguez, and Tito Puente, this Manhattan venue was dubbed "Home of the Mambo" in the American mainstream press in the early 1950s.[60] Despite this label, many other musical styles were performed there by a variety of group formations including the earlier rhumba-styled orchestras, son conjuntos (including Arsenio Rodríguez's New York–based Conjunto de Estrellas), and charangas. Musical styles performed at this time included rhumba (son), guaracha, son montuno, guajira, chachachá, bolero, mambo, and variations on these styles. The Cuban son and charanga groups of the Palladium (from New York and bands visiting from Havana) influenced the music of the larger Latin big bands, in that many musicians who played the Bronx venues in conjuntos, charangas, and guitar-based trios also performed in the Latin big bands. The mambo bands themselves developed through influence from the Cuban son conjuntos, charanga orquestas, and Havana-based larger orquestas and jazz bands of the 1940s. The question mark at the end of this section's title is not to negate the importance of the Palladium's music and dance culture/s, or the immense contributions made by renowned musicians, such as Mario Bauzá, Frank Grillo (aka Machito), Tito Puente, and Tito Rodríguez, but to widen the context to include a broader spectrum of influence.

As outlined earlier, the Palladium was not the only venue where Cuban dance music was performed in mid-twentieth-century New York. Research by David Garcia, Christina Abreu, and Elena Martínez and Roberta Singer, in particular, has demonstrated how the son and charanga groups that performed regularly in the Bronx social clubs and venues such as the Park Plaza and the Bronx Tropicana, can be seen as more representative of grassroots Latin music and culture.[61] Garcia has highlighted the fact that the focus on the Palladium has tended to preclude any consideration of other manifestations of Latin music and dance culture in the city:

> Its [the Palladium's] importance to the popularization of Latin dance music in the United States is undeniable, but, perhaps even more important, the Palladium and the music of its principal protagonists have constituted a dominant place in both the Latin imagery of American popular culture and the historical canon of Latino popular music and culture in the United States.[62]

Accounts of Cuban dance music history in New York often skip from the end of the Palladium mambo era to the búgalu of the late 1960s and then chart the subsequent rise of the Fania label with its controversially named *salsa* brand of Latin music. The fact that musicians such as Johnny Pacheco, Eddie and Charlie Palmieri, Ray Barretto, and Manny Oquendo were influenced by charanga and conjunto orquestas in the 1950s is not always brought to the fore. These musicians played the Palladium as part of the big bands and also performed in their own conjuntos and charangas. Musical aesthetics from the charanga and the conjunto informed their approach to Cuban dance music performance and this approach became known collectively as *salsa dura* in the 1970s and early 1980s. Pianist and arranger Alfredito Valdés, for example, wrote arrangements for Ray Barretto that were, he says, "very 'Arsenio.' [They] were all Arsenio ideas. Rather, they had that approach."[63] Big band mambo was an influence for them, but no more so than the son montuno and mambo diablos of Arsenio Rodríguez and the charanga mambos and pachangas of José Fajardo, Orquesta Aragón, Orquesta Sublime, and Arcaño y sus Maravillas. Sydney Hutchinson in her study "Mambo on 2" dancing cites the big band mambo as "salsa's most immediate precursor," but the story is far more complex, as I will demonstrate in the analyses in chapters 2, 5, and 8 on the mambo, pachanga, and bugalú, respectively.[64] The Palladium musicians and their audiences did not suddenly disappear in 1966, either; they simply moved to other clubs where Cuban dance music had always been performed, such as the Chez José in the Park Plaza Hotel. When that closed in 1970, the Corso Club (which opened as a Latin music venue in 1968) took over the scene, becoming known as the "Casa del Sonido Típico Latino" [The Home of the *Típico* Latin Sound].[65] These venues accommodated the "smaller" charanga and conjunto bands, accounting in some respects for the surge in their popularity in the 1960s. As the mambo big bands fell out of favor with the more mainstream American public in favor of rock 'n' roll in the 1960s, Cuban dance music was sustained through the support of the sizeable Latin population in the Bronx and Harlem venues and social clubs.

Journalists, music historians, Latin music scholars, and ethnographers such as Max Salazar (Latin Beat), Israel Sanchez Coll (Herencia Latina), John Child (Descarga), Roberta Singer and Elena Martínez (City Lore), Joe Conzo, David Pérez, David Carp, John Storm Roberts, and David Garcia, among others, have undertaken much-needed ethnographic work, particularly in terms of interviews with musicians from this era. Films such as Kevin Kaufman's documentary *The Palladium: Where Mambo Was King* and the somewhat stereotyped portrayal of the Palladium in Arne Glimcher's *The Mambo Kings* (1992), on the other hand, have disseminated a mainstream

Figure 1.14 Mark Weinstein at home in New Jersey, June 22, 2016. Copyright Sue Miller.

narrative of the venue's history.[66] As the work of Abreu, Garcia, and Singer and Martínez reveal, however, many innovations took place in the South Bronx and El Barrio at the grassroots level. Indeed, many musicians from these Bronx clubs played in the big bands of the Palladium, where changes were made only in terms of audience demographic and band orchestration. In terms of income and recognition by recording companies, performances for non-Latin audiences were important to Latin musicians' careers. Commenting on audience demographics for Latin music in the 1950s, Perfecta trombonist and Latin jazz flute player Mark Weinstein remarked:

MW: Here's what you have to understand. Latin music, starting in the fifties, was not played for Latin audiences. Latin musicians made a living playing mainly for Jews and secondarily for Italians. There were two venues where the bands like Tito Puente made a living, made their big money. In the summer, they played in the Catskill Mountains, and then in the winter they played out on the shore in Long Beach. After the summer season they'd play Long Beach. The bands either played for Jews in the Catskills—Machito played in the Concorde, Eddie [Palmieri] played in Kutsher's, all of these bands made nice money during the summer, and the La Playa Sextet was always on the shore. Then the other venues were church dances for Italians. . . . Saint Fortunato's was the big one in Brooklyn. . . . The first time that Latin bands were playing for predominantly Latin audiences was . . . Now, how can I say this? I want to say this right. The place that changed everything—there were venues in Harlem and in the South Bronx that played for Latin audiences, but these were mainly what the young guys called *gallego* bands ... they'd play a lot of merengues and a lot of boleros, although Machito always played in the Hunts Point Palace, right?

SM: Yes, I've heard about that, yes.

MW: The Hunts Point Palace had a Latin crowd. The Palladium had a Latin crowd, an African American crowd, and a Jewish/Italian crowd. Jews and Italians were—everything in New York was Jewish/Italian.... Anyway, the thing that changed everything was a little club down the block from Hunts Point Palace. A loft painted black ...

SM: Was that the Tritons Club?

MW: ... called the Tritons Club where Eddie Palmieri, Pacheco and ...

SM: Charlie Palmieri as well?

MW: No, not Charlie so much.... The three bands in the Tritons were Eddie, Pacheco, and Orlando Marín, they were the three bands, and they were the first bands that were playing for young Puerto Ricans.[67]

As Weinstein points out, the Manhattan-based Palladium drew crowds from a variety of backgrounds as opposed to the mainly Latin audiences of Spanish Harlem and the South Bronx. The disparaging term *gallego* probably refers in the main to Puerto Rican voice and guitar-led trios, as popularized by the composer and performer Rafael Hernández. These "pan-Caribbean" groups performed in cafes and clubs playing a variety of styles including Puerto Rican *aguinaldo*, Mexican *corrido*, Cuban *guajira*, *bolero*, and *son*, and the Cuban–Puerto Rican *guaracha*.[68] These earlier-generation trios were influential, and compositions by Rafael Hernández, for example, have become famous son, charanga, and salsa classics (e.g., "Silencio," "Lamento Borincano," and "El Cumbanchero").[69] It is also important to note that Eddie Palmieri, Orlando Marín, and Johnny Pacheco also performed at the Palladium and many working-class Puerto Ricans attended the mambo big band dances. Percussionist John Berdeguer celebrates the mix of people that attended the Palladium in the 1960s:

> Yes, the pachanga was danced with the mambo at the Palladium. It was like something you don't see nowadays where different cultures were there, they all danced together. There were Jewish people there, there were black people there, there were Italian people there, there were Latinos there.... a beautiful situation. Yes the music brought everyone together as people, not as "Oh, you're this" and "I'm that." Nowadays it doesn't happen that way.[70]

Figure 1.15 Percussionist John Berdeguer, New York, June 15, 2016. Copyright Sue Miller.

Eddy Zervigón performed at the Palladium after it had lost its liquor license at the end of 1962. Zervigón says only non-alcoholic beer was sold and people brought their own drinks to the dance:

> EZ: El Palladium cerró en el año 1967. Cuando yo llegué a Palladium no había bebida, no vendían bebida porque se la habían cancelado. Vendían cerveza sin alcohol y la gente traía su caneca y tomaba.
>
> [The Palladium closed in 1967. When I arrived at the Palladium there was no drink, they didn't sell drink because they lost their license. They sold non-alcoholic beer and so people brought their own hip flasks and drank from those.][71]

Orquesta Broadway secured a regular spot there after performing on a Friday under the heading "El Festival del Danzón," a name Zervigón used as he was afraid the new band name Orquesta Broadway (suggested to them by the Palladium promoter Catalino Rolón) might make dancers think the music was American and not Latin. Their one-year contract displaced Eddie Palmieri's band from their regular booking slot and Broadway performed that year on Wednesdays, Fridays, Saturdays and Sundays. Zervigón stated that musicians were paid $20 on a Wednesday, $24 on a Friday, $28 on a Saturday (although he got paid a little more at $32) and on Sunday between $20 and $24. Sundays were most popular with African Americans and Zervigón asserts that their preference was for the mambo, not the chachachá, although

Figure 1.16 Author David A. Pérez Sr., Brooklyn, June 11, 2016. Copyright Sue Miller.

they occasionally liked to dance to a guajira. He said these Sunday gigs were physically hard work as the mambo is so riff-based and always taken at a fast tempo. Saturdays he said attracted a mainly Puerto Rican crowd, with Friday attracting both Americans and Puerto Ricans. Wednesdays attracted more Americans, with many coming for the dance classes to learn the steps for guajira, chachachá, and merengue. When I asked if the Puerto Rican plena and bomba dances were also taught he said yes, also stating that elements from the bomba and plena did find their way into arrangements, although he was unable to musically define those elements to me himself. He did, however, comment that Cuban dance music was supported by the Puerto Rican population and that there were fewer Cubans in New York at this time. He explained that many Cuban exiles preferred Miami because of the warmer climate and the proximity of the home country.[72] The much-lauded racial integration fostered by the Palladium does need more nuanced analysis, as it is not clear whether much real integration took place if audience demographics were as differentiated by days of the week as Zervigón states.

Perspectives among those interviewed for this book varied depending on which community they were from, and in which era they attended the Palladium. New York–born Puerto Rican David Pérez, for example, grew up in Brooklyn and rarely went to the Bronx venues but attended the Palladium from 1959 as " basically people from Brooklyn and the Bronx do not see eye to eye—but we would meet in Manhattan."[73] Weinstein mentions that parents would allow their teenage sons and daughters to attend church dances and the Palladium but not the rougher uptown and Bronx venues.

Thus, Latin music was found in the clubs and venues of the South Bronx, Spanish Harlem, the Catskills resorts, Long Beach, and at Catholic church dances as well as in the downtown Manhattan venues. The audiences from Harlem and the Bronx and those from Brooklyn may well have met "halfway" at the Palladium but as Garcia points out, many working-class Cubans and Puerto Ricans living in the Bronx would not necessarily have attended the Palladium. A history of the music performed at the Park Plaza in El Barrio would perhaps reveal a different story from the canonical, more well-trodden histories of the Palladium, as Puerto Rican dancer Luis "Maquina" Flores remarks:

> The Palladium always got the fascination of people because it was situated on 53rd Street and Broadway. . . . The Plaza never got in the limelight because it was smack in the middle of the ghettos. . . . But I'll tell you one thing: Machito, Arsenio, all of these bands—you never heard these people swing like they swung when they were playing at the Plaza. Because the music belonged to the ghettos. . . . You could not have the same feeling in the Palladium. When you went to the Palladium you were more starchy, you know, a little more phony.[74]

The trajectory of histories of Cuban dance music in New York has tended to be Palladium-centric, but even accounts of the Palladium-based music often lack detailed musical analysis, which is needed if lines of influence are to be evidenced and developments better understood. The concept of "generation" also needs to be questioned, as many musicians from the "new" generation of Puerto Ricans, as mentioned by Weinstein, performed with older musicians in the earlier rhumba bands and mambo big bands before developing their own charangas and conjuntos. Tito Puente played in Cuban trumpeter Julio Cuevas's orquesta in the 1940s, for example, and Johnny Pacheco performed with Gilbert Valdés's charanga at the Bronx Tropicana alongside Cuban conga player Mongo Santamaría in the 1950s. Often, due to what Nancy Raquel Mirabal has termed the "exile model," Cuban influence from Cuban migrant musicians is assumed to start after the 1959 Cuban Revolution, despite an established presence of Cuban Americans in New York and Miami in the 1940s and '50s (including Mongo Santamaría, Julio Cuevas, and Gilberto Valdés).[75] While revolution did have major consequences for Cuban music in the United States, particularly with the influx of Cuban musicians in the early 1960s, reinforcing the charanga presence in particular, much of what came before paved the way for Cuban dance music to take hold in the United States.

Cuban dance music has played a central role in defining Latin New York. Despite a much smaller population size than the Puerto Rican one, the Cuban influence on Latin music's development here is due to several factors: the important role of the Cuban and Puerto Rican social clubs; the presence of influential Cuban musicians (such as Marcelino Guerra, Arsenio Rodríguez, Anselmo Sacasas, José Curbelo, René Hernández, Miguelito Valdés, and José Fajardo); the influence of visiting Cuban bands; and the dominance of Cuban music within the record industry.

The mambo has played a central role in defining Latin music in New York; but before examining how Puerto Rican musicians adopted and adapted this and other Cuban styles, it is important to understand the wider context of mambo's development by first considering the relationship between musicians in Havana, Mexico, and New York. This is done not to argue the case for its origins or to outline a strictly linear time frame for the mambo's development, but rather to explain in more musical depth the complex relationships between musical styles and their performance contexts.

Two important groups are cited when discussing the origins of mambo: Antonio Arcaño's charanga, Arcaño y sus Maravillas; and Arsenio Rodríguez's conjunto, both of which drew upon Afro-Cuban culture to develop their danzón-mambo and mambo-diablo "open" sections. In the next chapter I will demonstrate how these innovations were then creatively adopted by arrangers for the Havana big bands and exported to Mexico and New York, often via the very same arrangers, many of whom moved to New York in the mid- to late 1940s. Rather than focusing on who invented the mambo, I will instead be looking at lines of influence in the mambo genre's development, revealing the pervasive charanga thread that runs through the Palladium years from the 1940s through the 1950s, long before the charanga "boom" of the early 1960s, explored in chapter 5.

- 2 -

LOS TRES GRANDES

Redefining the Mambo Genre

LOS TRES GRANDES:
THE THREE GIANTS AND THE CUBAN JAZZ BANDS

The son (which includes rhumba and guaracha) and charanga ingredients in the mambo big bands hark back to the Cuban "Big Three" bands of the 1940s (David Garcia refers to them as "The Three Giants"). *Los Tres Grandes* consisted of Arsenio Rodríguez y Su Conjunto, Antonio Arcaño y Sus Maravillas (a charanga augmented to a larger Orquesta Radiofónica for radio broadcasts),[1] and the charanga Melodías del 40. All three bands performed in the black social clubs and cabarets of Havana and also performed live regularly on the Mil Díez radio station in Havana and therefore were influential in terms of reach across the island, especially in the 1940s.[2] Their fame may well have been why the Palladium bands of Tito Rodríguez, Tito Puente, and Machito were also named "The Big Three." While Arsenio Rodríguez performed his *diablo*-styled son montunos in the 1940s in the dance halls of Havana, and Arcaño's group were innovating with their *danzones de nuevo ritmo* and open mambo sections, the hotel big bands in Havana were also beginning to add mambo elements to their arrangements in the form of *guajeos mambeados*, inspired by these developments. The son montunos of Arsenio and the guarachas of the larger orquestas were not called "mambo" at the time, and Arcaño's "Mambo" was performed as part of a full danzón with a mambo section in 1938; it was only recorded much later in 1951 as the shorter "Mambo" featuring just the second half of the composition.[3] This was part of a wider trend to truncate the first section of the danzón and son styles and extend the open montuno section, which showcased vocal and instrumental improvisation.[4] New York musicians also focused on the montuno section with an improvisatory *descarga* (literally, discharge; loosely translates to "jam") aesthetic in performance inspired by these changes but perhaps also due to adjusting to English-speaking contexts. Mark Weinstein remarks: "a lot of the New York charangas never really played the songs. They just played an intro and a montuno."[5] This may perhaps have come about in order to adapt to Anglophone audiences, with 1930s and '40s hotel bands in Havana catering for American tourists; many Latin musicians performed to predominantly English-speaking audiences in 1950s venues and resort hotels in the USA. Weinstein notes that Jewish American musicians in the Latin bands of the Catskills resorts were only able to sing *coro*, not verses: "This was 1959 at the President Hotel and you played Latin dance music. All of the Jewish guys sang *coro*, all the Jewish guys, and they couldn't sing in Spanish, so all it was was intro and *coro*, intro and *coro*. Of course Machito played real music but . . ."[6]

Before the 1959 revolution there was regular interchange between Havana- and New York–based musicians, as Lise Waxer has pointed out in her article:

> In New York, musicians performing Cuban styles were exposed to audiences, performance contexts, musical resources, and economic constraints that differed from those in Cuba, all of which served to transform the Cuban sound. Back in Cuba, however, musicians were continually absorbing ideas and stylistic practices from North America (most importantly, jazz styles emanating from New York), a process that reframed the local Cuban music formation. These new sounds, in turn, would go back to New York and other North American cities, influencing further developments there. . . . Thus, in refining the standard narrative of Latin music history, Havana and New York are seen as two points of creativity in a circular process, each one responding, either directly or indirectly, to changes in the other.[7]

Arsenio Rodríguez's conjunto moved to New York permanently in 1952, bringing Arsenio's mambo-styled son montuno to the city.[8] New York–based Cuban performers and arrangers had also worked previously in the 1940s big bands of the Havana hotels catering for American tourists. Cuban pianist and arranger Anselmo Sacasas and singer Miguelito Valdés performed in Casino de La Playa before moving to New York in the 1940s to join Xavier Cugat's Latin band in New York. Pérez Prado arranged music for several Havana big bands including Casino de la Playa, and during a trip to New York in the mid-1940s he sold several arrangements to Xavier Cugat.[9] Anselmo Sacasas started his own group performing at La Conga Club and the Havana Madrid in New York,[10] having previously worked with Tata Pereira's charanga in the 1930s, an important group in the evolution of the charanga.[11] The Cuban arranger and pianist René Hernández worked in Julio Cueva's Orquesta, the first big band to play the mambo-styled montunos in Havana in 1944 before moving to New York in 1945 to arrange and perform in Machito and his Afro-Cubans (Bebo Valdés replaced him in Cueva's Orquesta).[12] Although Mario Bauzá was the musical director of Machito and his Afro-Cubans, Hernández wrote many of the band's arrangements and the *guajeos mambeados* of the saxophone lines were almost certainly introduced here by Hernández. As Ned Sublette explains:

> The big band mambo polyrhythmicized the jazz band. It was characterized by a new way of treating the sax section, which seems to have been devised by René Hernández, one of the most underappreciated figures in Latin music. The sax section became independent from the other horns, and more rhythmic in function . . . Whereas earlier Cuban jazz bands voiced their horns in the American style, with the whole horn section playing a single harmonized line, a new generation of Cuban arrangers—specifically, René Hernández, Ramón "Bebo" Valdés, and Dámaso Pérez Prado—started writing more idiomatically and in a more Cuban style.[13]

Differing from swing band arranging conventions, the approach taken for the mambo band orchestration was influenced by the performance practices of previous Cuban ensemble formats where saxophones emulated violin guajeos and conjunto tres guitar guajeo patterns. Trumpets followed both the *septeto* and conjunto performance conventions, and the timbales of the charanga became a mainstay of both the expanded conjunto and the big band. The characteristic bass trombone in Pérez Prado's mambos performed dominant pedal riffs which, in terms of function (rather than register and rhythm), replicated the function of the pedal guajeos performed by violins in the charanga mambo. The following analysis of "Mambo" by Arcaño y sus Maravillas demonstrates these stylistic elements that were later adapted in the mambo big bands.

DEFINING THE MAMBO GENRE: LINEUPS AND LINES OF INFLUENCE

THE CHARANGA MAMBO

At first listening one might presume that the charanga mambo of the late 1930s and '40s is not connected to the brash New York sounds of the

Palladium big band mambo, or indeed to the swing band mambos of Pérez Prado; this is, in part, due to the different instrumentation. The charanga lineup, while containing the expected timbales, congas, güiro, piano, and bass, also includes violins and the five-key wooden flute (now mostly replaced by the metal Boehm system flute). The precursor to the charanga was the brass and woodwind ensemble of the orquesta típica, which included two clarinets in C, two violins, a cornet, timpani, güiro, ophicleide (a precursor to tuba or euphonium), double bass, and valve trombone. The influence of jazz in the 1920s is partially responsible for the decreasing popularity of the orquesta típica as musicians left to join the more popular septetos and Cuban jazz bands; the charanga was formed from the remaining instruments of the orquesta típica, with the addition of flute and piano. For a time the clarinet and flute coexisted within the charanga format.[14]

In the transcriptions below of "Mambo" by Arcaño y sus Maravillas, musical connections between the charanga mambo and the big band mambo can be seen in terms of the mixolydian static harmony of the flute solo over D7 (see example 2.1), the mambo guajeos in the violins, the danzón-mambo-styled bassline (see examples 2.2 and 2.3), the piano montuno accompanied by the same line in vocal 2, a counter melody coro in vocal 1 (see example 2.4), and the now standard mambo/chachachá patterns in the percussion section (see example 2.5). These patterns contain aspects of Cuban son, chachachá, and danzón styles, forming a "mambo" of layered guajeos, tumbaos, and coro figures functioning as an exciting polyrhythmic final section. The rhythm of the main "Mambo" guajeo became the rhythmic template for many emblematic mambo-styled piano montunos and saxophone guajeos in the Latin big bands and orquestas, albeit with the insertion of a more chromatic descending line.[15]

The flute solo transcribed and annotated in example 2.1 I explore in more detail in *Cuban Flute Style*, where the development of the Cuban flute improvisational style is analyzed.[16] The example is given here in order to demonstrate the characteristic mambo soloing style with its static harmony (over D7) with occasional sharpened fourth note $g^{\#}_3$ and the prevalence of axis note a^3, the dominant degree of the mixolydian mode on d (in the key of G major).

The mambo of Pérez Prado is directly linked to the rhythm and contour of the specific guajeo of the "Mambo" composition by Arcaño's musicians, as shown in example 2.2. This rhythmic configuration was transplanted into the saxophone sections of the Cuban "jazz" and New York–based Latin big bands.[17]

Mambo
Flute Solo by Eulogio Ortiz

c. Orestes and Israel 'Cachao' López
transcribed and analysed by Sue Miller
From Danzón Mambo [1944–51] Tumbao Classics TCD–029CD Reissue

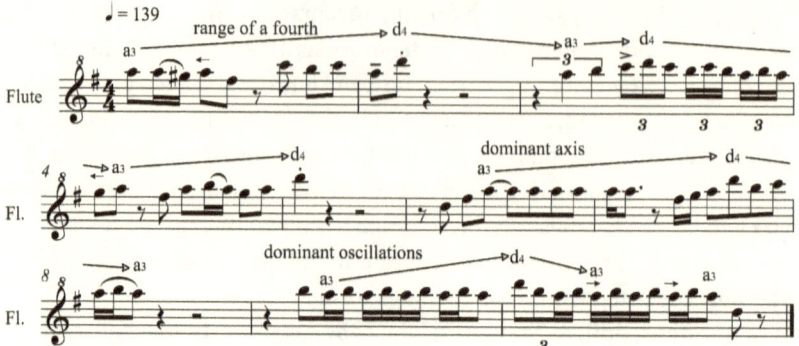

Example 2.1 Annotated transcription of the flute solo on "Mambo" by Eulogio Ortiz (over D7).

Example 2.2 String-section mambo guajeos and bass danzón-mambo-style tumbao in Arcaño y sus Maravillas recording of "Mambo."

Mirroring the main "Mambo" coro, the violins' incessant guajeos create a hypnotic effect where the bass line connects with their melo-rhythmic line on the 2+ beat of the 3-side of the clave, known as the *bombo*. This lack of convergence except on an important clave beat creates rhythmic tension, as does the absence/avoidance of a tonic note and the tonic chord of G. The bass line is characteristic of those played in the final open montuno sections of danzones in the charanga orquesta from the advent of Arcaño's charanga band "Mambo" onward into the 1940s and '50s. A similar bass line is employed by Tito Puente in his big band mambo composition "Mambo Gozón" (see example 2.8).

Another violin guajeo appears in the first section of "Mambo" functioning as a pedal on the e², the 9th of D7 and the 6th in G major (see example 2.3), which is characteristic of the style. Again this pedal effect emphasizes the static harmony and dissonant tension. The first part of this resembles the vamp used in the danzón-mambo "Chanchullo" by Israel López and in Tito Puente's static harmony chachachá "Oye Como Va."

Example 2.3 Violin pedal *guajeo* on "Mambo."

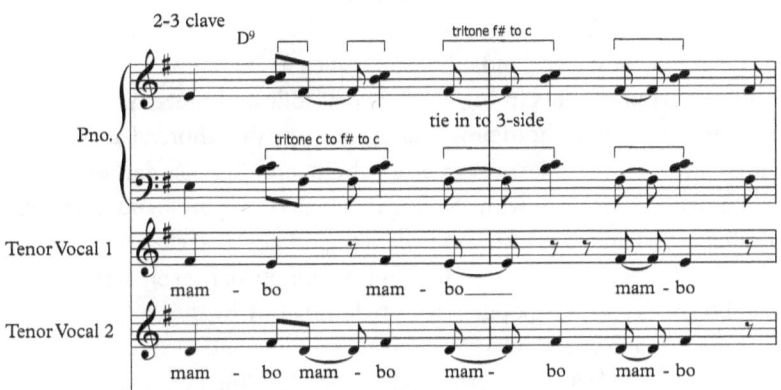

Example 2.4 Piano mambo figure with two variations on the mambo chant.

In example 2.4 the close intervals of minor and major seconds can be seen with the oscillation between the second (dissonant) and third (concordant) degree of the scale in Arcaño's "Mambo" (see examples 2.2 and 2.4). The repeated tritone interval of f♯ to c in the piano montuno adds to the tension and excitement. The use of the raised fourth g♯ in the flute solo gives the piece a whole tone inflection at times and adds further dissonance (see example 2.1).[18]

Through the adaptations of these elements in the mambo big bands, this composition and others like it may well have influenced the development of modal jazz in the USA, which in reality was a mix of functional and static harmonies. For example, the one-chord charanga mambo can be found in Mario Bauzá's "Tanga" from 1949. Indeed, Paul Austerlitz believes modal jazz may well have its roots in these mambo innovations:

Another pervasive Cuban influence on jazz and other forms of U.S. music was the use of static harmonies. North American popular music had traditionally utilized "common practice" chord progressions, but beginning in the 1950s, jazz and North American dance music increasingly used static harmonies. Jazz improvisation in this style was dubbed "modal improvisation" as it is confined to a single scale or mode, and this practice became extremely important in jazz. Its links, however, to Afro-Cuban music are rarely acknowledged.[19]

Some New York big band mambo arrangements kept the one-chord dominant seventh-based mambo of the charanga but introduced the chromatic Prado-styled descending mambo line, often incorporating jazz solos to accompany them (particularly in the case of Machito and his Afro-Cubans). The pedal figure as demonstrated in example 2.3 from Arcaño's "Mambo" has come to represent a New York style of chachachá, popularized by Tito Puente and then later by Latin rock band Santana.[20] Ray Barretto also made use of the device in "El Watusi" and other songs such as "El Bantu."[21]

Other arrangements in big band format followed more typical son or chachachá montuno chord progressions mostly using chords I and V, albeit with a larger range of keys to cater for the B♭ and E♭ brass and woodwind instruments. Certainly, with the larger forces of the big band, harmonic vocabulary expanded to include a wider range of keys and closer jazz harmonies. The chachachá followed on from the popularity of the son montuno and mambo styles and was popularized predominantly by the charanga bands in 1950s Havana (particularly Orquesta América and Orquesta Aragón) as well as by the larger orquestas and big bands.[22] The percussion patterns prevalent in the final section of *danzones de nuevo ritmo* became standard in the chachachá and mambo styles in both Havana and New York. The mambo pattern on the large timbale emphasizes the 2+ closed tone rather than the on-beat 2 of chachachá, and so the mambo can be viewed as slightly more syncopated in terms of percussion texture.

Example 2.5 Mambo percussion patterns.

The percussion section emphasizes clave direction through the in-clave *cierres* or "breaks" and within the solo improvisations where clave feel is demonstrated. The mambo elements developed in Arcaño's band came from the emphasis on the clave-outlining interwoven guajeo patterns over the D7 chord, which build the intensity of the music through repetition, dissonance, and the anticipated beat 4+, which tips into the 3-side of the clave. This intensity is something common to Afro-Cuban religious ceremony where the end point or climax is when the *orisha* (saint) "mounts" or possesses a devotee. In Arcaño's "Mambo," the vocal coro "mambo" has two versions sung in counterpoint, as do the two violin guajeos, reflecting the dialogic approach defined by the Bantú origins of the term and by the conversational aesthetic of Cuban music.[23] This mambo section extended in charanga form is similar to the final section in Arsenio Rodríguez's conjunto performances (he called his mambo final section *diablo*); the off-beat nature of the Arcaño "Mambo" violin guajeo pattern is similar to tres guitar guajeo patterning, and the violin and tres functions are identical in both contexts. Following these developments in the late 1930s and early 1940s, Cuban big bands and larger orquestas began to incorporate mambo sections into their arrangements and these became a major feature of the swing band–inspired Latin big bands of Pérez Prado and the New York Palladium groups. Many aspects of the charanga mambo from the late 1930s were incorporated into other varieties of the mambo genre, as was the contemporaneous *diablo* section of Arsenio Rodríguez's conjunto arrangements.

THE SON CONJUNTO AND ITS MAMBO DIABLO

In the son montunos of Arsenio Rodríguez's band, the climax is characterized by a shortened "half coro" (with the same function as the mambo coros in Arcaño's "Mambo"), and by the diablo figures of the trumpets including their off-beat shakes or stabs (used later by Pérez Prado's trumpet section); these are demonstrated in Arsenio Rodríguez's composition "El Reloj de Pastora" [Pastora's watch],[24] shown in example 2.6.

In this final section the three trumpets play semi-independent lines; a louder trumpet ad libs toward the end, finishing with an improvised *moña* riff before the final coro as coda. The reduced score in example 2.6 demonstrates the overlapping trumpet lines and the half coro repetitions characteristic of the diablo section. The relationship between Arcaño's "Mambo" and Arsenio's diablo section is apparent when comparing examples 2.2 and 2.4 with example 2.6. Both sections have the intensity of Afro-Cuban religious music and dance ceremony with their hypnotic confluence of

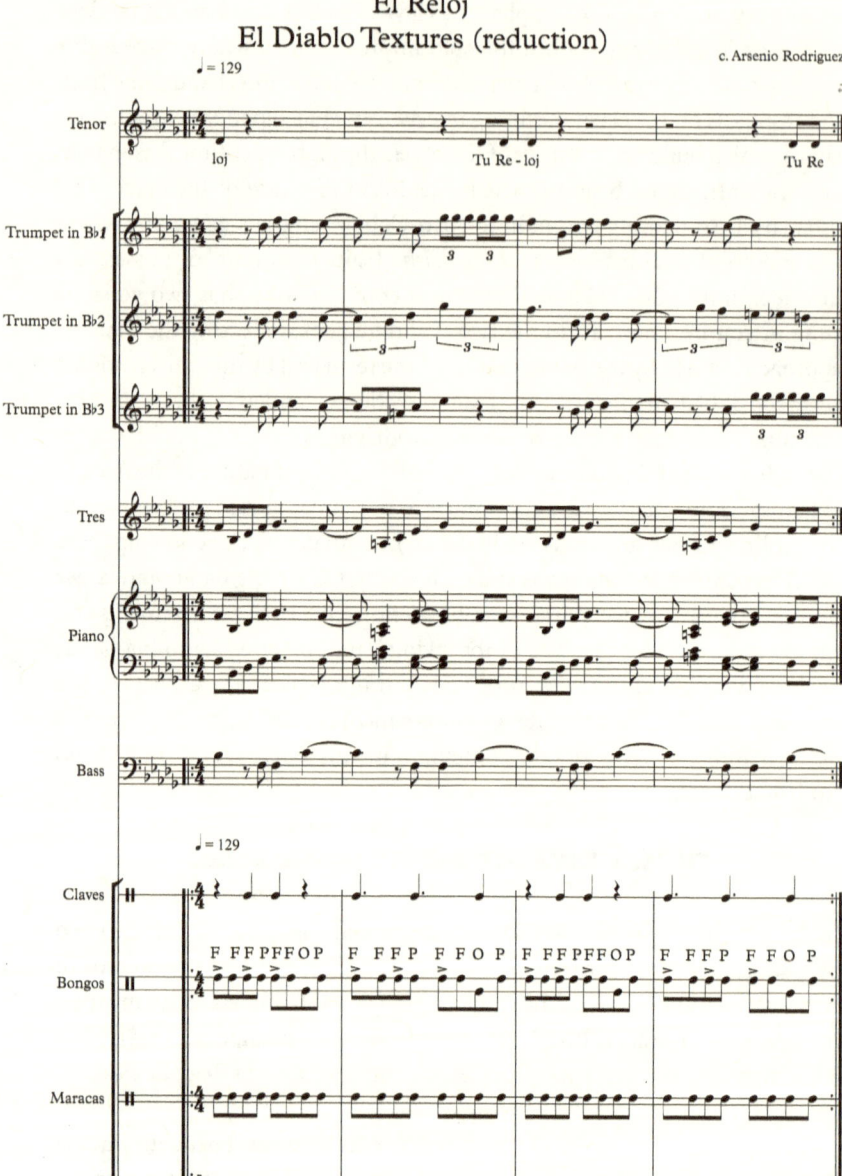

Example 2.6 Diablo textures in "El Reloj de Pastora" by Arsenio Rodriguez.

clave-organized figures. These off-beat interwoven clave-organized lines from Arcaño's danzón-mambo in his charanga orquesta and Arsenio's diablo in the son montuno played by his conjunto were influential on the Cuban big bands and through them on the US-based mambo bands. David Garcia draws attention to the use of the diablo trumpet figures from example 2.6 in later arrangements of Orquesta Casino de La Playa ("La Ultima Noche") and the use of Arcaño's charanga "Mambo" violin figures in Bebo Valdés's arrangement of "La Rareza del Siglo" in the saxophone lines.[25] Further examples of this process are discussed below in the context of both Havana-based and New York–based mambo big bands.

THE HAVANA BIG BANDS

Many mambo montunos take the rhythmic aspect of Arcaño's "Mambo" guajeo but introduce a descending chromatic line; these mambo figures are emblematic of the mid-twentieth-century mambo style associated in particular with Pérez Prado and Benny Moré's work in his Banda Gigante. Both the Arcaño mambo and Arsenio diablo section were adopted and adapted in the Havana hotel jazz bands and orquestas of the mid-1940s. Before the mambo big bands became popular in New York, the big bands and orquestas in Havana were busy incorporating elements from both types of mambo in their arrangements in a variety of styles, supporting Bebo Valdés's statement that many Cuban musicians were already playing in a mambo style in the 1940s:[26]

> Back in 1943 I was music arranger for the Orquesta Cubaney and Pérez Prado was its pianist. We certainly never played a mambo while, at the same time, Arsenio and his band already were playing mambos frequently. The first band to play mambo in a jazz arrangement was that of Julio Cueva, back in 1944, a wonderful arrangement by my friend René Hernández. But while René was in the exclusive services of the Cuevas band and I was under exclusive contract for Cubaney, Pérez Prado was a free agent and so, it was his arrangements which were printed and became more widely known.[27]

Leonardo Acosta describes Pérez Prado's orchestration style as one where the trumpet section is differentiated from the saxophone section by register, with each section playing in counterpoint to each other.[28] This is typical of Cuban arrangement aesthetics, which are driven by instrument function in relation to son clave.

In his book *Arsenio Rodríguez*, David Garcia examines the textures of Arsenio's son conjunto with its diablo section and compares them to those of La Sonora Matancera and to the mambo arrangements of Tito Puente and Pérez Prado. This reveals performance aesthetics related to attack (phrasing), and rhythmic placement in relation to dance movements and tempo. Issues of race, gender, and class inform evaluations of certain performance styles characterized by the Cuban terms *estilo negro* and *estilo blanco*[29] (often referred to in today's Cuba as *macho* or *hembra*). These essentially Cuban performance aesthetics also accord with the above evaluations of the downtown and uptown performances at the Park Plaza in the Bronx (*estilo negro*) and the Palladium (*estilo blanco*) in Manhattan, with the caveat that the musicians who played in the big bands at the Palladium also played the Bronx venues but adapted to their audiences' tastes. Garcia notes that the "black style" was applied to those musicians who played for Cuban audiences, whereas the "white style" referred to (often) mixed-race bands who played for white tourist audiences on holiday in Havana. Although there are parallels between performance styles in Havana in the 1940s with those in New York later in the 1950s, there are also differences in sound and approach. New York–based music historian René López, in conversation with Lise Waxer, has pointed out that by the late 1950s there was more social mobility among African Americans and Latinos and that they could afford the slightly higher admission prices of the downtown venues such as the Palladium.[30] The fire and excitement of a Tito Puente performance at the Palladium could not be adequately described as *estilo blanco*, although it would be interesting to compare his performances at the Palladium with those he gave at the Park Plaza.[31]

THE NEW YORK BIG BAND MAMBO

The New York mambo big bands from the 1940s onward can be seen as an extension of the 1930s and early '40s rhumba orchestras such as those led by Puerto Rican Noro Morales, Spanish Xavier Cugat, and Cuban José Curbelo. The earlier rhumba orquestas popular in the 1930s and '40s typically included piano, double bass, vocals, bongos, congas, vocals, trumpets, sometimes saxophones, a flute or clarinet, and maracas. The bands of Machito, Tito Puente, and Tito Rodríguez augmented the rhumba band lineup to include elements from the swing bands, while maintaining a Cuban aesthetic regarding instrumental function. The layout of the bands followed Cuban conventions to some extent but also those of the swing band. Tito Puente, inspired by Gene Krupa's jazz drumming, transformed the role of the timbales by placing them at the front of the band.[32] This placement does not work acoustically for the conjunto and charanga format with its smaller forces that, given the limited amplification of the time, needed to maintain a dynamic balance between the instruments often through a semicircular layout with the percussion section placed at the back.[33] Influenced by jazz styles of drumming (improvisation), Tito Puente changed the emphasis and to some extent the role of the timbales in Latin music. The fact that he was a dancer and able to perform on timbales while dancing in formation with other dancers introduced a new form of virtuosic showmanship. He certainly developed the timbales' improvisational style with his in-depth understanding of both Cuban dance music and jazz.

The full lineup for Tito Puente's orquesta included five trumpets, five saxophones (two alto, two tenor, and one baritone), four trombones, occasional flute, piano, bass, timbales, congas, maracas or güiro, bongos, and a lead vocalist. While drawing from American swing band instrumentation, his arrangements kept a more Cuban aesthetic following the charanga and conjunto open montuno conventions. The driving saxophones of Tito Puente's big band perform what Sublette terms the "*sobremontuno*" function as a "propulsive repeating rhythmic part";[34] these figures relate directly to both charanga and conjunto traditions within a modified swing band format. In example 2.7 the brass section of five trumpets and four trombones play clave-aligned dominant pedal figures derived from the charanga mambo; similarly, saxophone guajeo patterns are adapted from son conjunto tres *and* charanga violin figures. The transcribed reduced scores demonstrate these aspects and are based on a recording of "Mambo Gozón" by Tito Puente and his Orchestra recorded in 1958.[35]

In example 2.8 the violin guajeo pattern is present in the saxophone and trumpet lines where eighth-note pairs on beats 1 and 3 build up the excitement, as they would often do in a charanga orquesta performance of danzón in the 1950s. The pedal bass pattern is identical to that of Arcaño's "Mambo" arrangement (although transposed up a tone over the E7 chord) and is also reflected in the trombone parts, again referencing the charanga violin pedal function from "Mambo."

Both mambo sections build in intensity by drawing on elements from the son conjunto diablo section and from the charanga mambo, where violin guajeo rhythms are transplanted to the saxophone and trumpet lines, and where pedal figures are played by the brass emulating the violin pedal in Arcaño's "Mambo." Puente's "Mambo Gozón" thus demonstrates how elements from the son conjunto and the charanga are woven into the approach and textures of a big band mambo, with its mix of charanga danzón-mambo and chachachá patterns and conjunto-derived trumpet diablo melodies and ornamentations. Similarly, the breaks (known as *efectos* or *cierres*), derived

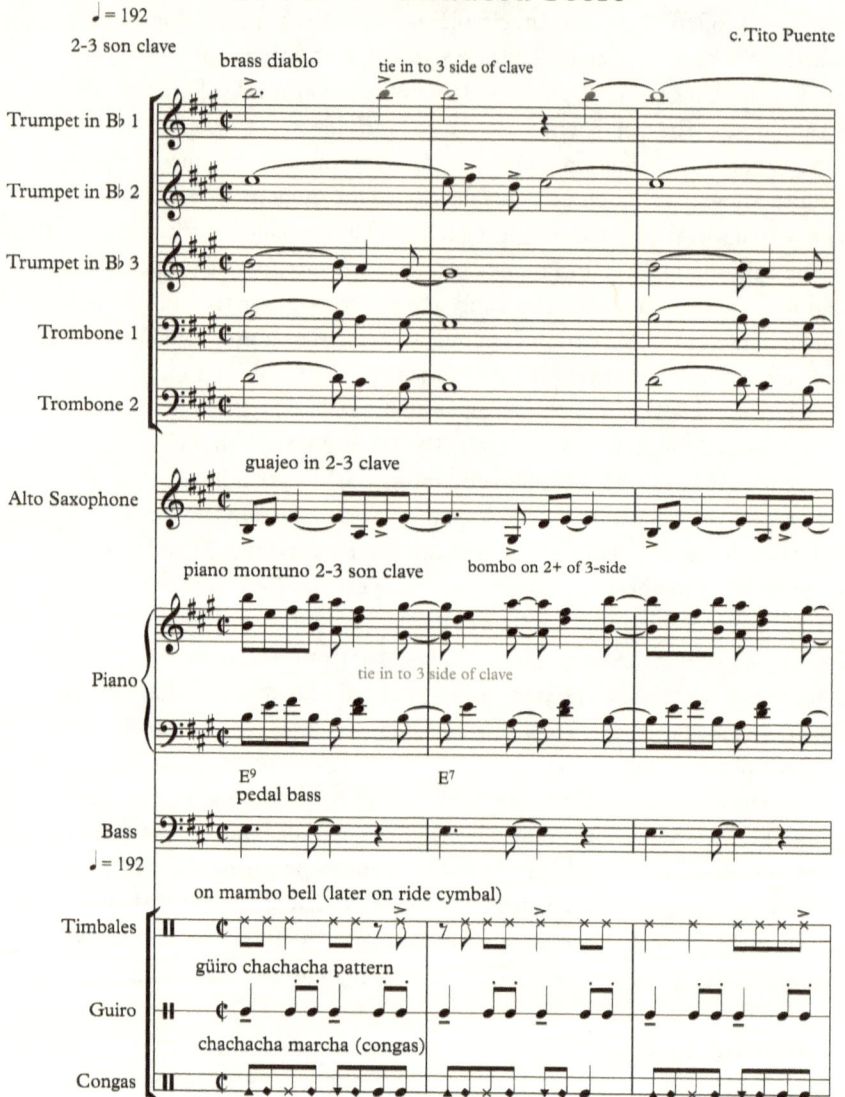

Example 2.7 Reduced score of mambo 1 in Tito Puente's "Mambo Gozón" demonstrating charanga and conjunto influence.

Mambo Gozon
Mambo 2 - Reduced Score

c. Tito Puente

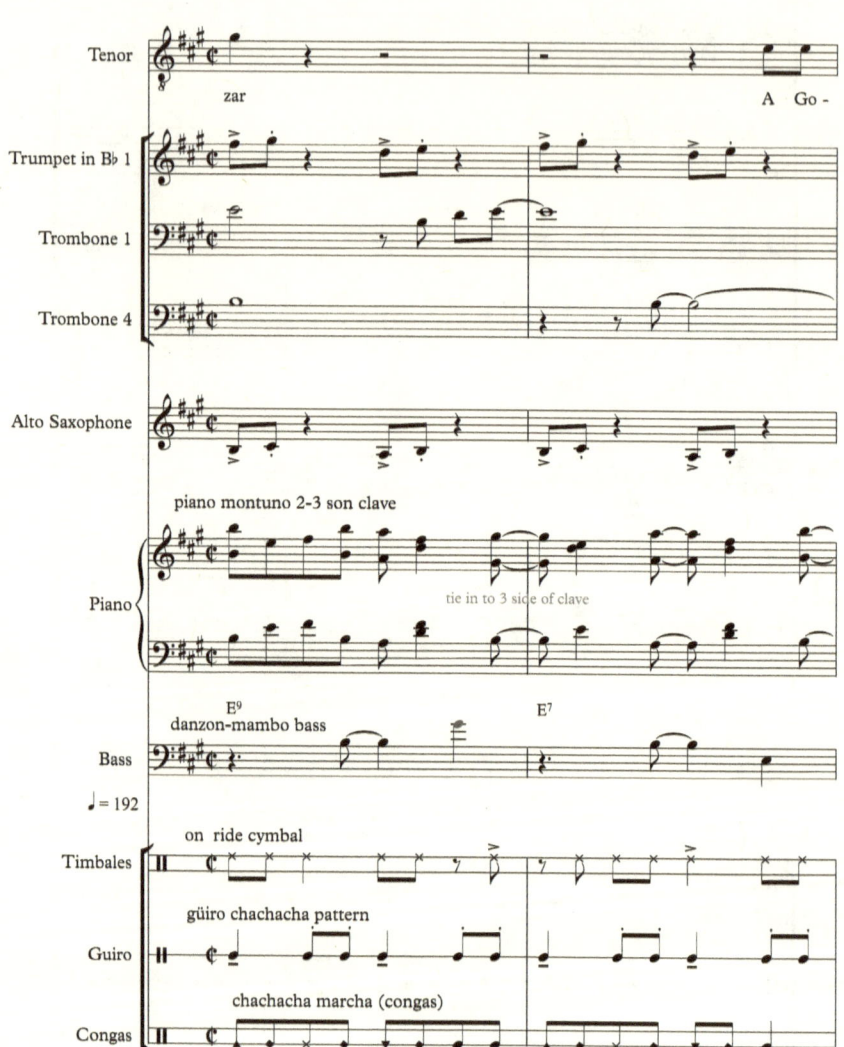

This annotated transcription (c) Sue Miller, Leeds, November 2017

Example 2.8 Second mambo in "Mambo Gozón" showing charanga-derived violin and bass patterns and half coro conjunto diablo influence.

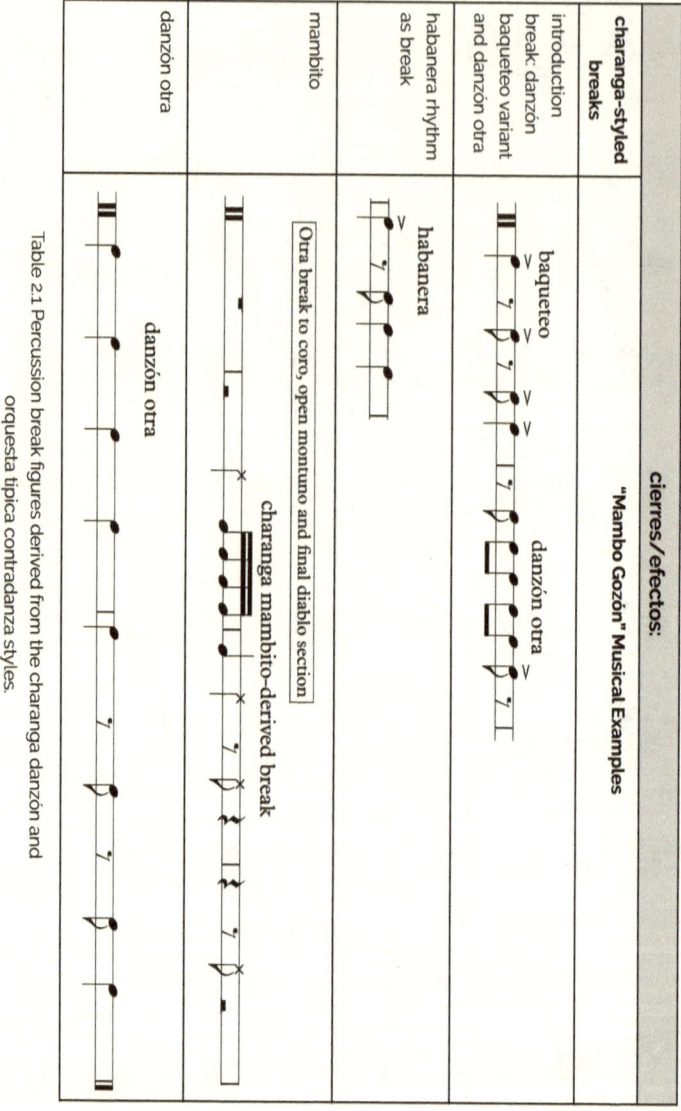

Table 2.1 Percussion break figures derived from the charanga danzón and orquesta típica contradanza styles.

from the Cuban charanga (for example danzón *otras*, *mambito* breaks, and *habanera* rhythms), are used in this big band mambo arrangement as shown in table 2.1.

Closer examination shows, therefore, that the mambo big bands and Havana jazz orquestas were influenced as much by son conjunto and charanga performance practice as by swing band conventions. In terms of jazz influence, "Mambo Gozón" has the instrumentation of a large swing band, more harmonization due, in part, to the larger brass and woodwind sections, and the addition of ride cymbal later in the arrangement—but the instrumental functions dictate a Cuban clave-organized performance aesthetic rather than a jazz approach.

The large orquestas and big bands in Havana grew out of each other and are related to each other through the musicians who passed through them. Cristobál Díaz Ayalla notes that Los Hermanos Castro, founded in 1930, gave rise to Orquesta Casino de la Playa (founded in 1937) and then to Orquesta Riverside (founded in 1938); these big bands were integral to the development of big band mambo in Havana during the 1940s, and later, in New York through the migration of Havana-based musicians.[36] For example, the pianist and composer José Curbelo, who cut his teeth with Orquesta Havana Riverside and Gilberto Valdés's orquesta, moved to New York to perform with the bands of Xavier Cugat, Juancito Sanabria, and Oscar de la Hoya before setting up his own orquesta in 1942, performing in New York at the Conga Club, the Havana-Madrid, the Zanzibar, and the Catskills resorts. Curbelo later became a music promoter, in 1959 creating Alpha Artists. Representing Charlie Palmieri, Tito Puente, Tito Rodríguez, Machito, Noro Morales, and Orquesta Broadway among others, Curbelo had a significant effect on the live Latin music scene in New York up until the early 1980s.[37] Tito Puente played in Curbelo's band in 1939 and again in 1945 as well as playing in Anselmo Sacasas's band in 1941, in Noro Morales's band, and in Machito's orchestra in 1942.[38] Thus musicians from the Cuban big bands of the 1930s and '40s, with their guarachas, sones, and *guajeos mambeados*, are linked directly to those in New York in the 1940s and '50s, particularly through music arranging work and the influence of Cuban musicians who migrated there.

As with many innovations in popular dance music, new musical styles cannot be attributed solely to one originator, even when there are many claims to the title of "Mambo King." Undoubtedly Orestes and Israel López in Arcaño y sus Maravillas, Arsenio Rodríguez, and Pérez Prado are all major figures in its evolution, as is Puerto Rican timbales virtuoso Tito Puente. Instead of one originator we have a complicated web of influence populated by some very gifted musicians who built on each others' contributions. Hettie Malcomson comments on this romantic desire to attribute new musical styles to one specific creator and questions this step change view of stylistic change.[39] Certainly musicians in Arcaño y Sus Maravillas and Arsenio's conjunto were innovating on the danzón and son forms, drawing upon religious Afro-Cuban culture; their influence fed into the Cuban big bands in Cuba and through them to the mambo bands in New York. Ruben López-Cano probes these connections, summarizing these practices to include this "ida y vuelta" [to and fro]:

During the 1940s, "mambo" was understood as a series of different musical practices among which stood out the peculiar way of playing the montuno section in the big band guarachas. The mambo, understood as the musical genre that made Pérez Prado famous, emerged from these disparate practices. However, historically, it was not the only set of musical practice that went by that name. It is very likely that Bebo Valdés, Anselmo Sacasas, and other Cuban musicians based in New York knew of these new tendencies from their travels to Havana (the historic and symbolic capital of Caribbean dance music) and hurried to introduce them in New York.[40]

Instrument function and performance practice form part of the genre's definition and, rather than "peculiar," I would characterize the montunos and guajeos in the mid- to late 1940s as showing increasing influence from Afro-Cuban religious practices (Santéria, Palo Monte, and Abakúa). This would seem a natural progression in that son and charanga musicians mutually influenced each other at this time (and musicians played in both formats); both the mambo section of the more up-tempo danzones de nuevo ritmo of the late 1930s and Arsenio Rodríguez's diablo section in his son montunos in the 1940s perform the same cathartic function as a *toque de santos*. Robin Moore has documented this gradual increase in Afro-Cuban influence in popular styles, with mixed-race bands gaining popularity particularly from the 1930s onward, when Afro-Cuban working-class music became more socially accepted in prestigious venues.[41]

Due to the *ida y vuelta* of Cuban musicians between Havana and New York (until 1962), defining a New York mambo style as opposed to a Cuban one equally poses difficulties. As López-Cano remarks under the header "Mambology," "the study of mambo raises some very controversial topics."[42] Issues of ownership and appropriation are often raised when comparing Cuban bands with those based in the USA and, since the Cuban revolution put an end to easy mutual interchange between musicians (particularly after the 1962 embargo), arguments over the genesis of the mambo have often become politicized and polarized. However, a nuanced musical investigation of mambo allows for all views on the mambo's development to be taken into account once intricate relationships and lines of influence are brought to the fore. If we examine not only stylistic elements common to the charanga, conjunto, and big band but also explore the *approaches* to performance and performance practice, influenced as they are by Afro-Cuban religious practices, then these interrelationships can be more easily understood.

THE MAMBO AESTHETIC: AFRO-CUBAN RITUAL AS COMMON THREAD

Many lines of influence can be drawn between the charanga mambo of the late 1930s, the son band's development from septeto to conjunto with its diablo-filled mambo sections, the Havana-based jazz-inflected bands and hotel orquestas of the mid-1940s, Pérez Prado's mambo big band in Mexico (from 1949), Benny Moré's Banda Gigante, and the mambo offerings from New York's Palladium bands. The transnational mambo has migrated across a variety of musical formats, but definitions of the mambo in musical terms are possible if these different ensemble types and their relationships to each other are taken into account, particularly if one looks at the Afro-Cuban ritual origin of the mambo term and the function of the riff-based sections within arrangements. Mambo, when seen as an overarching genre encompassing a variety of related styles, can then be viewed more holistically. Mambo as a genre has a certain performance aesthetic common to all manifestations, one which privileges idiomatic riff-based passages (organized by son clave) designed to heighten the excitement in a performance, a fast tempo, and an instrumental rather than vocal approach (or where vocal coros form part of the woven texture), and where improvisations respond dynamically to a dancing public. David Garcia defines the mambo as a "confluence of rhythms" and certainly Rodríguez's clave-organized *diablitos* fit this description. These diablo figures increase the intensity of the music and bring the music to a climax, following rumba and Afro-Cuban religious music and dance practices; the overlapping guajeo, montuno, and tumbao figures from the violins, piano, and bass in Arcaño's charanga mambo perform the same function. These melo-rhythmic figures were adapted from the patterns of the tres, violins, and trumpets of the charanga and son conjunto and subsequently fitted to the saxophone and trumpet lines of the mambo big bands. This "diablo" approach was later taken up by the trombone section in Eddie Palmieri's "trombanga" La Perfecta and in Manny Oquendo's band Conjunto Libre.

The origin of the term "mambo," referring to, as Ned Sublette states, "a complex of things involving communication—all of which, in traditional Bantú culture, involved singing,"[43] conforms to a call-and-response aesthetic typical of Cuban musical forms.[44] These melo-rhythmic contrapuntal figures appear in a variety of Cuban dance band lineups and were derived from patterns in both the son and the danzones de nuevo ritmo—hence the difficulties in defining the genre and the ensuing arguments over who invented it. The Palladium Three developed their sound from the earlier rhumba bands of the 1940s, incorporating elements from the son montuno, guaracha, chachachá, and the mambo. There was, however, a predominance of mambo-style figures in the air in the mid-1940s due in many respects to the influence of the US swing bands and the innovations of Arcaño y sus Maravillas, Arsenio Rodríguez, René Hernández, Bebo Valdés, and Pérez Prado, among others.

Pérez Prado himself categorized his mambos as being either son- or rumba-influenced, naming them mambo *caén* and mambo *batiri* respectively.[45] He also added performance practices associated with the swing bands (brass smears, slides, low pedals, and shakes as played in Ellington's "jungle jazz" of the 1920s and '30s).[46] His mostly Mexican trumpet section also added an exuberant flavor unique to the Prado band, and the band's recordings have been hugely influential. Similarly, the contributions of musicians in New York gave the US-based mambo a different flavor. The Cuban musicians who joined or formed Latin bands in New York brought their influence to bear through performance style, composition, arrangement, and musical direction. The common thread of Afro-Cuban religious music and dance pervades all these changes and is responsible for the continuing influence of mambo as a music and dance form in its own right and within other forms of Latin music.

CROSS-FERTILIZATION AND CREATIVE BORROWINGS

Traditional histories of Cuban music in New York have tended to outline a stylistic evolution from commercialized son known as rhumba[47] in the 1920s and '30s to mambo in the 1940s, chachachá in the 1950s (mostly in big band format), and then pachanga (in both charanga and big band formats) in the early 1960s. The influence of the US Latin big bands in the run-up to the 1960s cannot be overstated, but their relationship to the smaller formats of the charanga and the conjunto needs further elaboration. Many musicians involved in the Fania project were involved in charanga bands initially, and although their later instrumentation favored brass sections over strings, the charanga flute sound and the charanga feel was still present (often through the addition of the flute, or through the timbales and güiro playing styles). Charanga percussionist with SonSublime, Manny Rivera, notes that the timbale player Manny Oquendo in Conjunto Libre used charanga figures in his playing and had a charanga feel, using for example the *timbal* bell on the off-beats instead of the usual busier mambo bell ride figure.[48] The continued use of the Cuban flute in the mambo big bands and conjuntos exemplifies these charanga "survivals" (the flautist Mauricio Smith Sr. in the Machito band and Johnny Pacheco in Tito Puente's band are the most well-known). But perhaps rather than seeing charanga elements as survivals or residual culture[49] we could look at these elements from charanga, son, r(h)umba, and Afro-Cuban religious music as forming an integral part of the mambo genre within the Latin big band format.

Musicians do not always stay within the formats for which they are most known. Dividing musical innovators into representatives of their generations, although convenient, also obfuscates these complex musical changes. For example, son conjunto trumpet player Armando "Chocolate" Armenteros played in Fajardo's charanga in New York in the late 1950s,[50] and Eddy Zervigón has played in the conjuntos of Eddie Palmieri and Manny Oquendo, playing against trombones instead of violins. Musicians such as Charlie and Eddie Palmieri and Mongo Santamaría played in the Palladium mambo bands before creating their own charangas, conjuntos, and trombangas. Charanga music in the USA did not simply appear in the 1960s, either, but was present before the Cuban Revolution in the form of recordings, visiting Cuban groups such as Orquesta Aragón and José Fajardo's Estrellas, and in the form of the first US-based charanga led by Gilberto Valdés.[51] Cuban flute player Alberto Socarrás was also on the scene as a dance band leader from the late 1920s performing in both jazz and Cuban idioms. Socarrás, in fact, stated he had thought of the two idioms as completely separate, unlike Mario Bauzá who sought to unify them through their common African ancestry.[52]

Christina Abreu's research and much work on the Herencia Latina website provide essential alternative accounts of Cuban music and dance culture in twentieth-century New York;[53] indeed, the grassroots side of this story and how it intersected with music industry demands and the wider national and international scene is yet to be fully researched. As demonstrated here, the musical detail needs attention if lines of influence are to be traced more thoroughly.

SOME CONCLUSIONS

The artistry and exuberance of the "Palladium Three" is undeniable, but the legacy of the venue can only be understood within the wider context of Latin New York and its connections to Havana. The roots, shoots, branches, and flowerings (to paraphrase Connie Grossman) of Cuban dance music in New York provide fertile ground for music analysis. Rather than revisiting old polemics surrounding ownership and appropriation of Cuban popular dance music, an appreciation of the music as performed by talented Cuban, Puerto Rican, Dominican, Jewish, and Italian Americans requires analytical attention to style, arrangement, improvisation, and performance practice. As demonstrated with this analysis of the mambo style, there are many lines of influence to trace. The charanga and the conjunto are major trajectories in the development of mambo, pachanga, and bugalú in New York, and the influence of these performance traditions runs deep.

- 3 -

LA MECHA

Belisario López, José Fajardo, and Rolando Lozano

The rise of charanga in the early sixties in New York follows the upward trajectory of the *mecha*. *La mecha* [the fuse] is a percussion buildup of two to four measures of eighth notes through a crescendo (see example 3.1) leading to a new section of an arrangement, usually featuring a higher dynamic mambo or instrumental solo (this can also be an ensemble tutti break written into an arrangement). This device is used to raise the rhythmic intensity and level of excitement in the music and is known in Cuba as an *escalera* [staircase]. Three Cuban musicians in particular are associated with lighting the fuse and creating the initial excitement for the charanga orquesta in the USA: Rolando Lozano, José Fajardo, and Belisario López.

All three musicians found success in North America due to the ubiquity of Cuban RCA Victor and Columbia music recordings, the network of Cuban social clubs, and the popularity of visiting Cuban bands. In the 1950s Orquesta Aragón performed at the Palladium, the Cuban social clubs, and the Catskills resort hotels while on tour, and Fajardo himself performed with his Estrellas at the Palladium and the Waldorf Astoria. The ground had also already been prepared in the 1930s, '40s, and early '50s through the work of less well-known New York–based charanga-styled bands, such as those led by flute player Alberto Socarrás and pianist/composer Gilberto Valdés.[1]

The injection of *cubanía* from three established charanga musicians, two of whom were famous bandleaders, inspired several New York–based Latin musicians to set up their own charangas. These included Puerto Rican

Example 3.1 La mecha [the fuse].

Charlie Palmieri and Dominican Johnny Pacheco (see chapter 6). This spark that took the popular charanga music of 1950s Cuba into new US-based contexts is looked at here through analysis of the work of these three influential Cuban flute players. Danilo Lozano has analyzed his father Rolando's work to some extent in his masters dissertation on the Cuban charanga, and features informative interviews with Rolando himself;[2] an in-depth analysis of Fajardo's work in Cuba can be found in *Cuban Flute Style*.[3] Apart from various discographical entries, a biography on the Herencia Latina website by Sánchez-Coll,[4] and a brief overview of Belisario López's life and work in *Cuban Flute Style*,[5] Belisario's work in Cuba and the USA remains under-researched. Some analysis of his recordings made before he emigrated is undertaken here in order to ascertain whether any changes in his style of performance took place once he was US-based.

Although Fajardo, Lozano, and López hail from the charanga scene in Havana, each originated from a different generation and region (Pinar del Rio, Cienfuegos, and Matanzas, respectively). Belisario López is of the earlier generation of musicians who performed danzones and danzones del nuevo ritmo in the first part of the twentieth century, before later adapting to the chachachá and pachanga of the 1950s and '60s. Fajardo rose to prominence in the 1950s; his formative years in the 1940s were spent performing danzones, danzones de nuevo ritmo, and *danzonetes* in charanga orquestas such as those led by Paulina Álvarez, Neno González, Armando Valdespí, Antonio María Romeu, and Antonio Arcaño.[6] His own band Fajardo y sus Estrellas, formed in 1949, became the most sought-after band in the 1950s. Born in Cienfuegos, Rolando Lozano was Orquesta Aragón's second flute player (1952–54) and his playing features on their first set of recordings in 1953.[7] Following a further two years performing and recording film tracks in Mexico with Orquesta América, Lozano moved to Chicago and later to Los Angeles. His legacy in the USA is linked in particular to his work with Mongo Santamaría and Cal Tjader. He performed and recorded in New York in 1959 with the Chicago-based charanga Nuevo Ritmo de Cuba and is included in this chapter due to his role in igniting interest in charanga at that time.[8] All three Cuban musicians are steeped in the charanga tradition and had successful careers in both Cuba and the USA. In many ways their contribution lies in adding *cubanía* to the Latin music scene in New York in the mid-twentieth century. For all three, adapting to the North American context was not without its difficulties and compromises, as the following three analytical studies reveal.

PRUEBA MI SAZÓN [TRY MY SEASONING]— BELISARIO LÓPEZ IN HAVANA AND NEW YORK

Belisario López (1903–1969)[9] was an established performer and bandleader in Cuba before leaving Havana for New York in 1960 following the revolution. Signed to the Victor record label in Cuba, Belisario's group held a residency at the Tropical in Marianao from 1940 until 1957.[10] Older than most musicians who left Cuba in the early 1960s, he suffered from pulmonary disease and performed with only one lung in his later years. His recordings in New York on the Ansonia label spearheaded the mainstream interest in pachanga, and his influence has been rather underappreciated, at least in the context of Latin music in the USA. In New York his band held a regular residency at the Havana San Juan (previously the Monte Carlo Club) but his age and ill health meant he was less able to continue with the level of fame he had previously enjoyed in Havana. As Eddy Zervigón remarks:

> Era más un estilo de danzones antiguos. No improvisaba mucho. Sí improvisaba pero tenía su estilo diferente. Era un estilo más antiguo. Era muy bueno y grabó muchos danzones en Cuba, artista muy respetado, fue muy popular en Cuba.
>
> [He was more in the older danzón style. He didn't improvise much. Well yes he improvised but he had a different style. He had an older style of performance. He was very good and recorded many danzones in Cuba—a well-respected artist, he was very popular in Cuba.][11]

As Zervigón states, the majority of Belisario's work involved the performance of danzones in the earlier *florear* style.[12] His performances on the recordings made on the collection *Prueba Mi Sazón*[13] between 1942–48 and 1951–57 demonstrate an affinity with nuevo ritmo players such as those in Antonio Arcaño's Maravillas. The florear style of danzón performance alongside signifiers of el nuevo ritmo (for example, the use of congas, extended solo sections for the flute, raised fourths over a dominant seventh tumbao) show Belisario to be moving with the times but with a strong *danzonero* approach to interpretation and improvisation, using rubato and ornamentation on both composed and improvised figures. With a good tone and melodic interpretative styling, Belisario nevertheless adapted to the later chachachá and pachanga styles, recording many of these in the early 1960s for the US-based label Ansonia. Before analyzing his New York 1960s pachanga recordings, I will undertake an analysis of his earlier Havana-based 1956 guaracha "Prepárate

Para Bañarte" (from the compilation *Orquesta de Belisario López 1951–1957: Prueba Mi Sazón*)[14] in order to show how far Belisario adapted to the New York context.

In "Prepárate Para Bañarte," an up-tempo guaracha about the benefits of having a bath, Belisario uses the a³ dominant note throughout—the

Example 3.2 Transcription of "Prepárate Para Bañarte" flute solo by Belisario López.

decoration of this axis note is the main strategy undertaken to develop melodic material in the solo. The main motif 1 in measures 27–28 appears throughout in varied form either through variations in note density (repeated notes), differing articulations, through the application of rubato, use of ornamentation such as trills, acciaccaturas, turns (in addition to the one in the

Lola Catula

Example 3.3 Transcription of "Lola Catula" flute solo by Belisario López (clave superimposed).

motif), and interversion (rearrangement of the motif's pitches). References to the composition "Mambo" by Arcaño y sus Maravillas is clearly in evidence in motif 2, where the characteristic pedal violin motif on the dominant d note (in the key of G) and also on e (the sixth) is employed. The variety of time values (quarter, eighth, sixteenth notes, and triplet quarter- and eighth-note figures) and rubato applied to the ornamented melodic material gives this solo a late-1940s nuevo ritmo feel. The sharpened fourth also gives it the characteristic mambo bite. This solo demonstrates the older style referred to by Zervigón. Those accustomed to listening to solos by Richard Egües and José Fajardo, or to the later solos by Johnny Pacheco or George Castro, may not hear Belisario's *inspiraciones* as improvisation at first listen, but there is clearly a lot of subtle melodic decoration and motivic variation in Belisario's improvisations. He certainly brought to New York both an earlier danzón-based florear style alongside the faster mambo inflections of the nuevo ritmo charanga. The 1961 recording of "Lola Catula"[15] featured on the Ansonia label from the album *Pachangas Vol. 1* was recorded a year after López had immigrated to the United States and is analyzed below in the context of his New York recordings to evaluate whether he adapted his style to this new North American performance context.

Labeled as a pachanga, "Lola Catula" follows the guaracha V-V-I-I progression and the lyrics are once again humorous, about a female Cuban dancer whose bodily contortions delight and amaze. The annotated transcription of Belisario López's solo on "Lola Catula" (see example 3.3) once again demonstrates his use of melodic decorative devices. Melodic material in the opening four-measure phrase is repeated with variations using an axis on the sixth note a^3 in the key of C, following a 2–3 clave direction in which chord notes are outlined. The axis note varies between a^3 and g^3, the sixth and fifth in the key of C, with motif 1 alternating between the apex pitches d^4 and c^4 in the fourth register. The emphasis is on the sixth note a^3 throughout and only resolves briefly to the tonic note c in measure 7 before the coro entry. This is a simple but elegant improvisation in the Cuban style showing 2–3 clave alignment, except for the clave-neutral motif 1, which resolves in clave in measure 25. Perhaps the fast tempo (♩ = 200) did not allow López to embellish the melodic motifs as intricately as he had done in "Prepárate Para Bañarte" (♩ = 170) and in much of his earlier work. On these Ansonia recordings Belisario seems less comfortable with the increase in tempo, and the decorative *rubatiando* approach is less in evidence in these later works. Being from an older generation of players, perhaps Belisario was less able to adapt to the more exuberant performance aesthetics of 1960s New York than the younger José Fajardo who was already well known for his faster *callejero* or *de la calle* ["street"] style.

JOSÉ FAJARDO IN NEW YORK—
"LA FLAUTA MÁS ALTA DE CUBA"

José Fajardo (1919–2001), a virtuosic flute improviser and bandleader in Cuba, performed at the New York Palladium in 1958 and for John F. Kennedy's presidential campaign at the Waldorf Astoria in the late 1950s, before moving to the USA in 1961.[16] His 1958 Palladium performance at Thanksgiving showcased the repertoire from his recent highly acclaimed Cuban Panart release *Ritmo de Pollos*;[17] Fajardo moved to the USA in 1961 riding this crest of fame and popularity.[18] Although he also found success in the United States, he never managed to maintain the quality of his original Cuban band; he continued, however, to set the standard in terms of improvisation in the Cuban flute style for many contemporary players. His US recordings maintain the fluidity and invention of his previous work in Cuba although he adapted to US culture to some extent. He did not change his improvisational style, however, and he maintained his Cuban sabor throughout his career in Cuba, Puerto Rico, and the United States.

In *Cuban Flute Style* I demonstrate the link between Fajardo's improvisational style and the danzones del nuevo ritmo players in Arcaño y sus Maravillas. Fajardo extended this approach to soloing (romantic interpretation and embellishment techniques), adding sequential motivic ideas not simply at the ends of melodic phrases but around structural melodic points. His clave sensibility and sonero or streetwise callejero fluidity have set the bar not only for charanga flute improvisers but for all soloists of Cuban popular dance music. In chapter 8, which examines the Latin bugalú, I demonstrate how Fajardo maintains his cubanía and sabor in the USA while at the same time making playful reference to US popular culture and adapting traditional Cuban repertoire to North American popular styles and hit songs of the time. Fajardo's contribution is in many ways a point of reference for US-based Latin musicians wanting to play in a típico vein. Along with Richard Egües, he remains unsurpassed in terms of improvisational creativity and virtuosity within the Cuban flute tradition. Based in the USA for the latter part of his career, he was the main role model for Latin flute players and charanga bandleaders there.

ROLANDO LOZANO—EL NUEVO RITMO DE CUBA

As a celebrated bandleader and virtuoso soloist, Fajardo could to some extent maintain artistic control. Rolando Lozano, in contrast, was obliged to adapt to more Latin jazz contexts. Although Lozano was influential at the start of the pachanga's rise in popularity in the 1960s, he diversified later by playing more jazz-oriented material. Lozano (b. 1931) played initially with Orquesta Aragón (1950–54) in Cienfuegos and Havana before joining Ninon Mondejar's Orquesta América in Mexico City. He moved from Mexico City to Chicago in 1956, where he joined the newly formed Orquesta Nuevo Ritmo.[19] After some success in Chicago, his group performed at the New York Palladium in July 1959. According to Eddy Zervigón, this performance and their album *Heart of Cuba*[20] (recorded in August of the same year) sparked the demand for live Cuban charanga in New York City. Charlie Palmieri apparently heard the band while performing in Chicago's Ambassador West Hotel in 1958 and was inspired to take up the charanga format a year later. Orquesta Nuevo Ritmo did not last long, but some members of the group joined forces with Mongo Santamaría in New York and, according to Latin music historian Max Salazar, Santamaría became musical director of Nuevo Ritmo in 1961.[21] The group, with Lozano on flute, became known as La Sabrosa following the recording of his first charanga album *Sabroso!*[22] Before evaluating Lozano's playing in the USA, a brief overview of his work with Orquesta Aragón is needed to more easily identify his personal style before exploring possible adaptations to American popular music forms.

Lozano recorded six numbers with Orquesta Aragón in 1953: "El Agua de Clavelito," "Mambo Inspiracíon," "Mentiras Criollas," "Tres Lindas Cubanas," "Mambo Sensacional," and "Nunca."[23] While his US-based solos analyzed here contain flutter-tonguing and much chromaticism, these elements were also in evidence on these 1953 recordings ("Mambo Inspiración," for example, features flutter-tonguing). Lozano's playing also already contained elements of blues and jazz, as for example in his use of a blue note in his 1953 recording with Aragón "El Agua de Clavelito." Similarly, the blues-influenced "Mambo Sensacional" has blue notes written into the flute melody line. Although enharmonic, the use of the sharpened fourth in the mambo style is differentiated from the use of the blues flattened fifth in that in the Cuban dance music context these "foreign" elements are often used as a deliberate reference to American jazz.

In Nuevo Ritmo, Lozano continued his clave-based Cuban style, and the repertoire of this band was unsurprisingly very Aragón-influenced (including, for example, the Aragón song "Ritmo d'Azucar"). Nuevo Ritmo de Cuba was founded by conga player Armando Sánchez in 1956 with Lozano on flute, Cuban violinists Elizardo Aroche, José "Chombo" Silva, and Pupi Legaretta, singers Rudy Calzado, Leonel Bravet, and Pellín Rodríguez, Victor Venegas on bass, René Hernandez on piano, Julian Cabrera on güiro, and

Cuco Martínez on timbales.[24] Many of these musicians continued to play when Mongo Santamaría took over the band's leadership in New York in 1961. Some of these musicians also became Alegre label musicians integral to the New York charanga scene of the 1960s.[25] Nuevo Ritmo's 1959 repertoire featured mambitos and breaks on the flute and timbales, as for example in "Aguardiente" on the album *Heart of Cuba*, in which the flute makes considerable use of mambo augmented fourths and flutter-tonguing.[26] Lozano's solo on "Hasta Decir No Mas" is full of tutti breaks, mambitos, and top note "3 in a grid of 4" breaks. The use of a chromatic "continental" riff on "No Sé Que Siento" also suggest Lozano's taste for chromatic lines. Influenced by Antonio Arcaño, Lozano has a preference for pedal note figures common in the mambo violin guajeos, and for decorative romantic interpretation. His playing in Nuevo Ritmo can thus be seen as remaining emblematic of the Cuban flute style, drawing on his Arcaño influence and his experiences in Orquesta Aragón and Orquesta América. Nuevo Ritmo provided cubanía and inspiration to the musicians of the Bronx. However, in Mongo Santamaría's band Lozano could branch out due to Santamaría's more hybrid approach to charanga (which incorporated Afro-Cuban rumba and African American influences). The band included José "Chombo" Silva on violin and tenor saxophone; soloing in the band from both Silva and Lozano involved an increased use of chromaticism and jazz inflection, while both maintained a clave-based approach to improvisation.

The following annotated scores of Rolando Lozano's solos on the Santamaría charanga albums *Sabroso!* and *Arriba!* demonstrate clave sensibility and an increased use of flutter tonguing and descending chromatic lines phrased stylistically in couplets. In "Que Maravilloso" Lozano starts his solo with nine measures of flutter-tonguing on a gradually rising motif which ends with a chromatic descending line, all phrased in 2–3 clave until a "3 in a grid of 4" rhythmic figure resolves in clave before another final chromatic descent.

Lozano's improvisation on "Olga Pachanga" draws upon many of the rhythmic and melodic ideas in the arrangement. Particularly noteworthy is the chromatic introduction on the bass and piano, where the line begins with an octave leap on the tonic before descending chromatically in a syncopated line, leading back to low c for a repeat of the octave-outlining two-measure phrase as in example 3.6. In example 3.5, measures 11–14, Lozano extends this chromatic descent in classical fashion, as per the Cuban flute style of articulation.

Alternating between $b^\flat$ and $b^\natural$, Lozano accentuates the melodic and harmonic minor scale notes and adds bite through his use of the sharpened

Example 3.4 Transcription of "Que Maravilloso" flute solo by Rolando Lozano (clave superimposed).

Example 3.5 Transcription of "Olga Pachanga" flute solo by Rolando Lozano (clave superimposed).

Example 3.6 Transcription of "Olga Pachanga" bass introduction. Chromatic descent within a one-octave tessitura.

fourth f♯ in measures 6–8. These augmented fourths could be viewed as blue note flat fifths, but they function here as mambo signifiers of the danzón-mambo tradition through their crushed note acciaccatura use. The high note f♮⁴ leap down to the dissonant f♯³, in measures 7–8, gives the solo a Lydian flavor. Lozano's attempt at this altissimo octave leap could be viewed as a competitive gesture and it is certainly a playful one as it alternates with the melodic and harmonic scale, emphasizing the sharpened fourth of the charanga mambo; it could also be viewed as a striving for the dominant g⁴ to g³ leap, which is almost impossible even on the five-key flute (although Eddy Zervigón almost manages to do this in his solo on "Goza la Vida," analyzed in chapter 4). The prevalence of anacrusis on the three-side of the clave and the ties in to the 3-side of the clave demonstrate clave feel and, although there is a tie into the 2-side in measure 4, the "3 in a grid of 4" figure resolves in clave at the end of measure 7 with a tie into the 3-side. The use of call-and-response phrases in measures 15–20 demonstrate the *callejero* conversational approach that Rolando Lozano himself identifies with, as does the percussive solo triplet entry that mirrors the *cierre* or break by the congas at the start of the piece (using the triplet figure as anacrusis as in measure 8 in example 3.7).

Example 3.7 Conga solo figure on the introduction to "Olga Pachanga" as played by Mongo Santamaría.

In both solos Lozano maintains his cubanía throughout; elements already present in his earlier work with Orquesta Aragón are extended in the US context, and his predilection for chromatic lines and flutter-tonguing are expanded. His musically intuitive improvisations interact at a deep level with elements in the composition/arrangement. Perhaps his ability to do this enabled him to expand into areas of Latin jazz later with Mongo Santamaría and others.

SOME CONCLUSIONS

All three flute improvisers brought cubanía and sabor from the charanga tradition to the USA in the late 1950s and early 1960s and adapted their repertoire, if not their playing styles, to their new musical and cultural contexts. Highly influential in terms of spreading the Cuban improvisational style, Rolando Lozano proved to be the most adaptable to more hybrid forms, later making his name in the West Coast Latin jazz scene. Belisario López and José Fajardo, in contrast, made their mark in New York City and contributed to the Cuban dance music scene there mostly by performing traditional Cuban repertoire. The use of the blue note by Lozano is made mostly as a referencing gesture but is ever present in his style. Chromaticism associated more with jazz than with the diatonic Cuban dance music genres does increase in his soloing, but is still used directionally in relation to landing notes on the tonic and dominant chords of the montuno pattern, and always follows a clave aesthetic. Belisario López kept his Cuban style to the end but there are slight changes to his performance practice in terms of reduced rubato use and ornamentation; Fajardo maintained his cubanía and his faster callejero street style, enabling him to fit in with the faster pace of the 1960s pachanga scene, in contrast to Belisario López whose style remained of an earlier age. Rolando Lozano, in his son's terms, managed to negotiate both contexts by using "a blend of musicianship and stylistic nuances."[27]

In terms of influence, Fajardo certainly kept other soloists on their mettle through his virtuosic improvisations performed in the competitive context of Latin New York. López, by contrast, struggled to keep up with the new, fast pachanga performance aesthetic, whereas Lozano molded his cubanía to suit audiences (and fellow band members) whose tastes extended to jazz. All three play the five-key wooden charanga flute, an instrument whose features and ergonomic restrictions ensure an adherence to the Cuban flute style. The five-key wooden flute, rather than its replacement Boehm system metal flute, remains to this day emblematic of típico charanga performance. These players lit the fuse for charanga's rise in popularity; and although they performed with other Latin American and Caribbean musicians, they maintained and disseminated their Cuban sabor and clave sensibility. Their contribution has been made through injecting cubanía from the Cuban charanga tradition into the New York Cuban dance music scene and influencing other musicians in the process.

- 4 -

EXILE AND ADAPTATION

Eddy Zervigón and Orquesta Broadway

La Orquesta Broadway es una charanga más adaptada al ambiente de Nueva York, es más citadina; su base es el son montuno y sobre esta columna le agregamos las fusiones. Tu tienes que estar muy atento a lo que está sucediendo donde te mueves, debes tener olfato a los cambios que se desarrollan en una urbe. La clave del éxito es que mueves como lo hace la comunidad. A veces el exceso de pureza te lleva a no entender los propios cambios.

[Orquesta Broadway is a charanga that has adapted the most to the New York ambience, it's more urban; son montuno is its backbone and we added various fusions to it. You need to pay attention to what's going on where you're living and sniff out the changes going on in the city. The key to success is that you move with your community. Sometimes excessive purism leads to not understanding those changes.][2]

—EDDY ZERVIGÓN

Figure 4.1 Orquesta Broadway. Photograph courtesy of Eddy Zervigón.[1]

Unlike the established, older charanga flute players and bandleaders who left Cuba in the early 1960s, Eddy Zervigón had barely started his musical career before moving to the United States. He became famous in the USA, whereas José Fajardo and Belisario López, for example, were already well-known musicians in Cuba. Zervigón performed at dances in 1960 and 1961 in Güines (his home town) and then later in Havana, moving to Miami in 1962 before relocating to New York a few months later.[3] Born on July 7, 1940, Zervigón was twenty-one years old when he migrated to the USA. His professional career as a charanga flute player began in 1958 in Havana, when he and his brother Rudy co-led La Orquesta Ideal. He also played briefly in Estrellas Cubanas directed by Felix Reina before leaving Havana in 1962.[4] In New York he initially played in Lou Pérez's charanga, in Arsenio Rodríguez's son group at the Monte Carlo (later named the Havana San Juan), and in Alfredito Valdez Sr.'s charanga before forming his own band, drawing initially on his Cuban musician contacts.[5] Zervigón told me that in Havana, as a meteorologist, he was required to either join the army or the communist party after the revolution and he did not want to do either. He therefore left Cuba "with two suits and one dime to my name" to make a new life for himself in America.[6] His twin brother Rudy went with him to join his other brother Kelvin in Miami before moving to New York a few months later.[7] After performing with those other bands, Zervigón, together with singer Roberto Torres, set up Orquesta Broadway in 1962.[8] A staple of the New York Latin scene, the band performed a fiftieth anniversary concert at Lincoln Center in New York in 2012, and they continue to perform worldwide including regular tours to Venezuela, Colombia, Africa, and Europe. Although Zervigón's musical career is US-based, his formative years in Cuba inform his playing style, having had lessons from Cuban flute players in his home town (with Arnaldo "El Mulatón") before studying solfège and music theory with Eduardo Egües in Havana in the late 1950s.[9]

Zervigón heard all the popular bands of the day at dances and in the TV studios in Havana, where, as a meteorologist, he presented a ten-minute weather forecast before the *Show del Medio Día* (The Midday Show) on Canal 6. The program featured bands like Orquesta Aragón, Fajardo y sus Estrellas, and Pancho el Bravo y sus Candelas de Tira Tira.[10] Zervigón was therefore already immersed in the music and dance culture of the day before embarking on a professional musical career.

In this chapter, I analyze three solos by Zervigón in Orquesta Broadway in order to trace his influences, describe his own personal style or *sello*, and determine whether his mix of cubanía and Havana/New York sabor can be demonstrated in musical terms. The first, "Al Mirar No Me Vistes" from the

Figure 4.2 Eddy Zervigón, Güines, Cuba, aged 17. Photograph courtesy of Eddy Zervigón.

album *Paraíso*, demonstrates a percussive approach; the second, "Quinta Guajira" from the album *Como Me Gusta!*, exhibits a more Cuban romantic delivery; and the third solo, "Goza La Vida" from the same album, displays a conversational style reflecting Zervigón's sharp wit and nervous energy. In terms of cubanía in his improvisational style, Zervigón has always stated that both Cuban flute players José Fajardo and Richard Egües were major influences on his own playing:

> Lo que oí a Richard hacer en la flauta de cinco llaves, no creo que nadie lo pueda igualar.... Fajardo fue un gran amigo mío y lo admiré mucho también pero era otro estilo, más callejero.... Richard era más clásico y tenía un manantial de ideas increíbles. Richard fue el primer flautista que me inspiro a tocar ese instrumento, después fue Fajardo.... Lamentablemente mis dos flautistas favoritos ya no están con nosotros.
>
> [What I've heard Richard do on the five-key flute, I don't believe anyone could equal..... Fajardo was a great friend of mine and I admired him a lot as well but he had a different style, more "street."... Richard was more classical and had a wellspring of incredible ideas. Richard was the first flute player who inspired me to take up the flute, then it was Fajardo.... Regrettably both of my favorite flute players are no longer with us.][11]

Alongside these two major influences on his playing style, Zervigón has also expressed admiration for Julio Guerrero of Estrellas Cubanas and Belisario

López, both earlier Cuban flute players from Havana. In addition to these definite Cuban influences, New York's ambience almost certainly affected the young Zervigón in the early 1960s and it is interesting to see if a New York sabor distinct from or in addition to his Cuban sabor can be detected in his playing through close analysis of his recordings. The working hypothesis, which is tested through analysis of his improvised solos, is that Zervigón combines the influences of these Cuban players but with changes to suit a New York rather than Cuban audience. The opening quotation from Zervigón reveals an important aspect of Latin music performance practice after the 1959 exodus of many Cuban musicians to the USA: that in order to stay current you have to adapt to your new, "more urban" environment. It is also worth noting that although Havana was an urban environment, New York is perceived to be "more city" even by Cuban exiles such as Zervigón. Musical analysis and ethnographic research are combined here to test the hypothesis that Orquesta Broadway and the soloing style of Eddy Zervigón has a distinct "urban" New York Latin sound even within the traditional charanga format, one that developed through adaptation to New York audiences' tastes. Orquesta Broadway's music is the product not only of Cuban musicians such as Eddy, Rudy, and Kelvin Zervigón, and singers Roberto Torres and Felo Barrios, but also of Puerto Ricans such as pianist and arranger Gil Suárez, and Jewish American musicians (pianist Ira Hersher and his brother David Hersher on bass); the band therefore to some extent was bound to have a different sound or *sello* from the Havana-based charanga orquestas of the same era. In Zervigón's case his solos, the repertoire on which they are based, and the background of his band musicians need to be examined in order to answer the questions: can cubanía and a separate, distinctive New York sabor be defined in objective musical terms? Does the meaning of the term sabor change in the New York context? And how are concepts of cubanía and sabor related? Certainly Cuban performance conventions were changed through adaptation to New York audiences' expectations. In the following analysis of Zervigón's flute solos, I attempt to define cubanía, Cuban sabor, and a different but related New York sabor through detailed analysis of Zervigón's music, providing evidence to illustrate musical elements that are nostalgic or típico (exile) and elements that are more hybrid (New York adaptations).

The historical interconnections between Havana, Miami, and New York are complex, and the reverence for Cuban music and culture, particularly from the many Puerto Rican musicians interviewed, make for some interesting close readings of charanga flute improvisations. As Conzo and Pérez state when discussing Tito Puente's approach to Cuban music performance: "It was . . . very New York. It was his unique sound. It combined the best of the Yoruba traditions, Afro-Cuban dance music and American big band jazz influence. It sounded Cuban and it felt New York. The sound of the Tito Puente orchestra had a swagger and arrogance about it."[12] Although the mambo big bands such as Tito Puente's group were larger in size, with a full brass section, they were influenced by charanga performance practice and repertoire; and Orquesta Broadway, albeit with a different timbre,[13] also displays a confident sound that could be described in similar terms. In the following section three improvised solos by Zervigón are analyzed to investigate how these ideas of grit, swagger, arrogance, and aggression manifest themselves sonically.

In the first example of Zervigón's improvisational style on "Al Mirar No Me Vistes" [You Look But You Don't See Me], the influence of Fajardo's fast rhythmic style is readily apparent; but on further inspection Egües's melodic influence can also be heard. However, Zervigón's personal style is not purely defined by how his style fuses the styles of Fajardo and Egües. The annotated transcription of "Al Mirar No Me Vistes" (see example 4.1) demonstrates these influences alongside a more individual "hurricane-like" soloing style that perhaps captures the feeling of a faster-paced New York.[14] Later his improvisation on the slower tempo "Quinta Guajira" [Fifth *Guajira*] is examined for evidence of both "cubanía" and New York sabor. To finish, Zervigón's conversational approach on "Goza La Vida" [Enjoy Your Life] is examined with a view to demonstrating both his cubanía and perhaps his more New York–oriented competitive energy.

"AL MIRAR NO ME VISTES"

This solo has the energy of a Fajardo improvisation, particularly in terms of the range, with its predominance of top fourth register e^4s and use of up-tempo, clave-driven suspense (using "3 in a grid of 4" sequences). The use of the fourth register $f^{\sharp 4}$ above the range in measure 208 is a hallmark of both Fajardo's and Zervigón's styles. Zervigón has even occasionally played fourth register g^4 and could perhaps be considered the charanga flautist with the highest range. Zervigón's fingerings for these *altissimo* notes are illustrated in figure 4.3 and table 4.1; it is worth noting that most charanga flute players play up to d^4 or e^4 and rarely perform these higher altissimo notes (although Fajardo, George Castro, and Rolando Lozano do occasionally hit these). Performing an f or g in the fourth register is a competitive gesture (in the same vein as holding a note for the longest duration) and Zervigón has often employed the use of *altissimo* notes in descarga jam session environments

Al Mirar No Me Vistes

Transcribed from the album *Paraiso* by Orquesta Broadway

flute solo by Eddie Zervigón, transcribed and annotated by Sue Miller

Copyright © this transcription Sue Miller, Leeds, June 23, 2007, revised December 2010, annotated August 2018

Example 4.1 Transcribed and annotated score of "Al Mirar No Me Vistes" flute solo by Eddy Zervigón.

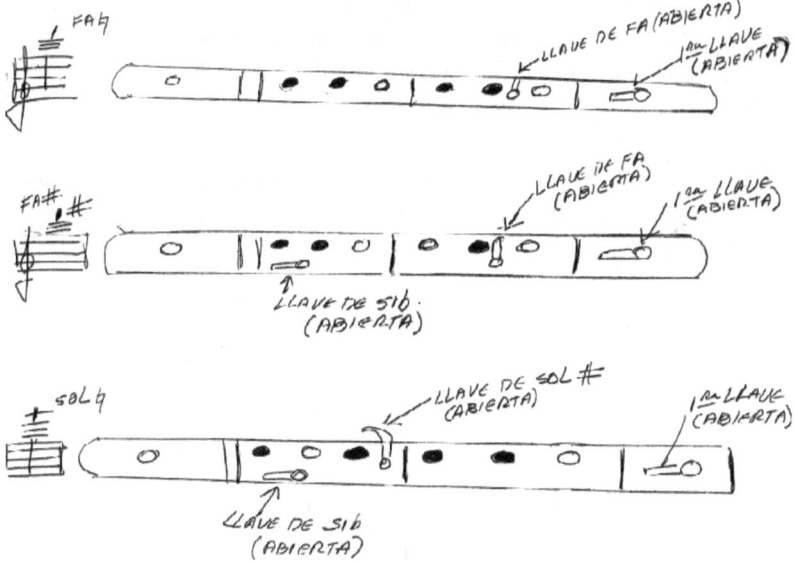

Figure 4.3 Eddy Zervigón's fourth-register "*sobre agudo*" altissimo notes. Drawing courtesy of Eddy Zervigón.

in order to throw down the gauntlet in these friendly Latin music "cutting" contests.

Zervigón sent a diagram drawing of these fingerings to me on August 6, 2018 (see figure 4.3) with performance guidance for reaching the f⁴ (*fa natural*):

> El fa natural es igual que el fa de la tercera escala, lo que tienes es que darle más duro, apretando la llave del fa (armónica) porque hay otra posición que usaba Richard (mas fácil para ejecución sin apretar la llave de fa), pero esa no sale el fa. Yo me puse a tratar de sacar el fa natural que nadie lo tenía y de milagro me salió el fa natural (una armónica) sobre agudo . . . pero tiene que estar la flauta bien ajustada . . . no muchas flautas se pueden lograr fa, fa♯, y sol sobre agudo—tienen que estar muy suaves.

> [The f natural is the same [fingering] as the third octave f natural— what you have to do is give it more strength, pressing the f key (harmonic) because there is another fingering which Richard [Egües] used to use (which was easier to finger without pressing the F key) but this doesn't get the f out. I tried to get the f natural which no one

could get and by some miracle an f natural harmonic came out in the altissimo register. But the flute needs to be well adjusted for this. Not many flutes are capable of producing f, f♯, and g in the altissimo range—they have to be very well made.]¹⁵

Table 4.1 gives Zervigón's fingerings showing where a key is present and depressed, thus venting the hole (open/*abierta*). Closed holes which are not in operation (closed/*cerrada*) are not shown.¹⁶

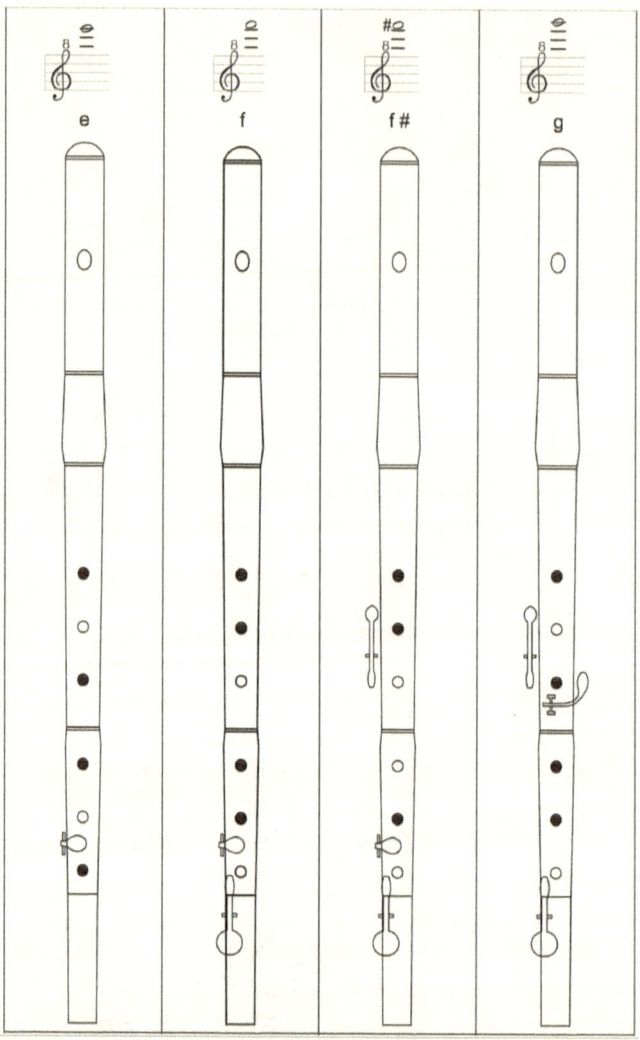

Table 4.1 Zervigón's altissimo fingerings for fourth-register e, f, f♯, and g. Courtesy of Nigel Humphreys of Jadenrange Ltd.¹⁷

The most striking feature of this long solo is the preference for fourth-octave playing with a tessitura of d³ to f#⁴ above the range. Many phrases hover between fourth-register e⁴ and d⁴ and are played with the strong attack characteristic of five-key flute playing. Virtuosic elements such as the fast sextuplets at measure 212 are a feature of both Egües's and Fajardo's styles, but the flutter-tongued fourth-octave c#⁴s and d⁴s in measures 260 and 261 are entirely Zervigón's. In many ways these sustained high-octave phrases mixed with virtuosic techniques exemplify Zervigón's style, revealing the brasher, energetic city ambience of New York which he claims his band reflects in the opening quotation to this chapter.

At first glance one could assume that Fajardo is Zervigón's main influence, but on closer investigation the influence of both Egües and Fajardo can be detected in Zervigón's style. Ornamentation and phrasing are very similar to Fajardo's, with frequent turns around g³ woven into a more continuous line than would be the case for Egües. On the other hand, the rise and fall of Zervigón's phrases are very much part of Egües's melodic call-and-response style in that they are developed motivically, often finishing with a descending phrase, as in example 4.2. Zervigón's motivic development is as melodic, rhythmic, and playful as Egües's style here, with chord tones outlined, as in this octave-leap charanga-style motif:

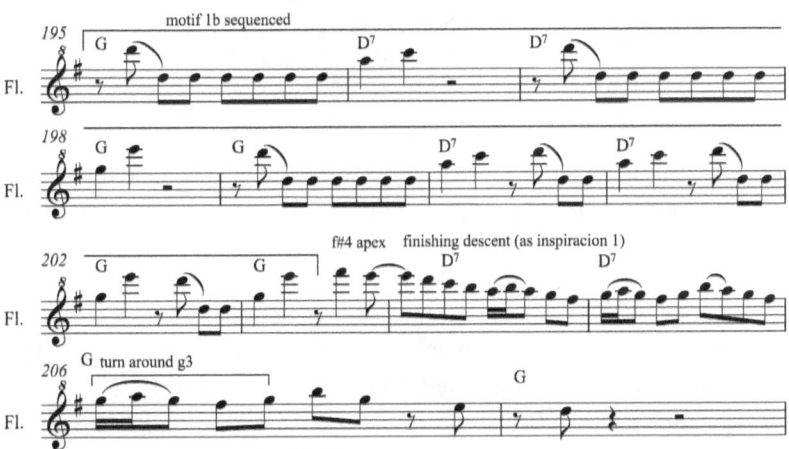

Example 4.2 Octave-leap motivic development "Egües-style" in flute solo by Eddy Zervigón.

This high-energy, exhilarating solo also relates, in subtle ways, to the composed elements of the piece—something Egües is renowned for in his *inspiraciones*. Zervigón, like Egües, responds to the coros in typical call-and-response fashion at rehearsal marks E, H, and I of the transcription (see example 4.1) in a similar vein to Egües in Orquesta Aragón.[18] Drawing on the percussive elements of the style, coro 2 has rhythms derived from the timbales cascara and Zervigón uses these patterns frequently in his inspiraciones (section H), as in example 4.3:

Example 4.3 Call and response in clave, referencing the 2–3 cascara pattern, in flute solo by Eddy Zervigón (clave superimposed).

Using ideas from the composed ensemble breaks, Zervigón uses motivic development in conjunction with clave organization to develop his improvised phrases. In terms of clave sensibility, the 2-side of the clave aligns with the on-beat phrases, and the 3-side with the off-beat ones (see example 4.3). The four straight quarter notes followed by the repeated eighth notes of break 1 in example 4.4 reference the *danzón baqueteo* pattern and the *danzón solo* pattern (played by the güiro and timbales, usually under a piano solo). These rhythmic motifs are then drawn upon throughout Zervigón's solo, and hence these percussive clave-organized patterns infuse Zervigón's motivic development and sequenced ideas. The references to Cuban danzón are therefore subtle and pervade both the composed elements of the arrangement and Zervigón's flute solo. The danzón patterns are outlined in examples 4.4 and 4.5 and the related composed break is in example 4.6.

2-3 danzon solo pattern

Example 4.4 The two-bar danzón pattern in 2–3 clave (in common time) usually played under piano solos.

2-3 danzon baqueteo pattern

Example 4.5 Danzón baqueteo (in 2–3 clave) featuring the cinquillo five-beat pattern in the second measure (in common time).

Example 4.6 "Al Mirar No Me Vistes" break 1: imitating danzón patterns.

Drawing on these patterns, Zervigón's improvised phrase in example 4.7 contains the full *cinquillo* (five-beat) 3-side of the *baqueteo* pattern delayed by an eighth note (starting on the off-beat), before playing the four downbeats of the 2-side:

Example 4.7 "Al Mirar No Me Vistes" flute solo by Eddy Zervigón, drawing on the composed break and danzón pattern: improvising in clave.

Zervigón frequently starts his phrases on the "and of one" (or 1+); these phrases sometimes function as anacrusis on the 3-side of the clave, often leading to breaks and new sections (as in measures 97, 139, 173, 195, 221 in example 4.1). Anacrusis on the 3-side is a feature of the style, and this is one way of detecting clave sensibility. There are no hard and fast rules for performance practice when it comes to Cuban flute improvisation (a few of Zervigón's phrases do not adhere to this on-beat/off-beat principle), but a 2–3 clave feel is present throughout the solo—this can be demonstrated in score even if the player's application in performance is intuitive. In example

4.8, Zervigón plays with the timbales cascara pattern and, in example 4.9, the basic cascara pattern is outlined alongside the clave to show how Zervigón's improvised sequence outlines the clave direction. Here the 3-side off-beat and 2-side on-beat align with clave and cascara accentuation.

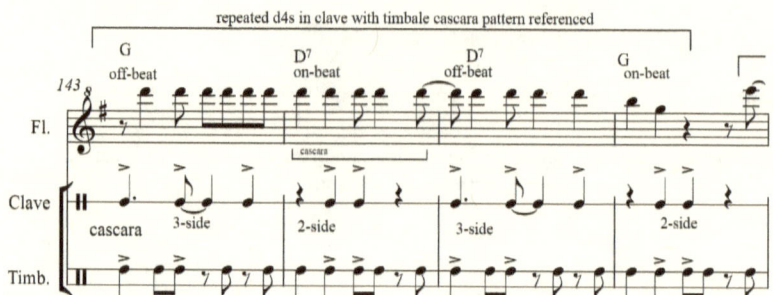

Example 4.8 Referencing the timbales' 2–3 cascara pattern in flute solo by Eddy Zervigón.

This improvised phrase follows a 2–3 clave direction (from measure 144) with the 2-side phrases placed on the beat at the beginning of the bar and with the 2-side of the timbales cascara pattern realized in full in measure 144. These intuitive references to percussion patterns that align in the main with clave direction (son clave, danzón *baqueteo* variants, and timbales' cascara patterns) show how Zervigón's solo relates closely to clave and also to the two-measure danzón baqueteo pattern, which also functions as a clave.[19] Zervigón has always insisted that, to play charanga típica, one needs a grounding in traditional Cuban danzón, and he often cites José Fajardo and Belisario López as good examples of all-round charanga players who have this solid foundation in danzón.[20] It is therefore not surprising that his solo here is informed by both son-clave and the danzón's organizing baqueteo two-measure pattern. This concept of an on-beat 2-side and more off-beat 3-side of the clave is in evidence in his solo on "Al Mirar No Me Vistes," and in his rhythmic play he shows an allegiance to Fajardo's *callejero* style, in keeping with an idea of "street" for the loud and busy sounds of New York City.[21]

"YO SIEMPRE HA SIDO UNA PERSONA MUY QUISQUILLOSA CON EL RITMO."

["I HAVE ALWAYS BEEN A REAL STICKLER WHEN IT COMES TO RHYTHM."][22]

Zervigón is indeed very attentive to rhythmic factors. In the "Al Mirar No Me Vistes" solo, in addition to adherence to clave and references to other percussion patterns such as the cascara and danzón baqueteo, he employs cross-rhythm devices for added tension. Some of these are in clave as, in example 4.9; others are clave neutral but eventually resolve in clave, as in example 4.10.

Example 4.9 Improvisation in clave in flute solo by Eddy Zervigón.

Example 4.10 Rhythmic tension and resolution—playing with clave in flute solo by Eddy Zervigón.

In example 4.10, Zervigón employs "out of clave" (or one-measure clave neutral) phrases that finally resolve in clave in measure 162. This tension-release device is also used frequently by José Fajardo.

In this solo Fajardo's influence is evident but Zervigón's subtle creative strategies are also indicative of Egües's melodic influence. Of course, both Egües and Fajardo have been fundamental to the development of the Cuban flute style in general. However, this solo is a reminder that the role of influence in the development of individual style is a complex affair, related not just to characteristic ornamentation and favored phrases but to broader elements such as creative strategies and expressive devices. Here, both Cuban influences are joined together but nevertheless reveal Zervigón's own individual voice in the way they are combined. The "hurricane-like" velocity, dense rhythmic structures, quick wit, and stamina required of frequently used high-register motifs (for example, fourth-register flutter-tonguing) embody a nervous energy that could be said to reflect the fast pace of New York City life as well as Zervigón's personality or his individual *sello*.[23]

In conversation with Zervigón at his home in 2007, he told me that most of Orquesta Broadway's repertoire was up-tempo to cater to New York audiences (he said the slower tempo chachachá songs like "El Bodeguero" bombed in the New York context),[24] but that he really enjoyed spreading out in slower styles like the *guajira* or in the slower montuno sections of certain danzones.

He sounded wistful, making me think of how he had needed to adapt to a faster pace of life and a new musical landscape very different from the life he had left behind in Cuba. His soloing on mid-tempo *guajira* is therefore explored next with a view to seeing how Cuban and New York sabor might coexist. Does he, for example, incorporate more nostalgic Cuban *"del monte"* ("from the mountains") rural elements in the slower *guajira* style?[25]

QUINTA GUAJIRA—CUBANÍA IN ZERVIGÓN'S IMPROVISATIONAL STYLE

In *Cuban Flute Style: Interpretation and Improvisation*, I analyze the "Quinta Guajira" piece, looking at how the main motif from the first movement of Beethoven's fifth symphony was "cubanized."[26] In this chapter I describe and analyze the flute improvisation to demonstrate how the slower tempo *guajira* style (here ♩ = 100) enables Zervigón to explore a Cuban *campesina* or country feel in contrast to his high-energy up-tempo improvisations on pieces such as "Al Mirar No Me Vistes." New York–born Puerto Rican Gil Suarez composed and arranged "Quinta Guajira" and plays piano on the Orquesta Broadway recording of the album *Como Me Gusta*! recorded in New York on May 25, 1972. The personnel on the recording include Eddy Zervigón on five-key flute, his brother Rudy on violin, Gil Suárez on piano,[27] Mike Amití on bass, Abraham Norman on violin, Carlos Rubio on congas, Enrique Vélez on timbales, and Felo Barrios and Vicente Dario on vocals.

Figure 4.4. Orquesta Broadway singer Felo Barrios, Miami, July 2016. Copyright Sue Miller.

In this analysis, elements showing cubanía and other aspects of Cuban or New York sabor are investigated to see if Zervigón's improvisational style demonstrates more of a Cuban or a New York charanga sound. Does he in fact "sound Cuban but feel New York," or does he play this solo with more cubanía in the campesina style by drawing on feelings of nostalgia for his homeland?[28]

Example 4.11 Full score of flute solo on "Quinta Guajira" by Eddy Zervigón.

This solo references the Cuban danzón and the guajira/*música campesina* traditions in that Zervigón quotes melodic material from the danzones "Isora Club" and "Angoa," delivered using both danzón and guajira expressive techniques such as rubato and vibrato. Zervigón's solo is built around the "Isora Club" melody, which is usually played by the flute at the beginning of this danzón in the open montuno section (see example 4.12).[29] In

Zervigón's solo at rehearsal mark B (see example 4.13), this melodic line is varied rhythmically through phrasing, use of rubato and vibrato, and through embellishment of the dominant axis note of g³. Zervigón improvises around this theme before he states it at A and then later throughout the solo from rehearsal mark C (measure 26), utilizing octave leaps, "3 in a grid of 4" cross rhythms, triplet mordents, and acciaccaturas. This solo draws repeatedly on the melodic structure of this danzón melody styled as a guajira.

Example 4.12 Melody preceding the piano solo at beginning of montuno section of "Isora Club," *Cachao Master Sessions*. Flute: Nestor Torres.

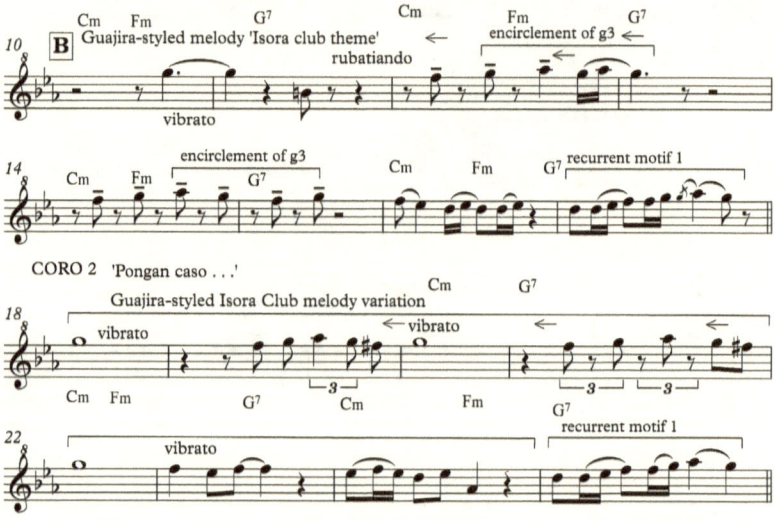

Example 4.13 "Isora Club" variation in "Quinta Guajira" with guajira-styled delivery. Flute: Eddy Zervigón.

The "Isora Club"–derived melody in example 4.13 is played twice with variation and is based around a dominant axis of g³. In the first rendition, the tessitura ranges from d³ to a♭³, and a♭² to a♭³, while the second uses a lower register tessitura reserved for slower romantic styles such as the guajira, bolero, and their hybrid versions such as guajira-son and bolero-son. The use of rubato and vibrato demonstrate a romantic expressive element common not only in the vocal guajira style but also in the danzón and danzón-mambo playing of Antonio Arcaño and other Cuban charanga flautists from the 1930s and '40s.[31] The melody consists of a turn around the dominant note g³, a turn around the third degree e♭³, and a rising figure finishing with the sixth resolving to the fifth note. The turnaround final phrase prevents the line from resolving to the tonic, allowing for more variations of the theme to take place (unlike the final bar of the "Isora Club" theme, which finishes on the tonic). Aside the final bar, this danzón melody in example 4.12 is structurally the same as the "Quinta Guajira" melody at B (see example 4.13); these danzón melodies, with their introductory or "bridge function," sometimes borrow melodies from son and guajira-son coros, as for example in the danzón "Tres Lindas Cubanas"; the "Tres Lindas Cubanas" melody is often mistakenly attributed to the bandleader, pianist, and composer Maria Antonio Romeu but the theme was a son melody incorporated into his larger danzón charanga orchestration.[32] The unresolved, plaintive guajira melody, with its associations of rural living, could perhaps be viewed as a sign of cubanía and also nostalgia for a lost homeland.[33]

The delivery of the melody at B is similar to the romantic interpretation of the guajira-style "Al Vaiven De Mi Carreta" melodies I learned from Richard Egües in 2000 and 2001;[34] in these lessons with Egües, a guajira-style phrasing including rubato was taught to me through oral transmission. These yearning phrases are similar to an *inspiracíon* Egües plays on Orquesta Aragón's homage to Beethoven's Fifth, "Voy Hablar Con Tu Papa," itself a guajira-inspired piece.[35] In "Voy Hablar Con Tu Papa," the slower tempo of guajira allows rubato and vibrato to be used to create a lyrical and somewhat plaintive mood that Havana-based flautist Joaquín Oliveros refers to as *monte adentro*.[36] Cuban music scholar Rebecca Bodenheimer has translated "*soy del monte adentro*" as "I'm from the boondocks" ("I'm from the sticks" in UK English) and she comments that the term is derogatory.[37] However, Oliveros said the term could also be one of praise,[38] stating that if you played "*monte adentro*" then you had cubanía, that is, an authentic "country" feel. Zervigón certainly does give this solo a more guajira feel in contrast to his playing on the faster, more insistent "Al Mirar No Me Vistes" solo. Perhaps nostalgia for his home town of Güines underlies his style of performance here. The push-and-pull *rubatiando* melodic approach is more akin to Cuba-based charanga than New York charanga versions of the style, but the tempo of this guajira is nevertheless faster than guajiras and guajira-son-styled recordings from mid-twentieth-century Cuba. Indeed, tempo has often been identified as a parameter that distinguishes Cuban charanga from New York–based groups. As outlined in chapter 3, Belisario López recorded slower-tempo danzones, danzón-*cha*, and chachachás in Cuba, although these were often faster than those of his contemporaries.[39] His recordings in New York on the Ansonia label are mainly up-tempo and at times sound a little rushed in comparison to his earlier Havana-based recordings.[40] Zervigón, in contrast, was in his twenties and full of youthful energy at this time. Tempo affects the type of improvisation produced whatever the age of the performer, in that certain stylistic elements no longer work when the speed is increased.[41] In this solo Zervigón plays with the texture using a wider variety of rhythmic values. Elements relating to clave feel, important in both Cuban and New York traditions, are present here with three different instances of "3 in a grid of 4" cross-rhythm patterns which increase the textural density of the solo. These push against the beat and against clave alignment but resolve in clave (see example 4.14).

Example 4.14 "3 in a grid of 4" cross-rhythms resolving in clave (m. 32) in "Quinta Guajira." Flute: Eddy Zervigón.

Zervigón's solo on "Quinta Guajira" takes place over the coros and over a Cm, Fm, G7 progression or i-iv-V7, a typical guajira progression. The basic violin guajeo, piano montuno, and bass tumbao under the solo are shown in example 4.15 (clave superimposed but not sounded):

Example 4.15 The main patterns underneath the flute solo on "Quinta Guajira."

There are a few minor variations on these patterns as shown in the following bass example, which alternates between guajira and chachachá stylings.

Example 4.16 Bass tumbao variant showing both guajira and chachachá influence on "Quinta Guajira."

This texture and phrasing of the traditional arpeggiated i-iv-V7 figures under the flute solo subtly influence the improvisation, with a romantic delivery common to 1930s and '40s charanga flute danzón performance practice, and a guajira vocal style associated with these underlying patterns. This romantic-styled solo (shown in full score in example 4.11) also references melodies from danzones "Angoa" (m. 44) as well as "Isora Club" (mm. 10–25 and their development in mm. 1–9). In terms of chachachá styling,

Zervigón employs embellishment techniques common to the danzón-chá *montuneando* style of soloing including ornamentation (turns, acciacaturas, encirclement of melody notes), triplet and "3 in a grid of 4" cross rhythms (mm. 26–31 and mm. 45–46), and anacrusis development (mm. 36–41), all of which are either in clave or resolve in clave. The busier textures from rehearsal mark C are possible due to the slower tempo. The improvisation keeps the unresolving guajira chord pattern in mind (a "chord loop" in Philip Tagg's terms)[42] by having an axis of the dominant note g^3 running throughout the whole solo. The solo only resolves to the tonic in the final bar when g^3 moves to tonic c^4, an ending more in keeping with the more "euroclassical" danzón tradition. A resolution to the tonic in guajira is considered a "gringo" ending and euroclassical ideas on resolution in the son and guajira-son tradition are therefore misplaced in those contexts. Here, though, the ending very definitely resolves to the tonic, inspired as it is by Beethoven's fifth symphony.

Zervigón certainly demonstrates cubanía in this guajira-son homage to Beethoven, reflecting his youth in Cuba, his formative training in Güines, and his brief professional debut in Havana, alongside his Cuban flute influences (Egües, Fajardo, Guerrero). New York–based Orquesta Broadway differed from Orquesta Ideal and Estrellas Cubanas in that this new band was formed from Cuban, Puerto Rican, and Jewish American musicians; the band had to adapt to the multicultural environment of New York, particularly in terms of tempo and dynamic. Zervigón's improvisational style is undoubtedly típico here, yet it still has a brash energy (swagger or nervous energy?) which could be labeled New York sabor. The tempo does seem to be a factor in defining difference between midcentury Cuban charanga playing and early 1960s New York charanga performance, reflected both in the performance of the repertoire and the improvisations that belong to them.[43] Zervigón likes this variety of texture and dynamic but told me that the more suave Cuban repertoire did not go down as well in New York. Any Cuban repertoire that did not get New York audiences up and dancing was taken out of the band's repertoire.[44]

The first solo "Al Mirar No Me Vistes" demonstrates Zervigón's main influences, namely Richard Egües's melodic approach and José Fajardo's continuous callejero style. The second example, "Quinta Guajira," perhaps contains elements from other charanga flautists from his formative years such as Rolando Lozano (from early Orquesta Aragón and Orquesta América) and Julio Guerrero from Estrellas Cubanas, both known for their sweeter sound and romantic approach. Undoubtedly the musicians in Zervigón's band also brought their own stylistic elements to bear on the overall effect of Orquesta Broadway, affecting the flute improvisations in turn, whether that be through tempo, phrasing, dynamic, attack, or choice of stylistic elements. The repertoire clearly had to change to meet the needs of a Pan-Latino audience. Zervigón confided to me in 2007 that New York audiences did not want slower chachachá dances, preferring more up-tempo music that related to the pace of their own lives.[45]

Working with other Cuban musicians but also with Puerto Rican, African American, Jewish, and Italian musicians Zervigón's style was bound to change over time. Nevertheless, "Quinta Guajira" is very similar to Orquesta Aragón's "Isora Club," and has its parallel with Aragón's "Voy Hablar con Tu Papa." However, the recording as a whole has a more "streetwise" attitude and a nervous energy. If "Al Mirar No Me Vistes" demonstrates New York sabor, then Zervigón's solo on "Quinta Guajira" has more cubanía, laced with a touch of homesickness and nostalgia for the Cuba he left behind. As an exile Zervigón found a "home from home" in Latin New York, but missed all that he lost after the 1959 revolution: following his move to the USA in 1962, he was never able to see his parents or wider extended family again. The creativity of his playing demonstrates Cuban sabor in terms of clave sensibility, call and response and melodic development, and his high-octave, hurricane-like densely textured sequences could be interpreted as displaying if not a swagger, then at least an assertiveness borne of the New York competitive environment. In the final solo analyzed here Zervigón's conversational and playful approach to improvisation incorporates both cubanía and a New York sabor in more equal measure. "Goza La Vida," from the album *Como Me Gusta*! was recorded on May 25, 1972, and exemplifies his hybrid New York Latin identity.

Goza La Vida!

La vida da muchas vueltas, mañana no sabes donde parar
Y por eso yo te canto este viejo refran
Goza la vida—que cuando vayas al hueco, no vuelves mas!

[Life goes round in circles, tomorrow you don't know where it'll stop
And so I sing to you this old refrain:
Enjoy your life—'cause once you're in the hole you ain't coming back!].
—LYRICS TO "GOZA LA VIDA"

This playful *carpe diem* guaracha is about living for the moment—a plea to seize the day and have fun, perhaps reflecting both the uncertainty and the excitement of being a Cuban exile in New York. A fusion of both Fajardo

Figure 4.5 Eddy Zervigón, by Manhattan Bridge, July 16, 2016. Copyright Sue Miller.

and Egües, Zervigón's sequential playing is very characteristic of Richard Egües's call-and-response approach, while the continuity of sound is more in keeping with Fajardo's callejero or street style (see example 4.17).

Zervigón reaches for the fourth-register g^4 in measures 142–144, playing a sharp f^4 natural altissimo note (as part of a characteristic octave leap from third to fourth register) in an attempt to complete the top octave tessitura from dominant g^3 to fourth-octave g^4. Most charanga flute players do not reach these altissimo notes (f^4, $f^{\#4}$, and g^4) and they are certainly a feature of Zervigón's individual style (as are the high flutter-tongued notes). This reaching higher can be viewed in terms of the New York competitive scene but also as a playful gesture—indeed, in all three solos his personality comes through as quick-witted and restless. Perhaps this nervous energy and striving form part of that New York competitive edge, and the faster tempos and dense textures even in the guajira are reflective of a more mechanized city soundscape. The high dynamic is also characteristic, and although Zervigón cues a lower dynamic with an octave leap from third register g^3 to a held trilled g^2 in measures 92–96, the rest of the band do not take the cue to accommodate his lower register trill and follow-on improvisations, as musicians would have done in Havana. Perhaps some of the subtler performance conventions of charanga were not adhered to as much by musicians from

Goza La Vida

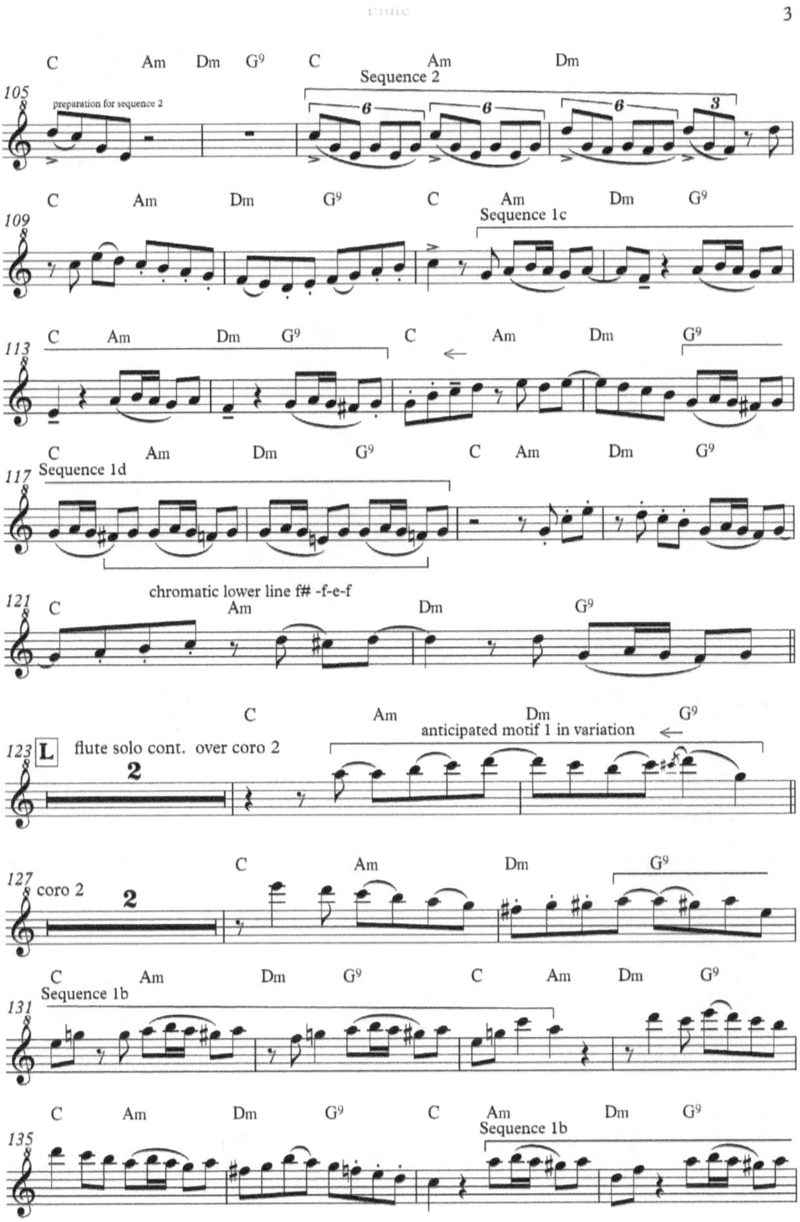
Flute
3
preparation for sequence 2
Sequence 2
Sequence 1c
Sequence 1d
chromatic lower line f# -f-e-f
L
flute solo cont. over coro 2
anticipated motif 1 in variation
coro 2
Sequence 1b
Sequence 1b

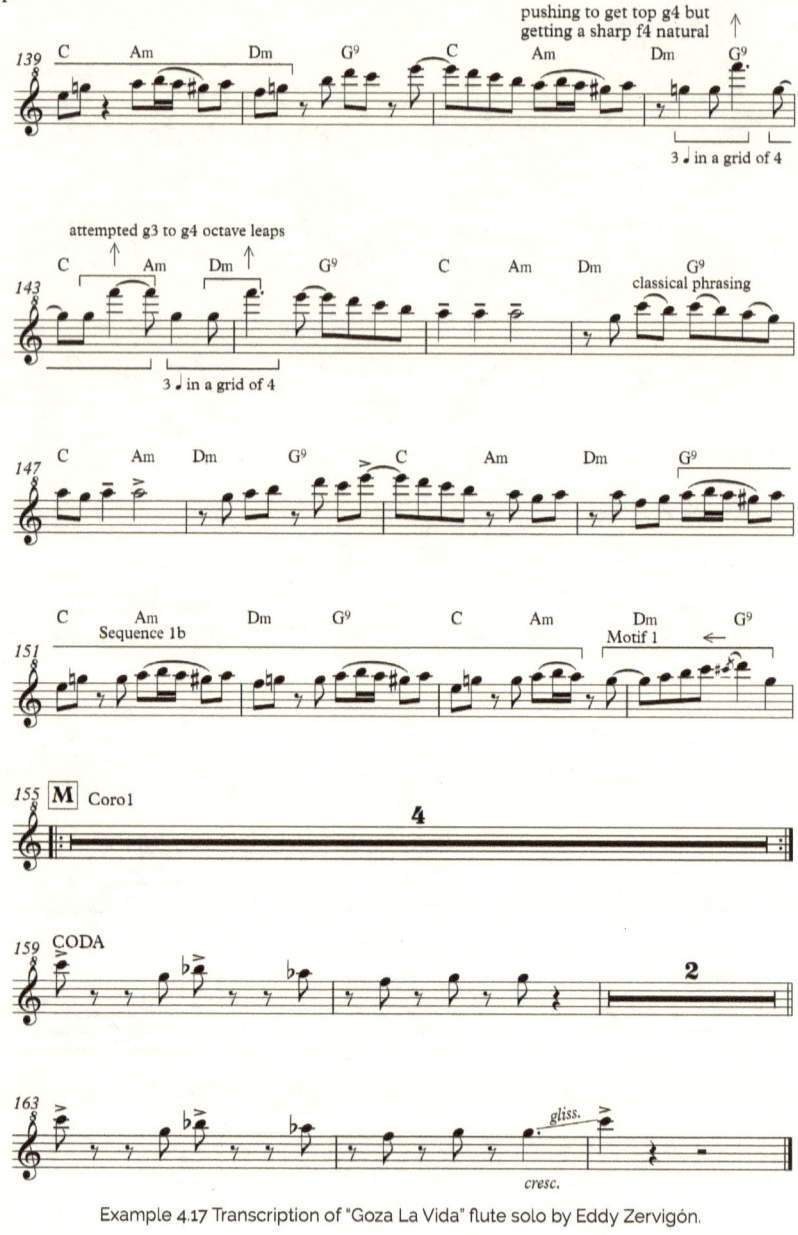

Example 4.17 Transcription of "Goza La Vida" flute solo by Eddy Zervigón.

Figure 4.6 Publicity poster for Orquesta Broadway's fiftieth anniversary performance at Lincoln Center, New York, 2012.

outside the Cuban tradition (or even for those Cuban musicians who may have relaxed a little once away from the home country), and some cues and *llamadas* [calls] may be missing in the later New York versions. This consistently high dynamic may have been a factor in Zervigón's usual louder fourth-register style. From this instance of an unwritten performance code not being followed, one could put forward the idea that New York charanga was less subtle in terms of dynamic shading than the Havana-based típico charanga orquestas.

In real life Zervigón is known for his sharp wit and top-octave energy. In performances with Eddie Palmieri's La Perfecta II and Manny Oquendo's Conjunto Libre, his flute powers out over a three- to five-strong trombone section. His experiences of the Cuban Revolution made him wary of politicians and conscious of how fortunes can change without warning (as the title of this piece asserts). His personality has been shaped by his experience as an exile, adapting his musicality to reflect his dual identity as a Cuban who established himself in New York. Orquesta Broadway is New York's longest-running charanga band (over fifty-eight years to date) and, as Latin music historian Rene López remarked in a live public interview with Zervigón, it is quite an achievement to maintain the level of quality it has done over such a long period of time.[46] Zervigón certainly injected a high dose of cubanía into the New York Latin music scene. In turn, New York gave his playing and that of his Orquesta Broadway a unique sound or *sello* which "sounded Cuban but felt New York."[47]

- 5 -

CHARANGA OR PACHANGA?

THE REBRANDING OF CUBAN DANCE MUSIC IN 1960S NEW YORK

When I was staying in a flat in Brooklyn in the summer of 2012, my hosts assured me it would be fine to play some charanga flute while they were out at work, and not to worry about the neighbors. So I rigged up a playback system and settled in to playing my flute in the third and fourth register along with tracks by some of my favorite New York charanga bands such as Orquesta Broadway, Charlie Palmieri's La Duboney, Mongo Santamaría's La Sabrosa, and Pacheco y Su Charanga. After about ten minutes of play there was a loud banging on the door and I froze—should I open the door not knowing who was there? Was it an angry neighbor armed and ready to shoot? I waited a moment before a voice piped up "don't worry, it's your neighbor Ruben here and I just want to say how much I love your music—it's old school pachanga!" I opened up and Ruben introduced himself to me as a Puerto Rican New Yorker who grew up listening to this music. His parents used to go dancing at the Palladium and play pachanga records and he had not heard this music in a while—it made him nostalgic. The fact that Ruben chose to call the music pachanga and not charanga highlights the music's history in New York City, where Johnny Pacheco's and Charlie Palmieri's charanga music (and others) was popularized as pachanga. As a stylistic term, pachanga has its origins in a 1959 composition by Eduardo Davidson, "La Pachanga" [The Party]. It initially was a hit for the Panart record label's group, Orquesta Sublime. Orchestrated by Orquesta Aragón's Richard Egües and also popularized by Fajardo y sus Estrellas, the style of subsequent pachangas recorded in its wake in Cuba were not always related to this initial composition by Davidson.

Che Guevara's slogan "revolución con pachanga" in the early days of the Cuban revolution is a little ironic given the fact that, after Eduardo Davidson's defection to the United States, his pachanga records were destroyed and his music no longer played on the radio.[1] Orquesta Sublime, however, continued to perform their hit which brought them fame as "La Pachanguera

Figure 5.1 Melquiades Fundora, flute player with Orquesta Sublime, at home in Habana Vieja, 2007. Copyright Sue Miller.

de Cuba." In an interview in 2001, Melquiades Fundora Dina (1926–2009), cofounder and flute player of Orquesta Sublime, related the history of the band as formed on January 21, 1956, by a group of young men who had no intention of earning a living from their music. Their first recordings "El Peletero" and "El Cartero," both chachachás, were well received and they subsequently recorded "Union Cienfueguera" (a danzón) and "Seis Perlas Cubanas" (a son).[2] With the success of "La Pachanga," the group became popular nationally and the band found they could earn a living through their performances and recordings.[3]

The word "pachanga," as with "rumba," initially denoted a "party," as Juan Flores has documented in his account of New York Latin music in the 1960s:

> ..."una pachanga" has long meant "party" in Spanish colloquial usage; in some contexts it is often used in the verb form, "pachanguear," meaning to have a party or dance or have a good time. The word then took on its more specific modern-day reference in 1959 as the title of an extremely popular song by the well-known Cuban librettist, composer and entertainer Eduardo Davidson. Indeed, the song "La Pachanga" as first performed in Havana by Orquesta Sublime and recorded by the most famous charanga band of the day, led by renowned flutist José Fajardo, generated a feverish craze in Cuba on

the eve of the 1959 revolution.... Right away the fever spread to New York, especially with the Fajardo recording of the song and its performance by none other than Orquesta Aragón at the Palladium and other prominent midtown venues.[4]

Flores also discusses the naming of the pachanga dance in New York, pinning its origin to Johnny Pacheco's dance, which, although based on elements of Rafael Bacallao's dancing with Orquesta Aragón, seems to have evolved at the Triton Club in 1960.[5] According to Flores (citing Al Santiago), Pacheco copied the small jumps that Rafael Bacallao performed in his dance routines, adding the waving of a handkerchief and a stomp on the downbeat inspired by the Puerto Rican dancers at the Bronx club. According to Max Salazar this dance was like a "sort of Latin Charleston" which had dancers "hopping and yelling 'a caballo' while waving a handkerchief around their heads."[6]

A committee of musicians and promoters decided to label this dance as pachanga to market Johnny Pacheco's charanga band and its music, and Palladium promoter Federico Pagani steered the decision to market it as pachanga.[7] Much of the confusion in New York between the term charanga for the name of the lineup of a charanga orquesta and the term pachanga denoting a new music and dance style was created at this time. To make things more complicated, musicians speak of a charanga style when discussing performance practice: a charanga feel requires knowledge of charanga music's codes of performance (instrument patterns, instrumental functions, knowledge of repertoire, characteristic playing techniques, distinct timbres, and other unwritten performance conventions). Added to this confusion between charanga and pachanga is that the pachanga style often remains undefined musically in relation to the chachachá or the Cuban son montuno or guaracha. Flores, for example, in his otherwise excellent account of New York Latin music of the 1960s generation, does not give musical detail about the style in his book *Salsa Rising* other than referring to the "musical trappings" of pachanga.[8]

The phrases "*vamos a rumbear*" and "*vamos a pachanguear*" in origin simply meant "let's party" before the rhumba and pachanga terms became associated with specific popular dance music forms. Just as charanga and pachanga were terms commonly confused in New York, so previously were the separate styles of Cuban rumba and Cuban son. American tourists enjoying Cuban son, rumba, guaracha, and *comparsa* in the 1920s and '30s would probably have heard the term *r(h)umba* applied to events in bars, clubs, and hotels where music and dance were present. Rhumba, then, is an example of a broader term representing a myriad of styles long before the salsa labeling controversy of the 1970s. In the early 1960s the often cited "La Pachanga Se Baila Así" by Charlie Palmieri and Joe Quijano attempted in song format to clear up the confusion between the charanga lineup and the pachanga dance style by explaining that you *dance* pachanga, a musical style with a distinctive pachanga rhythm, which is *played* by a charanga orquesta:

> *Hay una discusión en el barrio, de cómo se baila la pachanga*
> *hay una confusión en el barrio, se creen que charanga es pachanga.*
> *Una charanga es la orquesta que está de moda*
> *Y una pachanga es, el baile que se baila ahora.*
> *Esta orquesta es charanga*
> *Toca el ritmo de pachanga, nene*
> *Baile la pachanga*
> *Con esta charanga*
>
> *[There's an argument in el barrio on how to dance pachanga*
> *there's confusion in el barrio where they think charanga is pachanga.*
> *The charanga is the band that's in fashion*
> *and the pachanga is the new dance.*
> *This is a charanga band*
> *playing the pachanga rhythm, girl.*
> *Dance the pachanga*
> *with this charanga]*[9]

However, the song does not exactly clarify the meaning of the two terms. Although making it clear that the charanga is the name of the lineup, the lyrics describe pachanga as being both a dance and a rhythm. In fact, many of the pachangas listed on the album *Pachanga* are fast tempo chachachás with son- or mambo-style bass lines, chachachá güiro patterns, and typical charanga violin guajeo patterns. There are V-I montunos typical of the Cuban guaracha, often including mambo sections on one dominant seventh chord in the second part of an arrangement (as on "La Pachanga Se Baila Así") demonstrating stylistic hybridity. Ironically, the Alegre label is at the root of the charanga/pachanga controversy, as Johnny Pacheco's charanga was publicized by Al Santiago using the term *pachanga* (before the term *salsa*, which Pacheco co-invented for Fania Records, did much the same thing a few years later). Pacheco has even claimed that he created the word pachanga from a mix of his name Pacheco and the term "charanga" and that if the word was around before then it was just a coincidence![10] His claim as originator of the pachanga dance does seem to be borne out by those who attended the Triton club, but it is also worth bearing in mind that Al Santiago and Johnny Pacheco were adept at promoting and marketing their own music.

There were charanga musicians present in New York before the influx of charanga musicians following the Cuban revolution (such as pianist Gilberto Valdés and flautist Alberto Socarras). Visiting Cuban bands such as Orquesta Aragón and Fajardo y sus Estrellas also regularly performed at the Palladium and at the Cuban social clubs in the city, popularizing the charanga in the 1950s. Home-grown charanga bands were not well known in New York, however, until the advent of Charlie Palmieri's La Duboney and then Johnny Pacheco's charanga orquesta. The confusion between style of performance and musical style at this time in the late 1950s and early 1960s is therefore due in part to musicians referring to charanga style when they mean a performance *style* linked to the charanga lineup, and also in part due to a renaming of older musical styles for marketing purposes, as Cuban bandleader Eddy Zervigón asserts:

> EZ: No existe pachanga. La pachanga es de Davidson, que es como un merengue y después le pusieron pachanga por decir que es una cosa nueva, pero no era cierto. . . . aquí le pusieron pachanga a todo. En Cuba, la pachanga es un baile, una fiesta. . . . Aquí le decían pachanga a la música cubana. . . . Guaracha, le quitaron ese nombre de guaracha porque era un nombre antiguo y le pusieron pachanga para decir que era una cosa nueva. Lo mismo pasó con la salsa.

> [Pachanga does not exist. "The Pachanga" is by Davidson, which is like a merengue and after this they called everything pachanga to say it was something new. But that's not true. . . . here [in New York] they put the pachanga label on everything. In Cuba "pachanga" means "a dance or fiesta." Here they said all Cuban music was "pachanga." . . . Guaracha, they took away the name of guaracha because it was an old-fashioned term and replaced it with "pachanga" to say it was a new thing. The same happened with salsa.]

Zervigón also asserts that Pacheco did not invent the pachanga dance:

SM: Y Johnny Pacheco inventó un baile con pañuelo para la pachanga, ¿no?
EZ: La gente pone lo que quiere pero Pacheco no inventó ningún baile. La única pachanga que existe es la de Eduardo Davidson porque la creó. Es un merengue . . . pero esa fue su idea.

[SM: **And Johnny Pacheco invented a dance with a handkerchief to go with the pachanga, didn't he?**
EZ: People put whatever (label) they like on things but Pacheco did not invent any dance. The only pachanga that exists is the one by Eduardo Davidson because he created it. It's a merengue . . . but still it was his idea.][11]

For Zervigón, then, the pachanga was Davidson's composition "La Pachanga" only, and he asserts that the term was then used merely to relabel the older Cuban guaracha, defined as having a two-chord tonic to dominant montuno structure (V-I or I-V) taken at a mid- to fast tempo. Any style with a four-chord montuno he defined as being a son montuno rather than a guaracha. A running theme of adopting words for "enjoyment" [guarachear], and "fiestas" [rumbas, pachangas] to stand for musical styles therefore emerges when looking at the taxonomy of Cuban dance music genres in general. According to accounts such as the one by Flores, Pacheco's pachanga dance at the Triton did fuel the flames of the 1960s New York pachanga phenomenon regardless of however "new" the style of music and dance actually was:

> Johnny Pacheco had no doubts about being the originator of the pachanga craze, and that it all started in the Tritons Club. "I was the one that started the dance," he stated repeatedly, and went on to explain. "We call the music, the orchestra was called a charanga. And then I used to do the little hop with the hankie and people started watching me at the Tritons and that's where the dance started from, 'cause there was no dance. And that's what made it so popular, 'cause it was a very easy dance, and you hear the stomping of the people dancing, on the downbeat."[12]

Pacheco's dance in all certainty did develop in the South Bronx Latin scene, however derivative of Orquesta Aragón's dancer Rafael Bacallao it may have been, and it filtered through to other venues in Spanish Harlem and the Palladium in Manhattan, underlying the importance of live performance in the development of the Latin music scene in New York. Zervigón arrived in New York from Havana (via Miami) in 1962 and was not present in the early years of Charanga Duboney and Pacheco's charanga, so he may not have been aware of these local practices. There is no associated dance for pachanga in Cuba (as Zervigón states, "pachanga" meant a "dance" or "fiesta") and the idea of pachanga as a music/dance style is therefore very much a part of the grassroots Cuban dance music scene of the Bronx in the early 1960s.

The styles of subsequent pachangas recorded in the wake of Davidson's "La Pachanga" in both Cuba and the United States were not necessarily related musically to this composition either. Confusion has arisen due to the "invention" of a pachanga step (claimed by Pacheco and taught by Arthur Murray at the Roseland Ballroom)[13] and the music industry branding of all charanga styles as pachanga once Pacheco and others popularized the term in New York. When we met in Brooklyn in June 2016, Karen Joseph, flute player with Eddie Palmieri's Perfecta II, Charanga America, and Los Jovenes del Barrio, demonstrated the pachanga dance to me as a move from the center forward with knees bent, a small jump to the right followed by a shuffle back to the center. Joseph underlined the relationship between the style and Pacheco: "I associate Pacheco with pachanga and whenever it comes up there's always someone in the audience or someone somewhere in the club who starts to do this other little dance."[14]

The standard narrative of New York Latin music is one of a step change linear trajectory that favors individual male creators over messier, real world collective processes.[15] Malcomson critiques this standard form of historical narrative in the context of danzón:

> Markers characterizing genres are rarely initiated or brought together by one person/originator. . . . By emphasizing new generic names and originators, a "monumental" history of danzón is created which moves from originator to originator, from named genre to named genre, and neither transformations and diversities within genres, nor the collective nature of creative production are commemorated.[16]

Malcomson's points about the danzón's history can equally be applied to the stylistic changes in Latin music in the USA, with the usual narrative following the trajectory of rhumba in the 1930s and '40s to big band mambo in the mid-1950s to pachanga in the early 1960s. The story then usually leaps from the briefly popular Latin bugalú in the late 1960s to the popularity of salsa in the 1970s as an international genre. There is some truth in these time frames, but styles are never truly stable and the reality is, of course, far more complex.

CHARANGA AND PACHANGA: MUSICAL EXPLORATIONS

In this section I examine the rebranding of Cuban charanga for the New York Latin scene, first by analyzing Davidson's composition "La Pachanga" as recorded by Orquesta Sublime in Havana, and second by comparing it to "Bronx Pachanga" from Charlie Palmieri's Charanga Duboney. As will be demonstrated, industry labels do not necessarily correspond directly to musical elements of style. Before interrogating the pachanga, however, a brief explanation of charanga lineup and performance practice is needed, particularly as many Latin musicians interviewed described the pachanga style in terms of charanga *feel* rather than by specific stylistic markers. Charanga performance practice therefore informs the styles that originated in the lineup, such as danzón, mambo, chachachá, and pachanga as well as other Cuban popular styles adopted by the lineup, including son, son montuno, guajira, and bolero.

CHARANGA PERFORMANCE AESTHETICS

Cuban dance music as played by charanga orquestas has its own textural and timbral qualities that are not purely a result of the instrumentation—it has its own rhythmic patterns and performance codes. You do not even have to play a charanga instrument to have elements of the charanga feel in one's playing. Cienfuegos-born trumpet player Roberto Rodríguez, for example, played in Orquesta Broadway and is said to have had a charanga feel or sensibility in his choice of phrasing and stylistic vocabulary. Zervigón has often said that the charanga orquesta sound is simple but that it is incredibly difficult to get right. In New York some percussionists joining the early 1960s charanga orquestas were initially unfamiliar with the charanga style of performance and often played too busily. Manny Rivera, timbale player with New York's SonSublime, mentioned that timbales player Nicky Marrero, while not having the feel of a charanga timbale player, was an innovator in many other ways, particularly in terms of his soloing style in Típica Novel.[17] Eddy Zervigón has also talked about the different percussion playing styles for conjunto and charanga, emphasizing the more dynamic approach of charanga percussionists as opposed to the more "laid down" conjunto style. He cites Cuban conga player Carlos Rubio (Orquesta Broadway) as a dynamic conga player as he played with a strong black style (*estilo negro*) with correct tuning for the charanga orquesta's requirements.[18]

Instrumental roles play a part in the formulation of a charanga sound. For example, the piano and violin lines have to complement each other, with the strings dynamically above the piano. A pianist who dominates this balance destroys the charanga flavor. A jazz pianist who alters chords without listening to the largely diatonic violin guajeo patterns similarly destroys the charanga sound. Conga players need to ensure the conga and *tumba* drums are tuned correctly for charanga in order to be more dynamic; if they are tuned too high, there's a smaller range of dynamic.[19] Manny Rivera talks about percussionist Manny Oquendo (Orquesta Libre) as having a great sense of space and charanga sensibility, grooving with an off-beat timbal bell pattern rather than the more forceful mambo bell ride pattern; Rivera mentions space, subtlety, and dynamic variation as being essential to típico charanga performance while emphasizing that the feel is *macho* but not *machista* (forthright but not aggressive).[20] In addition to this there are typical breaks (*cierres* and *efectos*) from the danzón, chachachá, and mambo styles that permeate the transitions from composed to open montuno sections of an arrangement, where coro/*inspiración* and solos take center stage. Knowledge of the charanga repertoire (including the large number of danzón compositions) also informs the stylistic vocabulary chosen for soloing, inspiraciones, cierres (e.g., mambitos and *abanicos*), and *llamada* calls. In common with other lineups is the unifying concept of clave. Thus, a myriad of features linked to repertoire, arrangement, instrumentation, timbre, dynamic, and clave adherence define the charanga sound; the charanga style of performance is therefore more than the result of its violin- and flute-oriented instrumentation.

When asked to define the pachanga style, percussionist John Berdeguer did so in terms of dance step, commenting "pachanga was danced a certain way, the jumping. The mambo, they had the box step. The chachachá also." When pressed for specific musical definitions of the style, he stated it was characterized by a faster-paced *marcha* pattern on the congas and that the style was played with a charanga feel.[21] He added that the words of the lyrics probably defined a number as a pachanga and that it was pretty much the same as a chachachá. Similarly, Joe de Jesus of Charansalsa asserts that pachanga was a marketing label used to promote the charanga band using a dance craze to popularize it.[22] Even Orquesta Sublime's flute player Melquiades Fundora described the pachanga as being like a faster chachachá, despite the fact that his original rendition of Davidson's "Pachanga" was a Cubanized version of the Dominican merengue style, although, as demonstrated in the analysis below, there are elements of son-chá, *comparsa*, and merengue in this rendition.

Orquesta Sublime's La Pachanga

Señores que pachanga, Vamos pa' la pachanga
Que buena la pachanga, Me voy pa' la pachanga
Cubanos a la rumba—rumba, pachanga, que zumba!

[Ladies and gentlemen what a pachanga, Let's go to the pachanga
How good is the party, I'm off to party
Cubans to the rumba—rumba, pachanga, what a buzz!]

The composition "La Pachanga" by Eduardo Davidson for Orquesta Sublime, first recorded on August 5, 1959, for Panart Records in Havana,[23] is a clear invitation to a party, that is, to a rumba or a pachanga.[24] The cut common time signature, its emphasis on 1 and 3 and the use of the clarinet for the main theme all point to the Dominican merengue influence (although the clarinet also had a presence in early twentieth-century charangas).[25] The call and response between the vocals and flute/clarinet in the verse section, and later in the montuno section in the form of responsorial melodies to the coros, also point to similar structures in merengue. The merengue elements are particularly prominent in the groove where the timbale and conga patterns shown in example 5.2 relate closely to the basic merengue patterns outlined in example 5.1 with its güira, tambora drum, and dance band conga instrumentation:[26]

Example 5.1 Basic merengue patterns.

In merengue the tambora drum basic pattern includes open tones that emphasize beat 1 in the first measure and then beats 3+, 4 and 4+ in the second measure accompanied by the standard merengue dance band conga rhythm (see example 5.1). In Davidson's "La Pachanga" the congas start on beat 1+ and finish with a prominent open tone on beat 4 preceded by four sixteenth notes on beat 3 (see example 5.2), demonstrating a Cubanized version of the merengue pattern with its 1 and 3 emphasis (backbeat) and fourth open tone:

Example 5.2 Cubanized merengue variation in "La Pachanga."

"La Pachanga" has an affinity to the Cuban street conga or comparsa tradition with its communal function of getting people to join in the dancing and to party. When performing as an invited guest with Orquesta Sublime in El Convento de Belen in Habana Vieja in 2011, the band called for a conga line and all the old-age pensioners joined in a line to the coro of "el tren" [the train] where the cut common tempo and *güiro machete* rhythm accompanied the line of lively older dancers.[27] The güiro on the "La Pachanga" recording is the Cuban wooden güiro, not the Dominican metal güira, and the pattern played on it is a fast machete rhythm often used in cut common time in charanga performance, as in the band's 2011 performance fifty-two years later. Although not present in this recording of "La Pachanga," the merengue conga pattern is sometimes further embellished in performance to create the *a caballo* rhythm (see example 5.3), which salsa musician Rebecca Mauleon ascribes to the pachanga style.[28] Certainly the slap strokes on beats 1 and 3 and the open tone on beat 4 align with the dance band conga pattern of merengue, which is itself derived from the tambora figure.

Example 5.3 The *a caballo* [on horseback] conga pattern commonly ascribed to the pachanga style.

The bass on the Sublime recording mostly follows the strong beats on 1 and 3 as in the traditional merengue style, but it also performs a son-cha pattern in the B coro/inspiración section of the piece, supporting the rhythm of the vocal line on the words "cuan-do" and "sien-to" on beats 1 and 2+ respectively. Here there are touches of the chachachá/guaracha bassline pattern (see example 5.4).

Example 5.4 Son guaracha/son-chá-inflected bass line at B (in verse 2).

Melodically, the introduction is built from the descending couplets g^3 to $f\sharp^3$, and $f\sharp^3$ to e^3 in the top flute line played an octave above the written stave (see example 5.6), which is very characteristic melodic movement in charanga performance, particularly in the violin parts, as shown in example 5.5.

Example 5.5 Typical charanga violin figure for I–V–V–I montunos.

Example 5.6 "La Pachanga" introduction: call and response with characteristic charanga melodic movement (suspension).

This phrase encloses the piece, suggesting a 3–2 clave direction through direct reference to the 3-side clave rhythm in odd-numbered measures; but once the vocal line enters in measures 8 and 9, the vocal line is less characterized by this rhythm. Instead a rise-and-fall contour outlines the chord notes in a very on-beat quarter-note fashion, except for the final coro which implies a 2–3 clave direction through the tie into the second measure. The D^9-D^9-G^6-G^6 chord progression follows the V-I guaracha progression Eddy Zervigón mentioned earlier (in elongated form as V-V-I-I) and the violins perform charanga guajeos within the montuno sections of the piece, doubled by the piano. These patterns reference the main merengue rhythm, as shown in example 5.7.

The vocal coro "*Pachanga eh, Pachanga eh*" follows a 2–3 clave direction (see example 5.8), although the phrase starts with a *tresillo* as in the introduction and coda, contributing to clave ambiguity. Thus, due to the tresillo 3-side

Example 5.7 Piano and violin patterns supporting the merengue rhythm of the congas.

forming the first part of the coro 2 melody and the intro/outro, the piece is ambiguous in terms of clave as touches of clave direction are indicated only by ties into the 3-side in the coro and montuno/guajeo patterns and by way of anacrusis on the 3-side leading back to the 2-side.

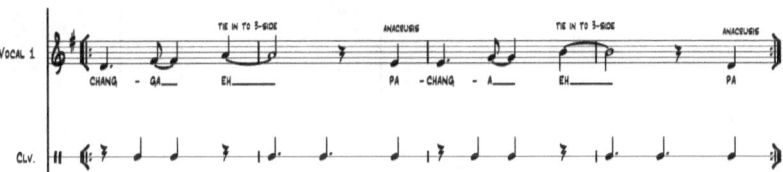

Example 5.8 Coro 2 with tresillo nevertheless outlining 2–3 clave through the tie into the second measure and the beat 4 anacrusis.

The introduction outlines 3–2 clave for nine measures before becoming 2–3 clave for the rest of the piece at A (verse 1) until the partial reiteration of the introduction in the coda. Cuban son compositions often open in 3–2 and change to 2–3 clave direction in the montuno sections, mostly by way of an odd number of bars. Here the vocals enter on an anacrusis with the lyric "Señores que pa," and in this respect "La Pachanga" resembles a Cuban guaracha. However, the clave direction is ambiguous in that the clarinet responses in measures 2, 4, and 6 are off-beat, which usually indicates a 3-side of the clave. The structure of the piece is summarized in Table 5.1 below to demonstrate this clave ambiguity and also to demonstrate the mix of Cuban and Dominican stylistic elements:

	INTRODUCTION	A Verse 1 "Señores que pachanga"	B Verse 2	C Bridge	D Coro and coro melody	CODA
Measures (m., mm.)	1-9	10-25	26-41	42-49		
Number of measures	9	16	16	8	16	4
Subdivision	6 call and clarinet response / 2 break / 1 anacrusis	8 mm. verse / 8 mm. melody on clarinet	8 (2mm. vocal x2mm. clarinet) x2 / 8 (2mm. vocal x2mm. flute) x2	4 4mm. vocal / 4 3mm. vocal + break + 1m anacrusis	8 coro / 8 flute and clarinet	2 as intro / 2 2mm. break
Tonal plan	G major; ii - V^9 - I^6	G major (D^9 - D^9 - G^6 - G^9) V - V - I - I	D^9 - D^9 - G^6 - G^6	D^9 - D^9 - G^6 - G^6	D^9 - D^9 - G^6 - G^6	G major; ii - V^9 - I^6
Cuban stylistic indicators	3-2 clave feel. Call and response (2,2) x 1½. Break (cierre) leading to 3-side of clave vocal anacrusis. Characteristic charanga melodic movement in flute and clarinet lines.	Güiro machete pattern. Lyrics refer to Cuban culture. Son/guaracha chord progression. 2-3 clave although mostly clave neutral	Güiro machete pattern. Lyrics refer to Cuban culture. Cuban guaracha/son bass line	Rubato style vocal + charanga break. Lyric references to Cubans. Cuban son, pachanga, and rumba	Coro use similar to Cuban comparsa (street party). Coro outlines 2-3 clave.	3-2 opening + typical charanga cierre
Dominican merengue indicators	Clarinet lead instrument	Conga and timbale merengue patterns. Merengue bass line on beats 1 and 3. Piano and violins emphasize merengue conga and timbale rhythm.	Conga and timbale merengue patterns. Fixed call and response between ensemble/vocal and clarinet/flute.	Merengue conga pattern can also be seen as an 'a caballo' figure. Use of Cuban slang "ique zumba!"	Conga and timbale merengue patterns. Variation on merengue conga line similar to fast sixteenth-note jaleo lines for clarinet/saxes in merengue.	Clarinet as lead melody instrument
Notes	Tempo is ♩=116 Cut common	Structure = Sections A-B-C (3X BEFORE D)				

Table 5.1 Structure of Orquesta Sublime's "La Pachanga"

This fusion of Cuban son/guaracha, chachachá, and merengue elements has led here to more clave ambiguity in the composition. These features perform the same function in terms of charanga performance conventions, but they also support the main merengue rhythm rather than outline clear clave direction for the most part. Interestingly, this piece is through-composed and there are no improvisations—even the clarinet and flute responses are fixed and recur three times. Perhaps this lack of clave consistency mitigates against the insertion of a more open montuno section, where soloing in clave might prove more difficult. It would seem that charanga performance conventions and certain rhythmic aspects of the merengue are combined and varied in Orquesta Sublime's "Pachanga" with the deliberate use of the pachanga term in the lyrics. In other pachangas the use of the conga *a caballo* pattern may also characterize the pachanga with its similarity to the main merengue pattern of the congas and tambora. The tempo (fast cut common) and the guaracha tonic and dominant two-chord structure may also be important. The merengue elements of the original Davidson composition may not be as integral, however, to the later New York pachanga. To investigate further, I next analyze "Bronx Pachanga" by Charlie Palmieri's La Duboney and compare it to Davidson's "La Pachanga," shedding more light on what Flores terms the "musical trappings" of pachanga in 1960s New York.

Charanga Duboney's Bronx Pachanga

Han sacado un nuevo baile, en el Bronx, en la USA
Y lo toca Palmieri, con su orquesta Duboney
En El Caravana se baila pachanga con Doña Juana

[There's a new dance out in the Bronx, in the USA
The one Palmieri plays with his Orquesta Duboney
In the Caravana (club) they're dancing pachanga with Doña Juana][29]

The Caravana club in the Bronx was, in many ways, as influential as the Triton, in that it was where Alegre Records formed and where the Alegre All Stars descarga projects took place under the direction of promoter Al Santiago, a producer who was instrumental to Latin music's development in the late 1950s and early 1960s. Charlie Palmieri also played at the Triton, but this "Bronx Pachanga" references the Duboney charanga orquesta at the Caravana as being at the forefront of the new pachanga dance craze, as the words to "Bronx Pachanga" by Charanga la Duboney attest (see examples 5.9 and 5.10).

Example 5.9 Coro 1 in 2–3 clave.

Example 5.10 Coro 2 in 2–3 clave.

The coros fit the rhythm of the violin and piano guajeo patterns in 2–3 clave with a more on-beat 2-side and ties into the 3-side, with an accent on the *bombo* 2+ beat on the 3-side of the clave on the vocal syllable "se" (see example 5.11)

Example 5.11 Violin and piano guajeo in 2–3 clave with mambo bass line.

The chord progression is I-V7 in G major (G-D7), a typical charanga progression which Zervigón defined as emblematic of the Cuban guaracha. The mambo bass line outlines the 2-3 clave and the I-V progression, anticipating the chord change on beat 4 as is usual in many Cuban popular dance styles.

The percussion patterns are chachachá ones, with the chachachá rhythm of the güiro used rather than the machete pattern despite the fast tempo. A timbale cha bell is played throughout on the quarter notes, and a typical 2-3 conga marcha pattern with a slap on beat 2, and open tones (often eighth-note beats) on the fourth beat of each measure forms part of the clave-organized percussive texture (see example 5.12).

Example 5.12 Chachachá-style percussion in "Bronx Pachanga."

The virtuoso conga player Patato Valdés performs fills, flourishes, and percussion breaks under the flute solo, which would not necessarily happen in the Cuban charangas, where the role of spontaneous fills and breaks is usually taken up by the timbales. Carlos "Patato" Valdés was a Cuban percussionist who played in Conjunto Casino and Conjunto Kubavana before moving from Havana to the USA in 1954.[30] Perhaps the flavor of Patato's playing was more in the conjunto vein, where more spontaneous fills from the congas would be the norm, lending a busier texture to the percussion section. He also played with Dizzy Gillespie, Machito, and Tito Puente, among others in the USA, and is therefore linked, through jazz influence, to his big band work in Havana and New York. The musical texture is full, but the style is Cuban with no elements of Dominican merengue present. The 2-3 clave organization is adhered to throughout and all ensemble and percussion breaks outline clave (which is superimposed in the score extract in example 5.13).

The flute solo by Rod Lewis (Luís) Sánchez is stylistic, but there is no room for the solo to develop; as Mark Weinstein has pointed out,[31] the role of the flute changed with this busier texture into one designed for punctuating the rhythm at the top end of the registral spectrum. The only element linking this pachanga to Davidson's is the lyric and the tempo (but not the meter). There is a breathless excitement to the piece, taken at ♩ = 208, not dissimilar to the

Example 5.13 Tutti break in 2–3 clave with final hit on the bombo (2+) on the three-side.

tempo of "La Pachanga" (although the cut common meter of Davidson's piece has fewer eighth-note phrases and therefore feels slower due to the decrease in rhythmic density). This piece, in contrast, is relentless in its fast repetition of the main riff (see example 5.11) in a fast 4/4 meter. Other pachangas on Charlie Palmieri's *Pachanga at the Caravan Club* similarly use chachachá percussion patterns, busy violin guajeos, and V-I or I-V chord progressions, supporting Zervigón's assertion that the pachanga was a relabeling of the Cuban guaracha. Whatever the claims for origins of the New York pachanga, the dance took off in the Bronx and was later taught by Arthur Murray in his chain of dance academies, and the charanga orquesta was certainly popularized through this mainstream marketing of charanga as pachanga.

SOME CONCLUSIONS

The pachanga was, as Zervigón and others state, a rebranding of the Cuban guaracha as performed by charanga orquestas. It cannot be easily defined as a music and dance style because it was an amalgam of styles from the outset and today it is played with or without the merengue elements of Davidson's composition or the *a caballo* conga pattern associated with the merengue feel. The chord sequence is that of the guaracha, but otherwise the pachanga is defined by the use of the term in the lyrics and by charanga performance conventions more generally, particularly those of the chachachá, mambo, and son/guaracha styles. The charanga, which became synonymous with the pachanga term in New York at this time, was popularized by the dance that evolved at the Tritons and Caravana clubs and, musically, was a charanga performance practice favoring faster tempos, improvisation, and interaction with a dancing audience. The pachanga craze is therefore an example of how a socially grounded performance practice spread from the Bronx to other areas of the city including the Palladium, dance academies, and other city venues and internationally through marketing and distribution. Marketing publicity can override the intricacies of more local music and dance practices and create confusion, affecting subsequent interpretations by musicians themselves as they seek to emulate those popular recordings; in this way, certain stylistic characteristics begin to emerge and become "fact" through the various processes of imitation and adaptation. Thus, for many Puerto Rican New Yorkers, like my Brooklyn neighbor Ruben, for whom Cuban culture forms part of their New York heritage, charanga *is* pachanga.

- 6 -

CHARANGA *EMBALAO*

Charlie Palmieri and Johnny Pacheco

The charangas of Johnny Pacheco and Charlie Palmieri, formed respectively in 1959 and 1960, paved the way for new US-based charanga groups in New York after the fresh influx of Cuban players following the Cuban Revolution. The success of Cuban-led bands such as Orquesta Broadway owed much to the previous popularity of both La Duboney and Johnny Pacheco y su Charanga. Charlie Palmieri set up La Duboney in 1959, having met Pacheco at the Monte Carlo Club in October 1958.[1] Pacheco played flute in La Duboney before setting up his own charanga band in 1960. Various accounts of this parting of the ways highlight differences between the performance aesthetics of the two groups. The promoter and Alegre Records producer Al Santiago asserted that musical differences were at the heart of the split; Charlie Palmieri preferred more harmonic complexity and a medium tempo whereas Johnny Pacheco chose harmonic simplicity and a faster tempo, stating "Johnny was into going *embalao* at a very fast tempo."[2] The term *embalao* is short for *embelado* and is Latin American Spanish slang for "in a hurry," "racing," "rapid," or "accelerated." In informal Cuban and Latin American Spanish a "d" is often omitted, and this "street" term certainly fits the feel of many of the early recordings by Pacheco. However, it also suits some of the repertoire of La Charanga Duboney (indeed, Palmieri and Pacheco's work are intertwined) and the song "Bronx Pachanga" by La Duboney could also be described as embalao with its ♩ = 208 tempo. This explanation by Santiago does hold true for some repertoire, but the differences between the two groups are not always as clearly pronounced in terms of montuno type or tempo, at least in the early years. The Alegre All Stars, led by Charlie Palmieri (co-led initially by both musicians) and formed with members of both groups, certainly combined the jamming descarga ethos and energy of both bands. Charlie Palmieri's accompaniments, montuno playing and, virtuosic solos were, however, more intricate than Pacheco's soloing; listen, for example, to his accompaniment to the bolero "Estuve Pensando" at 2:02

on the *Viva Palmieri* album from 1962, where he extemporizes exquisitely around the *West Side Story* song "One Hand One Heart."[3] In many ways the differences between the two groups come down to differences in the bandleader's instrumental work, with Charlie Palmieri's piano able to range further harmonically than Pacheco's flute; Palmieri also drew on a wider range of style and repertoire. The embalao concept is nevertheless relevant to this emerging New York charanga aesthetic. I next analyze two recordings by La Duboney, "Mack is Back" and "Bronx Pachanga," with a focus on the flute improvisations by Johnny Pacheco and Rod Lewis Sánchez (sometimes spelled Rodger Luís Sánchez) to further investigate sabor in the context of Nuyorican and Dominican interpretations of Cuban charanga. Before this analysis, some examination of both groups in the context of típico performance in New York is useful.

CHARLIE PALMIERI AND HIS CHARANGA LA DUBONEY

Charlie Palmieri's contribution as a pianist, bandleader, and improviser has been immense—to document his work more comprehensively would require a book in itself. In terms of Palmieri's ensemble and arranging skills, he was adept at combining several Cuban musical styles (danzón, mambo, chachachá, pachanga, son montuno) with the American Songbook and jazz traditions. His improvisations are virtuosic, not only in the often-cited harmonic sense but also in terms of melodic invention and clave-infused rhythmic dexterity, and they have yet to be analyzed in depth in academic literature or indeed elsewhere. Often overshadowed by his younger brother Eddie, Charlie prepared the way for the success of subsequent charanga orquestas in New York with his Charanga La Duboney. The first piece analyzed here, "Mack the Knife" (a reworking of the Brecht/Weill song), is from the album *Let's Dance the Charanga* by Charlie Palmieri and His Charanga La Duboney, recorded and released in 1959 on the United Artists label.[4] Personnel on the recording given in Andres Campo Uribe's discography include Dominican Johnny Pacheco on flute; Nuyorican Charlie Palmieri on piano; Puerto Rican singer Vitín Aviles and Cuban vocalist Leonel Bravet; Cuban violinists José Andreu, Rafael Muñoz, Daniel González, and Rafael Aroz; Cuban bassist Evaristo Baró; Cuban percussionist Julian Cabrera on guiro; Nuyorican José Rodríguez on timbales; and Puerto Rican John Palomo on congas. According to music historian David Pérez, Cuban singer Leonel Bravet was known as the Nat King Cole of Cuba and first recorded in Chicago with Orquesta Nuevo Ritmo. The Cuban violinists had performed with Antonio Arcaño in

Cuba in 1958 and so were directly related to the Cuban charanga and the danzón-mambo tradition. Similarly, Julian Cabrera played with Orquesta América in 1947 in Mexico and also with Orquesta Jorrín in Havana before leaving Cuba for the USA. Another singer on the recording missing from the Uribe discography is Puerto Rican Pellín Rodríguez, who later became famous in Puerto Rico's El Gran Combo.[5] The separation of Cuban- and New York–based charanga performance styles is therefore not so clear-cut, as demonstrated here by the strong presence of Cuban musicians from the charanga tradition (particularly the Cuban nuevo ritmo mambo violinists from Arcaño y sus Maravillas and the 1950s chachachá performers from Orquesta América). The second piece analyzed, "Bronx Pachanga," is from the album *Pachanga at the Caravana Club* by Charlie Palmieri and His Charanga La Duboney recorded on the Alegre label in 1961 (released 1962), which also features José Silva on violin, David Soyer on cello,[6] Roy Colindres replacing bassist Evaristo Baró,[7] and percussionists Julian Cabrera, Joe Rodríguez, Carlos "Patato" Valdés, and Tommy López. New vocalists added from the Alegre label included Antar Daly, Felo Brito, and Willie Torres, with coros sung by Rudy Calzado and Victor Velazco.

JOHNNY PACHECO Y SU CHARANGA

The personnel on Johnny Pacheco's debut Alegre recording of 1961 includes Pacheco on flute; Carlos Piantini, José "Chombo" Silva, and Daniel González on violins; Hector Pellot on piano; Julian Cabrera, John Palomo, and Manny Oquendo on percussion; Victor David Pérez on bass; Elliot Romero as lead vocalist; and Pedro Manuel Calzado on coro vocals. Unsurprisingly, there is some overlap of musicians in each charanga and with the Alegre All Stars; "Chombo" Silva, for example, performs in Pacheco's group on violin and on saxophone in the Alegre All Stars. Percussionist Julian Cabrera recorded with all three groups and Cuban Daniel González is on violin in both Pacheco's and Palmieri's charanga groups. Many of these musicians later appear in Ray Barretto's Charanga Moderna and Mongo Santamaría's La Sabrosa charanga, and some make an appearance in Eddie Palmieri's La Perfecta (for example, Manny Oquendo on percussion and Barry Rogers on trombone).

THE ALEGRE ALL STARS

Formed in 1961, the Alegre All Stars was a band produced by Al Santiago and led by Charlie Palmieri on piano. It was initially also co-led by Pacheco on flute until Santiago chose Charlie Palmieri over Pacheco to be the sole musical director of the group. Following this decision by Santiago, Pacheco left the Alegre label to set up his own rival Fania label with its own Fania All Stars, which Flores notes led to the "bifurcation of the musical history" of the genre. Certainly, without the Alegre projects the history of Latin music would have had a different mainstream narrative. Featuring bandleaders, singers, and instrumentalists signed to the Alegre label, the Alegre All Stars included Silva on tenor sax, Barry Rogers on trombone, Marcelino Valdés on congas, Julian Cabrera on güiro, Bobby Rodríguez on bass, Kako (aka Francisco Angel Bastar) on timbales, and Dioris Valladares, Rudy Calzado, and Puerto Rican Yayo el Indio (real name Gabriel Eladio Peguero Vega) on vocals.[8] Regular descarga (jam) sessions were held at the Tritons social club in the Bronx on Tuesday nights and the *descarga* album was recorded in 1961. Inspired by the Cuban Jam Sessions on the Cuban Panart record label from the 1950s, these sessions had a Bronx setting and a wider mix of ethnicity among the musicians (as Flores notes, that diversity did not extend to African American or female musicians). Flores remarks that the charangas of Charlie Palmieri and Johnny Pacheco were "the central bands of the charanga phase in Latin music history."[9] However, as outlined earlier, the popularity of the charanga among the grassroots of the Latin community did not disappear once the mainstream popularity of the pachanga was over.

All three groups were inspired by, on the one hand, Cuban charanga groups, many of which had performed in the Cuban social clubs, the Catskills resorts, and the Palladium (such as Orquesta Aragón and Fajardo y sus Estrellas), and on the other hand by the rhumba and mambo bands of Machito, Noro Morales, Tito Rodríguez, and Tito Puente. Before creating La Duboney, Charlie Palmieri started a conjunto in which Pacheco initially played timbales; both musicians shared a love for both traditional Cuban son and charanga.

EMBALAO EN TÍPICO—PACHECO'S PERFORMANCE AESTHETIC

The excitement of the Bronx Tritons and Caravana club scene in the early 1960s is conveyed on both Palmieri's and Pacheco's early recordings, reflecting the energy of the post-mambo era. Mark Weinstein makes the point that the flute's role in Cuban dance music, whether in the charanga, conjunto, or the modified trombone-led conjunto ensemble or *trombanga* of which he was a part (La Perfecta), was different in New York, particularly due to Pacheco's influence:

> George Castro [flute player with Eddie Palmieri's La Perfecta] played like Johnny Pacheco. Johnny Pacheco used the flute—he played little melodies but that wasn't the point. The flute was supposed to rhythmically punctuate from the top. These guys were swing players. You've got to understand that George's job was to keep the top filled while the bottom of the band was going crazy. George didn't have any room to be creative. George had to just find a way to fill up that top echelon of the acoustic sound, and so, again, forgive me, he was a very primitive flute player, as was Pacheco. These guys couldn't come close to a guy named Richard Egües. Or Fajardo. They were just a completely different league. These guys were not really flute players. These guys were whistle players. It was perfect for the energy of the New York sound.... The job of the flute was to keep that energy going against that tremendous volume of sound.[10]

As Weinstein remarks, this instrumental function was not the same in Cuba, where more space for flute soloists was provided through diversity of style, tempo, and texture. In New York the emphasis was on the montuno, the groove, and the improvisations over repeated coros.[11] Pacheco was not, however, "just a whistle player," as I will demonstrate later, although the energy, timbre, and speed of his playing does have this sonic effect to some extent. Pacheco's understanding of Cuban percussion through clave sensibility is demonstrated by his melodic-rhythmic use of typical *cierres* (breaks) and use of percussion patterns such as the *cinquillo* (five-beat danzón pattern) in his flute lines.

In general, the tempos of many pachanga numbers from the early Pacheco and Charlie Palmieri charanga recordings of the late 1950s and early '60s were taken faster than those in Cuba, forcing players, as Weinstein asserts, to punctuate the top part of the timbral register with continuous melodic-rhythmic embellishments. Al Santiago noted that Pacheco had a preference for "going embalao [racing],"[12] and I shall demonstrate shortly how Pacheco's fast *inspiraciones* (short improvisations in response to sung coros) reveal this high-energy percussive style that, while melodic, has a strong rhythmic sensibility due to his knowledge and skills as a percussionist.

Pacheco has often been described as an imitator rather than an innovator, which is a little unfair. This critique is, in part, I think due to Pacheco's less popular promotional activities, particularly following his rebranding of Cuban dance music as salsa in the latter part of the 1960s. John Storm Roberts, for example, seems to associate a New York City sound solely with brass and characterizes charanga as more tropical and Caribbean, describing Pacheco as an enthusiastic "revivalist":

> His music showed little or none of the big city drive of most New York bands, but reflected the Caribbean joy of its Cuban origins very closely—some said too closely, especially in the early days. Pacheco, in fact, was a little like the young jazz revivalists of the 1940s, whose relationship to their models was, according to your point of view, imitation or preservation. But Pacheco's band always conveyed the music's original verve, and as much as on his playing or creative innovation, his long-term success has rested on personal charisma and an instantly communicated enthusiasm for Latin music.[13]

Pacheco has also been criticized by Juan Flores as a "traditionalist."[14] Nevertheless, his music illustrates a particular New York performance aesthetic rooted in the rich musical culture of the Bronx, an aesthetic related to, but distinct from, earlier Cuban role models. Additionally, Roberts's assertion that Pacheco did not have "the big city drive" needs to be contested or at least given more nuance as he provides no supporting musical analyses to support his claim. Dominican-born and New York–raised, Pacheco could be described as conveying "Caribbean joyfulness" (albeit from a displaced Caribbean), but his music, whether from the early part of his career or later, cannot be said to be identical to the Havana-based bands he admired.[15] In terms of motivation, Roberts's citation above makes clear Pacheco's enthusiasm for Cuban music and his ability to convey its vitality. But what exactly does Roberts mean by "big city drive" or "Caribbean joy"? And how do these ideas manifest themselves musically? The answers lie partially in Pacheco's musical background in the Bronx, in the history of Cuban dance music in New York and its complex relationship to Havana, and also in the clave-driven performance aesthetic of Latin dance music. The New York sabor in típico charanga performance can, I argue, be defined in musical terms. By analyzing Pacheco's improvisations we can question claims by Roberts and others that Pacheco was simply an imitator. He certainly had strong Caribbean roots, but was also firmly embedded in the artistic life of the Bronx Latin music scene of the early 1960s.

Pacheco's father was a famous bandleader of Orquesta Santa Cecilia in the Dominican Republic before the family had to move to New York to escape the Trujillo dictatorship in 1946, when Johnny was eleven years old. Although often described as a "natural" musician,[16] Pacheco was taught music by his father (who played clarinet, violin, flute, and saxophone), and in his youth he focused mainly on percussion (congas, bongos, timbales, maracas, and güiro), studying piano for compositional purposes. He played percussion in recording studio sessions, in demand because of his ability to read charts.[17] In the early part of his career Pacheco recorded as a flute player and percussionist with Charlie Palmieri's Charanga La Duboney, his own group Pacheco y su Charanga, and then later with his own conjuntos. He also performed with Tito Puente's Palladium mambo band and earlier with New York's first charanga band (formed in 1951) led by Cuban bandleader Gilberto Valdés.[18] His Fania catalogue of recordings from the mid-1960s onward is extensive, so his musical success cannot be dismissed merely as a result of personal charisma and enthusiasm for Cuban music, at least not without some detailed scrutiny of his recorded output.

The generation of mainly Puerto Rican musicians who formed their own "smaller" conjuntos and charangas in the 1960s played clubs in the Bronx and Spanish Harlem, and at Catholic church dances in Brooklyn. Musicians such as Johnny Pacheco, Ray Barretto, Larry Harlow, Eddie Palmieri, and Charlie Palmieri emerged from this scene, and some of these musicians became mainstays of Pacheco's Fania record label in the 1970s. The faster tempos and the exuberance alluded to by Storm Roberts correlate with accounts of the Tritons and Caravana club performances in the Bronx at this time, and with the concurrent recordings put out by both Johnny Pacheco and Charlie Palmieri on Alegre. The faster, pushed tempos and the breathless energy of these performances could, therefore, be said to reflect a "big city drive," if one discounts the singular association of a swing-styled brass section as representing a New York City sound.

Johnny Pacheco has been at the forefront of a collective movement by Cuban, Puerto Rican, Jewish, and other Latin American musicians from the Bronx and other areas of New York (including Spanish Harlem and Brooklyn) in developing Latin music in New York and internationally. The fact that Pacheco promoted many forms of Cuban dance music first as pachanga and then as salsa in the mid- to late 1960s is still controversial (hence the many accusations of cultural appropriation), and music industry issues continue to obscure Pacheco's work as a performer and bandleader within this scene. Rather than examine his work as a record producer and entrepreneur (which has been more extensively documented), later in this chapter I explore Pacheco's earlier work as a charanga flute improviser to demonstrate, that, *pace* Roberts, Pacheco does indeed embody the energy and drive of New York

City, and to provide musical evidence to show how he has made changes to Cuban performance aesthetics in terms of the flute's soloing function. Mark Weinstein has pointed out that many New York flute players imitated Johnny Pacheco's style, including George Castro in La Perfecta and Rod Lewis Sánchez in La Duboney.[19]

By focusing on two examples by Charlie Palmieri's Charanga La Duboney featuring flute solos from both Johnny Pacheco and Rod Lewis Sánchez, I demonstrate below how típico performance in New York was not purely imitative and that new, often smaller innovations in performance style were brought in—changes that defined a New York sabor (or at least one variety of New York sabor) as distinct from the virtuosic Cuban role models of the 1950s.

STYLISTIC TRANSFORMATIONS: MACK IS BACK DOING THE *CHACHACHÁ*

The adaptation of Kurt Weill's "Mack the Knife" to a chachachá arrangement/composition (with mambo influence) by Charlie Palmieri and his Charanga La Duboney provides the backdrop to Pacheco's three flute *inspiraciones* outlined in the musical examples below. Latin versions of popular tunes from the musicals or films are part of the charanga tradition, and pianist Charlie Palmieri, who regularly performed American and Latin repertoire in a variety of bands, drew on both. Here we have German cabaret mixing with Cuban chachachá, son, and mambo, with the menace of the original somewhat diluted. A lighthearted dance version recorded by La Duboney in 1959, it features Johnny Pacheco on the five-key charanga flute. Before analyzing his three-part solo, it is important to analyze the arrangement to see how his soloing functions within these textures, as Pacheco draws on the melodic-rhythmic ingredients of the composition as well as adhering to clave direction throughout.

In example 6.1 the new coro section (not composed by Weill) features chachachá percussion patterns, a mambo string guajeo-based section outlining 2–3 clave, a 2–3 piano montuno pattern replicating this descending "d-c-b" "Mack the Knife" motif or m1 (later utilized in Pacheco's flute solo), and a typical Arcaño mambo-styled bass line derived from the danzón-mambo, emphasizing beats 2+ and 4. The coro outlines clave by being on-beat on the 2-side and off-beat on the 3-side, as shown in example 6.2, where the *bombo* beat (on the 2+ beat on the 3-side of the clave) aligns with the lyric "Do" and where the coro lyric "Mack" marks the downbeat on the 2-side of the clave.

Example 6.1 Transcribed score for the coro section in Charanga La Duboney's "Mack the Knife."

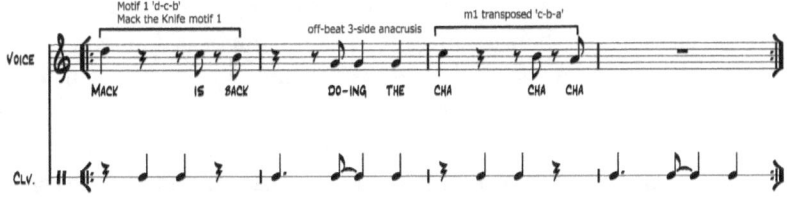

Example 6.2 Coro of "Mack the Knife" in 2–3 clave alignment.

The piano plays son montunos throughout except under the flute inspiraciones, where the off-beats are emphasized in a chachachá pattern. The usual pattern for the right hand has on-beat quarter notes on beats 1 and 3 (see example 6.3), but Charlie Palmieri replicates the left-hand off-beat pattern in both hands on this recording (see example 6.4), perhaps to give the texture even more of a syncopated feel. It is not a convention usually followed by Cuban pianists.

Example 6.3 Conventional piano chachachá pattern with on-beat right hand.

Example 6.4 Charlie Palmieri's "Mack the Knife" off-beat chachachá pattern: off-beats in both hands.

The chachachá has often been described as less syncopated and frantic than the mambo style and the timbale low drum does emphasize beat 2 rather than 2+ in this piece. However, the stylistic elements of son, chachachá, and mambo are integrated here, revealing not only the nonlinear relationship of these styles brought together on a pachanga album, but the hybrid nature of musical style and Palmieri's mastery of them all. Perhaps the recording could also be said to have a particular New York aesthetic in that it brings several Cuban styles together within a Broadway show tune by a German Jewish composer exiled in New York, and is performed by a New York–based band formed of Cubans, Dominicans, and Puerto Ricans. Elements from the Cuban son style include the piano montuno and the overall adherence to clave direction in the arrangement (with verses in 3–2 clave and breaks of uneven measure numbers to enter the open montuno section in 2–3 clave direction). The violin guajeo pattern (see example 6.1) has the same contour as the main guajeo from the original "Mambo" composition created in the late 1930s by charanga Arcaño y sus Maravillas, a contour motif later adapted by big band arrangers such as René Hernández and Pérez Prado in the 1940s. This mambo figure also complements the direct reference to big band mambo as popularized by Pérez Prado in the piano accompaniment to the verses (see example 6.5). The original "Mack the Knife" lyrics are changed into new Spanish lyrics and the well-known melody is transformed into a mambo-styled 3–2 son.

Example 6.5 Pérez Prado's mambo style in Charlie Palmieri's piano accompaniment.

Here I analyze the three improvised flute inspiraciones by Pacheco, made in response to the coros, followed by an analysis of his clave feel and creative process.

PACHECO IN *TÍPICO*

The first solo inspiración (see example 6.6) is típico in that Pacheco uses a tessitura of one octave from fourth-register "d" to third-register "d," taking the "Mack Is Back" melody notes "d-c-b" to define the contour of his phrases and using the dominant note g^3 (in C major) as an axis note around which típico ornamentation of mordents and turns are based. The first two phrases are in call-and-response form followed by a figure based around the turn on the dominant note repeated three times, finishing in a characteristic danzón percussion break (a final "*otra*" or "last time" measure).

All these elements are typical of the Cuban flute style of improvisation (therefore típico) and are executed with clave feel, as Pacheco aligns his phrases with the tendency for on-beat 2-side of the clave figures and more off-beat 3-side phrases. The coro melody is embellished through rhythmic transformation and uses the first motif "Mack Is Back" theme (m1) and its

Mack The Knife
Flute Solo by Johnny Pacheco
from Palmieri, Charlie and His Charanga "La Duboney"—*Mack The Knife*— *Let's Dance The Charanga*, United Artists UAL 3082, 1959.

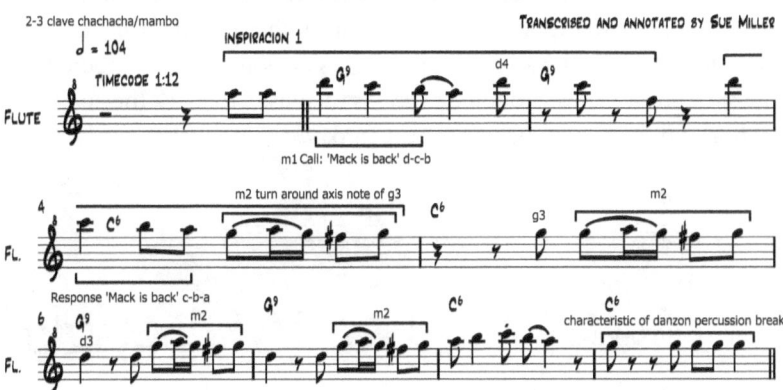

Example 6.6 Pacheco's flute inspiración 1 on "Mack the Knife" (clave superimposed).

transposition down a tone to "c-b-a" in measures 4 and 8. The inspiración follows the contour of the coro in call-and-response variation, leading to the dominant-note danzón break that announces the next coro entry.

Inspiración 2 (see example 6.7) similarly draws on the melodic ingredients of the coro with an extended tessitura of d^4 to g^2 and plentiful use of anacrusis on the 3-side of the clave demonstrating clave awareness. This time motif 3 is repeated, finishing with motif 1 repeated and extended. These repeated motifs grouped in "3 ♩s within a frame of 4" in measures 21–23 (motif 3 x3) create rhythmic tension; these phrases play with the clave in that phrases stay off the beat until the resolution which here occurs on beat four of measure 23 and then via motif 1 on beat 1 of the next coro in bar 26.

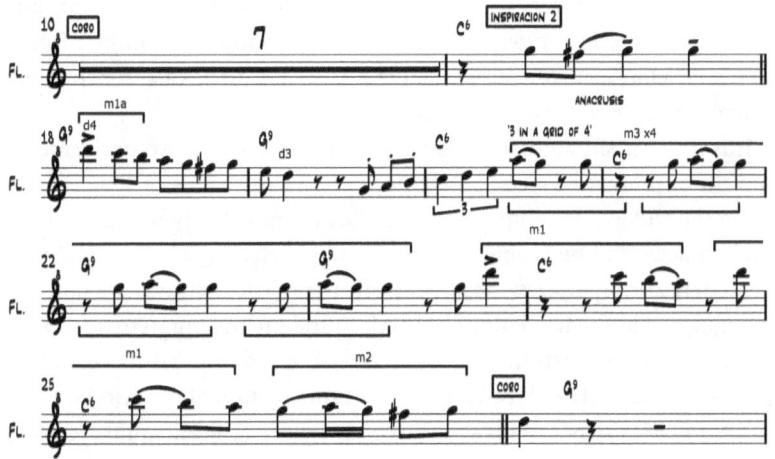

Example 6.7 Pacheco's flute inspiración 2 on "Mack the Knife": playing with clave.

The third inspiración (see example 6.8) is rhythmically developed further with a fourth melodic idea (m. 4) played slowly and then in double time. Motif 1 is varied through delay and through a texturally denser scalar descent of d^4 to g^3. Similarly, motif 2 comes back in another varied form, played five times to resolve on the fourth beat of the 3-side of the clave. The percussion cierre or break (called a double *ponce*) is then used to mark the end of this section and the beginning of the next coro.

Example 6.8 Pacheco's flute inspiración 3 on "Mack the Knife": playing with double time and delay.

The tempo of the song is very fast, and it is easy to dismiss this improvisation as "whistle playing" as it is over so quickly. Closer scrutiny, however, reveals Pacheco's complete understanding of the style, the clave timeline organization and the relationship between melody, rhythm, and arrangement texture. Pacheco's short flute solo on "Mack the Knife" on Charanga La Duboney's 1959 version reveals that he has absorbed the Cuban flute style of improvisation with its typical one-octave tessitura from fourth to third register, its clave feel, typical ornamentation around the dominant note, motivic development, use of repeated motifs of "3 in a grid of 4" for rhythmic tension, and its percussion-informed *cierres*.

This analysis shows that while Pacheco is a not a virtuoso performer in the vein of renowned Cuban flute players Richard Egües or José Fajardo within the wider Cuban flute tradition,[20] he cannot simply be dismissed as purely imitative as he is able to generate new material from the repertoire that coheres firmly to clave aesthetics. His improvised phrases are not simply regurgitated from memory but link to the melodic ingredients of the arrangement, demonstrating a command of the idiom and its generative creative processes. His clave-feel and rhythmic treatment of melodic material are ample evidence of his stylistic competence, musicality, and creativity.

The performances on this recording have the undeniable energy, or "sonic signature," of New York's *barrios* through their breathless speed and energy. In the next song I analyze, "Bronx Pachanga," this breathless energy is also in evidence—but now Charlie Palmieri's La Duboney has a new flute soloist.

BRONX PACHANGA

The second piece analyzed here, "Bronx Pachanga," from the 1961 album *Pachanga at the Caravana Club* by Charlie Palmieri and His Charanga La Duboney, features the new flute player Rod Lewis Sánchez.[21] Following in Pacheco's footsteps, Sánchez embraces the embalao approach but is less adept than Pacheco in terms of overall melodic and rhythmic coherence; nevertheless, he draws on Cuban flute stylistic vocabulary and típico generative devices. Sánchez plays the metal Boehm system flute on this recording rather than the traditional five-key wooden flute used by Pacheco. This results in a slight difference in timbre, with the metal flute of Sánchez ringing a little more stridently than Pacheco's wooden timbre in the fourth register. The assertive attack nevertheless emulates the sound of the five-key flute in his phrasing. In record cover images Sánchez is seen holding a metal flute, and David Pérez confirms that Sánchez was a metal flute player.[22]

The arrangement of "Bronx Pachanga" analyzed in chapter 5 demonstrates the descarga aesthetic most clearly, built as it is on one fast riff or guajeo broken up by two different coros, with one cierre used to signal section changes and the final coda. It bears no relation to the pachanga of Orquesta Sublime's "La Pachanga" and is based around a I-V guaracha progression in 2–3 clave. In many ways it shares elements of the fast charanga mambo style with its insistent violin riffing throughout. It is noteworthy that the Cuban violinists José Andreu, Rafael Muñoz, Daniel González, and Rafael Aroz on this recording had played in Cuba with the original danzón-mambo innovators in Arcaño y sus Maravillas before emigrating to the USA. The flute improvises over most of the arrangement, demonstrating Weinstein's point that the Latin flute players of New York had no other option than to fill out the textures at the top over such a barrage of sound from below. In example 6.9, Sánchez's flute solo demonstrates his knowledge of the Cuban flute style with most movement between the tessitura of fourth-octave d^4 to d^3 on the dominant note, with an apex note of e^4. There are many short motifs using mordents in the style of Pacheco, echoes of Eulogio Ortíz's solo on Arcaño y sus Maravillas' recording of "Mambo" (in m. 36), and characteristic sequences outlining the chord notes in the style of Richard Egües, although

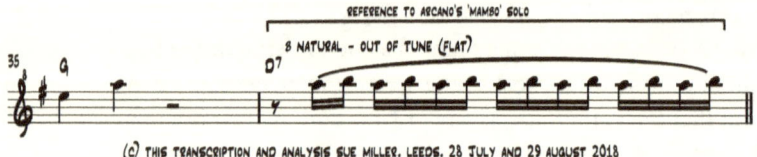

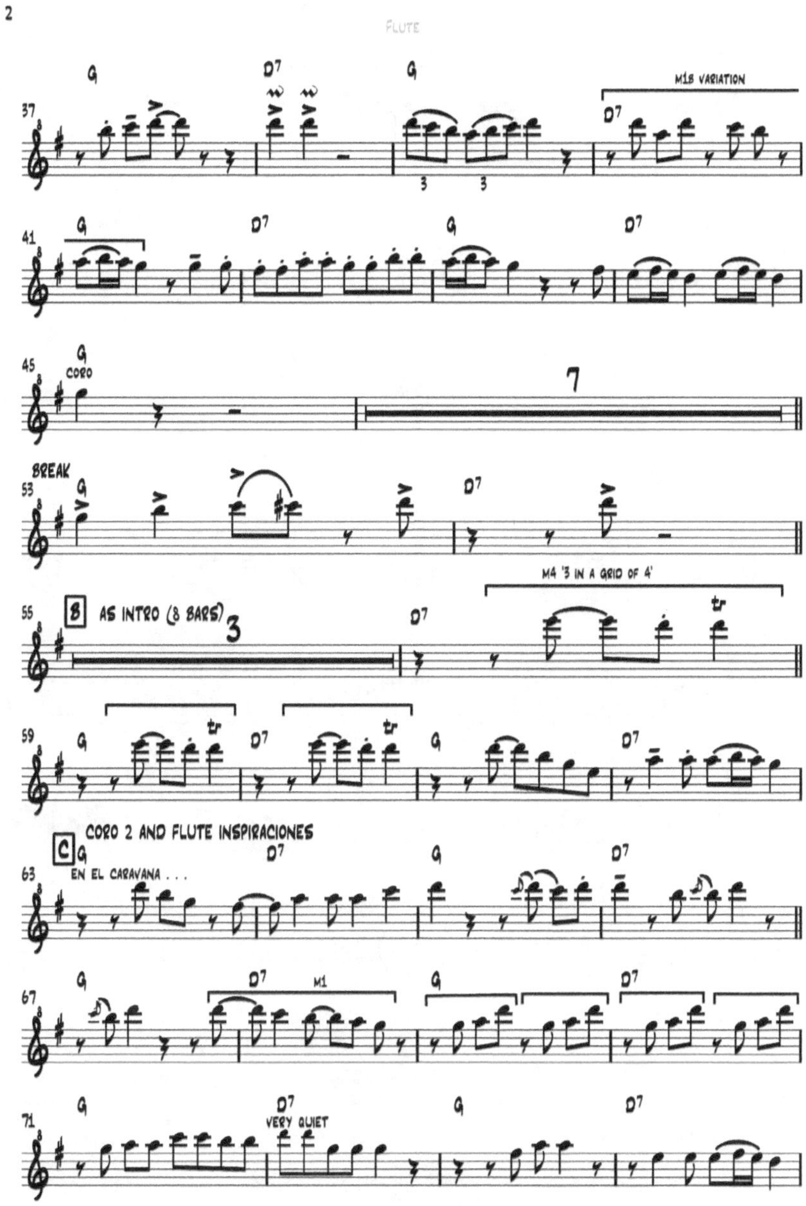
2
FLUTE
M1B VARIATION
CORO
BREAK
B AS INTRO (8 BARS)
M4 '3 IN A GRID OF 4'
C CORO 2 AND FLUTE INSPIRACIONES
EN EL CARAVANA . . .
M1
VERY QUIET

Example 6.9 Flute solo by Rod Lewis Sánchez on "Bronx Pachanga."

there are a few mistakes in this regard in Sánchez's performance here. As Pacheco's style draws on both Arcaño's and Richard Egües's work, Sánchez may have learned some of these characteristic elements secondhand from Pacheco as well as from Cuban recordings. As Mark Weinstein has pointed out, all New York–based (mainly Puerto Rican) flute players were influenced by Pacheco. Not much is known about Rod Lewis Sánchez other than that he played flute in La Duboney. David A. Pérez mentioned that Sánchez was a Puerto Rican flute player much in demand as a session player and had a background playing in conjunto groups, recording with pianist and arranger Hector Rivera in 1961.[23]

This solo has a very live feel, due to imperfections such as the out of tune trill in measure 36, the harmonic clashes with the coro in measures 75–78 (see example 6.10), split or weaker notes (mm. 72 and 127, and the missed chord change in measure 89 (see example 6.11).

Example 6.10 Pedal figure on the ninth in the flute solo clashes with the string guajeo, coro 2, and piano montuno over the G tonic chords.

These small errors where intervals of major seconds clash (i.e., the a^3 and g^3, and b^3 and a^3 in measures 75 and 77, and the d^3 and e^3 throughout in example 6.10) do not obstruct the overall rhythmic effect and in many ways demonstrate liveness. In terms of providing a pedal against the percussion break and the violin and piano patterns, this phrase is stylistic in approach, but a Cuban player such as Egües would perhaps have ensured the pattern was slightly modified over the tonic chord to outline the changes.

There are many repeated rhythmic phrases in this solo, some successfully using the "3 in a grid of 4" clave tension-and-release technique, although some of these repeated phrases are less clave-aligned or developed (see example 6.11).

In example 6.11, the "3 in a grid of 4" motif plays against the clave before resolving with a new descending phrase starting on the bombo beat (2+

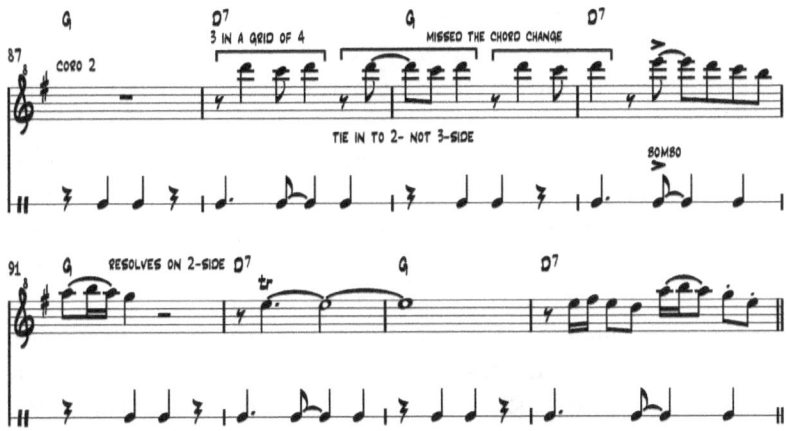

Example 6.11 "3 in a grid of 4" thrice repeated figures that resolve on the two-side of the clave.

played on the 3-side of the clave) in measure 90 and resolving squarely on the 2-side in measure 91. With the missed chord change and the tie-in to the 2-side of the clave, it could be viewed either as playing with clave for tension or as cross-clave. Other similar figures employed by Sánchez do not always resolve in clave (such as in mm. 58–62), and although there is a clave sensibility throughout it is not as consistent as Pacheco's clave feel. Nevertheless, the solo bubbles away energetically at the top end. Although containing melodic movement outlining the chord notes as arpeggios or in thirds, many of the phrases are based on motif 1, a scalar descending figure from d^4 to g^3. If anything, the frequent resolving to tonic g in this motif gives the solo less coherence as it starts and stops, but the development of this main motif 1 throughout does reveal Sánchez's ability to develop the solo thematically. Less assured than Pacheco and lacking the fluidity and coherence of Egües and Fajardo, Sánchez nevertheless illustrates the change in performance aesthetic highlighted by Mark Weinstein—típico in style but also embalao in approach. There is a breathless excitement in this performance where minor mistakes add to the live feel of the performance, underlying the more descarga or "jamming" quality of the New York charangas at this time.

INNOVATION OR IMITATION? CREATIVITY REDEFINED

Imitation is a process whereby a style is absorbed, as Nuyorican bassist Andy González of Conjunto Libre and Grupo Folklórico y Experimental Nuevayorkino asserts: "Music is like a language and once you learn the basic rules and vocabulary of that language you can have a conversation. The more you understand the vocabulary and rules and the way words can be combined to express different ideas the more you can vary the conversation in expressive ways."[24]

Johnny Pacheco's early work in the late 1950s and 1960s within the Cuban charanga format was not part of any revival but was rather part of a continuation and natural development of Cuban music performance in the South Bronx and Spanish Harlem. For his work to be "revivalist" there would have had to have been a discontinuity in the tradition of Latin music performance in the city. The ethnographic work of Roberta Singer and Elena Martínez (2004) alongside recent work by Christina Abreu (2015), on the Cuban/Interamericano social clubs in New York and Miami from the 1940s to the 1960s, outlines the centrality of Cuban dance music in the forging of Latin identity in the city, long before the Cuban Revolution. Similarly, ethnomusicologist David Garcia (2004, 2006) has highlighted the importance of son and charanga in the Bronx venues and social clubs of the 1940s and '50s and critiques the standard narrative of Latin music history in the USA with its focus on the downtown Manhattan venues to the exclusion of the Latin communities in the South Bronx and Spanish Harlem. Juan Flores, in his account of the rise of salsa, similarly highlights the wider diversity of Latin performance in the city prior to the dominance of the Fania label.

While the Cuban role models are clearly in evidence in Pacheco's playing in the examples given here and elsewhere, Pacheco does add a different sabor to the típico style. He captures the essence of the music, as Storm Roberts concedes, but there is more to his playing than imitation or a desire for charanga preservation. The creative process is in evidence when his solos are looked at in detail. It is admittedly easy to miss the detail, as many of his recordings are taken at very fast tempos ("Mack the Knife" is ♩ = 208) and in many instances the vocal coros are sung throughout his inspiraciones. The same applies to Sánchez's solo, although his playing aligns more clearly with Weinstein's assertion that development within a solo was not possible in the new, loud, and busy sonic environment of the New York Latin music scene. Thus, the listener is not drawn toward the solo in the same way as they are to solos by Richard Egües or José Fajardo. When compared to those two esteemed Cuban flute improvisers, Sánchez's creativity and virtuosity is not as apparent; but if we evaluate styles of performance within the New York context, different aspects of creativity in performance can be more fully appreciated. Johnny Pacheco and Charlie Palmieri soaked up the típico style of charanga performance, synthesized the main elements, and created a faster, louder, and more breathless version, leaving a path for others to follow.

Charanga flute players Rod Lewis Sánchez and George Castro certainly followed Pacheco's performance style in terms of Cuban flute improvisation in the New York context.

When asked by Peter Westbrook why the charanga's popularity waned in later years, Latin flute player Nestor Torres replied: "it faded because it's not a very pleasant sound—a high pitched, slightly out-of-tune flute with high pitched, same sounding out-of-tune violins."[25] In a personal communication with Torres in October 2017, I reminded him of his comments and we discussed the sabor of the early charanga bands of the 1960s such as the one led by Johnny Pacheco. He professed his love for charanga music, as it was one of his own formative influences, stating that some of these bands were more polished than others and suggesting that even the roughness and out-of-tune sharp intonation of the flute and violins of these early New York charangas might perhaps be part of its aesthetic.[26] As he and many others underline, this music is intended to get people to dance, and rhythm, rather than tuning, is the most important aspect of dance music performance practice.

A NEW PERFORMANCE AESTHETIC

Small changes in performance practice within típico charanga performance from the late 1950s and early 1960s in New York led to new ways of performing what was essentially traditional Cuban dance music. Through their club performances, led by Johnny Pacheco and Charlie Palmieri among others, a new trajectory for this music was born (building on the New York rhumba and mambo bands that preceded it). In the context of the improvisation tradition embedded within these styles, the imitation of Cuban musical elements also involved the ability to understand clave aesthetics and to absorb the performance codes and generative processes. As Andy González asserts, this enabled a meaningful communication with a dancing audience of Cuban, Puerto Rican, and other Latin American migrants in the city.

Creativity within stylistic boundaries can be better defined once stylistic parameters and approaches to melodic and rhythmic material are analyzed and evidenced. The analysis of Johnny Pacheco's and Rod Lewis Sánchez's flute improvisations in Charlie Palmieri's Charanga La Duboney presented here provide evidence that creativity can exist in music adopted and adapted from a "different" culture, and that evaluation of an individual's contribution needs to be undertaken within the wider communal context in which they perform. Small innovations can often be the most interesting. These may not be related to virtuosity or to deliberate fusions of musical format or instrumentation but rather involve variations in performance delivery. Pacheco, with his embalao approach, chose to improvise with rhythmic concepts to the fore. He has been highly influential through his work in the mambo bands, charangas, conjuntos, and finally his salsa productions in New York. He may not have been one of the top virtuoso flute players within the charanga tradition as a whole (or even the most innovative in terms of melodic-rhythmic ideas), but he developed a style of his own by reworking Cuban material with a Bronx-infused performance aesthetic. A catalyst for musical change, Pacheco was not the sole creator of a New York Latin sound by any means, but he has been an important figure within the context of Latin music in the USA and internationally. Embroiled as he has been in the sometimes murky world of music promotion, he is also a musician and performer; more attention should be paid to his extensive musical output in order to evaluate his musical contribution to Latin music more fairly. He did borrow extensively from Cuban music repertoire, but remade it (with others) for a New York Latin and later international audience, and always, as Roberts stated at the outset, with loving enthusiasm for Cuban music.

It is important to revisit arguments put forward to support claims of cultural appropriation or creativity in order to evaluate US-based Cuban dance music more inclusively. Accounts that pit the Cuban charanga (and indeed the son conjunto) against the US versions often do so in terms of the binaries "rural/urban," "traditional/modern," "less percussive/more percussive," "faster/slower," or "aggressive/laid back."[27] The cultural appropriation discourse in which US-based Latin forms are regarded as weaker/paler imitations of earlier Cuban music forms are sometimes put forward, often fueled by the Derechos Reservados or DR [Rights Reserved] copyright evasions rife after the 1959 revolution.[28] It is also worth reiterating that many of the US-based charangas included Cuban players and that these bands were often a mix of Cuban, Puerto Rican, Jewish American, and Dominican musicians. As Willie Rodríguez is at pains to point out, differences between the two need more nuance:

SM: When I ask people to define New York sabor, a lot of them have talked about the music having to be more aggressive. I don't know if you agree with that.

WR: Well aggressive is a hard word. I need a softer word that means aggressive but not the way most people think of aggressive, because it's more driving if you will perhaps.

SM: I think that's a nicer term because so many people said aggressive...

WR: It's more city. You see don't forget it's not country. It's an in-your-face city sound, pushy, brassy if you will.[29]

Some, like Andrea Brachfeld and John Storm Roberts, characterize the Cuban sound as "tropical" and opine that the winters in New York made for a harder sound; David Pérez describes the Cuban sound as "more laid back and confident," due to Cuban musicians being the originators of the style (and therefore more natural and self-assured). He thought that Puerto Ricans' need to forge a strong identity more stridently within an often hostile English-speaking nation had accounted for the more aggressive sound. Many of those interviewed erroneously associated charanga in Cuba with a rural feel; charanga is an almost entirely urban creation, albeit with the participation of musicians who migrated from other parts of the island to Havana and other larger towns. New York is nevertheless seen as more city than Havana, as Zervigón notes in chapter 4. Charlie Palmieri's Charanga Duboney and Pacheco's charanga did create an embalao style of performance in the late 1950s and early 1960s and their sabor could be characterized as sounding loud, fast, and driving. Not all charangas in New York had the same approach, however, and not all groups played without dynamic variation.

Willie Rodríguez stresses that it is important to keep in mind who is playing the music and who they are playing it for, emphasizing that the music is essentially interactive dance music. Music and dance evolved together in mid-century Cuba and also in New York, but within different contexts. After the revolution, Cuban music continued to develop in some ways that were parallel to US developments (Havana-based Los Van Van and later *timba* groups, for example, drew on African American forms such as disco and funk), but these changes were largely cut off from the US mainstream following the political and economic embargo. The Cuban influence in New York therefore has come, in the main, from Cuban idioms popular before 1959, giving New York–based Cuban dance music an altogether different trajectory in the long term from popular music in post-revolutionary Cuba.

In answer to critiques by Roberts, Flores, and others that Pacheco was a revivalist and a traditionalist, I concede that he is an imitator (but with the caveat that without imitation there is no stylistic tradition) and an appropriator (for example, his ability to commercialize and popularize Latin music has often led to promotion of Cuban music without acknowledgment of sources). He is also, however, an innovator, particularly in terms of Latin performance aesthetics, and as such his work as a charanga flute improviser, Latin percussionist, and arranger merits further research. Academic research on Charlie Palmieri's improvisational style is also long overdue. Charlie Palmieri and

Johnny Pacheco created an exciting, breathless New York sound associated with the charanga lineup, which was highly influential. Characterized by a change in performance aesthetic to encompass a faster embalao approach, both Pacheco and Palmieri demonstrate, in the examples analyzed in this chapter, their ability to fuse Cuban forms into arrangements that reflect the excitement of the Bronx club scene of the late 1950s and early 1960s. A big city sound is often assumed to contain brass instruments (particularly trombones), but Pacheco and Charlie Palmieri brought Caribbean joy and a driving big city sound through their charanga performances and recordings. The subtle features of the Cuban charangas were largely absent in their music, but in their place was a sound adapted to a more pan-Latin American audience. As Mark Weinstein remarked, they created music that sonically represented the busy sounds of New York City, performing a less polished but driving charanga repertoire that catered to a mixed Caribbean/Latin American New York–based audience.[30]

- 7 -

CHARANGUEA'O EN TÍPICO

Eddie Palmieri's La Perfecta

Juan Flores credits Eddie Palmieri with being one of the most important innovators in Latin music by combining the conjunto and charanga lineups in La Perfecta, describing it as "two bands in one, without adding or changing personnel: for any given number he [Eddie] had either a conjunto, with trombones and bongo, or what he calls 'charanguea'o,' that is, with the charanga feel, combining flute, trombones and timbales."[1] Although leaving out the timbales for the more son-oriented repertoire and replacing it with bongos signifies the traditional conjunto approach,[2] La Perfecta was not the only band combining charanga and conjunto aesthetics. Contrary to Flores's distinction that Pacheco abandoned the charanga for a conservative típico approach with his conjunto Nuevo Tumbao, Pacheco also continued to combine a charanguea'o approach with a conjunto lineup—but the connections are perhaps less apparent when the lineup does not include a flute (or violins). Pacheco's arrangement of "El Bodeguero" on his *Early Rhythms* album, for example, features the brass section performing the traditional charanga violin guajeo patterns. Understanding the nuances of the two different but related approaches is, therefore, key to understanding where innovation or change is taking place. A change of instrumentation is observed more readily than more subtle indications of charanga or conjunto features, or of specific performance aesthetics associated with the two traditions. Cuban trumpeter Roberto Rodríguez improvised in a charanguea'o manner in Orquesta Broadway because he understood the charanga conventions of performance. Palmieri's La Perfecta made instrumental lineup changes but, like Pacheco, combined elements from the charanga and conjunto in other subtle ways. Palmieri's jazz inflections were more modern than Pacheco's, however, with jazz-styled chord progressions (more ii-V-I) and greater use of chord extensions. The jazz-influenced Perfecta charts came about through trombonist Barry Rogers's knowledge of both idioms and by Eddie Palmieri's gradual expansion into jazz-styled harmonic language.

The original La Perfecta band was formed in 1961 by Eddie Palmieri. The lineup varied at first, but it mostly featured Eddie Palmieri on piano, Manny Oquendo on timbales and bongo, Tommy López on congas, Bobby Rodríguez on bass, Barry Rogers, José Rodrígues, and Mark Weinstein on trombones, Ismael Quintana on vocals, and George (Jorge)[3] Castro on five-key wooden flute. In the sleeve notes to La Perfecta's debut album in 1962,[4] Charlie Palmieri calls the band a "trombanga" even though La Perfecta only had four numbers on the record featuring the flute and trombone format (the rest of the repertoire featured either four trumpets and two trombones or four trumpets).[5] Eddie Palmieri had initially wanted a four-trumpet brass section, but good trumpet players were hard to find—they were much in demand in the mambo big bands of the day.[6] Subsequently Barry Rogers, Manny Oquendo, and Eddie Palmieri worked closely together on the band's arrangements to adapt to a slightly less conventional trombone-led conjunto with accompanying charanga flute. Barry Rogers is universally credited with defining La Perfecta's trombone section sound, which was high in register and usually very loud. Mark Weinstein has described how many of the trombone lines were improvised *moñas* (riffs), which Barry would invent and sing to each player to imitate:

> Barry would call me over and would sing into my ear the vamp that he wanted played and I had to pick up. Sometimes I'd say "Do it again" with my hand but if I didn't pick it up in two times I didn't have the job. I had to pick up the vamp, so I'd start the vamp and then Barry would keep on singing. Jorge would start to play. Barry would start to play the vamp in unison with me, maybe correcting my phrasing, and then he'd start to play it in harmony. Then he would start to play almost like Dixieland, a second line, and that's when the band would take off.[7]

Barry Rogers was influenced by the 1950s trombone duets of jazz players J. J. Johnson and Kai Winding[8] and knew the earlier tailgating styles too; in turn, Eddie Palmieri was very influenced by Rogers. Palmieri later drew on work by McCoy Tyner and Chick Corea in his own improvisations, but in La Perfecta neither Rogers nor Palmieri deviated from the main function of the clave-based music and followed a dance imperative. In many ways the interlocking improvised lines of early jazz were aligned with the conjunto's diablos and charanga mambos in terms of function (building up the rhythmic intensity). La Perfecta II was set up in 2002 using the same charts and

Eddy Zervigón, Karen Joseph, and Dave Valentín all recorded flute solos for these Perfecta II recordings. As Weinstein states:

> They are still playing the same La Perfecta charts. They're playing the same half a dozen potboilers. I'm sure they're playing other stuff too. . . . Well, they're great charts . . . but Eddie never had a working band like La Perfecta. . . . The La Perfecta band—that was the best band I think he [Eddie Palmieri] had, and it was a very short period of time that he had that band, which had Bobby Rodríguez on bass, Tommy López and Manny Oquendo, and that was a band. . . . When Eddie resuscitated La Perfecta Eddy [Zervigón] played sometimes but Karen Joseph was the main flute player when it resuscitated. Karen, like Connie Grossman, plays the style. . . . Barry [Rogers] was the greatest musician in the world, and he was always leaving Eddie, because playing with Eddie was too hard on his chops. Then he would come back to do recordings, and if you see live performances with Eddie, he had just all sorts of mixed musicians.[9]

Mark Weinstein told me that both he and Barry Rogers never referred to the trombone simply as "the trombone," it was always "the fucking trombone" because the force required for the loud Perfecta trombone section was hard on their lips.[10] Although there are only two written parts for trombone, the early Perfecta albums featured the three trombones of Weinstein, Rogers, and Rodrígues. The use of three trombones to cover two parts was due to Rogers singing coro and also to give players a chance to either rest their lips during the moña sections or to extemporize over the two lines as part of a final diablo section.

Prior to 1960, Eddie Palmieri had performed on piano with the Tito Rodríguez band, with Pete Terrace's charanga orquesta, and with the conjunto band of Vicentico Valdés, where he worked with percussionist Manny Oquendo (who played both bongos and timbales).[11] Many of these 1950s performance opportunities were provided for him by his older brother Charlie Palmieri before Eddie started his own band. Overshadowed initially by his then more famous brother, Eddie is now the more internationally well-known of the two, particularly as a piano improviser, popular in the salsa as well as the jazz community. His work as a soloist is not analyzed here but, as with his brother Charlie, more academic research is needed to fully understand his work as both bandleader and virtuosic piano soloist in the Cuban dance music context. It is not surprising that Eddie Palmieri, with a background in charanga, conjunto, and mambo, combines these elements in his own band, and consequently influences the soloists within it. The following analyses of flute improvisations by George Castro, Eddy Zervigón, and Dave Valentín in La Perfecta and La Perfecta II, demonstrate how all these players solo *charangueando en típico*, drawing on the chromatic lines of the composed melodies and responding to the conjunto and charanga elements of the arrangement. George Castro improvises on the five-key flute with the original La Perfecta (1962 and 1964), and Eddy Zervigón, also on the five-key flute, solos with La Perfecta II in 2003. Dave Valentín plays the metal Boehm system flute with La Perfecta II in 2002. The difference in terms of recording dates allows some reflection on performance practice changes from the 1960s to the early 2000s. The following four analyses reveal Cuban and New York sabor and, in the case of Valentín, the extended techniques of free and avant-garde jazz.

RITMO CALIENTE—*EL RITMO CON SALSA, CON TROMBÓN Y FLAUTA*

El Ritmo Caliente

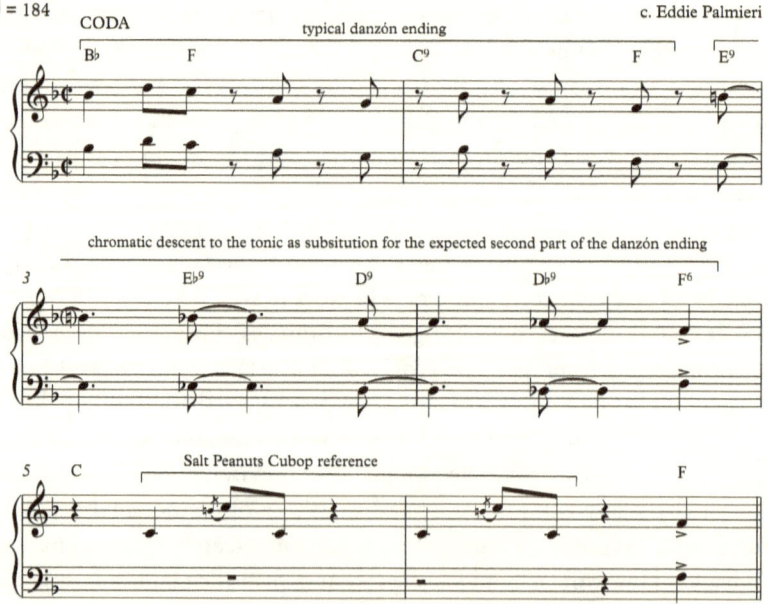

Example 7.1 Coda for "Ritmo Caliente": combining charanga with jazz-inflected son and Cubop.

In the final coda to both versions of "Ritmo Caliente" by La Perfecta I and II, elements from the Cuban danzón and jazz-inflected Cuban son lines are combined before a cheeky reference to Cubop ("Salt Peanuts") concludes the piece. This quotation is more than a simple reference to Dizzy Gillespie's composition, however, as it outlines the characteristic Cuban one-octave tessitura on the dominant note and also alludes to the most famous Cuban son composition, "El Manicero" [The Peanut Vendor] by Moisés Simons.[12] This example, therefore, succinctly demonstrates how Eddie Palmieri understands clave function, a variety of Cuban performance traditions (*charangeando en típico*), and the significance of the Cubop quotation. This is not simple imitation of Cuban models: this is synthesis. Palmieri's understanding of style and function enables the music to work as both a conjunto and a charanga with a combination of their features (see example 7.1). The use of extended chords and the insertion of more jazz-oriented progressions in La Perfecta arrangements influences the style of improvisation to some extent; even in the five-key flute solos by Castro and Zervigón some of these more chromatic composed melodic ingredients surface. In the arrangement and the related improvisations, however, the tonic to dominant relationship and clave alignment are never sacrificed and the music remains Cuban dance music in essence. The flute improvises over the 2–3 clave-organized piano montunos (with ties into the 3-side) and also over the trombone moña lines, which emphasize the bomba 2+ beat and the open beat 4 on the 3-side, as demonstrated in example 7.2.

Example 7.2 Trombone moña, piano montuno, and bass tumbao patterns on "Ritmo Caliente."

In the La Perfecta II version there is also a second montuno section over which Eddy Zervigón solos against a pedal montuno, outlining the sixth note d played by the piano and bass before the piano returns to the first montuno. The trombones then enter with a new improvised moña in the vein of an Arsenio Rodríguez diablo figure, bringing the solo to a climax before the final coro and coda.

Example 7.3 Pedal-based montuno and tumbao on sixth note d on "Ritmo Caliente II."

Both Castro and Zervigón perform improvisations over these melodic-rhythmic textures, which are firmly rooted in the Cuban flute style while nevertheless reflecting elements of the arrangement, as demonstrated in the analysis below.

GEORGE CASTRO'S 1962 SOLO ON "RITMO CALIENTE" BY LA PERFECTA

According to Mark Weinstein, George Castro emulated Johnny Pacheco's improvisational style, with its busy and energetic Bronx aesthetic.[13] The solo here certainly matches Pacheco's energy and volume, but it is less ornamented and not as percussive as Pacheco's playing.[14] Not much is known about the background of George Castro, although many interviewed for this book assume he was Cuban due to his surname. He later moved from New York, possibly to Los Angeles, some say, due to family issues.[15] Weinstein has remarked that Castro played at a high volume level—he would certainly have developed strong diaphragm muscles performing his high-register flute lines over the La Perfecta trombone section. Castro's improvisation, while rhythmic and clave-based, does not always follow the tonic-to-dominant chord changes in this solo as he bases most of his lines on the notes of the C7 chord, sometimes missing the changes to the tonic F chord (this improves midway through the solo).[16] The energy and fire of the band are matched by the flute's rhythmic energy, but this is less developed than later La Perfecta flute players such as Zervigón and Karen Joseph. However, Castro was the original La Perfecta flute player, and his style is clave-aligned and firmly rooted in the Cuban flute tradition. His less decorative loud, fast soloing, as Weinstein notes in chapter 6, was perfect for the energy and busy New York sounds of the homegrown Latin music scene.

Example 7.4 "Ritmo Caliente" flute solo by George Castro.

The chromatic rising line of "3 in a grid of 4" eighth notes in measures 5–9 could be viewed as derived from the opening composed figures under the coro, but more likely they emerge from Eddie Palmieri's preceding piano solo with its rising chromatic figure at 1:21. Improvisers do not play in a vacuum, but feed off the ideas in the arrangement, including the solos of fellow band members. This rising chromatic line is used by Castro in his solo on "Tu Tu Ta Ta"; it is also favored by Rolando Lozano (see chapter 3), however, and so could also be viewed simply as stylistic vocabulary. Castro uses motivic variation, sequencing (e.g., motif 2 in mm. 13–16), and an anacrusis motif on the dominant c^4 (m2 in mm. 16, and 21–22), which Zervigón extends in his 2003 version shown below.

EDDY ZERVIGÓN'S SOLO ON "RITMO CALIENTE" IN LA PERFECTA II

Karen Joseph asserts that Eddy Zervigón was the original La Perfecta II flute player but also that Eddy had not wanted to continue with the band and had recommended her to take his place.[17] Joseph plays the Boehm system flute and is now one of the most well-known charanga flute players on the New York scene today.[18] Although there is no credit given for the flute player on "Ritmo Caliente II," it is clearly Zervigón's playing (he is listed as a guest).[19] On this 2003 Concord release *Ritmo Caliente*, Zervigón is credited as the flute player on "Lázaro y su Microfono,"[20] and Karen Joseph on "Grandpa Semi-Tone Blues," "Leapfrog To Harlem," and "Gígue (Bach Goes Bata)," with "Lo Que Traigo Es Sabroso II" credited to them both.[21] It seems that in this twenty-first-century version Palmieri favors Zervigón for the more típico charanga improvisations and Joseph for the blues, jazz, and classically inflected material. The fact that Palmieri also engaged Dave Valentín for the 2002 recording shows how Palmieri can incorporate soloists from very different musical backgrounds who respond to the Perfecta arrangements with charanga, conjunto típico, and jazz/free stylings without taking away from the music's danceability.

In this solo Zervigón improvises over two different trombone moñas and over a piano and bass pedal–styled montuno and tumbao on the sixth note (see example 7.3), which starts in measure 16 in the flute solo score (see example 7.5). Here Zervigón follows this change in harmony by using a "3 in a grid of 4" figure based around d^4 and moving between d^4 and c^4. When Palmieri restates the first montuno on chords I and V (F and C), Zervigón gradually adjusts to this motif (missing one chord change in the process)

El Ritmo Caliente

Example 7.5 "Ritmo Caliente" flute solo by Eddy Zervigón.

and returns to outlining the tonic to dominant chord changes from measure 40. When the trombones re-enter, they perform a new moña figure which gradually builds to a diablo multi-layered moña typical of the conjunto. Zervigón responds by increasing the density of his syncopated pedal motif (m1 originally in mm. 13–21 and now extended in mm. 59–66) before finishing with an insistent eighth-note figure around top c^4 played three times as a lead-in to the final coro section. This is a direct extension of Castro's motif 3, showing how elements of an earlier solo can be recycled in a later version. Zervigón also echoes aspects of the chromatic pedal bassline (c^4-$c^{\#4}$-d^4) in measures 32–34 and 71–75. There is a strong clave feel throughout, with use of anacrusis on the 3-side of the clave, phrasing following an on-beat 2-side and off-beat 3-side, and "3 in a grid of 4" figures that play against clave but resolve rhythmically (mm. 15–20). The solo is more cohesive in terms of motivic and textural development than Castro's, although the 1964 original captures the energy level and charangueaó en típico aesthetic. Both Zervigón and Castro play idiomatically within the clave-based Cuban flute tradition and draw on elements of the arrangement. Both are Cuban five-key flute players and as such demonstrate cubanía but are also responsive to the jazz-inflected elements of the arrangement.

In the next two examples on "Tu Tu Ta Ta," two very different improvisational styles are contrasted. George Castro represents a louder, brasher cubanía with both Cuban and New York sabor in evidence while Dave Valentín displays the same level of intensity in terms of energy and speed but breaks many of the stylistic rules of clave-based improvisation so one might not describe his playing as having sabor (and perhaps therefore need to evaluate with a different aesthetic in mind). As Zervigón states in the introduction, sabor is not "la velocidad de 8,000 notas por minuto" [not 8,000 notes a minute][22] and Valentín does play very fast runs using approaches more common in contemporary classical and free jazz idioms.

"TU TU TA TA"

GEORGE CASTRO AND DAVE VALENTÍN— FROM HIGH ENERGY TO HIGH JINKS

The title "Tu Tu Ta Ta" by its very sound suggests call-and-response phrasing, and in the composition the trombones call and the flute responds in addition to the usual coro/*pregón* and inspiraciones. Both Castro's and Valentín's solos also respond in this conversational way. The flute improvises over D9 montunos and trombone moña riffs as shown in example 7.6 and the trombone lines in La Perfecta's "Tu Tu Ta Ta" are clearly modelled on typical charanga violin guajeo patterns.

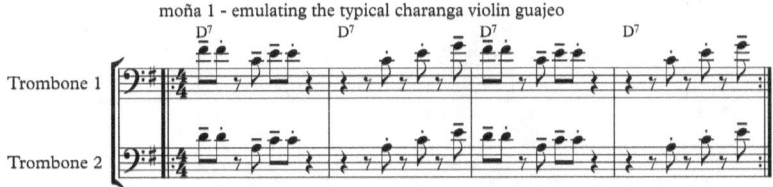

Example 7.6 Trombone moña 1 in "Tu Tu Ta Ta": imitating charanga violin guajeo lines.

There are also flute inspiraciones over D7 and $E^\flat 7$ on the introduction (see example 7.7) and Castro's flutter-tonguing here is taken up and extended by Valentín in his 2002 version. This shifting up and down by a semitone makes "Tu Tu Ta Ta" a very different type of charanga mambo in style, perhaps allowing Latin jazz players like Valentín to introduce more elements from free jazz.

Example 7.7 George Castro's inspiraciones on the introduction to "Tu Tu Ta Ta."

These inspiraciones by Castro respond to the trombones' "Tu Tu, Ta Ta" melody with the sharpened fourth crushed into the dominant note and octave leaps over D7, and he plays safer with longer flutter-tongued notes over the E♭ tonic chords (E♭ is not a good key for the charanga five-key flute and may explain the less developed E♭ sections by Castro).[23] In the first moña, the flute line starts each time with a rising scale (D mixolydian scale) and is answered by an octave leap mambito figure as shown in example 7.8. The opening scale by Castro is not only extended by Valentín but has since become a set part of the arrangement.

Example 7.8 Mixolydian scale and mambito: call and response. Flute: George Castro.

Castro's main solo in example 7.9 contains the standard hallmarks of the Cuban flute style with in-clave motivic sequencing, octave leaps on the dominant, a one-octave high-register tessitura and use of the sharpened fourth (g♯) as a stylistic indicator for the mambo style. He also manages an octave leap from $f^{\sharp}3$ to $f^{\sharp}4$ above the range (m. 3), a note only rarely played by Fajardo and Zervigón, demonstrating the sheer power in his playing. This improvisation demonstrates clave feel as the majority of Castro's phrases cohere to a more on-beat 2-side and an off-beat 3-side with some "3 in a grid of 4" non-clave aligned stylistic figures which resolve in clave for the purpose of creating rhythmic tension and release (mm. 16–17, 18–20). The solo ends weakly, however, perhaps due to uncertainty over the cueing out of the solo and/or moving away from the microphone.[24]

Tu Tu Ta Ta

c. Eddie Palmieri. Flute Solo c. George Castro in La Perfecta 1964.

©This Annotated Transcription Sue Miller, Leeds, 26 December 2018.

Example 7.9 "Tu Tu Ta Ta" flute solo by George Castro.

Castro's playing on the 1964 La Perfecta recording is very sharp and out of tune; as Weinstein has stated, George was a loud flute player (he had to be) and that he "tended to play very, very sharp." Like many five-key players, George Castro made the embouchure hole larger to make a bigger sound; as Weinstein remarked, "he had opened up the hole with a knife." This alters the tuning but makes the flute louder.[25] The main solo occurs over the dominant seventh chord D7 in the key of G; the tuning on the recording is sharp enough to sound almost a semitone higher (over D#7). Perhaps La Perfecta's characteristic loud trombone and flute section is responsible for this sharp intonation.[26] The introduction alternates between D7 and E♭ major chords, so this sharper tuning might also reflect this aspect of the arrangement.

On the moña 2 section of the 1964 version, the trombones are high in the mix. Their c and e notes obscure the d root note of the D9 chord in the bass, giving it a C Lydian flavor (see example 7.10). The high volume level of the trombone section, collectively known as the "roaring elephants,"[27] may explain why Castro missed some of the chord changes from tonic to dominant.

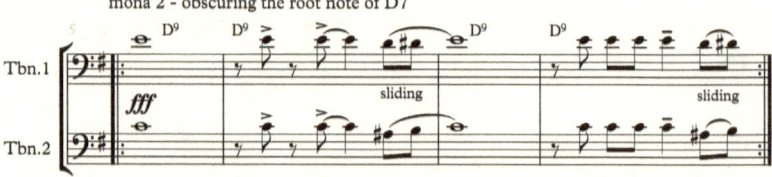

Example 7.10 Trombone moña 2 on "Tu Tu Ta Ta." Notes c and e mask the bass root note d.

DAVE VALENTÍN'S "TU TU TA TA II" SOLO WITH LA PERFECTA II

Dave Valentín's live performances are renowned for their excitement and exuberance; in this solo from 2002, that energy bursts out over the trombone moñas with a more contemporary fusion of styles.[28] Extended techniques are used such as singing down the flute while playing simultaneously (a technique also employed by Jethro Tull's Ian Anderson, for example), flutter-tonguing, percussive sounds, and tongue clicks. There are some characteristic Cuban rhythms present, abundant use of acciaccaturas (but fewer mordents and turns), and a conversational approach, although Valentín does not venture above b^3 in his solo (he only plays d^4 on the set breaks). The timbre of his metal Boehm system flute is also different from that of Castro. Many charanga flute players draw attention to the fact that the Boehm system flute is easier to play and has more technical possibilities (including slurring,

Eddie Palmieri's La Perfecta

Tu Tu Ta Ta II

Flute Solo - Dave Valentín in La Perfecta II, 2002

©This annotated transcription Sue Miller, Leeds 30 December 2018.

Example 7.11 "Tu Tu Ta Ta II" flute solo by Dave Valentín.

technical effects, and fluidity in all keys—not just the charanga keys, which are usually G, D, F, C, A, and E majors and minors). But they also say that the timbre and range is not as good on the metal flute and that it does not have the típico sound. Valentín is certainly taking the opportunity to demonstrate the advantages of the metal flute here, singing through the flute while performing fast nonuplets (mm. 11–12), key slapping for open and closed effects (mm. 154–56), flutter-tonguing, triple-tonguing (mm. 87–88), slap tonguing (mm. 15, 47–48, 94–95, 109–11, and 123–24), wailing over a quotation of "Fatima's Dance" from *Show Boat* (mm. 125–26) and using vibrato on lower sustained notes. This solo is crazy but also fits the energy of La Perfecta very well, thereby conforming to some extent to Pacheco's embalao approach. However, Valentín is rarely in clave and perhaps therefore has less sabor. Due perhaps to the prevalence of triplet quarter notes, Valentín is not even playing against clave in order to resolve in 2–3 direction at a later stage, as Castro and Zervigón do. In example 7.12 the solo is cross-clave with only one bar corresponding to the all-important bomba 2+ beat on the 3-side of the clave in measure 112. Overall there is very little correspondence between 2-side on-beat and 3-side off-beat phrasing, with on-beat 3-sides and off-beat 2-sides revealing very little clave sensibility.

Example 7.12 Valentín's less clave-aligned phrasing.

SOME CONCLUSIONS

While George Castro's playing is not as virtuosic as Cuban players such as Fajardo, Egües, or Zervigón, his solos are nevertheless clave-based and within the Cuban style (Cuban sabor) while reflecting the heat, excitement, and volume of the first version of La Perfecta. Later recordings of La Perfecta II feature more virtuosic soloing from Zervigón and Valentín, but Zervigón is in style and in clave whereas Valentín is not playing in clave or in style (although there are Cuban elements thrown into the mix). While some enjoy Valentín's exuberance, others critique his playing as "clowning around," viewing the extended techniques as a cover for not knowing the Cuban style well enough. Perhaps, as Zervigón remarks in the introduction, the speed and velocity is irrelevant if you do not have sabor (and sabor includes adherence to clave). Sabor, then, requires adherence to clave direction and a clave sensibility in improvisation. Elements of the Cuban improvisation style include stylistic vocabulary but also adherence to stylistic performance conventions and a deep knowledge of Cuban repertoire. The cultural references inherent in much of the stylistic vocabulary are what I would term aspects of cubanía and these aspects are subsumed under the concept of sabor. Players such as Zervigón and Castro, I would argue, demonstrate cubanía and both a Cuban and a New York sabor. Valentín, while having *Latinidad*, is more of a fusionist. Those who enjoy jazz (free and bebop) as well as Cuban music may, however, appreciate Valentín's solo more if they disregard the lack of clave feel and top-octave tessitura. Valentín's inventive and virtuosic solo is infused with palpable excitement and the energy is infectious. Palmieri's inclusion of four very different soloists in La Perfecta suggests he is able to appreciate the variety of approaches to Cuban/Latin jazz improvisation. The tight rhythm section and trombone moñas keep the music danceable even when a soloist such as Valentín flouts some of the stylistic conventions.

La Perfecta of the 1960s was certainly a catalyst for innovation, and in many ways the group represents a certain type of New York sabor with its fiery trombone and flute combination. One could view Valentín's work as a harbinger of things to come as many more contemporary Latin flute players have diversified into Latin jazz and other more hybrid styles (for example, Artie Webb, Nestor Torres, Andrea Brachfeld).[29] The experimental playing of Eddie Palmieri himself certainly paved the way for soloists such as Joseph and Valentín to innovate with jazz inflection within the Cuban dance music context. Eddie Palmieri continued to use charanga concepts within a conjunto-oriented format beyond the life of La Perfecta, adhering to típico practices all the while with an experimental approach. For example, his Latin jazz-styled "Un Día Bonito"[30] nevertheless features charanga violins and his repertoire continues to draw upon both the Cuban son and charanga traditions—charangueaó en típico—synthesizing aspects of African American jazz subtlety into the dance mix.

- 8 -

I DON'T LIKE IT LIKE THAT!

The Latin Bugalú

Nosotros grabamos "Black Is Black." ¿Sabes lo que ha pasado con la risa, con la Broadway, cuando grabamos en bugalú? Porque la pronunciación era tan desastrosa que empezamos a reírnos y dijimos "vamos a dejar esa risa ahí"—eso es lo que gustó mucho del disco ese. En ese tiempo, el conjunto que era muy popular fue el de Pete Rodríguez, el pianista. Ese era el conjunto más malo que había. Pero metieron el bugalú y listo. El que no tocaba bugalú se moría de hambre. Entonces nosotros grabamos "Black Is Black" y fue un temazo, y después grabamos "I Dig Rock and Roll" y entonces nos levantamos. Aquí todo el mundo tuvo que grabar un bugalú, sino te morías de hambre.

[We recorded "Black Is Black." Do you know how the laughing happened with Broadway, when we recorded our bugalú? Our [English] pronunciation was so bad that we started to laugh and we decided to keep this [the laughing] in and that's what people like best about this record. At this time the most popular band was pianist Pete Rodríguez's conjunto. That was the baddest conjunto around. But they did a bugalú and then they were set. So we recorded "Black Is Black" and it was a hit, and after this we recorded "I Dig Rock and Roll" and so we went up in popularity. Here everyone had to record a bugalú, if you didn't you would starve to death.][1]

The Latin *boogaloo*, written in Spanish as bugalú (although variously spelled), was a mix of African American soul elements (claps on beats 2 and 4, use of tambourine, blues/soul infection, blue notes, a slower groove, sometimes modified chord progressions and English lyrics) combined with Cuban son montuno, guajira, chachachá, a descarga aesthetic and other Cuban dance music elements (montuno, tumbao, guajeos, clave adherence), creating a celebratory party groove that was less frantic than the faster pachangas which preceded them. Sometimes known as "Latin soul,"[2] those Puerto Rican musicians who were teenagers in the 1960s were enthusiastic about the style and spoke of how much fun they had playing it at parties and in the clubs.[3] Older Latin musicians, in contrast, talk of the style as something they had to do to stay current. Many, like Eddy Zervigón, felt uncomfortable with the English lyrics but liked the income from the record sales—as he states above, everyone had to record a bugalú, otherwise they "would starve to death."

Pete Rodríguez ("I Like It Like That," 1967),[4] Ricardo Ray ("Lookie Lookie," 1967),[5] and Joe Cuba ("Bang Bang," 1966)[6] recorded perhaps the most well-known bugalú songs, although Ray Barretto's descarga "El Watusi," first recorded in 1962, is cited by Juan Flores and others as a forerunner. Other more established Latin artists also turned their hand to bugalú in the mid- to late 1960s, often from economic necessity, as Zervigón states. Manny Rivera, New York Puerto Rican percussionist with the contemporary New York charanga SonSublime, was a teenager at the time of the bugalú and, in contrast to slightly older Latin musicians like Zervigón, loved the bugalú as well as the music of the Beatles and was inspired to become a percussionist watching the Afro-Nuyorican Lebrón Brothers perform at a club on the Lower East Side (below 14th Street). He also went to clubs with a slightly older clientèle where charangas and conjuntos performed (El Corso), gaining a simultaneous love for charanga.[7] Similarly, Puerto Rican percussionist John Berdeguer, while inspired by Tito Puente and the Palladium bands, describes seeing the Lebrón Brothers in Brooklyn and performing bugalú at parties in the late 1960s.[8] Berdeguer recorded with Chollo Rivera and the Latin Soul Drives for Cotique Records, run by producer George Goldner, who led the way in recording Spanish and English bugalú and Latin soul artists:[9]

> The bugalú was hot in that era [late 1960s]. You had Johnny Colón, the "Boogaloo Blues;"[10] at that time they were really, really hot. Who else? The TnT, which is Tito and Tony;[11] they had a lot of hits, who else? Joe Bataan was really hot at that time . . . Those guys recorded with Cotique Records. Yes it was all through Cotique Records. That band that I recorded with, Chollo Rivera and Soul Drive, they also did Cotique Records and George Goldner was our producer. We had a couple of nice hits—we had "I Could Never Hurt You Girl" and we were in the process of a second album and then everything just blew off. Yes I don't know what happened, yes . . . George Goldner passed away and everything was gone.[12]

The bugalús of the conjunto groups were a result of direct cultural engagement with African American dancers, whereas older-generation Latin musicians, many from the charanga tradition, were less connected to this organic development. Reasons given for the bugalú's decline by Roberts, Salazar, Flores, and other leading Latin music scholars often cite those younger musicians of the bugalú era complaining that they were not given airplay or performance opportunities. Undoubtedly, as with Fania Records in the next decade, channels for diffusion and distribution will have been controlled by record producers and promoters with vested interests in their own signed artists. Berdeguer notes that Eddie Palmieri grudgingly recorded a bugalú called "African Twist"[13] and that it was "incredible." La Perfecta trombonist Mark Weinstein, in addition to playing with Eddie Palmieri's conjunto, also played with Ricardo Ray's band in Brooklyn, where the ambience he describes in chapter 1 is further characterized by local crowds of young Puerto Ricans:

MW: There was a venue on Flatbush Avenue Extension, right before you get onto the Manhattan Bridge. There was a loft right next to a car wash place, and that's where all the Brooklyn kids went. I never even knew the name of it, but I played with Ricardo Ray a lot there.[14] He had a two trumpet band, and one of the trumpet players was his brother Ray Maldonado, who ended up being the trumpet player for Stevie Wonder. Ray, until he died, had a wonderful career. Ray and I had played with the La Playa Sextet, and so Ray talked his brother into using a trumpet and trombone instead of two trumpets because Ray was so loud you couldn't hear the second trumpet player. I was so loud that the two of us . . .

SM: Oh it was a perfect match, right?!

MW: The two of us were a perfect match, and that was for the Brooklyn kids. It was still very much [local]—besides for the Palladium, which was a cosmopolitan place—but the dancer scene was a local dance scene but it wasn't the church dancers. It was moving out of the comfort zone of letting your adolescent kids go to a church dance and to letting your adolescent kids go to a place where people might have whisky in a paper bag and maybe sneak outside and smoke a little of this and that. It was the whole start of a Latin counterculture among the youth. The first generation of the bands were the ones who started it and then very quickly was the second generation of bands. The second generation of bands, Willie Colón and all of those guys, that was the maturation of those kids who came to those dances.[15]

Figure 8.1 Willie Rodríguez, Lehman Center, the Bronx, June 21, 2016. Copyright Sue Miller.

Some conjunto groups became known as bugalú bands, whereas others did not stake their reputation on the style but nevertheless threw in a couple of bugalús into their sets for purely commercial reasons. The influence of bugalú on those musicians growing up as teenagers in the 1960s also contributed to musical change further down the line, as Weinstein mentions above. Willie Rodríguez, initially pianist in percussionist Pete "El Conde" Rodríguez's group in the 1970s, has performed with conjuntos (Conjunto Libre), charangas (Orquesta Broadway, Charanga América), Latin big bands (Machito), and smaller Latin jazz ensembles. Although too young to join the bugalú bands of the late 1960s, he grew up in the Bronx surrounded by a rich mix of Latin and African American musical forms and asserts that African American styles were also part of his musical background:

> I am a product of the Bronx and we were saturated with music from our neighbors who were doing R&B, our other neighbors who were doing popular music, doo-wop stuff, that we just heard everything. And I'm the youngest of three so my older brother and sister were into music because everybody had their record players. So I listened to all their stuff plus whatever I liked. So all of those things influenced what you ultimately did.[16]

According to Juan Flores, the bugalú style came into being due to African Americans requesting soul elements from Latin bands playing in the

Palm Gardens during Sunday dances attended by black teenagers (a venue which later became the Cheetah Club).[17] This dance-floor interaction almost certainly lies at the root of this musical style for the younger bugalú era Nuyorican musicians.

"I Like It Like That" by African American Chris Kenner was recorded in 1961[18] and was covered (some say quite badly) by the Dave Clark Five in 1965. The Pete Rodríguez song bears no resemblance to the Dave Clark Five version and has only a few affinities with the Kenner song, in that a few of the gospel/soul elements are taken into the Afro-Cuban fabric of their bugalú number. The title lyric may have proved popular, however, perhaps due to the song title's familiarity with African American audiences. Boogaloo as an African American genre is said to have developed from a hit single in 1965 entitled "Boo-Ga-Loo" by a "light" soul band from Chicago called Tom and Jerry-o.[19] Certainly the party atmosphere, the shouted interjections, and backbeat handclaps are in evidence in most Latin bugalús; but there are differences between those bands who developed their Latin soul in dialogue with African American dancers and those who adopted the style to keep up to date and popular in the wake of the bugalú bands' success.

In the next part of this chapter, I compare Pete Rodríguez's famous bugalú "I Like It Like That" with José Fajardo's "Batman *Bugalú*" to demonstrate the two very different approaches to bugalú performance, and to provide some answers as to why the bugalú style was short-lived and so hated by many Latin musicians who were not themselves teenagers in New York in the mid- to late 1960s.

"I Like It Like That' by Pete Rodríguez and his Conjunto

Here and now, let's get this straight
Bugalú baby—I've made it great!
Because I gave it the Latin Beat
You know child I'm kinda hard to beat!

When Pete Rodríguez recorded "I Like It Like That" for Al Santiago's Alegre Records in 1967, they became known for their performances of the bugalú style and marketed themselves as a bugalú band. Composed by Tony Pabón and Manny Rodríguez (Pete's brother), the song is similar to Ray Barretto's 1962 hit "El Watusi" in that it is built initially on a similar repeated riff accompanied by hand claps on beats 2 and 4 (see example 8.1). Despite the soul backbeat, clave direction is outlined via anacrusis and the bombo beat convergence on the 3-side in the piano and bass parts.

Example 8.1 The Introduction to 'I Like It Like That'—a Cuban *Guajira*/bluesy chord progression outlining 2-3 *clave*.

Ray Barretto's original 1962 recording of "El Watusi," on the album *Ray Barretto Charanga Moderna*, has handclaps only on beat 4 (a more Cuban emphasis), whereas "Watusi '65" on his album *Viva Watusi* has more bugalú elements including claps on 2 and 4, trumpet lines under a new coro, and a soul-styled trumpet line played against the string pedal guajeo.

Example 8.2 Reduced score of Ray Barretto's "El Watusi," the 1962 Tico release.

Simultaneously combining soul and Cuban guaracha elements through stylistic convergence, the 1965 version has more of a party feel about it with less of a Cuban guaracha "Espirtu Burlón" reference to banishing evil spirits (including the *aguadiente* firewater variety).[20] This later version (see example 8.3) has a coro inviting the audience to dance the Watusi, a popular R&B

dance from the early 1960s said to have been inspired by an African Tutsi dance in the film *King Solomon's Mines* from the 1950s (the film trailer states in sensational style "see the sacred dance of the giant Watusi").[21] Sometimes known as the "African Twist," the Watusi dance was probably an African American sendup of the racial stereotyping in the film and was as popular as the twist at this point in the 1960s. Barretto's vocalists call out "Ven a bailar Watusi, Watusi pa' mi; Ven a gozar Watusi, Watusi pa' ti" in a Latinized version of "Do the Watusi."[22]

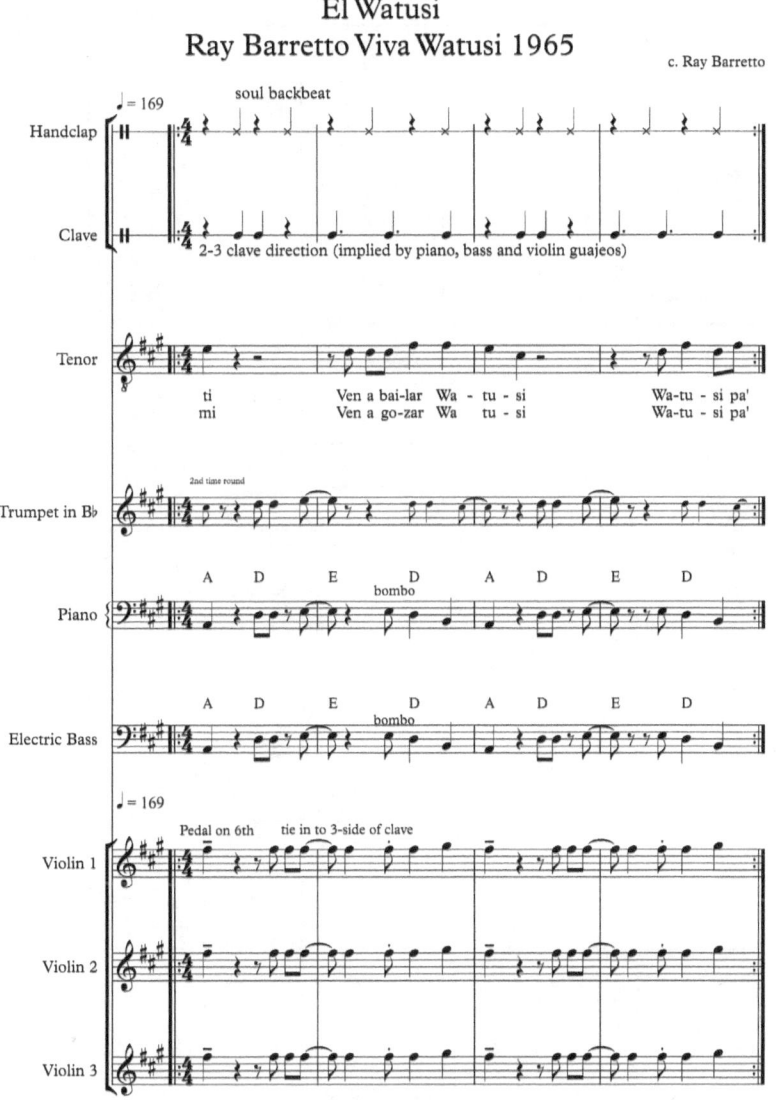

Example 8.3 A second, more boogaloo-infused "Watusi '65" by Barretto's band in 1965.

	INTRO	A VERSES	B BREAK	C CORO 1 "I Like It Like That" female vocals/lead male vocal pregón	D CORO 2 "Stomp your Feet" Male vocals	E MAMBO Brass section
Measures	Pickup + 1–4	5–20	21–22	23–40	41–48	49–62
Number of measures	5	16	2	18	8	14
Subdivision		4 | 4 | 4 | 4		4 | 4 | 4 | 4 | 2	4 Male coro | 2 Coro + percussion escalera | 2 Coro + Mambo starts	2 | 4 | 4 Last 8 bars played up an octave | 4
Tonal Plan F minor	Fm pick up into main riff E♭–D♭–C–Fm	E♭–D –C–Fm	G–C– C–Fm	Fm–Gm♭5–C–Gm♭5– Fm I–ii–V–ii–i	Fm–Gm♭5–C–Gm♭5–Fm 2 bar son montuno in 2-3 clave	Fm–Gm♭5–C–Gm♭5–Fm
Notes	Guajira chord progression VII–VI–V–i			Son montuno progression common to conjuntos	Mambo starts early in Bar 47. The crescendo on the escalera starts in bar 45. two measures early.	A 16 bar mambo which starts early in section D (overlaps)

	F Coro 1 male and female vocals	G Coro 2 "Stomp your feet" male vocals	H Mambo brass section	I Lead vocal ad libs	J Coro 3 Shout "I like it, I like it, I like it like that"	K Mambo	L Coro 1 to fade
Measures	63–78	79–86	87–102	103–112	113–122	123–138	139–fade
Number of measures	16	8	16	10	10	16	4+
Subdivision	4.4.4.4	4 Male coro / 4 Coro + escalera	4.4.4.4 Last 8 played an octave higher	4 Voc + / 4 / 2 percussion break	4 Coro 3 / 4 Coro 3 + percussion break / 2 Coro 3 + escalera	4.4.4.4	4+
Tonal Plan F minor		Fm – Gm♭5 – C – Gm♭5 – Fm					
Notes		The 2mm. escalera cues in the mambo – this time coming in at the beginning of the four measures.		The last two measures "join the party, say like I say" introduces the audience participation.	Male and female vocalists join together to give the impression of the audience joining in. Final 2mm. escalera cues in the mambo section (K)		The fade gives the impression of a party that never ends.

Table 8.1a and 8.1b Introduction to "I Like It Like That": a Cuban guajira/bluesy chord progression outlining 2–3 clave.

The correspondence between "El Watusi" and "I Like It Like That" can be clearly seen in the above examples, although "I Like It Like That" has a bluesier main riff and "El Watusi" a more blues/rock 'n' roll–styled I-IV-V-IV progression. A previous bugalú by Tony Pabón, "Pete's Boogaloo," used a chromatic bassline derived from Peggy Lee's version of "Fever";[23] "El Watusi" similarly uses a unison descending line on piano and bass, which is also characteristic of the Cuban guajira style, as shown in example 8.1. Here the piano and bass unison patterns outline a typical guajira chord progression emphasizing the 2+ on the 3-side of the clave (bombo), thus outlining 2–3 clave direction. In terms of soul, "I Like It Like That" has the hand claps on beats 2 and 4, directly relating to Chicago soul, as does "Watusi '65." The style of delivery therefore draws on both Chicago soul and Cuban performance aesthetics, but there is a conflict in terms of backbeat (the Latin backbeat is 1 and 3 not the 2 and 4 of soul). Certainly the descarga aesthetic is at play in both "El Watusi" and "I Like It Like That," with vocal ad libs and added mambos and guajeos. "I Like It Like That" departs from the opening riff (unlike "El Watusi," which is based on one continuous repeated mambo-style pattern) and could equally be seen as a Latin treatment of a soul tune or as a bluesy version of a guajira montuno pattern.

The 4,4,2 divisions reveal the oral arranging process whereby the percussion two-measure/four-measure escalera [stairs] break of repeated eighth notes cues in the mambo section each time, resulting in the mambo starting two measures early in section D (see example 8.4).

These 4,4,2 divisions do not necessarily interrupt the flow of the music (even measures mean the song stays in 2–3 clave) in that the montuno pattern is of two-measure duration. However, written arranging conventions do not usually break up the four-measure cycle. This disruption of the usual four-measure segment therefore adds to the feeling of spontaneity in this recording, something seen by Flores as one of the defining features of the bugalú.[24] While acknowledging that the earlier Alegre *descarga* sessions also cultivated this emphasis on the open, more improvised montuno sections, Flores characterizes the Latin boogaloo aesthetic as one that encourages spontaneity, put together by ear rather than through the use of written arrangements:

> ... the very aesthetics of boogaloo and Latin soul illustrate this descarga sensibility and can best be appreciated as part of that lineage within the Latin music tradition. In fact, Willie Torres, who had been a vocalist with the Alegre All-Stars until they chose to start using arrangements, moved back to the Joe Cuba group (he had been part of

Example 8.4 The two-measure turned four-measure percussion escalera cueing an early mambo (with overlapping second half of the coro).

the original group in the 1950s) for precisely that reason: he preferred the informal, improvisational mode as being most in tune with his jazz-inspired and jamming creativity.[35]

Approaches to arrangement can vary depending on the type of musicians involved, however, and stylistic differences cannot purely be explained through a written-versus-oral approach. It is easy to classify "street" as non-notational and "middle class/bourgeois/white" as notation-bound, but the reality is much more complex. Many Latin working-class players, for example, were both good readers and improvisers. While "I Like It Like That" seems to have been put together by ear, there would probably have been some form of charts for it, however rough, used by some of the band musicians at some stage. Spontaneity can also be "faked" in the studio through the use of vocal shouts and handclaps while underneath there is a good deal of musical experience and skill employed in the recording. Flores gives Joe Cuba's account of how his hit "El Pito" was recorded, revealing that constraints on studio time led to musicians drawing on their knowledge of the repertoire (chachachá, mambo, Cubop, and son) and also on their experience of live performance:[26]

> The piano vamp is based on a melody taken from Tito Puente's "Oye Como Va" and then used by Charlie Palmieri as a sign-off; the refrain "I'll never go back to Georgia" was from a line by Dizzy Gillespie in "Manteca"; and the sound of whistles in the song were provided by composer/percussionist Henry Alvarez. The whole composition was put together hastily in a recording session just as the allotted studio time was running out. With pianist Nick Jiménez playing the vamp over and over, Sonny recalls, "I got Henry Alvarez, Willie Torres, Jimmy Sabater and the singers doing coros and I said, 'Go in the booth and sing the chorus "Asi se goza." Make all kinds of noise, stomp your feet, clap your hands. This is going to be a party record."'[27]

Similarly, "I Like It Like That" simulates live performance in its production but the song is supported by a knowledge of conjunto performance aesthetics. Incidentally this "Manteca" line is one cited by Weinstein as often subject to "creative" double-entendre reworkings by Latin musicians in New York: "When Joe Cuba's band would say, 'We'll never go back to Georgia,' they would never say, 'Georgia.' They'd say, 'We'd never go back to chocha,' which is the Cuban rude term for the female [sexual] organs. Boys will be boys. Boys will be boys."[28]

While the bugalú bands responded to their African American audiences' soul ad libs and calls for "black power," the cultural meanings of never going back to the American South by Gillespie in the 1950s may not have had such resonance with Puerto Rican youth in the 1960s, at least in this nightclub setting.[29] However, Max Salazar cites musician Tommy Berrios recounting the creation of Joe Cuba's "Bang Bang" in response to a call and response with black teenagers at the Riverside Plaza where, in addition to cries of "bang bang" and "beep beep," there were "black power" calls which were adopted by the band and greeted with black power clenched fist salutes. The record producer Morris Levy, however, did not allow the black power call to be recorded.[30]

Pete Rodríguez's bugalú does draw on both African American soul and Latin dance music elements and was a product of dance-floor interaction during the "black" dances at the Palm Gardens, where Latin musicians responded to the tastes of their mostly African American audience. While the bugalú was a mainly conjunto-led development, Ray Barretto's charanga was a forerunner of the style. In contrast, José Fajardo's "Batman Bugalú"[31] is a response by an established Cuban charanga player to the fashion for bugalú in the late 1960s.

JOSÉ FAJARDO'S "BATMAN BOOGALOO"

Recorded in 1968 for Kubaney Records on the album *Fajardo's Boogaloo*, the arrangement is playful with the theme from the *Batman* TV show intertwined with elements from "El Baile Suavito," a son-chá written by Cuban composer María Aurora Gómez and made famous by Orquesta Aragón. This well-known Cuban montuno runs the length of the track accompanied by a son bass line, congas, ride cymbal, cascara, mambo bell eighth notes, tambourine, and handclaps on beats 2 and 4, as shown in example 8.5.

With tight breaks, coros about Batman dancing the boogaloo, and a virtuosic blues-inflected charanga flute solo, this bugalú does not have the soul party sounds or ambiance of "I Like It Like That." The soul/gospel backbeat and use of the tambourine are the only African American markers here. The arrangement is tight, with well-timed breaks where the element of spontaneity is contained within the vocal and flute improvisations, typical of Cuban performance aesthetics. There are no missed cues or shouted ad libs and the main indicators of the bugalú style are the lyric "Batman Baila Boogaloo, Boogaloo Boogaloo," together with the *Batman* TV theme in the introduction

Example 8.5 Reduced score of the open montuno section of Fajardo's "Batman Bugalú."

and the coda. The flute solo is in the Cuban charanga style but with some playful blues inflections. Having moved to the USA from Cuba in 1961 as an established flute virtuoso and bandleader, Fajardo's attempt to stay current was this album of boogaloos, in much the same way as Orquesta Broadway's "Black Is Black" and Eddie Palmieri and his Orquesta's "African Twist."

"BATMAN BOOGALOO" IMPROVISATION—*CUBANÍA* IN THE CONTEXT OF IMITATION LATIN SOUL

In Fajardo's "Batman Boogaloo" solo he acknowledges African American and American mainstream culture, but maintains his cubanía with a solo that remains firmly in the charanga performance tradition, as demonstrated in example 8.6.[32]

This solo on "Batman Boogaloo"—a rather superficial rendering of "Baile Suavito" adapted to the *Batman* theme with bugalú signifiers (such as handclaps on beats 2 and 4)—nevertheless demonstrates all the elements of Fajardo's soloing style through his use of motivic development, sequential playing, and use of rubato on the romantic "Russian" theme in measures 61–65.[33] Quotation also takes the form of a bugle call, signifying the military. Fajardo uses the bugle call twice (mm. 27, 65–66) and although used regularly in Cuban improvisation (the orquesta típica and charanga have their roots in military brass bands) Fajardo may perhaps be commenting humorously on Batman's combative role.[34] The call and response in measures 47–48 show his percussive aesthetic with timbales-styled figures where the high and low drum head hits are replicated through octave contrasts. The rising sequence m1 in measures 51–55 demonstrates motivic development typical of the style as it rises to the apex d^4 and back to d^3 at the end of the sequence; motif 2 (mm. 55–59) follows a similar trajectory in reverse, moving down from d^4 to d^3. This top-octave tessitura between dominant notes is typical of the style and the level of invention, and the artistry lies in how inventive players are in moving between these two points. Creative variation in terms of motifs and varied rhythmic values and what I term "directional chromaticism" (where diatonic harmonies and clave organization underpin melodic movement) are in evidence particularly in the first part of the solo (mm. 20–26). Later Fajardo plays with the d to $d^♭$ blues—the sharp 4th is a characteristic of the charanga mambo but here it is used to reference the blues/soul and the North American mainstream (mm. 66–69). The recording of "Batman Boogaloo" can therefore be seen as the Cuban chachachá "Baile Suavito" reworked for a different kind of North American audience. The solo, with its tip of the

Batman Boogaloo

Example 8.6 "Batman Bugalú" flute solo by José Fajardo.

hat to blues and soul, still represents cubanía but is situated in the USA. "Batman Boogaloo" is therefore a good example of a commercial boogaloo rather than one forged through live interaction with a soul audience, as was the case with "I Like It Like That."

The distinctions made by Flores are useful here in that the original bugalú bands were born out of direct dialogue by young Puerto Ricans with African American youth on the dance floor. The bugalú style was further propagated through the style's adoption by other types of Latin bands, many of which did not sit comfortably with the 2 and 4 backbeat and English lyrics (which often conflicted with clave). The Latin boogaloo era spanned both types of approach and also later encompassed Latin soul groups such as the Lebrón Brothers and work by Joe Bataan in the 1970s. Traditionally, Cuban dance music forms draw upon popular culture and Fajardo's track is no exception, although the incorporation of the *Batman* theme and superficial signifiers of boogaloo could be seen as jumping on a bandwagon. Many bugalú pieces reliant on a superficial rendering of soul-tinged Cuban dance music, while fun and often brilliantly executed, do quickly fall out of favor. Latin musicians' groans at the mere mention of bugalú may very well relate to these more commercial bugalú versions that they had to play, which did not evolve from direct, socially grounded contexts such as the one in the Palm Gardens scene of the mid-1960s. Fajardo's boogaloo does, however, have energy and spontaneity and still reflects something of those times, but it is not really connected to African American culture in the same way as the younger bugalú bands' work. The recording does however showcase Fajardo's virtuosity and clave-based improvisational style and demonstrates his ability to reference popular American culture in a lighthearted and humorous way.

The mixing of African American and Latin styles inevitably increased with second- and third-generation Latin musicians as they drew on the eclectic mix of musical styles they grew up with in the Bronx, as Willie Rodríguez notes earlier. The younger bugalú bands (rather than the conjuntos and charangas who reluctantly took on the new style) were at the forefront of these developments and, even though the bugalú era was short-lived, these groups were a sign of changes to come. Ray Barretto, who had ushered in this bugalú era with his charanga-styled "El Watusi," continued to experiment with Cuban music by adding jazz, soul, and blues inflection to his music. Similar to Eddie Palmieri, Barretto's adherence to both a típico aesthetic and experimentation with African American styles led to a smoother but no less driving version of New York sabor, as the next chapter demonstrates.

- 9 -

LA CHARANGA MODERNA AND THE MODERN CHARANGA

RAY BARRETTO'S CHARANGA MODERNA: *COCINANDO SUAVE*

Barretto's La Charanga Moderna began life in 1961 as an extension of Johnny Pacheco y su Charanga and Charlie Palmieri's Charanga Duboney. Band members initially included Rod Lewis Sánchez on flute from La Duboney (replaced by Joe [José] Canoura in 1962), Cuban violinists Daniel González, José Andreu, and "Chombo" Silva; and Eliot Romero and Rudy Calzado on vocals. The Palladium star Tito Rodríguez is also on coro for the Riverside recordings of La Charanga Moderna.[1] Puerto Rican pianist and arranger Hector Rivera played piano on the debut Riverside Records release *Pachanga with Barretto/Barretto Para Bailar*,[2] and was replaced by Cuban pianist Alfredo Valdés Junior in 1962.

Orrin Keepnews, the owner of Riverside Records, approached Barretto to suggest he form his own charanga to record pachangas (at the time he had just left Tito Puente's band), underlining the importance of promoters, agencies, and record producers in the development of Latin music in New York.[3] José Curbelo, a successful Cuban pianist and bandleader in New York in the 1940s and '50s, set up the Alpha Artists agency in 1959 to represent Latin musicians and acted for all the now well-known names in Latin music, including Noro Morales, La Playa Sextet, Tito Puente, Tito Rodríguez, Machito, Pete Terrace, Ray Barretto, Vicentico Valdés, and Orquesta Broadway. Al Santiago's Alegre Records was also influential (as outlined in chapters 5 and 6) and his label was later bought by the Tico label. Thus, many of these musicians played together and recorded together; the same roster of Latin musicians therefore appear in different combinations in a variety of bands—if not on stage then on record. Latin arrangers were also part of the New York charanga scene, although it is not always clear on recording credit lines who actually arranged the pieces; bandleaders are often credited (or take the credit) when arrangements have actually been written down beforehand and brought to life through collective band rehearsal. Louie Ramirez arranged for Pacheco y su Charanga, and Puerto Rican pianist Hector Rivera arranged music for Ray Barretto's Charanga Moderna, and these arrangements played a major part in both the *sello* [individual sound] of each group and in the success of these bands.[4] As Charanga Moderna developed, Barretto's openness to jazz and soul led to a different type of charanga-conjunto sound, one that, like Eddie Palmieri's La Perfecta, understood both traditions and wove the two approaches together to form a distinctive New York sabor.

In Cuba, many older musicians active in the 1950s and '60s lament the fact that contemporary dance bands all have the same sound and that it is difficult to tell these groups apart (most modern Cuban musicians train at ENA and ISA conservatories, so some homogeneity is inevitable). As with mid-twentieth-century Havana, 1960s New York had a plentiful supply of charangas, conjuntos, mambo big bands, and bugalú groups, each with their own distinctive sounds (although there was some overlap, particularly with Pacheco's charanga and Charlie Palmieri's La Duboney). In La Charanga Moderna, elements of the charanga and conjunto were combined, as with La Perfecta, but Barretto's band was a different beast. The brass and saxophone additions to some of the Hector Rivera arrangements (with Cuban trumpet player Alejandro "El Negro" Vivar and Cuban pianist Alfredo Valdés Jr. adding cubanía) possessed a different type of jazz sensibility. This differently styled jazz flavoring is in part down to Barretto's dual identity as both a Latin and jazz musician. Barretto (1929–2006) grew up alongside Eddie and Charlie Palmieri in the Bronx in the 1940s; he knew Arsenio Rodríguez and his brothers and went to local dance halls to hear Machito and Marcelino Guerra perform at the Gran Plaza.[5] He became interested in jazz while in the army serving in Munich (1946–49)[6] and, inspired by Dizzy Gillespie and Chano Pozo's "Manteca," he bought some conga drums and started frequenting jazz jam sessions. On his return to New York he performed with Charlie Parker and was much in demand as a session player on both jazz and Latin recordings. He played initially in José Curbelo's band before joining Tito Puente's band at the Palladium, replacing Cuban *conguero* Mongo Santamaría, and was therefore thoroughly versed in Cuban music styles and techniques. Barretto maintains that there is no such thing as "Latin Jazz" or "Jazz Latin" and that "Latin with jazz" is a more accurate description of his work.[7] When asked by Aurora Flores why he kept his charanga going when he was in demand as a jazz session player, Barretto responded passionately with "because I love my music, I'm a Latino, man" but that it was "only part of who I am." He thus identifies strongly with charanga music as a Latino while remaining open to other influences.[8]

Barretto's Charanga Moderna released two albums with Riverside Records during the 1961–62 period before signing to Tico Records, where he recorded a further six Charanga Moderna albums. His "El Watusi" became a mainstream hit, anticipating the Latin bugalú by three years.[9] Although Barretto refers to "El Watusi" as "actually a pretty dumb tune," the interactivity of the piece, dance groove, and live feel gave it a wide mainstream appeal. Barretto talks about how he was inspired to create "El Watusi" in response to a line dance he saw at the Palladium where they were doing little jumps and handclaps; he describes how the band's singer/güiro player Wito Kortwright worked with the dancers in the audience, inspiring the band to respond musically to their steps and handclaps.[10] This same interaction produced the bugalú music of Ricardo Ray, Pete Rodríguez, and Joe Cuba. Although Barretto does not state the day of the week on which this Palladium line dance took place, it may well have been at one of the Sunday African American matinee dances described in chapter 8.

Charanga del Norte pianist Kim Burton describes "El Watusi" as the quintessentially perfect groove which makes her "smile hugely and want to jump up and down." She analyzes why this is the case more technically:

> It ["El Watusi's" groove] is perfect (and I am thinking of the piano/bass pattern primarily) because although skeletal, it encompasses the flexibility of the clave pattern: bar one first interlocking on beats one and two, coinciding through presence on beat three, and then through absence in beat four. In bar two it underlines the ambiguity of the tresillo, explicitly stating the third beat that is only implied in the clave, while outlining the syncopation. All of this is set against the handclap on the last beat of the phrase (or is it an anticipated first beat?), and the implied syncopation of the ostensibly four-square pattern supports the more formal syncopation of the string part, the freedom of the flute solo, and the flexible speech rhythms of the dialogue. The melodic elegance of the figure, which then becomes a faintly ambiguous harmonic underpinning (are the last two beats simply an elaboration of V^9, or is the ii chord doing its own harmonic work to undercut the boldness of the dominant?), combines with the rhythmic uncertainty in an intensely satisfying way.[11]

This groove is analyzed in chapter 8, and I argue here that Barretto's charanga is a fluid synthesis of New York sabor, cubanía, and jazz sensibility that maintains a dance imperative that is perhaps less fiery but more sensual than La Perfecta.[12] This melodic elegance is demonstrated in the next example, "Te

Traigo Guajira," from the 1963 album *On Fire Again/Encendido Otra Vez*.[13] The charanga sound is maintained through the typical pizzicato guajira lines and bowed chachachá-style guajeos in the violins—but Barretto gives the Cuban guajira a subtle New York drive. Here the tempo is a touch faster than a Cuban guajira and evocations of rural life are distinctly lacking. The lyrics refer to the singer as a vagabond (of the first degree!) and also to Ray Barretto himself, grounding the Cuban guajira in a New York barrio performance context. Although more "street" lyrically, the flute solo by Joe Canoura, in contrast, is much less *callejero* in approach and more melodic in concept, perhaps due to the more romantic guajira style. It is not without some cubanía but it has a different effect from the solos analyzed in the preceding chapters. The analysis below suggests that Barretto's Charanga Moderna was more *suavecito* [smoother] in approach due, in part, to the jazz and soul sensibilities of some of his players.

"TE TRAIGO GUAJIRA"[14]

Joe (José) Canoura was La Moderna's main flute player and, like Valentín, he played the metal Boehm system flute.[15] Eddy Zervigón described him as a "*galleguito de español*," a short Spaniard who was a good player on both metal and wooden Boehm system flutes.[16] DJ Al Angeloro also believes Canoura was Spanish.[17] Most of my interviewees did not know much about Canoura, but in an interview for *OffBeat*, Honduran singer Fredy Omar states that Canoura was a flute and saxophone player adept at both jazz and Latin styles who moved down to New Orleans after his stint with Barretto's charanga.[18]

Canoura plays more in the Cuban style than Dave Valentín, with characteristic vocabulary and phrasing throughout; but although there are moments where there is clave sensibility, his soloing is not always clave-aligned. Canoura's solo on "Te Traigo Guajira" is melodic and motivically cohesive, however, and it has Cuban stylistic elements within it including octave leaps, "3-in a grid of 4" figures, some clave-outlining phrasing although with less of a *callejero* on-beat 2-side and off-beat 3-side alignment. Much more in the style of melodists like Richard Egües, Canoura follows the chord progression throughout, with arpeggiated phrases on the Gm, Cm, and D7 chords following the rise and fall of the piano montuno and violin guajeo (shown in examples 9.1 and 9.2). It has less of the Cuban guajira feel but is very sensual and in keeping with Barretto's more "suave" or smooth band sound. There is less attack in the phrasings, however, so it is not in keeping with the usual Cuban flute style performance aesthetic.[19] Perhaps due to his jazz

La Charanga Moderna and the Modern Charanga   211

Example 9.1 "Te Traigo Guajira" textures: coro/pregón section.

Example 9.2 "Te Traigo Guajira" textures under the flute solo, outlining 2–3 clave.

Figure 9.1 Andrea Brachfeld at home in New Jersey, June 17, 2016. Copyright Sue Miller.

background, Canoura negotiates well the use of chromatic variation around the diatonic underpinning of the i-iv-V7 guajira progression,[20] alternating the e^b note of the harmonic minor scale with the $e^\natural$ of the melodic minor scale. As Andrea Brachfeld explains, "most Cuban charanga music is very diatonic and jazz is more chromatic, but the higher-level players in Cuban music play more chromatic, although they keep it to a diatonic kind of vibe."[21]

Clave feel manifests itself in a variety of ways in improvisation, and Canoura's style cannot be said to be without sabor. But it is not "*de la calle*"; the callejero style exemplified by Fajardo and Zervigón has a strong on-beat/off-beat correspondence and a tendency for anacrusis on the 3-side of the clave; beat 4 is often emphasized on the 3-side especially and the bombo (beat 2+) is often an important landing point in phrasing. Cubanía is also revealed through the choice of stylistic vocabulary, the rise and fall within the one-octave high-register tessitura, the style of ornamentation (mordents, turns, and acciaccaturas), the phrasing, and the frequency and placement of percussive figures such as octave leaps, *cinquillos*, danzón *otra* figures, *ponce*, and mambito breaks. Quotations of melodies from the danzón, son, guajira, and chachachá repertoires, alongside American songbook melodies popular in the 1930s and '40s in Cuba, also form part of this *cubanidad*. Canoura's solo contains motivic development, turns and acciaccaturas, and some indicators of clave direction. There is classic couplet phrasing of the chromatic scale and some octave-leap figures in the "3 in a grid of 4" figure characteristic of the style as demonstrated in example 9.3.

Example 9.3 "Te Traigo Guajira" flute solo by Joe Canoura (clave superimposed).

The sequential motivic nature of this solo entails a more on-beat phrasing, less *sonero* or callejero but elegantly melodic and suited to Barretto's approach. Flute players who later recorded and performed with Barretto's bands include the Egües-influenced Cuban flute player Don Fernando González (who recorded on the 1964 album *La Moderna de Siempre*), who presented more technically virtuosic improvisations. González played the metal flute, as did the more jazz-inclined Art Webb, who joined Barretto's Fania label band in 1967. Barretto may perhaps have embraced flute players with a more melodic approach with some jazz inflection and a softer attack in terms of phrasing. The flute became less of a feature in later US-based Cuban dance music, perhaps through a taste for less "aggressive" high flute sounds; additionally, high frequencies have not been caught well by modern recording technologies, and in fact were better recorded in the 1950s and early '60s than in later years.[22] The five-key wooden flute sounds less piercing in the top octave, and metal flute players have to ensure a staccato attack that emulates the wooden flute sound to be stylistic. Joe Canoura therefore has elements of the Cuban improvisational style but less of the attack and intensity of a Cuban five-key flute player; his improvisation is nevertheless well suited to Barretto's smoother charanga sound. Barretto's combining of charanga and conjunto elements with jazz, blues, and soul inflections produced a distinctive *suavecito sello* for La Charanga Moderna, one with a New York sabor different from Orquesta Broadway's assertive cubanía, Pacheco's embalao approach, and Eddie Palmieri's fiery charangueaó en típico sound.

CHARANGA, MODERNITY, AND THE MODERN CHARANGA

In an interview with Aurora Flores, Johnny Pacheco was disparaging about modern groups who add a violin or flute to a conjunto lineup and subsequently name them charangas without understanding how the charanga sound is formed. And it is interesting that Pacheco blended aspects of charanga and conjunto performance within the conjunto formation and did not blend the two traditions with brass, flute, and/or strings in the same ways as Eddie Palmieri or Ray Barretto. Eddy Zervigón has remarked that the charanga sound appears to be simple but is incredibly difficult to get right; this is due to specific culturally rooted performance practices, some of which have been identified both here and in *Cuban Flute Style*. Bandleader and vocalist Jesse Herrero (Pupy y su Charanga, Sublime, and SonSublime) has also stressed his allegiance to the traditional charanga sound, insisting that he keeps his Cuban culture close and is against putting brass in the band, as that loses the charanga essence. He asserts that his band does not sound New York but has *cubanidad*.[23] It is not clear why Barretto labeled his charanga La Charanga Moderna, although presumably the name had something to do with the addition of brass on some recordings and an added jazz inflection. Barretto, with his openness to other musical styles, has often been cast in the role of Latin music pioneer, but what he achieved in Charanga Moderna was, like Eddie Palmieri's La Perfecta, a creative blend of charanga and conjunto practices with jazz and street rumba flavoring. With its associations with classical music, the violin suffers from the perception that it is old-fashioned, so perhaps Barretto wanted to prove that charanga violins "swing á la moderna."[24] Jazz has certainly been used as a symbol of modernity, particularly in the 1920s Jazz Age, and perhaps Barretto's work in jazz, recording initially with Riverside Records (a jazz label), entailed adopting the idea of "jazz as progress." Although Barretto moved away from the charanga format from 1965, his work has always contained elements from the charanga tradition, and many of the musicians from La Charanga Moderna contribute to later albums on the Fania salsa label.

Not all musicians gave up on the charanga format, however, and charanga musicians still performing today talk of work being plentiful in the 1970s and '80s but starting to dry up in the following decade. Some say this was because small venues at the grassroots level could not afford new health and safety regulations and licenses. However, there was a resurgence of bookings of bands for non-Latin audiences in the 2000s following the success of *Buena Vista Social Club*. The grassroots support for this music also persists, with many educational talks and performances taking place at the Hostos Center for the Arts and Culture in the South Bronx, Lehman College Center in the Bronx, summer council events, and dances run by church-run groups and Cuban and Puerto Rican social clubs. Veteran charanga orquestas still playing today include Orquesta Broadway and Típica Novel; Orquesta Broadway continues to perform at the Lincoln Center and other prestigious events and to tour internationally to Europe, Latin America, and Africa, and is held up as an example of traditional Cuban charanga (despite its occasional use of trumpet or trombone).

The charanga-conjunto blends of Típica 73, Charansalsa, and Manny Rivera's Son del Monte are still popular on the Latin scene, and world fusion charanga is provided by Charanga Soleil (produced by DJ Al Angeloro).

Recently, more traditional-styled charanga is being performed by the charangas SonSublime, Yerason, Los Más Valientes, Charanga 76 with Andrea Brachfeld, and Charanga América. At the time of writing, Eddie Palmieri is still performing and the mambo bands continue their legacy with the Mambo

Figure 9.2 Members of Charanga Soleil at the Brooklyn Commons Café, June 2016. Cathy López—vocals; Connie Grossman—flute; Lewis Kahn—violin. Copyright Sue Miller.

Legends, Victor Rendon's Connexión, the Spanish Harlem Orchestra, and Bobby Sanabria's Latin big band at CUNY, among others. The "*Ven tú*" [you come] pickup session jobs in Latin function bands also continue to provide work for Latin musicians at venues such as the Floredita, some with charanga elements and others more conjunto in flavor; but fewer clubs are putting on live Latin music. The shortage of good charanga violinists who can play with the right attack and clave feel may account for the demise of the charanga violin section, and many of the New York bands contain only one violin. Lewis Kahn, a Fania label musician, performs on violin and trombone and a younger violinist in today's Orquesta Broadway also doubles on trombone. The fact that a charanga violin section is not the medium for stardom, reliant as it is on a collective ethos (essential for the rhythmic unison phrasing), means that violinists seeking recognition as soloists look for other idioms in which to make their name. Johnny Pacheco claims his Cuban violinists went to Washington hoping to make their fortunes in classical music, and that was why he turned to the conjunto lineup.[25] The legacy of the mambo big bands means there are still a lot of good Latin brass players on the scene (sustained by several mambo legacy big bands), but there are fewer violinists conversant with the Cuban style of playing. The Cuban violin legacy, in many ways, is instead embedded within Latin arrangements where violin guajeo patterns and phrasings have been transferred to brass and woodwind parts.

The success of the Fania label and its associated musicians has led to the horn section becoming the salsa norm. Joe de Jesus, trombone player

Figure 9.3 Trombonist Joe de Jesus. Copyright Sue Miller.

with Ray Barretto's band in the 1980s, describes the standard salsa band as containing "two trumpets, two trombones, maybe sometimes the sax; the arrangements with the rhythm just going straight through."[26] He talks about how Latin music in the salsa mold has become predictable and formulaic.

Other musicians, such as the musical director of the charanga SonSublime, Jesse Herrero, have also mentioned how arrangements now center around the vocalist and that today there is less of a focus on improvisation and the instrumental side of Cuban dance music.[27] The lack of radio play and the fact that promoters are no longer knowledgeable about Latin music (as producers and promoters José Curbelo and Al Santiago once were) has led to the demise of Cuban dance music in general in the city. However, the smaller radio stations (such as WBAI, with programs led by Chico Álvarez and Al Angeloro) continue to play Cuban dance music, and grassroots community support is still keeping the music alive to some extent through the organization of community dances and events.

While the charanga lineup is no longer as prevalent as it was before the 1990s, its performance aesthetics continue to be relevant to more contemporary forms of Cuban dance music in the city. The analyses of Cuban flute improvisations in these seminal charanga and charanga-conjunto hybrid bands have revealed aspects of sabor in the New York context. The soloists featured reveal elements of cubanía, a Cuban sabor, and/or a New York sabor modified by a long performance history in the city. The final chapter sums up some of the findings of this research, evaluating the contribution of New York–based musicians to the development of Cuban dance music in New York, the USA, and internationally.

Conclusion

DEFINING NEW YORK *SABOR*

The típico concept remains important in the New York context, where clave sensibility is passionately preserved. New York sabor contains elements of cubanía—a quality infused at the outset by influential Cuban musicians—but has a different inflection in New York. Bands were primarily (but not exclusively) made up of Cubans, Puerto Ricans, Dominicans, and American Jewish and Italian musicians, all with a tremendous love and respect for Cuban dance music forms. Cubanía, however, is a lived experience and can be heard most clearly in the improvisations of Cuban players such as Belisario López, José Fajardo, Alfredo "Chocolate" Armenteros, Rolando Lozano, and Eddy Zervigón, whose work I have profiled here. New York Dominican Johnny Pacheco and Puerto Ricans like Tito Puente, Ray Barretto, and Eddie and Charlie Palmieri performed and trained with Cuban musicians; they absorbed the styles, drew on elements of cubanía and, through interaction with a variety of New York audiences at grassroots and more mainstream

Figure C.1 Eddy Zervigón, Brooklyn Bridge, New York, July 16, 2016. Copyright Sue Miller.

venues, created a new performance aesthetic to meet the tastes of their audiences. This New York sabor is by no means uniform, and subtle differences between bands and musicians have been revealed through detailed musical analysis in this book.

Cuban dance music in New York thus followed a related but different trajectory to its island counterpart, one not entirely captured by the mainstream narratives in circulation, such as the Fania-led story of salsa. In terms of a band's sello, one could conclude that Orquesta Broadway had both Cuban and New York sabor with elements of cubanía emanating in particular from the flute soloing style of Eddy Zervigón and the subtle charanga dynamics of conga players such as Carlos Rubio. Pacheco's charanga and Charlie Palmieri's Charanga La Duboney both had an embalao approach, producing sabor with a breathless energy and fizz perfect for the Bronx clubs of the early 1960s. Barretto's Charanga La Moderna produced a smoother combination of charanga and conjunto aesthetics than Eddie Palmieri's fiery trombanga La Perfecta but both were charangueaó en típico. Both groups could be said to have a Cuban sabor with added jazz and blues inflection, and Barretto and Eddie Palmieri demonstrate allegiance to the típico aesthetic of both charanga and conjunto traditions while remaining open to experimentation. The addition of the trombone section plus flute in La Perfecta could be seen as combining the Cuban sabor of the charanga flute with the hard-driving New York sabor associated with the loud moñas of the trombones, which replaced the conjunto trumpet diablo effect; the flute soloist could either add Cuban sabor (Eddy Zervigón and George Castro) or a freer Latin jazz style to the mix (as Dave Valentín did in La Perfecta II). Indeed this tradition continues in the form of Son del Monte, whose latest album image illustrates this hybridity with an image of a violin crossed by a bow-like five-key flute and trombone.

In this book I have shown, through ethnographic work and detailed musical analysis, how the mambo big band, charanga, and conjunto practices are interrelated, and how they developed in the cohesive and artistically rich community of the Bronx over three decades preceding the economic problems of the 1970s. Cuban music made in New York has taken a different path from that within Cuba itself, because, while intrinsically related to pre-Castro popular Cuban musical forms, it developed its own sound and aesthetic through local performance practices. As demonstrated in the earlier chapters of the book, grassroots performances in less well-known venues lie at the root of this popular art form.

There has, to date, been less consideration of Cuban musicians' influence on the development of popular Cuban dance music in New York, with little

Figure C.2 Son del Monte album [*A Charanga with Something More*].
Image courtesy of Manny and Mirna Rivera.

thought given to the power dynamics within bands formed predominantly of Cuban, Puerto Rican, Dominican, Jewish, and Italian musicians (particularly in the mambo big bands), all of whom have shaped the development of Cuban dance music in the city. As Willie Rodríguez has stated, there was immense respect for Cuban music among Puerto Ricans, many learning the idiom from resident Cuban musicians in their own bands, or from bandleaders whose apprenticeships were undertaken in Cuban-led bands (as well as from recordings). The focus here has been on the adoption and adaptation of Cuban musical forms in New York, examining the social contexts for its performance in the city. The complex processes of musical change have been analyzed, particularly through improvisation. To some extent this book complements Juan Flores's *Salsa Rising* in that it brings music analysis and contemporary comment from New York–based Latin musicians together to examine in more musical detail the history and development of Cuban dance music in the city at this time. This is not to say that the standard narrative of Latin music is incorrect, but that the history needs to be understood from a multiplicity of perspectives.

Internationalization of a style without the support of a local, socially grounded context can result eventually in more formulaic and homogenized music, as some contributors to this book have suggested has happened in the case of contemporary salsa. Cuban dance music needs prolonged interaction with a dancing public to develop, and this has been the case in New York, where a Latin community still supports live Latin dance music events in the city. Commenting on the exhibition salsa dance scene, Joe de Jesus underlines the fact that dancing is a communal activity, not a regimented routine-based one:

> Well, here's a thing about dancing. Really, it's supposed to be like a freeform thing. You're supposed to actually improvise on the dance floor, and the man leads, and the woman follows, and he improvises, and so if he feels like turning the girl, he turns her, or the lady. If he feels like separating, or dancing holding each other, you know, it's up to him. So it's not a thing of routines and something that you learn and, "Okay, remember routine number one, routine number two."[1]

I have witnessed the dancing at the Mamoncillo Festival events in New York where this freer, more interactive social dancing takes place; these are the type of performance events where musical change can happen. Connie Grossman, for example, describes how improvisation interacts with a dancing public, demonstrating how an improvisatory style evolves through shared musical movement:

> I know there are differences in dance style, but for me, I notice more in terms of the old-school dancers versus the more modern dancers. One thing that I learned from Eddy [Zervigón], and that I love doing—it's loads of fun—is to have an interchange with the dancers. So I'll watch their feet and if I do notice some of the old-school dancers, I'll key into them and I'll do my riffs along with their feet or sometimes I'll do my riffs to inspire them to move a certain way because I'll see them starting to move in a certain way. So I'll try to keep that going with the riffs that I do, like the rhythm and punches that I'll put in my solos. So it's like the call and response on me, it's like call and response between the flute and the dancer.[2]

The internationalization of Cuban dance music, primarily through Pacheco's Fania label project from the 1970s onward, is blamed by some for the demise of this crucial live interaction. Without grassroots community support in local venues, this dynamic shaping of the music is no longer prevalent. This is perhaps part of the reason why so many Latin musicians avoid the term "salsa" and lament the homogenization of a diverse set of clave-based musical practices. Many prefer to use the term típico and all those interviewed preferred to speak of "Cuban" or "Afro-Cuban" dance music rather than salsa. There is a need to question the continued use of the *salsa* term to refer to such variety of performance practices. If "Cuban dance music" feels less marketable, perhaps a return to típico as a label might be more in keeping with musicians' perspectives. Whatever the label, however, it is time for a review of the standard narrative on the evolution of Latin music in the USA, one more inclusive and evidence-based. Of course even the perspectives put forward in this book are not complete; much more research remains to be done to evaluate and understand these US-based trajectories of popular Cuban dance music.

Alongside dancing, improvisation has been central to the development of Latin music in New York and is an integral part of the music; as noted by Grossman, players interact directly with each other on stage and with a dancing public. As demonstrated in the introduction with the analysis of Alfredo Armenteros's solo on "Bilongo," essential ingredients of the Cuban flute style are also applicable to other instruments (trumpet and trombone in particular) where a clave–driven melodic-rhythmic approach forms part of the típico aesthetic. Weinstein maintains that a melodic approach is the dominant one: "Well, the Cuban trumpet players are melodists. The Cuban flute players are melodists. The Cuban singers are melodists. The only people who play harmony are the piano players. The piano players are allowed to break out of the diatonic model."[3]

As shown in table I.1 in the introduction, stylistic ingredients for Latin improvisation include clave sensibility, "3 in a grid of 4" sequences that resolve in clave, a one-octave tessitura usually from dominant to dominant note (or sixth), characteristic vocabulary (including movement in thirds and sixths), classical ornamentation (turns and mordents often used motivically), and other set performance conventions. These ingredients create sabor and are firmly related to a Latin performance aesthetic. Peter Manuel has discussed various issues involved in trying to define a unified aesthetic for clave-based Latin dance music improvisation and concludes that to do so it is useful to collate specific common technical features, related as they are to "the percussive orientation of modern piano and even wind instrument styles."[4] Certainly the attack in the phrasings of both flute and trumpet, representing *bandas municipales* and orquesta típica roots in the Cuban danzón, have been formative in the creation of a Latin music performance aesthetic.

In terms of musical quotation, Cuban players favor tunes such as "Alagrimo," "El Manicero," "El Gallo Canta," "Dile a Catalina," bugle calls, melodies from the danzón repertoire, and American songbook tunes such as "Blue Moon." José Fajardo's callejero improvisational style, where fewer overt citations are used, rather than Richard Egües's more melodic classical style, seems to be the model most players have followed in the city. This may in part be due to the actual presence of Fajardo in New York while Egües remained in Havana with Orquesta Aragón after the revolution.[5] The callejero street style of improvisation also suited the up-tempo, brasher renditions of Cuban music performed by Johnny Pacheco y su Charanga and La Duboney among others. The New York approach cannot be codified completely, but there is generally an increase in tempo and volume where players' preferences for either melodic sequential playing or more callejero rhythmic practices further differentiate individual styles. Some players have less clave feel but are nevertheless either inventive through experimental free jazz approaches (e.g., Dave Valentín) or more jazz/soul-inflected in terms of approach (e.g., Joe Canoura). Certainly drive, energy, and a dance imperative are common to all of the bands profiled in this book. In tables C.1 and C.2 I outline the differences between the bands and soloists studied here and attempt a summary of each band's distinctive *sello*, where specific musical elements give a variety of nuance to their Cuban and/or New York sabor. In the tables (x), x, xx, and xxx denote the presence of these elements: (x) = sometimes present, x = present, xx = strong presence, and xxx = very representative.

	Fajardo y sus Estrellas	La Sabrosa	Orquesta Broadway	La Duboney + Johnny Pacheco	La Perfecta I	La Perfecta II	La Charanga Moderna
Clave adherence	xx	x	x	x	x	x	x
Embalao				xxx	(x)		
Suavecito/smooth		x					x
Charanga elements	x	x	x	x	x	x	x
Conjunto elements		(x)	(x)		x	x	x
Mambo big band elements				x	x	x	x
Cuban repertoire	x	x	x	x	x	x	
New York repertoire		x	xx	xxx	xx	xx	xx
Jazz inflection		x		(x)	x	xx	xx
Blues/soul inflection		x	(x)			x	xx

Table C.1 Elements of *Sabor* in US-based Latin Dance Bands.

The summary above demonstrates how certain groups maintained their cubanía and Cuban sabor through an older *florear* approach or through Cuban repertoire use, and how the conjunto influence (including the use of trombones), the embalao approach adopted by Pacheco, and elements added from jazz, blues, and soul gave sabor a New York inflection. Not all groups played fast but all adhered to a driving, energetic feel where improvisation was a major part of the overall aesthetic. Eddie Palmieri and Ray Barretto combined Cuban conjunto and charanga performance aesthetics in different ways; Orquesta Broadway added some conjunto inflection (through occasional use of bongo and, in later years, Roberto Rodríguez on trumpet) while maintaining the charanga dynamic, albeit with perhaps a bit more of an assertive articulation than their 1950s Cuban charanga models. As Zervigón has noted, charanga aesthetics differ from those of the conjunto, and a wider range of dynamic is required for the charanga to really groove (particularly in the percussion section). *Conjunto* aesthetics are more often described as having a driving but generally more uniform dynamic. That is not to say that the charanga lacks drive but that its dance impetus is punctuated by the different tuning and voicing of the percussion breaks and associated section dynamics. It is therefore not accurate to characterise all US-based Latin music as purely fast and loud.

In Table C.2 some general differences in improvisational approach are outlined to demonstrate differences between players, which, in general, reflect generational and cultural differences.

Obviously Tables C.1 and C.2 are only extracting the generalities drawn from this study, and the details and more nuance are given in the annotated transcriptions in the previous chapters. The sounds or sellos of the orquestas

	clave sensibility	*florear* melodic approach	*mambear* rhythmic approach	top-octave tessitura	embalao	jazz/blues elements
Belisario López	x	xxx		x		
José Fajardo	xx	x	x	xxx		
Rolando Lozano	x	xx	x	x		x
Eddy Zervigón	xx	x	xx	xxx		
Johnny Pacheco	x	x	xx	x	xxx	
Rod Luís Sánchez	x		x	x	xx	
George Castro	x	x	xx	x	(x)	
Dave Valentín			x		xx	xx
Joe Canoura	x	x		x		x

Table C.2 Elements of Cuban and New York *Sabor* in Improvisational Style.

studied depend on the musicians involved, and also depend on the type of instrumentation involved—the metal flute, for example, adds a different timbre that, unless heavily tongued, is less típico than the five-key wooden charanga flute. Production values and recording technologies are also factors to take into account when describing sellos or sonic signatures.[6]

The level of virtuosity and invention within the Cuban flute tradition in the USA does not match those of either Fajardo or Egües, but Zervigón comes close. Players like Pacheco introduced a new performance aesthetic—embalao—that was also very influential. These "whistleblowers," in Weinstein's terms, were not "primitive," however, as they absorbed the main elements of the style and played, for the most part, in clave. The zestful energy of Johnny Pacheco and Rod Lewis Sánchez's improvisations, the powerful punchiness of George Castro, and the melodic elegance of the more jazz-influenced Joe Canoura complemented the sounds of the New York bands they belonged to. The free jazz approach of Dave Valentín belongs to a different but related Latin jazz trajectory. More study of improvisations by Esy Morales, Hubert Laws, Art Webb, Karen Joseph, Andrea Brachfeld, Nestor Torres, and Herbie Mann are needed to situate these developments within that context. The cubanía and virtuosity of Cuban flute players Rolando Lozano, Belisario López, José Fajardo, and Eddy Zervigón, in particular, have been influential on Latin improvisers both in New York and internationally. In terms of the conjunto, Alfredo "Chocolate" Armenteros's improvisational style on the trumpet has also been hugely inspirational.

Even when performed by Cubans, in New York the charanga strings tend to be busier than Cuba-based bands, and there is a slight difference in terms of attack (in Pacheco's band the Cuban violinists perhaps play a little more loosely than they did in Cuba, for example). Cuban musicians in New York also adapted to their environment, as Eddy Zervigón states in chapter 4, and they were receptive to African American musical styles and to changes in audience demographic. Connie Grossman highlights the fact that there are different approaches within the New York Latin scene itself that further distinguish a band's unique sello, and she makes the important point that influence is not always a conscious thing but one that permeates through depending on one's own musical background and performance context:

SM: I want your thoughts on if you think there's a New York flavor to the traditional Cuban music played in New York? I'm not talking about the Latin jazz fusion so much as the charanga . . .
CG: That's an interesting question because it really depends on the bandleader and what they're wanting to create, and their age maybe.

The musical age, not the biological age, but kind of where their preferences live and what era, because you have young people who have a musical age in the '50s and then you have some older bandleaders that, their musical age is always looking for something new. They're all good and we need them all, just like you need peaches and strawberries and raspberries and blackberries to make a fruit salad (and melon and mango), but I think that if I were to describe something about the New York style, that's like . . . Hmm, okay. . . . There's an element, again depending on what era, I'm thinking like the '60s— Orquesta Broadway, which I think kind of defines and started the whole New York charanga thing, but then there are orchestras like SonSublime. I believe Jesse [Herrero], his goal is really to stick to an Aragón kind of tradition, but I think there's an element, maybe of jazz, but definitely R&B that somehow filters in. Even the more traditional, because you have your rhythm section players, especially if they're a little bit younger, that grew up listening to that. So even if they're not necessarily putting R&B into the arrangement, there's something there.[7]

SonSublime's timbale player, Manny Rivera, while adhering to a charanga típica aesthetic, has played a lot of bugalú and some of that inflection may be part of what Grossman alludes to here. However, it would be a generalization to say that all New York–based bands are more urban, aggressive, driving, grittier, jazzier, louder, and faster. Johnny Pacheco's embalao approach certainly gave his music an energy in keeping with the faster pace of New York City life, and this was taken through in La Perfecta. More jazz inflection was apparent in the piano soloing styles of Charlie and Eddie Palmieri and in the jazz- and blues-influenced improvisations of Rolando Lozano's later work and Dave Valentín's freer style. In Table C.2, you can see that not all players followed the embalao approach of Pacheco and Sánchez in La Duboney. Eddy Zervigón was obliged to play more up-tempo repertoire in Orquesta Broadway but it was not embalao. Eddie Palmieri's charangueaó en típico approach epitomized a fiery New York jazz-tinged energy, whereas Barretto's Charanga Moderna with its different charanga and conjunto combination is more *suave* [smooth]. Orquesta Broadway perhaps best exemplifies the blend of cubanía and New York sabor, with its charanga aesthetic responsive to New York audiences' tastes. There is no clear divide between Havana- and New York–based bands; but, as Karen Joseph remarks, "you play yourself, you play your environment,"[8] and the environment of 1960s New York in particular reshaped Cuban dance music, building on earlier representations of rhumba and swing-infused mambo in the city. Performance aesthetics changed as musicians adopted and adapted típico approaches to suit both their local audiences and their appeal to promoters and recording industry entrepreneurs. The various combinations of charanga and conjunto performance practice in many ways characterize the differences in sound between these New York bands.

There are several important bands and musicians not included here, due, in part, to geographical restrictions, and to the need for analytical depth, necessitating fewer case studies. The focus has also been on the charanga format, which has consistently been underrepresented in previous historical accounts. There are, of course, many more Latin flute players worthy of study and analysis who are part of this New York story, including Esy Morales (who performed in his brother Noro Morales's rhumba band), Panamanians Mauricio Smith Sr. (Mario Bauzá and Tito Rodríguez) and Mauricio Smith Jr. (Típica Novel), and Miami-based musicians who also worked in New York such as Gustavo Cruz (Charanga América and previously in Havana-based Orquesta Sensación), Andy Harlow/Kahn, and Nestor Torres (Típica Novel).

Important connections between New York and Miami have been mentioned only briefly here; the complex *ida y vuelta* [back-and-forth] relationship Cuban musicians have maintained between the two cities is important. As a first base for many Cuban musicians (and often later a place of retirement), Miami has a different sabor and has played an equally important part in the history of traditional Cuban and more contemporary Latin music forms; Miami-based charanga flute players such as Gustavo Cruz (Hansel y Raul), René Lorente (ex–Orquesta Aragón) (see figure C.3), and Nestor Torres (Cachao Master Sessions recordings) have been highly influential. Many Cuban musicians have settled in Miami, as Zervigón states, as it is closer to the mother country and the climate is similar. Nestor Torres made his name in New York in the 1970s before moving to Miami and is an international Latin Grammy award winner who tours regularly. Gustavo Cruz moved from New York, after many years with Charanga América, to perform with Hansel y Raul. On a local level, Eduardo Aguirre runs hybrid charanga group Típica Tropical in Miami. Bassist Robert Heredia and charanga flute player Andy Harlow run the *Fusion Latina* radio show on WDNA, regularly promoting charanga and other Cuban dance music forms. Robert Heredia runs regular descarga jam sessions at the Hot Spot, led by leading Latin performers, keeping the Cuban traditions alive. Rene Lorente, former flute player with Orquesta Aragón, emigrated to the USA in the 1990s but his performance style remains rooted in traditional Cuban charanga performance.[9] Much more research is needed into Cuban dance music performance in Miami;

Figure C.3 Gustavo Cruz and René Lorente—*Cubanía* in Miami, July 2, 2016. Copyright Sue Miller.

the *ida y vuelta* relationship between New York and Miami certainly needs further exploration.

Outside the mid-twentieth-century focus of this work, more research is needed to evaluate the work of Latin musicians from the 1970s to the present day in New York. A male-dominated history of the music is inevitably reflected here, given the time frame; more analysis of contemporary players would include work by female Latin flute players such as Connie Grossman, Andrea Brachfeld, and Karen Joseph, but this lies beyond the remit of this current work.[10] Similarly the contribution of African American musicians to Latin music in the city needs further elaboration, and not only in the context of bugalú. Pictured in figure C.4, for example, is one of the few African American musicians on the Latin scene today, the wonderful cellist John Henry Robinson III (in addition to higher profile musicians such as Karen Joseph and Art Webb).[11]

Building on the mambo, chachachá, and guaracha styles, New York–based versions of Cuban dance music could be seen as purely imitative or watered down, and some see the appropriation of Cuban repertoire as proof of a "smash-and-grab" approach.[12] Whatever exploitative record industry practices undoubtedly occurred, the considerable recorded output of New York–based Latin musicians is testament to the creative adoption and adaptation of Cuban music produced for a socially cohesive Latin community in

Figure C.4 Charansalsa's John Henry Robinson III on cello at Fiesta de San Juan Bautista, Foley Square, New York, June 26, 2016. Copyright Sue Miller.

New York's barrios. Many of the musicians involved were also Cuban and the music was therefore directly part of their culture. *Distinto y diferente*, these New York–based bands have developed their own performance aesthetic and sello while simultaneously maintaining a típico aesthetic: *Tienen sabor, sabor, sabor—y mucho más.*

GLOSSARY

Abakúa
An Afro-Cuban secret society from within the Palo Monte Afro-Cuban religious practice.

a caballo
A conga pattern commonly used in the pachanga. Meaning "on your horse," the sounds imitate a galloping horse.

aguinaldo
A Puerto Rican musical form of jíbaro or "peasant" origin characterized by décima poetic lyrics and an instrumentation of Puerto Rican cuatro, guitar, güiro, and bongos.

bachata
A style of music and dance music from the Dominican Republic originating in the 1960s and popularized internationally in the 1980s and 1990s.

barrio
A term meaning suburb that is often used in the form of *El Barrio*, meaning Spanish Harlem, where a Latin, largely Puerto Rican population migrated from the 1920s onwards, replacing Irish and Jewish populations. While many moved to other areas of the Bronx and Brooklyn, this part of East Harlem has traditionally been seen to represent the quintessence of Hispanic/Latin New York. This *barrio latino* in East Harlem is conceived as being located between 96th Street and 140th Street before merging with the South Bronx.

bandas municipales
Wind and brass bands common in late nineteenth-century Cuba, often derived from bands attached to the military, the police service, or fire brigade, with a close relationship to the orquesta típica.

bomba
An Afro–Puerto Rican music and dance genre characterized by call-and-response singing (coro and lead vocal), improvised vocal responses, and the use of bomba drums (a goat-skin drum called a *cúa* and a large maraca). Congas are sometimes used in lieu of the bomba drum.

bombo
The 2+ beat on the 3-side of the clave. This beat is often the one place where all the rhythmic and melo-rhythmic clave-organized patterns coincide.

Borinquen
The indigenous Taino Indian name of Puerto Rico before the Spanish conquest. A *Boriqua* is someone from Puerto Rico.

bugalú
Also spelled *boogaloo* or *bugaloo*, a fusion of African American soul and Cuban dance music that emerged from the New York–based conjuntos and was popular in the late 1960s.

callejero
Meaning "of the street," this term is used to characterize a musician's rhythmic improvisational style as opposed to a more melodic or "classical" approach.

charanga
Traditionally a lineup of violins, flute, piano, bass, güiro, timbales, congas, and singers. This formation developed the danzón from the late nineteenth century, creating the new danzón del nuevo ritmo and subsequently the mambo in the 1940s, and spawning the chachachá style in the 1950s. A very popular format in early 1960s New York, promoted under the banner of the pachanga "style."

charanga típica
The heyday of charanga was in the 1950s in Cuba and the early 1960s in New York. The charanga típica style is generally acknowledged as having its definitive form during the 1940s–early 1960s. In New York the term *típico* refers to performance aesthetics within this lineup and also within son sexteto, septeto, and more traditional conjunto lineups.

cierres
Ensemble "breaks" (unison rhythms designed to punctuate the music's structure), used to announce a change of section or soloist. Sometimes tutti breaks are called *efectos*, and unison "breaks" by the timbales and the flute are called mambitos (little mambos).

cinquillo
The five-note rhythm that characterizes the danzón.

civicas
Social clubs in 1920s and '30s New York, often specifically for Puerto Rican and/or Cuban clientele.

clave
The two-measure rhythm that acts as a timeline or organizing principle of Cuban music. Consisting of one measure that is more syncopated and another more "on-beat" it is played either in 2–3 or 3–2 direction. *Claves* are the two wooden sticks that play this rhythm in a Cuban son lineup; in other dance band lineups, the clave rhythm is often implied by the patterns of the other instruments or melody but not overtly stated.

comparsa
A percussion and vocal Afro-Cuban style incorporating the *corneta china* and/or brass and woodwind melody instruments.

conga dance
A nightclub version of the comparsa street parade.

conjunto
The son conjunto developed from the sextetos and septetos of the 1920s and 1930s. Arsenio Rodríguez is credited with the expansion of the son sextetos as he added congas and piano to the format. The conjunto is considered more *estilo negro* than the sonora and is characterized by higher register trumpet lines and diablo figures. The sonora lineup is the same but features lower-register, smoother trumpet lines.

corrido
A Mexican song traditionally in the form of a ballad with vocals accompanied by one or more guitars.

danzón
A Cuban music and dance style developed in the nineteenth century from the contradanza or habanera. "Las Alturas de Simpson" is an example of an early danzón in orquesta típica style (through-composed and with no montuno section). "Bodas de Oro" is an example of a later danzón that incorporates the chachachá style within the montuno section. The *danzonete* and danzón-chá were popularized by the charangas of the 1940s and '50s. The danzón is characterized by its rondo form with an introductory *paseo* [walking] section followed by sections for violins and flute. A montuno section was added in the 1930s.

danzón del nuevo ritmo
The extended Cuban danzón form invented by Orquesta Arcaño y sus Maravillas in the late 1930s and '40s. A more syncopated section was added to the recorded danzón "Mambo."

danzón-mambo
A danzón which finishes with a mambo-style open vamp section, as in the "Mambo" composition by Orestes López recorded by Arcaño y sus Maravillas.

descarga
Cuban jam session.

descargar
To improvise. Literally meaning "to offload," this is the term most used for improvisation by Cuban musicians. Contained in this word is the meaning of "release." Other terms for flute improvisation used by players are *florear, hacer floreos, montunear,* and *mambear*.[1]

diablo
The name given by tres player and composer Arsenio Rodríguez for a trumpet line of a mambo section usually lasting sixteen measures, which is either written or improvised and is used to heighten the intensity of a performance and often to conclude a piece. The name *diablo* makes reference to Afro-Cuban Palo Monte religion, in particular the masked dancers or "diablitos" of the Abakúa ritual.[2]

diablitos/diablos
Mambo figures ("little devils" or "devils") at the end of an arrangement used to bring the song to a climax. This build in intensity imitates the *toques de santos* rituals of Afro-Cuban religious music and dance. Arsenio Rodríguez claims to have introduced this mambo section to the son montuno form.

efectos
Whole-band breaks, usually composed and part of the arrangement.

Elegua
Cuban Orisha (spirit) also known as *Elegbá* and *Esu-Elegua* from the Lucumí religion—a trickster, interpreter, and god of the crossroads. All *Toques de Santos* (Santería ceremonies) start with a call to Elegua, the opener of pathways. See **Santería**.

escalera
"Stairs," also known as **mecha** in the USA. A break primarily employed by the rhythm section to build up intensity, starting piano (quietly) and building up to forte (loud), often following a mambito break or cierre.

estilo blanco
A style associated with bands in Cuba who played for predominantly white Cubans and tourists.[3] See **hembra**.

estilo negro
A style of performance associated with bands playing for Afro-Cuban working-class audiences. See **macho**.[4]

estudiantinas
A band formation that originated in the late nineteenth century, usually consisting of a tres, two guitars, one trumpet, a double bass, timbales, cowbell, güiro, and three singers. Said to have originally been composed of university students. Can be seen as a prequel to the septeto in terms of instrumentation, but features musical elements from the son, típica, and charanga traditions. Characterized by the use of the cinquillo and baqueteo to perform danzón and son repertoire.

flauta de cinco llaves/five-key flute
The five-key pre–Boehm system flute probably came into Cuba via the French after the Haitian revolution of 1789, when French colonialists and

their African slaves fled Haiti and settled in Santiago de Cuba. Until modern times, most charanga flute players played this flute. Many flute players today insist that the real sound of charanga can only be achieved with the *flauta de cinco llaves*, it being very loud in the top register, ideal for percussive altissimo playing, and having less sustain than the Boehm system flute.

florear
To improvise or embellish.

folklórico
Term introduced by musicologist Fernando Ortíz and mainly applied to Afro-Cuban religious music and dance. Ortíz is well known for several books on Afro-Cuban music, including *La Africania de la Música Folklórica de Cuba* (1965).

gallego
Term used to describe lighter-skinned Latinos. Also a stock character from the Cuban *teatro bufo*.

guajeo
The term for a repetitive, rhythmic violin riff, usually lasting two or four measures, which fits around the clave timeline and locks into the rhythm section patterns of the piano, bass, congas, and timbales.

guajira
A style of music similar to the bolero, often featuring an arpeggiated montuno with anacrusis. Lyrics usually describe an idyllic life in the countryside (related to *música campesina*).

guaguancó
Rumba dance involving a male dancer *el gallo* (the cockerel) and a female dancer *la gallina* (hen), which enacts courtship and insemination (*vacunao*, euphemistically called "vaccination").

guaracha
The early guaracha was associated with the *teatro bufo* vernacular theater. The more well-known guaracha-son is similar musically to the son style, and this form is usually associated with humorous stories. Cuban classic "Pare Cochero" is typical of the genre—it describes a bumpy ride on a bus with a delicate traveler ("*chico delicado*") complaining he is about to lose

all his internal organs if the driver does not stop the bus and let him get off. Often all that distinguishes a son from a guaracha is the latter's slightly faster tempo and the lyrical content. Eddy Zervigón defines the guaracha as having a two-chord tonic-to-dominant montuno structure (V-I or I-V) taken at a mid- to fast tempo.

güira
Metal scraper used in Dominican merengue.

güiro
A gourd or gourd-shaped scraper (in wood or plastic) that provides the rhythmic impetus in Cuban music, especially in charanga.

habanera
A Cuban *danza* dating from the mid-nineteenth century, containing the tango rhythm. The precursor to (some say the same as) the contradanza and subsequently the danzón. The word contradanza was sometimes shortened to *danza*, later becoming the longer danzón (the suffix "ón" means "large").

hembra
Another term for **estilo blanco**. A gendered term to imply a weaker performance, one less infused with Afro-Cuban culture. Also the name for the larger drum in the bongo set.

inspiración/guía
The term for the short improvisations in between coros in the montuno section—these can be vocal or instrumental.

jíbaro
Música jíbara or "peasant music" is Puerto Rican country music, with aguinaldo and seis the main styles associated with the term.

llamada
Literally "the call," where the soloist plays the tune (often of the coro) to signal the end of the solo and/or as a cue to the next section.

machete
Fast pattern played on the güiro imitating the sound of a machete cutting down the cane.

macho
Another term for **estilo negro**. Another gendered term to imply a stronger performance. Also the name for the smaller drum in the bongo set.

mambo
1. The name for a genre of music. Several styles of mambo are generally acknowledged. The charanga mambo by the López brothers in the charanga orquesta Arcaño y sus Maravillas was contemporaneous with the son conjunto mambo with its final diablo section, pioneered by Arsenio Rodríguez. The big band mambo of Pérez Prado, Benny Moré, and the Havana big bands of the mid- to late 1940s incorporated aspects of both the charanga and conjunto mambo. The New York big bands of Machito, Tito Rodríguez, and Tito Puente in the late 1940s and 1950s were influenced by all three mambo formats (charanga, conjunto, and big band mambo styles).
2. An eight- or sixteen-measure figure, usually played in the montuno section by brass instruments, used to break up sections of an arrangement in order to increase intensity. This is also sometimes referred to as moña. This section derives from the diablo section as developed by Arsenio Rodríguez.
3. A dance popularized in the Latin big bands and made famous by the Palladium dancers.

mambo batiri
A category of mambo identified by Pérez Prado to denote rumba-influenced mambo.

mambo caén
A category of mambo identified by Pérez Prado to denote son-influenced mambo.

mambito
A highly rhythmic break (or "little mambo") on the dominant note played by the flute and percussion section to create suspense in the middle of a flute solo.

marcha
Another term for the basic conga pattern or tumbao. This pattern also changes according to the direction of the clave.

mecha
A percussion buildup (literally, the "fuse") of repeated eighth notes starting quietly and making a crescendo usually over four to eight measures into a new section (usually a solo section from a brass or wind instrument). See **escalera**.

merengue
A Dominican Republic music and dance style characterized by an instrumentation of guitar and cuatro or button accordion, the double-headed tambora drum, a metal scraper known as a güira, and an alto saxophone. Conga drums and electric bass were added in the latter part of the twentieth century.

moña
An improvised eight- or sixteen-measure mambo played toward the end of an arrangement in the montuno section and functioning in a similar way to Arsenio Rodríguez's diablo.

montuno
1. montuno section
   The open section where coro/inspiración and solo improvisations take place.
2. piano montuno
   The piano montuno is the two-measure pattern based around clave, which has two forms: 2–3 and 3–2. A 2–3 montuno typically starts on the beat on the 2-side of the clave and ties over by an eighth-note on the 3-side. This is reversed for 3–2 montunos.

nuevo ritmo
A new rhythm developed by musicians in Antonio Arcaño's charanga Arcaño y Sus Maravillas in the 1930s in Havana, which became the prototype for the ensuing variety of mambo styles in the 1940s and '50s. See **danzón de nuevo ritmo**.

Nuyorican
A Puerto Rican born in the United Sates. This can be spelt as "Newyorican," "Nu-Yorican," and in Spanish, "Neoyorikan." Not all New York–born Puerto Ricans use this term to describe themselves; some prefer to say they are New York–born Puerto Ricans.

ophicleide
A brass-woodwind hybrid instrument invented in 1817 in Paris, used in military bands and adapted to the Cuban orquesta típica.

orquesta típica
The orquesta típica played contradanzas and, later, danzones. It usually is composed of two clarinets, two violins, a cornet, timpani, güiro, ophicleide, double bass, valve trombone, and a tuba.

pachanga
A popular "style" that followed the chachachá in the late 1950s, inspired in part by Cuban Eduardo Davidson's composition "La Pachanga" ("The Party"), written for Orquesta Sublime in 1959 and later popularized by José Fajardo. Stylistically, the pachanga is very much like (identical to, in some cases) a fast guaracha with optional added rhythmic elements in the percussion section borrowed from merengue. In the USA the term was used to market most Cuban dance music styles played by charanga orquestas in the early 1960s. Early pachanga renditions modelled on Davidson's composition are distinguished by a cut common "two" feel like a merengue and an a caballo conga pattern. However, many New York pachangas of the 1960s do not conform to this model.

Palo Monte
Afro-Cuban syncretic religion involving music (usually percussion and vocals only) and dance. This is a Congo religion (Bantú tribes from Angola and the Congo) as opposed to Santería, which is associated with the Yoruba religion (Lucumí tribes from Nigeria).

plena
An Afro–Puerto Rican music and dance style related to the **bomba** and originating in the late nineteenth century. Instrumentation consists of responsorial vocals and the *pandero* handheld drum. In more commercialized form, the instrumentation expands to include guitar, accordion, güiro, congas and trumpet, and, later in big band form, timbales, piano, bass, and saxophone.

pregón
Vocal improvisations in between coros in the montuno section.

rumba
Percussion, dance, and vocal secular form of Afro-Cuban music, usually divided into the three main styles of guaguancó, yambú, and columbia.

rhumba
Term that originated in the United States in the 1920s and was in use mainly in the first part of the twentieth century to refer to commercialized Cuban son styles of music and dance. Originally meaning "party," rhumba covered musical stylings associated with Cuban son, tourist comparsa (the conga dance), and Afro-Cuban elements embedded within the son. Arthur Murray and others taught and popularized the rhumba and later styles in their dance academies.

sabor
A multifaceted term used to describe "feel" or "swing" in Latin music. Often used to describe clave feel and "in style" improvisational performance.

salsa
Originally a marketing term for Cuban music meaning "sauce," the salsa name for Cuban dance music originated in the latter part of the 1960s in New York (although a Venezuelan DJ is said to have coined the term). It has since come to denote a particular style of Latin dance music developed in the main by Puerto Ricans in New York. The genre is now transnational with many different performance practices (in both music and dance) internationally.

salsa dura [hard salsa]
Cuban dance music performed by a generation of New York–born, mainly Puerto Rican musicians. The salsa dura aesthetic foregrounded improvisation, mambo/moña/diablo sections, and call and response within the open montuno section. It can be seen as growing out of the charanga and conjunto scene in New York in the late 1950s and early 1960s. The term is often used in contrast to the later **salsa romántica**, which downplayed the importance of improvisation and the diablo climax.

salsa romántica
A smoother style of salsa privileging sung verses and uniform tempos. Characterized as less hard-driving and with an emphasis on romantic love rather than barrio commentary, it has been critiqued by some as **salsa monga**. The form emerged when the Fania label was on the wane and when merengue

and Latin pop were becoming more in vogue. There are not always clear differences between music characterized as classic/dura or romántica.

salsa monga [limp salsa]
A derogatory term for **salsa romántica**.

Santería
Afro-Cuban religion involving music (usually only percussion and vocals) and dance. This is the religion of the Yoruba tribes (Nigeria). Also referred to as *La Regla de Ocha*.

sello
Literally meaning "seal," this term is used to describe a band's unique distinguishing sound.

son
The traditional son lineup included maracas, claves, bongo, guitar, tres, double bass, and vocals.

son conjunto
An enlarged son lineup that includes piano, congas, three trumpets, tres, maracas, bongo, bass, and vocals.

son montuno
A son style using a larger lineup, usually with piano. Also used to describe the more montuno-based arrangements of son, where introductions and verses tend to be truncated and the emphasis is on the open section and improvisations.

sonero
Male vocalist in the son lineup who improvises inspiraciones/pregones as well as longer extended solos or *guías*.

sonora
A son lineup that includes piano, congas, three trumpets, *tres*, *maracas*, *bongo*, bass, and vocals. Said to be smoother than the son conjunto with lower-register trumpet lines featured in their arrangements.

tambora
A double-headed drum used in Dominican merengue.

toques de santos
Religious ceremonies on saints' days.

trombanga
A term said to have been invented by Charlie Palmieri when referring to his brother's band La Perfecta, which utilized trombones instead of violins (charanga) or trumpets. Fusing charanga elements such as the Cuban flute with the conjunto lineup, Eddie Palmieri created a hybrid format in La Perfecta of the 1960s that paved the way for the standard salsa lineup in the 1970s. This instrumentation was also employed by percussionist and bandleader Manny Oquendo in his Orquesta/Conjunto Libre.

tumbao
Tumbao can simply mean "pattern" but is mainly used for the bass and conga patterns. Both bass and conga tumbaos emphasize the "and" of beat 2 (2+) and beat 4.

NOTES

Preface

1. Sue Miller, *Cuban Flute Style: Interpretation and Improvisation* (Lanham, MD: Scarecrow Press, 2014). See also Sue Miller, "Flute Improvisation in Cuban Charanga Performance: with a specific focus on the work of Richard Egües and Orquesta Aragón," PhD thesis, University of Leeds, December 2010.

2. According to DJ Lubi, between 1995 and 2002 the "Casa Latina was probably the best live salsa, Cuban, or Latin session outside London, probably even better than most London nights." Personal correspondence from Lubi Jovanovic August 27, 2013. The club moved to the Wardrobe, Leeds, in September 1999 and continued to put on live bands from Cuba and the USA, although less frequently after 2002.

3. Mongo Santamaría, "Olga Pachanga," *Arriba* (Fantasy 8067, 1963).

4. Mongo Santamaría, "Que Maravilloso," ¡*Sabroso!* (Fantasy 8058, 1960; CD reissue, OJC Records B000000YFS, 1991).

5. Ray Barretto, "Esa es La Del Solar," *Viva Watusi* (Sonodisc CDW 4058, 1990).

6. Charanga del Norte, "Violin Pachanguero," *Charanga del Norte—Everybody Salsa Volume 1* (Avid Records, BMG, AVC 636, 1998).

7. Al Angeloro, DJ, radio presenter, and Latin music promoter. He regularly featured Orquesta Broadway on his WBAI show *Montuno* (John Child, "Orquesta Broadway," in Colin Larkin [ed.], *The Guinness Encyclopedia of Popular Music* [New York: Guinness World Records Publishing, 1992]).

8. Miller, *Cuban Flute Style*.

9. The *mamoncillo* is a tropical lime green fruit with a creamy pulp inside. According to Eddy Zervigón, a festival was traditionally held for the mamoncillo harvest in Cuba in the Polar Cervecería gardens (telephone conversations, August 2006). Also in Israel Sánchez-Coll and Nestor Emiro Gómez, "En Casa de Eddy Zervigón," *Herencia Latina*, 2003. http://herencialatina.com/Zervigon/Zervigon.htm, accessed August 14, 2012. This tradition started in 1930s Cuba and has continued in New York for the last forty years, according to the Fiesta del Mamoncillo website. http://www.fiestadelmamoncillo.org/mamoncillo_002.htm, accessed August 27, 2013]. According to this website, the tradition started across the road in the Tropical Gardens in Havana.

10. Eduardo Egües senior also taught the famous trumpet player Alfredo "Chocolate" Armenteros in Las Villas, alongside Richard Egües. See Rick Davies, *Trompeta: Chappottín, Chocolate and the Afro-Cuban Trumpet Style* (Lanham, MD: Scarecrow Press, 2003), 172.

11. Fajardo y sus Estrellas performed at the Waldorf Astoria in 1959 for John Kennedy's presidential campaign. The success of this performance quickly led to a Palladium engagement for the band. After these performances Fajardo went back to Cuba but returned to New York in 1961, having decided to leave Cuba for good after the 1959 revolution. Once in the USA, Fajardo set up his own US-based charanga bands and performed with all the leading Latin musicians of the time, such as the Alegre All Stars, Johnny Pacheco, Belisario López, Ray Barretto, Mongo Santamaría, Machito, and the Palladium bands of Tito Puente and Tito Rodríguez (among others). See Miller, *Cuban Flute Style*, 15–16; John Child, "Fajardo, José Antonio" in Donald Clarke (ed.), *The Penguin Encyclopedia of Popular Music*, 2nd ed. (London: Penguin Books, 1998); and Gaspar Marrero, "José Antonio Fajardo: Evocación," paper given at the conference Encuentro Nacional de Orquestas Charangas Rafael Lay in Memoriam, *Palma Soriano* XIV, 1998.

12. Raúl Fernández, *Latin Jazz: The Perfect Combination/La Combinación Perfecta* (San Francisco: Chronicle Books/Smithsonian Institution, 2002), 27–28.

13. John Storm Roberts, *The Latin Tinge: The Impact of Latin American Music on the United States* (New York: Oxford University Press, 1979), 132.

14. Max Salazar, *Mambo Kingdom, Latin Music in New York* (New York: Schirmer Trade Books, 2002), 182; Ed Morales, *The Latin Beat: The Rhythms and Roots of Latin Music from Bossa Nova to Salsa and Beyond* (Cambridge, MA: Da Capo Press, 2003), 58.

15. Christina Abreu, *Rhythms of Race: Cuban Musicians and the Making of Latino New York City and Miami, 1940–1960* (Chapel Hill: University of North Carolina Press, 2015), 6, 60–61.

16. Sánchez-Coll and Gómez, "En Casa de Eddy Zervigón."

17. *Trombanga* was the term Charlie Palmieri used to describe his brother Eddie's new band La Perfecta with its lineup of trombones and flute.

Introduction

1. "Tiene Sabor" was composed by Ignacio Piñeiro and Rolando Valdés. It has been recorded by innumerable artists, including Abelardo Barroso and Orquesta Sensación, *Cha Cha Cha (with Orquesta Sensación)*, available on the reissue CDs *Charangas de Siempre—Orquesta Sensacíon* (Egrem CD 0846, 2006) and *Abelardo Barroso With Orquesta Sensación—Cha Cha Cha* (World Circuit WCV-088, 2014); Charlie Palmieri y su Charanga La Duboney, *Salsa Na' Ma'* (Alegre LPA 810, 1967) and *Charlie Palmieri & His Orchestra—The Heavyweight* (Tico Records LPS-88.974, Alegre Records–LPS-88974, 1978); Típica (Orquesta) Novel, *Tipicante* (TR Records 114X, TLP 00600 X, 1973); and Omara Portuondo, *Cuba Lost and Found* (World Circuit B00SSJIAXE, 2015).

2. M. Juanita Berríos, Anna Carol Dudley, and Eva Pallán Habell, *American Sabor: Latinos and Latinas in US Popular Music/Latinos y Latinas en La Música Popular Estadounidense*, trans. Angie Berríos-Miranda (Seattle and London: University of Washington Press, 2018), 19, 21.

3. Janice Mahinka, in reader review correspondence for this book in August 2019, put forward the term "savor" but prefers sabor to stand untranslated to account for its multiple meanings.

4. See Sánchez-Coll and Gómez, "En Casa de Eddy Zervigón."

5. Personal correspondence with Eddy Zervigón through WhatsApp, August 2019.

6. See Salazar, *Mambo Kingdom*, 209.

7. In a phone conversation with the author August 14, 2019, Eddy Zervigón defined sabor in terms of rhythmic placement and attack, citing flute player Joseíto Valdés's one-note solos in Orquesta Ideal as having sabor because of this "locked-in" approach.

8. See, for example, Lise Waxer (ed.), *Situating Salsa: Global Markets and Local Meaning in Latin Popular Music* (New York and London: Routledge, 2002).

9. Interest in Afro-Cuban religion and Cuban rumba, particularly from the mid-1960s onward and especially in the 1970s, coincided with political struggles by marginalized Latin communities (e.g., the Young Lords). The famous Central Park drumming groups brought together Cubans, Puerto Ricans, and others, rekindling and building on Machito's Pan-African approach to music making. The term *Afro-Cuban* signified a valorization of the music's African roots. See Berta Jottar, "From Central Park—Rumba with Love," *Voices: Journal of New York Folklore* (New York Folklore Society) 37, no. 1–2 (Spring–Summer 2011): 24–31.

10. See Joe Conzo and David A. Pérez, *Mambo Diablo: My Journey with Tito Puente* (Milwaukee: Backbeat Books, 2010), 277–308.

11. *Rumba* is the term usually used for Cuban styles of music and dance—*guaguancó, columbia,* and *yambú,* among others—and is a genre that uses percussion and vocals. The term originally meant "party" and has also been used as a term for commercialized forms of son (including guaracha) popular in the late 1920s and 1930s in the United States and internationally (following the tango's popularity in the 1910s). When used with this meaning, the term is often spelled with an "h," *rhumba.*

12. Christian Weaver, "The Voice of the Drum in the Vision of the Dispossessed: Social Context, Musical Language and Participation in Cuban Rumba" (PhD thesis, University of Salford, 2009), 9.

13. Paul Austerlitz cites an interview with Bauzá by Anthony Brown. Paul Austerlitz, *Jazz Consciousness: Music, Race, and Humanity* (Middletown, CT: Wesleyan University Press, 2005), 59.

14. Austerlitz, *Jazz Consciousness*, 59.

15. Weaver (2009) also notes that Cuban rumba is both contemporary and popular inside Cuba. For further discussion on this issue of terminology, see also Miller, *Cuban Flute Style*, xxv–xxvi.

16. For a critique of the Fania All Stars phenomenon, see Christopher Washburne, *Sounding Salsa: Performing Latin Music in New York City* (Philadelphia: Temple University Press, 2008). For the standard salsa narrative, see the DVD *Latin Music USA*, Volumes 1 & 2, dir. Daniel McCabe (PBS LMUS601, 2009).

17. Abreu, *Rhythms of Race*, 13.

18. David. F. Garcia, *Arsenio Rodríguez and the Transnational Flows of Latin Popular Music* (Philadelphia: Temple University Press, 2006).

19. See Peter Manuel, "Representations of New York City in Latin Music," in *Island Sounds in the Global City: Caribbean Popular Music and Identity in New York*, ed. Ray Allen and Lois Wilcken (New York: New York Folklore Society, 1998), 23–43.

20. Mario Bauzá, cited in Conzo and Pérez, *Mambo Diablo*, 302.

21. The term *música folklórico* was a result of Cuban musicologists' work valorizing Afro-Cuban culture in the twentieth century as exemplified by Fernando Ortíz. See Robin D.

Moore, ed., *Fernando Ortiz on Music: Selected Writing on Afro-Cuban Culture* (Philadelphia: Temple University Press, 2018).

22. Roberta L. Singer and Elena Martínez, "Tradition and Innovation in Contemporary Latin Popular Music in New York City," *Latin American Music Review/Revista de Música Latinoamericana* 4/2 (1983): 183–202, 99.

23. Several musicians who emigrated to the United States and Europe had formative training in Tata Pereira's charanga and municipal bands, including Emilio Barretto, who made a name for himself as a bandleader in Paris from 1926 until 1997. See Alain Boulanger, *La Havane á Paris—Musiciens Cubains á Paris (1925–1955)* (Saint-Etienne-du-Rouvray, France: Jazzedit, 2018), 43. For more on Tata Pereira, see Miller, *Cuban Flute Style*, 64–70.

24. Salazar, *Mambo Kingdom*, 59.

25. Abreu, *Rhythms of Race*, 56–81.

26. For many Latin musicians the Boy's Harbor conservatory is no longer a grassroots organization connected directly to the Latin music community. It has since been taken over by Berklee Music City Network and is now called Boys & Girls Harbor Performing Arts Academy. See https://www.theharbor.org/performing-arts-academy/, accessed January 24, 2019.

27. Ry Cooder, sleeve notes to Buena Vista Social Club, *Buena Vista Social Club at Carnegie Hall* (World Circuit Production, WCD 080, 2008).

28. Interview with Willie Rodríguez, June 21, 2016.

29. For more on Eduardo Egües's legacy as a music educator, see Miller, *Cuban Flute Style*, 196–97.

30. For more on Armenteros's career, see Davies, *Trompeta*, 171–76.

31. Davies, *Trompeta*, 171.

32. Eddie Palmieri and his Orchestra, *Bilongo* (Tico T-574. 1968).

33. See Miller, *Cuban Flute Style*, 65–97, for a detailed explanation of these earlier approaches to improvisation in the danzón and danzón de nuevo ritmo.

34. For more on the relationship between quotation and repertoire in Cuban dance music, see Miller, *Cuban Flute Style*, 165–92.

35. Eddy Zervigón, Queens, New York, 2012.

36. Conzo and Pérez, *Mambo Diablo*, 197.

37. Research on Cuban charangas and their soloists after the revolution within Cuba is also deserving of further attention but is outside the scope of this current work.

38. The terms "aggressive" and "driving" were used to characterize the New York sabor by David Pérez (interview, June 11, 2016) and Andrea Brachfeld (interview, June 17, 2016).

39. For example, Raul Fernández, *Latin Jazz: The Perfect Combination* (San Francisco: Chronicle Books, 2002), and Vernon Boggs, *Salsiology: Afrocuban Music and the Evolution of Salsa in New York City* (New York: Excelsior Music, 1992).

40. See David Garcia, "Contesting That Damned Mambo: Arsenio Rodríguez, Authenticity and the People of El Barrio and the Bronx in the 1950s," *Centro Journal* XI, no. 1 (Spring 2004): 155–75. See also Garcia, *Arsenio Rodríguez and the Transnational Flows*.

41. Garcia 2004, 157.

42. The sonora is similar to the son conjunto with its lineup of trumpets, tres, piano, congas, güiro, bongos, bass, and vocalists but with lower-register trumpet lines and a smoother sound, as epitomized by Sonora Matancera.

43. The whole area of Latin music improvisation studies is ripe for expansion and has only begun to be explored academically over the last two decades. For more on the Latin trumpet tradition, see Davies, *Trompeta*.

44. Readers interested in these aspects can consult chapter 5, "Real and Imagined Representations of (Afro-) Cubanness and Latinness," in Abreu, *Rhythms of Race*, 141–83.

45. This Chicago-based charanga performed and recorded in New York in 1959.

46. Fajardo defected to the USA in 1961. Miller, *Cuban Flute Style*, 16.

47. John Storm Roberts, *Latin Jazz: The First of the Fusions, 1880s to Today* (New York: Schirmer Books, 1999), John Storm Roberts, *Black Music of Two Worlds* (London: Allen Lane, 1973); John Storm Roberts, *The Latin Tinge: The Impact of Latin American Music on the United States* (1979; New York: Original Music, 1985); Juan Flores, *Salsa Rising: New York Latin Music of the Sixties Generation* (New York: Oxford University Press, 2016).

48. Abreu, *Rhythms of Race*.

49. Catskills resort venues included the Concord, Grossinger's, and Kutsher's.

50. Orquesta Nuevo Ritmo de Cuba, *The Heart Of Cuba: Pachangas & Charangas* (GNP Crescendo GNP 47, 1959). See also Salazar, *Mambo Kingdom*, 183. José Fajardo's late-1950s performances alongside guest performances with pre-1959 Orquesta Aragón were also key to the rise in charanga's popularity at the turn of the 1960s. In an interview with Eddy Zervigón in Queens, June 18, 2016, he stated that Orquesta Nuevo Ritmo started the interest in charanga bands in New York.

51. Ernesto Lechner, sleeve notes to Johnny Pacheco, *Pacheco y su Charanga* (1961; Fania Records 773 130 219-2 CD Reissue Emusica Records, 2007).

52. Flores, *Salsa Rising*, 101–2; Roberts, *The Latin Tinge*, 164.

53. For my own reflections on this male dominance, see Sue Miller, "Perceptions of Authenticity in the Performance of Cuban Popular Music in the UK: 'globalised incuriosity' in the promotion and reception of UK-based Charanga del Norte's music since 1998," *Journal of European Popular Culture* 4, no.1 (2013): 99–116.

Chapter 1

1. See Frank M. Figueroa, "New York's Latin Music Landmarks," in Claudio Ivan Remeseira, *Hispanic New York: A Sourcebook* (New York: Columbia University Press, 2010), 366.

2. Bandleader Joe de Jesus told me he enjoyed putting timba into the mix but that New York audiences did not usually respond well to these elements.

3. Charansalsa's website has more detailed biographies of the band members. http://www.charansalsa.com/biographies.php, accessed November 28, 2016.

4. Christine Abreu, *Rhythms of Race: Cuban Musicians and the Making of Latino New York City and Miami, 1940–1960* (Chapel Hill NC: The University of North Carolina Press, 2015).

5. Interview with Eddy Zervigón, Queens, New York, June 18, 2016.

6. Abreu, *Rhythms of Race*, 61–64 and 84–91.

7. Abreu, *Rhythms of Race*, 82–91.

8. Abreu, *Rhythms of Race*, 61.

9. For more on the history of record companies and labels promoting mid-twentieth century Cuban music see Cristobál Díaz Ayala, *Música Cubana del Areyto al Rap Cubano*, 4ta Edición (Miami: Fundación Musicalia, 2003) [1981], 263–87.

10. Interview with Connie Grossman, Tarrytown, New York, June 18, 2016.
11. Singer, Roberta, L., and Elena Martínez, "A South Bronx Latin Music Tale," *Centro Journal* XVI, no. 1, (Spring, 2004):177–201. Herencia Latina, http://www.herencialatina.com/South_Bronx_Latin/Latin_Music_Bronx.htm, accessed October 24, 2016.
12. See Figueroa, "New York's Latin Music Landmarks," 362–63, and Salazar, *Mambo Kingdom*, 107, 33.
13. Conzo and Pérez, *Mambo Diablo*.
14. Singer and Martínez, "A South Bronx Latin Music Tale," 5.
15. Singer and Martínez, "A South Bronx Latin Music Tale."
16. Morales, *The Latin Beat*; Ed Morales, "The Story of Nuyorican Salsa," in Claudio Ivan Remeseira (ed.), *Hispanic New York: A Sourcebook* (New York: Columbia University Press, 2010); Rondón, *The Book of Salsa*.
17. Eddy Zervigón, November 4, 2016.
18. Conzo and Pérez, *Mambo Diablo*, 122.
19. Salazar, *Mambo Kingdom*, 71.
20. Eddy Zervigón, November 4, 2016.
21. Interview with Eddy Zervigón, New York, June 18, 2016.
22. Eddy Zervigón, November 4, 2016.
23. Eddy Zervigón, November 4, 2016.
24. The rhumba scene also requires more detailed research. Salazar profiles many of the musicians famous in this era including Noro Morales, Alberto Iznaga, Alberto Socarrás, Anselmo Sacasas, and José Curbelo, but their musical development is not given any analytical detail. For a detailed analysis of Cuban son and its US forms, see also Sue Miller, "Cuban Son," in *The Continuum Encyclopedia of Popular Music of the World (EPMOW): Part 3, Genres (Caribbean and Latin American Genres)* (London: Bloomsbury, 2014).
25. Email correspondence with architect Jonathan Lindt of Leeds Environmental Design, Leeds, November 7, 2016.
26. Will Jones, *How to Read New York: A Crash Course in Big Apple Architecture* (Brighton: Ivy Press, 2016), 140.
27. See Morales, *The Latin Beat*, 58.
28. Singer and Martínez, "A South Bronx Latin Music Tale," 6.
29. Mickie Meléndez conversation with Juan Flores, April 1, 2013. Cited in Flores, *Salsa Rising*, 39.
30. Al Santiago founded Alegre Records in 1956 and created the Alegre All Stars from members of Charlie Palmieri's Charanga Duboney and associates of Johnny Pacheco. Santiago set up a historic jam session recording (imitating the Cuban Jam Session recording by Panart) at the Triton Social Club in the Bronx in the autumn of 1961. Fostering a live improvisatory aesthetic that would continue in the following decade with the Fania All Stars, Santiago was instrumental in the development of Cuban dance music in New York. Salazar, *Mambo Kingdom*, 50, 199.
31. Charlie Palmieri and His Charanga La Duboney, *Pachanga at the Caravana Club* (Sonido LPA-8040, 1999 CD reissue of the original Alegre recording of 1962).
32. Interview with Eddy Zervigón, June 18, 2016.

33. Laura Shaine Cunningham, "Ghosts of El Morocco," *New York Times*, September 5, 2004. http://www.nytimes.com/2004/09/05/nyregion/thecity/ghosts-of-el-morocco.html, accessed October, 28, 2016.

34. Conzo and Pérez, *Mambo Diablo*, 122.

35. Eddy Zervigón, November 4, 2016.

36. See Garcia, "Contesting That Damned Mambo," 163.

37. Israel Sánchez-Coll, "Tributo a Lou Pérez: Una Entrevista," *Herencia Latina*, January 6, 2004. http://www.herencialatina.com/Lou_Perez/Lou_Perez%20I.htm, accessed November, 4, 2016. Recording details: Lou Perez, "Pa' Fricasé Los Pollos," *Tamboleo: Lou Perez y Su Charanga* (Corredor CLP 780, 1964; Cobo Music CD reissue, 2009).

38. Interviews with Eddy Zervigón, July 14, 2007, 2012, 2015, and June 18, 2016.

39. Salazar, *Mambo Kingdom*, 35, 183; Morales, *The Latin Beat*, 58.

40. Interview with Eddy Zervigón, June 18, 2016. Also see Figueroa, "New York's Latin Music Landmarks," 362; Salazar, *Mambo Kingdom*, 35, 183.

41. Eddy Zervigón in personal email correspondence with the author, November 4, 2016.

42. Salazar, *Mambo Kingdom*, 197; Flores, *Salsa Rising*, 50. Flores notes that the two met in the Monte Carlo and that Pacheco had played timbales in Gilberto Valdés's charanga.

43. Figueroa, "New York's Latin Music Landmarks," 363.

44. Salazar, *Mambo Kingdom*, 4, 54.

45. Josephine Powell, *When the Drums Are Dreaming* (Bloomington, IN: AuthorHouse, 2007), 42.

46. Abreu, *Rhythms of Race*, 67.

47. Figueroa, "New York's Latin Music Landmarks," 362.

48. Interview with Eddy Zervigón, June 18, 2016.

49. Interview with Eddy Zervigón, June 18, 2016.

50. Salazar, *Mambo Kingdom*, 2.

51. Salazar, *Mambo Kingdom*, 43.

52. Interview with Eddy Zervigón, June 18, 2016.

53. Salazar, *Mambo Kingdom*, 113, 144.

54. Salazar, *Mambo Kingdom*, 2.

55. Willie Torres in Salazar, *Mambo Kingdom*, 239.

56. Salazar, *Mambo Kingdom*, 2002.

57. See City Lore Municipal Arts Society website, http://www.placematters.net/, accessed October 20, 2016.

58. Interview with percussionist John Berdeguer, Brooklyn, New York, June 15, 2016.

59. Miguel Rondón notes that the venue changed its name to the Palladium in 1948 when promoter Max Hyman bought the ballroom. Latin music nights were hosted from 1947. Miguel Rondón, *El Libro de La Salsa: Crónico de la Música del Caribe Urbano* (Caracas: Editorial Arte, 1980), 30. Cited in Austerlitz, *Jazz Consciousness*, 84. See also Salazar, *Mambo Kingdom*, 87.

60. Garcia, *Arsenio Rodríguez and the Transnational Flows of Latin Popular Music*, 64.

61. See, for example, Singer, and Martínez," A South Bronx Latin Music Tale"; Herencia Latina, http://www.herencialatina.com/South_Bronx_Latin/Latin_Music_Bronx.htm, accessed October 24, 2016. See also Abreu, *Rhythms of Race*.

62. Garcia, "Contesting That Damned Mambo."

63. Alfredito Valdés Jr., cited in Garcia, *Arsenio Rodríguez*, 120.

64. Sydney Hutchinson, "*Mambo* On 2: The Birth of a New Form of Dance in New York City," *Centro Journal* XVI, no. 2 (Fall 2004): 110.

65. Max Salazar, "La Casa del Sonido Típico Latino," Version al español de Ian Seda, Herencia Latina. http://www.herencialatina.com/Corso/Corso.htm, accessed October 26, 2016. The article is taken from chapter 41 of Salazar, *Mambo Kingdom*, 265–68.

66. *The Palladium: Where Mambo Was King*. Dir. Kevin Kaufman, 2002. Documentary. *The Mambo Kings*. Dir. Arne Glimcher, 1992. See Abreu, *Rhythms of Race*, 141–84, for a considered critique of representations of Cubanness and Latinness in the American mainstream media in the 1950s.

67. Interview with Mark Weinstein, New Jersey, June 22, 2016.

68. See Peter Manuel, "Puerto Rican Music and Cultural Identity: Creative Appropriation of Cuban Sources from Danza to Salsa," *Ethnomusicology* 38, no. 2, Music and Politics (Spring–Summer 1994): 249–80.

69. For more on Puerto Rican music's relationship to Cuban dance music, see Manuel, "Puerto Rican Music and Cultural Identity."

70. Interview with percussionist John Berdeguer, Brooklyn, New York, June 15, 2016.

71. Interview with Eddy Zervigón, Queens, New York, June 18, 2016.

72. Interview with Eddy Zervigón, June 18, 2016.

73. Interview with David A. Pérez, Brooklyn, June 11, 2016.

74. Interview with Luis "Máquina" Flores, by David Carp, Riverdale, New York, October 22, 1993. Cited in Garcia, "Contesting That Damned Mambo," 163.

75. Nancy Raquel Mirabal, cited in Abreu, *Rhythms of Race*, 6.

Chapter 2

1. Miller, *Cuban Flute Style*, 14. Also see Helio Orovio, *Diccionario de la Música Cubana, Biográfico y Técnico* (Havana: Letras Cubanas, 1981), 36.

2. Although the radio stations CMQ and RHC-Cadena Azul were the most popular. See Garcia, *Arsenio Rodríguez*, 39.

3. Arcaño y Sus Maravillas, "Mambo," *Danzón Mambo [1944–51]* (Tumbao Classics TCD-029, reissue 1993).

4. The rhythmic textures changed little in the Cuban chachachá, as opposed to the more intense weave of the mambo/diablo figures of the charanga and conjunto, something Garcia analyzes when he examines the music of Arsenio's conjunto and its relationship to the mambos of Pérez Prado, Machito, and Tito Puente. See Garcia, *Arsenio Rodríguez*, chapters 2 and 3.

5. Interview with Mark Weinstein, New Jersey, June 22, 2016.

6. Interview with Weinstein, 2016.

7. Lise Waxer, "Of Mambo Kings and Songs of Love: Dance Music in Havana and New York from the 1930s to the 1950s," *Latin American Music Review/Revista de Música Latinoamericana* 15, no. 2 (Autumn–Winter 1994): 141.

8. Garcia, *Arsenio Rodríguez*, 68.

9. Xavier Cugat bought several of Pérez Prado's arrangements in 1947. Salazar, *Mambo Kingdom*, 107.

10. Salazar, *Mambo Kingdom*, 61.

11. For more information on Juan Francisco "Tata" Pereira, see Miller, *Cuban Flute Style*, 65–97.

12. This is according to Ned Sublette, Bebo Valdés, and Rubén López-Cano. See Ned Sublette, *Cuba and Its Music: From the First Drums to the Mambo* (Chicago: Chicago Review Press, 2004), 508. Ruben López-Cano, "Mambo," in *The Continuum Encyclopedia of Popular Music of the World*, *(EPMOW): Part 3, Genres (Caribbean and Latin American Genres)* (London: Bloomsbury, 2014), 435; Ruben López-Cano, "Notes for a Prehistory of Mambo," in Javier F. Léon and Helena Simonett (eds.), *Views from the South: A Latin American Music Reader* (Urbana and Chicago: University of Illinois Press, 2016).

13. René Hernández, an arranger who worked with Pérez Prado, played in Julio Cueva's mambo-styled orquesta in the 1940s in Havana before becoming Machito's pianist for a while and Tito Rodríguez's arranger. Sublette, *Cuba and Its Music*, 508.

14. For more detail on these transitions, see Miller, *Cuban Flute Style*, 1–5.

15. According to Eddy Zervigón, Cuban bands were referred to as orquestas if they had either violin or saxophone sections. If not, the conjunto label was used. Interview with Eddy Zervigón, Queens, New York, 2012.

16. See Sue Miller, *Cuban Flute Style*, 65–98.

17. See Ruben López-Cano, "Mambo," in *The Continuum Encyclopedia of Popular Music of the World (EPMOW)* and López-Cano, "Notes for a Prehistory of Mambo."

18. Although you can view this piece as being in the mixolydian mode (d-e-f$^\sharp$-g-a-b-c-d) disrupted occasionally by the raised fourth (g$^\sharp$) in the flute solo to give a whole-tone/lydian mode flavor, the improvisation would not be seen as modal by típico performers, who conceive of it more as clave-driven rhythmic tension over a dominant D7 chord in the key of G major.

19. Austerlitz, *Jazz Consciousness*, 96.

20. Santana, "Oye Como Va," *Abraxas* (CBS KC-30130, 1970).

21. The pedal strings begin at 0:50 on Ray Barretto, "El Bantu," *On Fire Again—Encendido Otra Vez* (Tico LP 1096, 1963).

22. While these styles often originated within one particular instrumental/vocal format, once established they were played by a mix of band types. Thus, mambo and chachachá are said to originate in the charanga but are also played by Latin big bands and son groups. Son groups may focus on son and son montuno but also play bolero, guajira, afro, chachachá. Estudiantinas would play danzones with extended son sections and sones accompanied by the danzón cinquillo rather than the son clave.

23. See Sublette, *Cuba and Its Music*, 53–54; Garcia, *Arsenio Rodríguez*, 49.

24. Arsenio Rodríguez, "El Reloj," *El Rey Del Son Montuno* (Rice Records RRS-001, 2004). Recorded June 21, 1946, in Havana for RCA Victor 23-0470-B, TCD-031.

25. Garcia, *Arsenio Rodríguez*, 49.

26. Bebo Valdés in an interview with Diego Salazar for Club Cultura, March 3, 2005. Cited by López-Cano, "Mambo," in *The Continuum Encyclopedia of Popular Music of the World (EPMOW)*, 438.

27. Bebo Valdés, cited in Sublette, *Cuba and Its Music*, 509.

28. Leonardo Acosta, *Descarga Cubana: El Jazz En Cuba 1900–1950* [Cuban Jam Sessions: Jazz in Cuba 1900–1950] (Havana: Ediciones Unión, 2000). Cited in López-Cano, "Mambo," in *The Continuum Encyclopedia of Popular Music of the World (EPMOW)*, 438.

29. Garcia, *Arsenio Rodríguez*, 32–92.

30. Waxer, "Of Mambo Kings and Songs of Love," 157.

31. Performances at the Park Plaza and other uptown venues have not been researched and documented in as much detail as those of the Palladium.

32. Josephine Powell notes this style of presentation had only occurred once before in Xavier Cugat's band in 1936, when timbale player Maño López joined the front line to play and dance to the number "Go West, Young Man." See Josephine Powell, *Tito Puente: When the Drums Are Dreaming* (Bloomington, IN: Author House, 2007), 75.

33. Eddie Palmieri reverted to this traditional layout in his 1960s band La Perfecta (see Chapter 7).

34. Sublette, *Cuba and Its Music*, 508.

35. Tito Puente, "Mambo Gozón," *Mambo Gozón Tito Puente and His Orchestra* (RCA International 901 017, France, 1958).

36. See Cristóbal Díaz Ayala, "La Década de los Años Treinta," in *Música Cubana del Areyto al Rap Cubano*, 4ta Edición (Miami: Fundación Musicalia, 2003 [1981]), 187.

37. Salazar, *Mambo Kingdom*, 95–99.

38. Salazar, *Mambo Kingdom*, 126.

39. See Hettie Malcomson, "The 'Routes' and 'Roots' of *Danzón*: A Critique of the History of a Genre," *Popular Music* 30, no. 2 (2011): 263–78.

40. López-Cano, "Notes for a Prehistory of Mambo."

41. See Robin D. Moore, *Nationalizing Blackness: Afrocubanismo and Artistic Revolution in Havana, 1920–1940*. (Pittsburgh, PA: University of Pittsburgh Press, 1997), 223.

42. López-Cano, "Mambo," 438.

43. Sublette, *Cuba and Its Music*, 53.

44. Miller, *Cuban Flute Style*, 166–71.

45. Radamés Giro, *Música Popular Cubana* (Vedado, Cuba: Editorial José Martí, 2007), 68.

46. Giro, *Música Popular Cubana*, 68; López-Cano, "Mambo," 437.

47. *Rhumba*, a misspelling of *rumba*, is a term that originated in the United States in the 1920s and was in use mainly in the first part of the twentieth century to refer to commercialized Cuban son styles of music. Originally meaning "party," r(h)umba covered musical stylings associated with Cuban son, tourist comparsa (the conga), and Afro-Cuban elements embedded within the son. Cuban rumba is an Afro-Cuban genre of percussion, dance, and vocal secular music, usually divided into the three main styles of guaguancó, yambú, and columbia.

48. Interview with Manny Rivera, New York, June 27, 2016.

49. John P. Murphy, "The Charanga in New York and the Persistence of the Típico Style," in Peter Manuel (ed.), *Essays on Cuban Music: North American and Cuban Perspectives* (Lanham, MD, and London: University Press of America, 1991), 115–36.

50. Fernández, *Latin Jazz*, 136.

51. The charanga of Cuban-born Gilberto Valdés was set up in 1952, performing danzón-mambo repertoire similar to Arcaño y sus Maravillas at the Bronx Tropicana Club. Both Max Salazar (2002, 182) and David Pérez (in an interview with the author, July 2016) state the group failed to ignite interest in the charanga format at this time. Valdés became musical

director for the Katherine Dunham Dance Company in 1953 and Afro-Cuban violinist Alberto Iznaga then directed the band until 1957 (Salazar, *Mambo Kingdom*, 35).

52. Interview between Alberto Socarrás and Max Salazar cited in Salazar, *Mambo Kingdom*, 57. See also Austerlitz, *Jazz Consciousness*, 92–93.

53. The Herencia Latina website is available here: http://www.herencialatina.com/, accessed November 9, 2019.

Chapter 3

1. Gilberto Valdés, a Cuban flute player, started a charanga in 1952 at New York's Bronx Tropical, which Cuban violinist Alberto Iznaga directed from 1953 when Valdés left to become musical director for the Katherine Dunham Theatre Company. Alberto Socarrás led the house band at El Club Cubanacán. See Salazar, *Mambo Kingdom*, 54–57.

2. Danilo Lozano, "The Charanga Tradition in Cuba: History, Style and Ideology," MA thesis (University of California, Los Angeles, 1990), 128–79. Danilo analyzes "Baila Vicente" by Orquesta Aragón (*Primeras Grabaciones*), although the flute solo is attributed to Richard Egües not Lozano in the recording sleeve notes and in the Diaz discography. He also analyzes a later descarga recording of "Descarga 69" made with Orquesta Nuevo Ritmo on their seminal album *Heart of Cuba* in 1959, where he highlights Rolando's use of the flattened fifth as a blue note influence.

3. Miller, *Cuban Flute Style*, 131–64.

4. See Israel Sánchez-Coll, "Belisario López Rossi (1903–1969): El Rey del Danzón Puro" (n.d.), http://www.herencialatina.com/Belisario_Lopez/Belisario.htm, accessed August 9, 2012.

5. Miller, *Cuban Flute Style*, 19.

6. Miller, *Cuban Flute Style*, 132.

7. Orquesta Aragón, *Primeras Grabaciones 1953–1955* (Tumbao Cuban Classics TCD 110, CD reissue, 1997). Originally recorded by CMQ radio, Havana, LPDBL-1-5011, 1953.

8. Orquesta Nuevo Ritmo de Cuba, *The Heart Of Cuba: Pachangas & Charangas* (GNP Crescendo–GNP 47, 1959).

9. Cristóbal Díaz Ayala, in his *Enciclopedia Discográfica de la Música Cubana Volume 2*, 118–24, states a birth year of 1913. If this date is correct, Belisario would have commenced his professional performing career as a young teenager. However, others such as Israel Sánchez Coll cite the year of his birth as 1903, which would make more sense. See Israel Sánchez-Coll, "Belisario López Rossi (1903–1969): El Rey del Danzón Puro," n.d. www.herencialatina.com/Belisario_Lopez/Belisario.htm, accessed August 9, 2012.

10. See Miller, *Cuban Flute Style*, 19, for a brief biography of Belisario López.

11. Eddy Zervigón, Queens, New York, June 18, 2016.

12. See Miller, *Cuban Flute Style*, chapter 3, for more on this earlier performance style.

13. Belisario López, *Orquesta de Belisario López 1942–1948 Prueba Mi Sazón* (Tumbao Cuban Classics, TCD 069, CD reissue, 1995).

14. Belisario López, "Prepárate Para Bañarte," *Orquesta de Belisario López 1951–1957 Prueba Mi Sazón*. Recorded in Havana, September 19, 1956 [CU 9839/19/56V 23-7107 CU DBM 1-5804].

15. Belisario López, "Lola Catula," *A Bailar la Pachanga* (Ansonia ALP 1288, US, 1961).

16. Miller, *Cuban Flute Style*, 15–16.
17. José Fajardo, *Ritmo De Pollos* (Panart LP-3051, Cuba, 1959).
18. Salazar, *Mambo Kingdom*, 180.
19. Lozano, "The Charanga Tradition in Cuba," 129, 131, 133–35.
20. Orquesta Nuevo Ritmo de Cuba, *The Heart of Cuba: Pachangas & Charangas* (GNP Crescendo–GNP 47, August 31, 1959).
21. Salazar, *Mambo Kingdom*, 183.
22. Mongo Santamaría, "Que Maravilloso," *Sabroso!* (Fantasy 8058, 1961).
23. Orquesta Aragón, *Primeras Grabaciones 1953–1955* (Tumbao Cuban Classics TCD 110, CD reissue, 1997). Tracks 1–6 originally recorded by CMQ radio, Havana, LPDBL-1-5011, 1953.
24. Salazar, *Mambo Kingdom*, 183.
25. Juan Flores, *Salsa Rising: New York Latin Music of the Sixties Generation* (New York: Oxford University Press, 2016), 59.
26. Orquesta Nuevo Ritmo de Cuba, *The Heart of Cuba*.
27. Lozano, "The Charanga Tradition in Cuba."

Chapter 4

1. Lineup of Orquesta Broadway (l-r): flute: Eddy Zervigón; güiro: Kelvin Zervigón; piano: Ira Herscher; timbales: Enrique Vélez; vocals: Helio Romero and Roberto Torres; congas: José Valente; bass: David Herscher; violins: Abraham Norman and Rudy Zervigón. Photograph courtesy of Eddy Zervigón. Further biographical detail on Orquesta Broadway can be found in the entry by John Child in *The Penguin Encyclopedia of Popular Music*, edited by Donald Clarke, 2nd ed. (London: Penguin Books, 1998). Available online at http://www.donaldclarkemusicbox.com/encyclopedia/detail.php?s=370, accessed August 9, 2018.
2. Sánchez-Coll and Gómez, "Entrevista a Eddy Zervigón."
3. Eddy Zervigón, telephone conversation with the author, August 22, 2006.
4. Salazar, *Mambo Kingdom*, 210.
5. Interview with Eddy Zervigón, Queens, New York, June 18, 2016.
6. Interview with Eddy Zervigón, July 14, 2007.
7. Sánchez-Coll and Gómez, "Entrevista a Eddy Zervigón."
8. John Child, "Fajardo, José Antonio," in Clarke (ed.), *The Penguin Encyclopedia of Popular Music*.
9. Interview with Eddy Zervigón, July 14, 2007.
10. For further biographical details on Eddy Zervigón, see Miller, *Cuban Flute Style*, 19–20.
11. Eddy Zervigón, email correspondence with the author, June 14, 2007.
12. Conzo and Pérez, *Mambo Diablo*, 197.
13. Although Orquesta Broadway has a typical charanga lineup, it incorporated Cuban trumpeter Roberto Rodríguez in the late 1970s to take on half the soloing duties, as the number of gigs put undue physical pressure on Eddy Zervigón; according to Max Salazar, Zervigón developed a herniated esophagus. See Salazar, *Mambo Kingdom*, 215. Recently the band has incorporated a trombone player who also doubles on violin (Lewis Kahn also doubled violin and trombone in Larry Harlow's orchestra and with the Fania All Stars).

14. Orquesta Broadway, "Al Mirar No Me Vistes," *Paraíso* (Musical Productions, CD reissue, 1991). Originally recorded 1981 for Coco Records.

15. Email correspondence with Eddy Zervigón, August 6, 2018.

16. These fingerings are presented in the five-key flute fingering charts in *Cuban Flute Style* but $f^{\sharp}_4$ and g^4 have since been amended here by Zervigón. His third-register $c^{\sharp}_4$ is not as shown in the original chart on page 61 in my earlier book but is instead the same as the fingerings shown in the charts for Polo Tamayo and Joaquin Oliveros. See Miller, *Cuban Flute Style*, 29–63.

17. Technical drawings of the five-key flute (including charts) courtesy of Nigel Humphreys of Jadenrange Ltd. The table is included as a correction ($f^{\sharp}_4$ and g^4) to the fingering charts for Eddy Zervigón in Miller, *Cuban Flute Style*, 62.

18. For a good example of this, listen to how Egües's inspiraciones respond to the coros on Orquesta Aragón's "Charlas del Momento," *Los Aragones en la Onda de la Alegria Vol. 2*, Sonido Inc Fondo Sonoro de Archivo Instituto Cubano de Radio y Televisión (Barbaro B218, CD reissue, 1998). Originally recorded 1963 (Héctor German, *Orquesta Aragón* [Havana: Editorial Unión de Periodistas de Cuba, 2004], 246). See Miller, *Cuban Flute Style*, 114–21, for more examples of the use of coro melody call and response in the improvisations of Richard Egües.

19. See Miller, *Cuban Flute Style*, for further discussion of clave forms and clave sensibility.

20. Eddy Zervigón in conversation with the author, New York, July 2007 and June 2012.

21. As demonstrated in Miller, *Cuban Flute Style*, 131–64.

22. Sánchez-Coll and Gómez, "Entrevista a Eddy Zervigón."

23. *Sello* literally means "seal" or "stamp" (as in historical letter seals stamped in wax) and would be translated as "voice" in English. The development of your own voice as an improviser (through imitation and adaptation) is a common theme in jazz and Latin improvisation practice.

24. However, the chachachá was very popular in the late 1950s in the Catskill resorts, particularly among Jewish American clientèle.

25. In interviews with the author in Havana in 2006 and 2009, flute player Joaquín Oliveros talked about a Cuban "country" feel known as "del monte" (from the mountains/hills) or "monte adentro" (pure country). Richard Egües also talked about guajira-style playing in a similar way (during lessons with the author in 2000 and 2001). See Miller, *Cuban Flute Style*, chapters 4, 7, and 8.

26. Henry Louis Gates Jr., *The Signifying Monkey: A Theory of African-American Literary Criticism* (New York: Oxford University Press, 1989). Samuel A. Floyd Jr., *The Power of Black Music: Interpreting Its History from Africa to the United States* (New York: Oxford University Press, 1995). Orquesta Broadway, "Quinta Guajira," *Como Me Gusta!* (West Side Latino Records, CD reissue, 1998). Composed by Gil Suárez and originally recorded by Orquesta Broadway in New York, May 25, 1972.

27. According to Jesse Herrero of New York–based Charanga SonSublime, Gil Suárez was born in New York of Puerto Rican descent. His obituary is available at http://www.havananewyork.com/ads/hvny_nf_suarez_9_13/, accessed November 14, 2015.

28. Conzo and Pérez, *Mambo Diablo*.

29. As for example on the recording Orquesta Aragón, "Isora Club," *Danzones de Ayer y de Hoy* [Vol. 1] (RCA Victor LPD 515, 1960; CD reissue: Discuba West Side Sound, 1990). The melody is played at 1:49–2:08.

30. Israel López Cachao, "Isora Club," *Cachao Master Sessions*, Vol. 1 (Epic Records CD EK 64320, 1994).

31. Miller, *Cuban Flute Style*, 77–84.

32. See Miller, *Cuban Flute Style*, 84 and 97, for more on the provenance of the "Tres Lindas Cubanas" theme.

33. For more information on the guajira style, see Miller, "Música Guajira," in *The Continuum Encyclopedia of Popular Music of the World (EPMOW)*.

34. The author took lessons in improvisation from Richard Egües in Havana in 2000 and 2001 as documented in Miller, "Flute Improvisation in Cuban Charanga Performance."

35. See Miller, *Cuban Flute Style*, 179, example 6.9. Also refer to the recording Orquesta Aragón, "Al Vaiven de Mi Carreta," *That Cuban Cha-Cha-Cha* (RCA Tropical Series 2446-2-RL, 1956; remastered for CD, 1990). Recorded in Havana 1955–56.

36. Interview with Joaquín Oliveros, Havana, April 3, 2009.

37. Rebecca M. Bodenheimer, *Geographies of Cubanidad: Place, Race, and Musical Performance in Contemporary Cuba* (Jackson: University Press of Mississippi, 2015).

38. Interview with Joaquín Oliveros, Havana, December 29, 2011.

39. In a 2001 interview Melquiades Fundora mentions Belisario López as one of the innovators of the danzón, particularly in terms of livelier interpretations of the danzón style before the chachachá of the 1950s became popular.

40. Interview with Eddy Zervigón, Queens, New York, 2015.

41. One could suggest that Belisario López did not adapt as easily to New York musical life as did the younger Eddy Zervigón. His solos sound a little hurried at the faster tempos of the 1963 and 1965 Ansonia recordings, whereas Zervigón seems positively to enjoy the velocity on "Al Mirar No Me Vistes." On "Pregón de la Montaña," for example, from the album *Belisario López y Su Orquesta* on the Ansonia label, the song is played at ♩ = 176, as is "Buscate un Chino" on his album *Tu No Estas En Na*. This contrasts with his performances on earlier recordings, such as those on Orquesta de Belisario López, *1942–1948 Prueba Mi Sazón*, on the Tumbao label. His solo on the montuno of "Yo Soy Manuel Garcia," for example, is played at ♩ = 144. Stylistic and generational differences aside, Belisario López sometimes sounds uncomfortable with the tempo of his New York–based band. While virtuosic and energetic, his improvisation does sound more brusque in contrast to his earlier, more suave recordings made in Havana. In New York, López was in his sixties and performing with only one lung. Charanga flute requires considerable physical exertion, so these recordings, while of a high standard, were not made in his prime. See Belisario López, « Buscate un Chino," *Orquesta de Belisario López Tu No Estas En Na* (Ansonia ALP1410, 1965); "Pregón de La Montaña," *Belisario López y su Orquesta* (Ansonia ALP1318, 1963); *Orquesta de Belisario López 1942–1948 Prueba Mi Sazón* (Tumbao Cuban Classics, TCD 069, CD reissue, 1995).

42. See Philip Tagg, *Everyday Tonality II—Towards a Tonal Theory of What Most People Hear* (New York and Huddersfield: MMMSP, 2018), 428; "Guantanamera Endings," Etymophony channel, YouTube. https://www.youtube.com/watch?v=7CStNSlNGfo, accessed August 9, 2018. For more on the guajira style, see Miller, "Música Guajira," *The Continuum Encyclopedia of Popular Music of the World (EPMOW)*.

43. Cuban charanga took a variety of trajectories within Cuba after the 1959 revolution, which were not identical to New York developments. More detailed research into the music of these post-revolution charanga groups is needed.

44. Eddy Zervigón telephone conversation with the author, August 11 and 13, 2019.

45. Eddy Zervigón conversation with the author, New York, July 2007.

46. Interview with Eddy Zervigón by Rene López, "Rene López interviews Eddy Zervigón" Salsa-101, YouTube, October 28, 2007. https://www.youtube.com/watch?v=H-egoIlBeHk, accessed August 8, 2018.

47. Conzo and Pérez, *Mambo Diablo*, 197.

Chapter 5

1. Peter Manuel, *Caribbean Currents: Caribbean Music from Rumba to Reggae* (London: Latin America Bureau, 1995), 54.

2. Orquesta Sublime, "El Peletero" (Cuba 45rpm, Panart 1898, 1957; Cuba LP, Panart 3018); "Los Carteros" (Cuba 45rpm, Panart 1898, 1957; Cuba LP, V. Lay 2026); "Seis Perlas Cubanas" (Cuba 45rpm, Panart 1913, 1957; LP, Panart 3018). All available on *A la Pachanga con la Sublime* (CD, Egrem/Artex 20, Cuba, 1994). Ayala, *Enciclopedia Discográfica de la Música Cubana Volume 2, 1925–1960*.

3. Interviews with Melquiades Fundora, Havana, April 2001 and March 28, 2007.

4. Flores, *Salsa Rising*, 47.

5. Orquesta Aragón, formed in 1939, rose to fame nationally in Cuba in the mid-1950s. The band's prolific output with the RCA Victor, together with performances, international tours, and TV and radio appearances, make the group one of the premier popular Cuban music dance bands of the mid-twentieth century. Miller, *Cuban Flute Style*, 9–11. Rafael Bacallao (born in 1935 in Cienfuegos) started his career as a singer and was a singer and dancer in José Fajardo's charanga before joining Orquesta Aragón in 1959.

6. Salazar, *Mambo Kingdom*, 198.

7. Flores, *Salsa Rising*, 46–48. Flores is citing an interview with Al Santiago in Vernon W. Boggs, *Salsiology: Afrocuban Music and the Evolution of Salsa in New York City* (New York: Excelsior Music, 1992), 220.

8. Flores, *Salsa Rising*, 57.

9. Charlie Palmieri and His Charanga La Duboney, *Pachanga at the Caravana Club* (Alegre, 1962; Sonido LPA-8040, CD reissue, 1999).

10. Interview with Johnny Pacheco with Aurora Flores, https://www.youtube.com/watch?v=Bq2wmKk2fwE, accessed November 27, 2017.

11. Interview with Eddy Zervigón, June 18, 2016.

12. Flores, *Salsa Rising*, 46. Flores also cites an interview with Johnny Pacheco by David Carp on May 12, 1997, published on the now defunct Descarga.com website. The interview is titled "A Visit with Maestro Johnny Pacheco."

13. Pacheco claims he invented the dance step (Flores, *Salsa Rising*, 46). Latin music DJ Al Angeloro saw Arthur Murray teach a regimented pachanga dance class using the handkerchief gesture and jump Pacheco claims he invented. Murray, who had a chain of dancing academies, would have undoubtedly popularized the step. There is a 1961 recording titled *Arthur Murray's Music for Dancing Pachangas* (RCA Victor LSP 2448) recorded by a band led by Mario Bauzá and Rene Hernández and featuring most of the musicians from the Machito band; the record cover features a photograph of a rather awkward-looking Arthur

Murray dancing a pachanga. The recording begins with a big band version of Pacheco's hit for Alegre Records "El Güiro de Macorina."

14. Interview with Karen Joseph by the author, Brooklyn, June 24, 2016.

15. This account of Cuban dance music is almost exclusively made up of male musicians, for a variety of historical and social reasons. Musicologist Alicia Valdés has undertaken research into women in Cuban music in *Con Música, Textos y Presencia de Mujer: Diccionario de Mujeres Notables en la Música Cubana* (Havana: Ediciones Unión, 2000); flute player Jessica Valiente has written about the more contemporary-styled female charanga flute players Andrea Brachfeld, Karen Joseph, and Connie Grossman in her DMA thesis "Siento una Flauta: Improvisational Idiom, Style, and Performance Practice of Charanga Flutists in New York from 1960 to 2000" (CUNY, 2015). However, until women are an equal presence on the Latin music scene with equal access to music industry promotion and dissemination, the history will continue to remain dominated by men.

16. Hettie Malcomson, "The 'Routes' and 'Roots' of *Danzón*: A Critique of the History of a Genre," *Popular Music* 30, no. 2 (2011): 269.

17. Interview with Manny Rivera, June 27, 2016.

18. Interview by phone with Eddy Zervigón, August 13, 2019.

19. Interview by phone with Eddy Zervigón, August 13, 2019.

20. Interview with Manny Rivera, SonSublime percussionist, New York, June 27, 2016. Rivera means that performers of charanga are assertive but not aggressive. For more on performance aesthetics in Latin music, see Garcia, *Arsenio Rodríguez and the Transnational Flows of Latin Popular Music*, chapter 2, "Negro y Macho."

21. Interview with John Berdeguer, Brooklyn, New York, June 15, 2016.

22. Interview with Joe De Jesus, New York, June 27, 2016.

23. Orquesta Sublime, "La Pachanga" (45rpm, Panart 2211, 1959; LP, Panart 2048; CD, Egrem/Artex 20, 1994).

24. Orquesta Sublime, "La Pachanga," *A La Pachanga con la Sublime* (Artex Canada, 1956–1960 recordings, 1994).

25. For more on the clarinet in the contradanza and danzón in Cuba, see Miller, *Cuban Flute Style*, xxv, 1.

26. See Moore, *Music in the Hispanic Caribbean*, 87.

27. Orquesta Sublime with Sue Miller, performance at the Convento de Belen, Habana Vieja, December 2011. https://www.youtube.com/watch?v=yNlJuiB5RK0, accessed January 22, 2018.

28. Rebeca Mauléon, *Salsa Guidebook for Piano and Ensemble* (Petaluma, CA: Sher Music, 1993), 207.

29. Doña Juana was not a person but rather stands for "Maria Juana"—a euphemism for marijuana.

30. Helio Orovio, *Diccionario de la Música Cubana, Biográfico y Técnico* (Havana: Letras Cubanas, 1981), 490.

31. Interview with Mark Weinstein, New Jersey, June 22, 2016.

Chapter 6

1. Salazar, *Mambo Kingdom*, 197.

2. Boggs, *Salsiology*, 222, cited in Flores, *Salsa Rising*, 53.

3. Charlie Palmieri and His Charanga La Duboney, *Viva Palmieri* (Alegre LPA 8160, 1962; CD reissue Sonido, 1998).

4. Charlie Palmieri and His Charanga La Duboney, "Mack the Knife," *Let's Dance the Charanga* (United Artists UAL 3082, 1959).

5. Thanks to author David A. Pérez Sr. for further elaboration on the recording's personnel, providing nationalities and correcting the Uribe information on John Palomo and Julian Cabrera. David A. Pérez, email correspondence, August 16, 2017.

6. New York–based cellist David Soyer was a well-known quartet player. Thanks to cellist Dr. George Kennaway for this information. See also Soyer's obituary in the *New York Times*, https://www.nytimes.com/2010/02/27/arts/music/27soyer.html, accessed October 23, 2018.

7. Cuban bassist Evaristo Baró is the father of Orquesta Broadway singer Ronnie Baró.

8. A profile of Yayo el Indio can be found on the Herencia Latina website, http://www.herencialatina.com/yayo%20el%20indio/yayo%20el%20indio.htm, accessed September 24, 2018.

9. Flores, *Salsa Rising*, 57.

10. Interview with Mark Weinstein by the author, New Jersey, June 22, 2016. Weinstein was a trombonist with Eddie Palmieri's La Perfecta from 1961–63. He later became a jazz/world music flute player and an academic specializing in philosophy.

11. See Singer and Martínez, "A South Bronx Latin Music Tale." See also Abreu, *Rhythms of Race*, for detailed ethnographies of the South Bronx in relation to grassroots Afro-Cuban dance music performance from the 1940s to the 1960s.

12. Cited in Flores, *Salsa Rising*, 53, originally in Boggs, *Salsiology*, 222.

13. Roberts, *The Latin Tinge*, 164.

14. Flores, *Salsa Rising*, 101–2.

15. Issues of copyright of Cuban works following the Cuban Revolution are not examined here. See Robin D. Moore, *Music and Revolution: Cultural Change in Socialist Cuba* (Berkeley and Los Angeles: University of California Press, 2006), 73–77. Copyright was abolished by the Cuban government in 1967, benefiting US record companies to the detriment of Cuban artists.

16. Eddy Zervigón, for example, describes Johnny Pacheco as being "born to improvise." Interview with Eddy Zervigón, Queens, New York, June 18, 2016.

17. Interview with Johnny Pacheco by Mimi Ortiz Martín, "La Clave del Rey: En Casa de Johnny Pacheco. Patriarca de la Música Latina," *El Nuevo Día* (Puerto Rico), April 15, 2007. Available from the Herencia Latina website.

18. Flores, *Salsa Rising*, 50. Flores notes that Pacheco had played timbales in Gilberto Valdés's charanga, which was formed in 1952.

19. Interview with Mark Weinstein, New Jersey, June 22, 2016.

20. See Miller, *Cuban Flute Style*, for an exposition and detailed analysis of the improvisational styles of Richard Egües, José Fajardo, and Antonio Arcaño, among others.

21. Charlie Palmieri and His Charanga La Duboney, "Bronx Pachanga," *Pachanga at the Caravana Club* (Alegre, 1961; Sonido 8040, CD reissue, 1999).

22. See David A. Pérez, *The Five Key Charanga Flute*. 2009. Article on the Descarga.com website (now defunct), http://www.descarga.com/cgi-bin/db/archives/Article15, accessed September 24, 2018.

23. Interview with David A. Pérez, Brooklyn, June 11, 2016.

24. Interview with Andy González in Singer, "Tradition and Innovation in Contemporary Latin Popular Music in New York City," 194.

25. Peter Westbrook, *The Flute in Jazz: Window on World Music* (Rockville, MD: Harmonia Books, 2009), 331.

26. Nestor Torres, Interview via Skype, October 18, 2017.

27. See Laudan Nooshin, "Improvisation as 'Other': Creativity, Knowledge and Power—The Case of Iranian Classical Music," *Journal of the Royal Music Association* 128/2 (2003): 242–96.

28. See Moore, *Music and Revolution*.

29. Interview with pianist Willie Rodríguez, Lehman College, New York, June 21, 2016.

30. Interview with Mark Weinstein, New Jersey, June 22, 2016.

Chapter 7

1. Flores, *Salsa Rising*, 85.

2. Timbales were added to the son conjunto in Cuba, too, so this is not such a unique US phenomenon. The Cuban sonora, for example, incorporated timbales into the son conjunto lineup and is said to have smoother, lower-register trumpet lines.

3. Weinstein states that no one called George "Jorge" and that the band often called him Georgie. Interview with Mark Weinstein, New Jersey, June 22, 2016.

4. Eddie Palmieri, *Eddie Palmieri y Su Conjunto—La Perfecta* (Alegre LPA 817, 1962).

5. Flores, *Salsa Rising*, 84. Eddie Palmieri, "Ritmo Caliente," *Eddie Palmieri y Su Conjunto—La Perfecta* (Alegre LPA 817, 1962).

6. Flores *Salsa Rising*, 76. In an interview in Spanish with Patricia Rengel for the University of Wisconsin-Madison, Department of Spanish and Portuguese (as part of their series "Personalidades de la Cultura Hispánica"), Eddie Palmieri explains his love of the conjunto formation as in Orquesta Casino from Cuba (interview #2 at 2:30). Here he talks about how he adapted to the lack of available Latin trumpet players by using Barry Rogers on trombone and George Castro on charanga flute. He also talks about his interest in the charanga and the Cuban orquesta típica sound. The broadcast was possibly in 2006 (the UW feed is no longer available and was archived in 2016—the podcast is marked as having been posted "12 years ago").

7. Interview with Mark Weinstein, New Jersey, June 22, 2016.

8. Roberts, *Latin Jazz*, 144.

9. Interview with Mark Weinstein, New Jersey, June 22, 2016.

10. In his 2016 interview, Weinstein mentions that Barry Rogers interviewed him for the now defunct Descarga website, in which both talked about the volume and stamina required for the Perfecta trombone section sound.

11. Flores, *Salsa Rising*, 73.

12. For more on the history and significance of this song see Sue Miller, "Cuban Son," in *The Continuum Encyclopedia of Popular Music of the World (EPMOW): Part 3, Genres (Caribbean and Latin American Genres)* (London: Bloomsbury, 2014), 786–87, 790–91.

13. Both Pacheco and Castro performed in the first New York-based charanga led initially by Gilberto Valdés in the 1950s. Although this first US charanga was not commercially successful, more research into this seminal New York charanga is needed to understand

its significance before dismissing it as unimportant in the music's history; Johnny Pacheco, George Castro, and Mongo Santamaría all performed in this charanga in the 1950s.

14. Eddie Palmieri, "Ritmo Caliente," *Eddie Palmieri y Su Conjunto "La Perfecta"* (Alegre LPA 817, 1962).

15. Weinstein has said Castro is not a Puerto Rican name, and that he moved away from New York to Los Angeles (Weinstein, 2016). Karen Joseph said Castro was still on the scene when she was starting out as a musician, and that she saw him play with Eddie Palmieri. She has heard on the grapevine that someone in his family had asthma and that he had moved away for health reasons, but cannot verify this. Interview with Karen Joseph, Brooklyn, June 24, 2016.

16. Castro was perhaps influenced by Arcaño y sus Maravillas, as there is also some charanga mambo influence in his solo on "Tu Tu Ta Ta." However, his playing in these two solos is less ornamented than these earlier players', probably due to the faster tempos. Pacheco, in contrast, manages to ornament his lines despite the fast tempos.

17. Interview with Karen Joseph, 2016.

18. See chapter 6 in Jessica Valiente, "Siento una Flauta," for an analysis of Joseph's soloing style.

19. Eddie Palmieri, "Ritmo Caliente II," *Ritmo Caliente* (Concord Picante CCD-2180-2, 2003).

20. Zervigón explained that Eddie Palmieri liked to record the band live and that, on "Lazaro y su Microfono," there were eleven takes. The band played until Palmieri was happy with his piano solo, which was tiring for a charanga flute player performing in the top register. Eddy Zervigón, August 13, 2019, personal correspondence with the author by telephone.

21. Eddie Palmieri, *Ritmo Caliente II*, 2003.

22. See Sánchez-Coll and Gómez, "Entrevista a Eddy Zervigón."

23. Charanga keys are usually those with fewer sharps and flats including C, G, D, A, F, and E majors, and C, G, A, E, and D minors. For more on five-key flute ergonomics and charanga keys, see Miller, *Cuban Flute Style*, 29–63; and Miller, "Flute Improvisation in Cuban Charanga Performance."

24. Eddie Palmieri, "Tu Tu Ta Ta," *Echando Pa'lante [Straight Ahead]* (Tico 1113, 1964).

25. Interview with Mark Weinstein, 2016.

26. Flores cites David Carp regarding Mon Rivera's trombonist Joe Orange and Mark Weinstein's comments on the Perfecta's higher trombone range. See Flores, *Salsa Rising*, 81.

27. Flores, *Salsa Rising*, 88.

28. Eddie Palmieri, "Tu Tu Ta Ta II," *Eddie Palmieri—La Perfecta II* (Concord CCD-2136-2, 2002).

29. Of course, Herbie Mann is also part of this Latin fusion narrative, but he is outside the scope of this book since the focus is on popular Latin dance music. For more on Latin jazz and fusion see Roberts, *Latin Jazz*. See also Cary Ginell, *The Evolution of Mann: Herbie Mann and the Flute in Jazz* (Milwaukee, WI: Hal Leonard Books, 2014). See also Peter Westbrook, *The Flute in Jazz: Window on World Music* (Rockville, MD: Harmonia Books, 2009).

30. Eddie Palmieri, "Un Día Bonito," *Eddie Palmieri—The Sun of Latin Music* (Coco CLP 109, France, 1974).

Chapter 8

1. Interview with Eddy Zervigón, Queens, New York, June 18, 2016.
2. John Storm Roberts and others cite Latin soul as being an offshoot of bugalú as pioneered by Joe Bataan in the 1970s. See Roberts, *The Latin Tinge*.
3. The late 1960s and 1970s saw a resurgence of pan-Africanism and an increasing interest in Afro-Cuban rumba and religious musics with Afro-Cuban drumming a feature in New York's Central Park. This younger generation of Puerto Ricans were more politically engaged and drawn toward African American cultural movements (e.g., the Puerto Rican Young Lords were allies of the Black Panther movement). The preference for the term "Afro-Cuban music" for Cuban popular dance styles spoken of by percussionist John Berdeguer reflects this pan-African philosophy.
4. Pete Rodríguez, "I Like It Like That," *I Like It Like That* (Alegre LPA 855, 1967).
5. Ricardo Ray, "Lookie Lookie," *Se Solto'—On the Loose* (Alegre LPA 850, 1967). Vinyl, USA.
6. Joe Cuba Sextet, "Bang! Bang!" (45, Tico T-475, 1966).
7. Manny Rivera, telephone interview, New York, June 27, 2016.
8. Interview with John Berdeguer, Brooklyn, New York, June 15, 2016.
9. Chollo Rivera & Latin Soul Drives, "I Could Never Hurt You Girl" (45, Cotique C-149, 1969).
10. "Boogaloo Blues" was a hit for Johnny Colón in 1967.
11. Tito and Tony were Tito Ramos and Tony Rojas, members of Johnny Colón's band, described by Flores as "Harlem street-corner harmonizers" (Flores, *Salsa Rising*, 117).
12. Interview with John Berdeguer, Brooklyn, New York, June 15, 2016.
13. Eddie Palmieri, "African Twist," *Champagne—Eddie Palmieri and His Orchestra* (Tico LP 1165, 1968).
14. This venue could possibly be the 3-and-1 Club. See Flores, *Salsa Rising*, 2016, 114.
15. Interview with Mark Weinstein, New Jersey, June 22, 2016.
16. Interview with Willie Rodríguez, Lehman Center for the Performing Arts, New York, June 21, 2016.
17. Flores, *Salsa Rising*, 110.
18. Chris Kenner, "I Like It Like That" (45, Instant Records (6) VR-3229, 1961).
19. Flores, *Salsa Rising*, 107.
20. "Espiritu Burlón" by Orquesta Aragón, recorded July 30, 1957, was very popular and was covered by Johnny Pacheco in 1961. Orquesta Aragón, "Espíritu Burlón" (CU 1167, V 23-7313, CU VLPM 1609 TH VCD 3204-2RL). Also on *Orquesta Aragón Legends of Cuban Music* (Nostalgia for Cuba Records CD G50 5030, 2001). Johnny Pacheco, "Espiritu Burlón," *Pacheco y su Charanga, Vol. 2* (Alegre LPA 805, 1961).
21. *King Solomon's Mines*, dir. Compton Bennett and Andrew Marton, MGM. 1950. The official film trailer can be viewed here: https://www.youtube.com/watch?v=tmXgC7k-QB0&list=PLLGOsLEp2nzuVBgZ8B4ZohMwcxfMsKAq-, accessed February 13, 2018.
22. Ray Barrretto, "El Watusi," *Charanga Moderna* (Tico LP 1087, 1962); "Watusi '65," *Viva Watusi!* (United Artists HiFi UAL 3445, 1965).
23. Flores, *Salsa Rising*, 111.

24. Musicologist Janice Mahinka notes that dancers of bugalú also value this spontaneity and describe their approach to dance this way.

25. Flores, *Salsa Rising*, 121.

26. According to Flores, Joe Cuba's nickname was "Sonny." His real name was Gilbert Calderón and Joe Cuba was his stage name.

27. Cited in Flores, *Salsa Rising*, 120. Originally in Mary Kent, *Salsa Talks: A Musical Heritage Uncovered* (Altamonte Springs, FL: Digital Domain, 2005), 260.

28. Mark Weinstein, New Jersey, June 22, 2016. It is outside the scope of this book to look at the gender aspects of the idiom, but this comment by Weinstein demonstrates the male-dominated environment of the scene. For my own perspectives on gender in Latin music performance, see Miller, "Perceptions of Authenticity in the Performance of Cuban Popular Music in the UK."

29. Dizzy Gillespie, "Manteca," *Afro* (Norgran Records, MG N-1003, 1954).

30. Salazar, *Mambo Kingdom*, 236.

31. José Fajardo, "Batman Boogaloo," *Fajardo's Boogaloo* (Kubaney LP MT-335, 1968).

32. José Fajardo, "Batman Boogaloo."

33. This "Russian" melody appears in solos frequently as a well-loved quotation. It appears in the piano solo at 5:05 for example on Rubén González, "Mandinga," *Introducing Rubén González* (World Circuit WCD 049). It is associated with the song "Ojos Negros," with lyrics by Russian-Ukranian composer Yevhen Hrebinka and music by German composer Florian Hermann, and a popular version by Italian-British composer Adalgiso Ferraris. The song is part of tzigane/gypsy repertoire and was performed to me in 2019 near Budapest by a tzigane trio of violin, cimbalom, and double bass. See Alfredo and His Gypsy Band (1934) for an entertaining version close to Fajardo's quotation https://www.youtube.com/watch?v=57c5utLEyyU, accessed August 31, 2019.

34. See Miller, *Cuban Flute Style*, 170–71, for more on the significance of the bugle call in Cuban music.

Chapter 9

1. Barretto's first charanga album featured Tito Rodríguez on vocals; and of the three Palladium bandleaders, Rodríguez is said by some interviewed for this book to have had the most cubanía in his music (interviews with Eddy Zervigón, Queens, June 18, 2016; Manny Rivera, New York, June 27, 2016; and David Pérez, Brooklyn, June 11, 2016).

2. Ray Barretto Charanga Band, *Barretto Para Bailar* (Riverside Records RLP 93531, 1961). Ray Barretto and His Charanga Orchestra, *Pachanga with Barretto* (Riverside RLP 97506, 1961).

3. Andrés Campo Uribe, "Ray Barretto. Que Viva La Música!" Herencia Latina, May 2006. http://www.herencialatina.com/Ray_Baretto_campo/Ray_Barretto.htm, accessed January 10, 2019.

4. In his interview with Aurora Flores, for example, Pacheco says he wrote most of the arrangements for Charlie Palmieri's La Duboney because Charlie was lazy! "Johnny Pacheco," interview by Aurora Flores at the Boy's Harbor Conservatory in 2003. https://www.youtube.com/watch?v=Bq2wmKk2fwE, accessed November 27, 2017. Pacheco does, however, credit Louis Ramírez for arranging his hit numbers "Oyeme Mulata" and "El Güiro de Macorina."

5. "Ray Barretto interview 2003," interview by Aurora Flores at the Boy's Harbor Conservatory in 2003. https://www.youtube.com/watch?v=Br53oh67IQE, accessed November 27, 2017.
6. Uribe, "Ray Barretto. Que Viva La Música!"
7. "Ray Barretto interview 2003," at 44:20.
8. "Ray Barretto interview 2003," at 22:45.
9. Ray Barretto, "El Watusi."
10. Uribe, "Ray Barretto. Que Viva La Música!"
11. Kim Burton, email correspondence with the author, January 12 and 13, 2019.
12. The characteristic violin pedal in "El Watusi" recurs frequently in Barretto's work and is related to the "Oye Como Va" vamp as examined in chapter 2, further demonstrating a New York interpretation of Cuban music performance practice.
13. Ray Barretto, "Te Traigo Guajira," *On Fire Again—Encendido Otra Vez* (Tico LP 1096, 1963).
14. Ray Barretto, "Te Traigo Guajira."
15. Canoura appears with a metal flute on the cover of *Viva Watusi!* but with a five-key wooden flute on the cover of the 1962 *Latino!* album. It sounds as if he is playing the five-key charanga flute on this recording. Here, on the track "Sugar's Delight," Canoura's playing features a little more jazz inflection in terms of some added blue notes and a quote of Gershwin's "I Got Plenty o' Nuttin'" at 2:23 alongside a Cuban melody quotation to finish. Although lauded by Uribe (2006) as "estupendo" [fantastic], this solo is less fluid than his solo on "Te Traigo Guajira." Perhaps Canoura is new to playing the five-key flute on this recording.
16. Interview with Eddy Zervigón, Queens, New York, June 18, 2016.
17. Interview with Al Angeloro, New York, June 21, 2016.
18. Bunny Matthews, "Fredy Omar: The Latin King of Frenchmen Street," *OffBeat Magazine*, December 1, 2002.
19. The slow-burning "Dulce Cha Cha Cha" from *Viva Watusi!* is a good example of Barretto's more sensual take on Cuban music.
20. For more on the Cuban guajira progression see Miller, *Cuban Flute Style*, 178. See also Miller, "Música Guajira," 337–41.
21. Interview with Andrea Brachfeld, New Jersey, June 17, 2016.
22. Rolando Lozano has complained about US-based sound engineers turning him down in the mix; see Danilo Lozano, "The Charanga Tradition in Cuba: History, Style and Ideology" (MA thesis, University of California, Los Angeles, 1990), 137.
23. Telephone interview with Jesse Herrero, New York, June 22, 2016.
24. Ray Barretto, "Swing La Moderna," *Guajira y Guaguancó* (Tico LP 1114, 1965).
25. Interview with Johnny Pacheco by Aurora Flores at the Boy's Harbor Conservatory in 2003.
26. Interview with Joe De Jesus, New York, June 27, 2016.
27. Interview with Jesse Herrero, June 22, 2016.

Conclusion

1. Interview with Joe De Jesus, New York, June 27, 2016.
2. Interview with Connie Grossman, Tarrytown, New York, June 18, 2016.

3. Interview with Mark Weinstein, New Jersey, June 22, 2016.

4. Peter Manuel, "Improvisation in Latin Dance Music," in Bruno Nettl and Melinda Russell (eds.), *In the Course of Performance: Studies in the World of Musical Improvisation* (Chicago: University of Chicago Press, 1998), 143–44.

5. It has been noted by some that fewer black and mixed-race charanga musicians emigrated to the USA following the Cuban Revolution and US embargo. As Joe de Jesus states: "They [white Cubans] were more privileged, and they owned businesses, and were more educated, and they were able to travel, and those who weren't as educated and weren't as wealthy weren't able to travel. Even if they created or perfected a style, they didn't have the opportunities." Interview with Joe de Jesus, New York, June 27, 2016. Richard Egües, as an Afro-Cuban, may well have feared racial prejudice in the USA even though Orquesta Aragón was famous and he was a star and well off at the time of the revolution. Nevertheless, the mixed-race charanga bands of 1940s and '50s Cuba became generally less mixed in the US context. The 1940s–'60s in the USA was a period rife with racial prejudice and discrimination and there are many tales of Machito and Tito Puente encountering problems with promoters who insisted on the segregation of white and black players (particularly while on tour in the American South).

6. See Sue Miller and Paul Thompson's work on the British Academy–funded project "An Investigation of Mid-Twentieth-Century Recording Techniques and Aesthetics in Latin Music Performance and Production." Published online. https://www.charangasue.com/british-academy-research-project/, accessed June 19, 2020.

7. Interview with Connie Grossman, Tarrytown, New York, June 18, 2016.

8. Interview with Karen Joseph, Brooklyn, June 24, 2016.

9. For more details on the Cuban flute style given by Lorente, see Ruth "Sunni" Witmer, "Cuban Charanga: Class, Popular Music, and the Creation of National Identity" (PhD diss., University of Florida, Gainesville, 2011).

10. For some analysis of the playing styles of Connie Grossman, Karen Joseph, and Andrea Brachfeld, see Chapter 6 of Valiente, "Siento una Flauta."

11. John Storm Roberts has documented this to some extent in *Latin Jazz*. The Jewish contribution has been explored further in Amalia Ran and Moshe Morad (eds.), *Mazal Tov, Amigos! Jews and Popular Music in the Americas* (Leiden and Boston: Brill, 2016).

12. Cuban flute player René Lorente believes that Latin dance music in New York is a watered-down version of Cuban music, possibly due to the lack of virtuosity of New York–based flute players as compared to Richard Egües in Orquesta Aragón. Interview with René Lorente, Miami, July 2, 2016.

Glossary

1. For more on improvisatory approach, see Miller, *Cuban Flute Style*, 65.
2. See Garcia, *Arsenio Rodríguez*, 47–55.
3. Garcia, *Arsenio Rodríguez*, 57.
4. Garcia, *Arsenio Rodríguez*, 57.

BIBLIOGRAPHY

Abreu, Christina D. *Rhythms of Race: Cuban Musicians and the Making of Latino New York City and Miami, 1940–1960*. Chapel Hill: University of North Carolina Press, 2015.
Acosta, Leonardo. *Del Tambor al Sintetizador*. La Habana: Editorial Letras Cubanas, 1983.
Acosta, Leonardo. *Descarga Cubana: El Jazz En Cuba 1900–1950* [Cuban Jam Sessions: Jazz in Cuba 1900–1950]. Havana: Ediciones Unión, 2000.
Acosta, Leonardo. *Cubano Be, Cubano Bop: One Hundred Years of Jazz in Cuba*. Foreword by Paquito D'Rivera, preface by Raúl Fernández, translated by Daniel S. Whitesell. Washington, DC: Smithsonian Books, 2003.
Agawu, Kofi V. *Representing African Music: Postcolonial Notes, Queries, Positions*. New York: Routledge, 2003.
Agawu, Kofi V. *The African Imagination in Music*. New York: Oxford University Press, 2016.
Aparicio, Frances R. *Listening to Salsa: Gender, Latin Popular Music, and Puerto Rican Cultures*. Middletown, CT: Wesleyan University Press, 1998.
Austerlitz, Paul. *Merengue: Dominican Music and Dominican Identity*. Philadelphia: Temple University Press, 1997.
Austerlitz, Paul. *Jazz Consciousness: Music, Race and Humanity*. Middletown, Connecticut: Wesleyan University Press, 2005.
Badger, Reid. *A Life in Ragtime: A Biography of James Reese Europe*. New York: Oxford University Press, 1995.
Bailey, Derek. *Improvisation: its Nature and Practice in Music*. Ashbourne, Derbyshire: Moorland Publishing, 1980.
Berliner, Paul. *Thinking in Jazz: The Infinite Art of Improvisation*. Chicago and London: University of Chicago Press, 1994.
Berríos, M. Juanita, Anna Carol Dudley, and Eva Pallán Habell. Trans. Angie Berríos-Miranda. *American Sabor: Latinos and Latinas in US Popular Music/Latinos y Latinas en La Música Popular Estadounidense*. Seattle and London: University of Washington Press, 2018.
Bodenheimer, Rebecca M. *Geographies of Cubanidad: Place, Race, and Musical Performance in Contemporary Cuba*. Jackson: University Press of Mississippi, 2015.
Boggs, Vernon. *Salsiology: Afrocuban Music and the Evolution of Salsa in New York City*. New York: Excelsior Music, 1992.
Boulanger, Alain. *La Havane á Paris—Musiciens Cubains á Paris (1925–1955)*. Saint-Etienne-du-Rouvray, France: Jazzedit, 2018.

Brown, Howard Mayer. *Embellishing 16th-Century Music*. Early Music Series 1. London: Oxford University Press, 1976.

Buckland, Theresa Jill (ed.). *Dancing from Past to Present: Nation, Culture, Identities*. Madison: University of Wisconsin Press, 2006.

Burnard, P. *Musical Creativities in Practice*. Oxford: Oxford University Press, 2012.

Burnard, P., and Elisabeth Haddon (eds.). *Activating Diverse Creativities for Changing Higher Music Education: Contemporary Research and Practices*. London: Bloomsbury, 2015.

Cerchiari, Luca, Laurent Cugny, and Franz Kerschbaumer (eds.). *Eurojazzland: Jazz and European Sources, Dynamics, and Contexts*. Boston: Northeastern University Press, 2012.

Chase, Gilbert. *America's Music: From the Pilgrims to the Present*. New York: McGraw-Hill, 1955.

Chasteen, John Charles. *National Rhythms, African Roots: The Deep History of Latin American Popular Dance*. Albuquerque: University of New Mexico Press, 2004.

Chernoff, John Miller. *African Rhythm and African Sensibility: Aesthetics and Social Action in African Musical Idioms*. Chicago and London: University of Chicago Press, 1979.

Child, John. "Fajardo, José Antonio." In Donald Clarke (ed.), *The Penguin Encyclopedia of Popular Music*. 2nd ed. London: Penguin Books, 1998.

Child, John. "Fajardo the Charanga Flute King Dies." April 15, 2002. http://www.descarga.com/cgi-bin/db/archives/Profile70, accessed July 18, 2010.

Clark, Walter Aaron (ed.). *From Tejano to Tango*. New York and London: Routledge, 2002.

Conzo, Joe, and David A. Pérez. *Mambo Diablo: My Journey with Tito Puente*. Milwaukee: Backbeat Books, 2010.

Cunningham, Laura Shaine. "Ghosts of El Morocco." *New York Times*, September 5, 2004. http://www.nytimes.com/2004/09/05/nyregion/thecity/ghosts-of-elmorocco.html, accessed October 28, 2016.

Dalmace, Patrick. *La Musique Cubaine á Paris entre 1930 et la Seconde Guerre Mondiale et Autres Textes*. Saint-Denis, France: Edilivre, 2017.

Davies, Rick. *Trompeta: Chappottín, Chocolate, and the Afro-Cuban Trumpet Style*. Lanham, MD: Scarecrow Press, 2003.

Díaz Ayala, Cristóbal. *Música Cubana del Areyto al Rap Cubano*. 4ta Edición. Miami: Fundación Musicalia, 2003 [1981].

Díaz Ayala, Cristóbal. *Enciclopedia Discográfica de la Música Cubana Volume 2, 1925–1960*. [Encyclopedic Discography of Cuban Music vol. 2, 1925–1960]. Florida International University, 2002. http://latinpop.fiu.edu/downloadfiles2.html, accessed January 22, 2018.

Doleac, Benjamin. "Strictly Second Line: Funk, Jazz and the New Orleans Beat." *Ethnomusicology Review* 18 (2013). https://ethnomusicologyreview.ucla.edu/journal/volume/18/piece/699, accessed January 29, 2019.

Dunlap, L., and Rebecca Mauleon (eds). *The Latin Real Book*. Petaluma, CA: Sher Music, 1997.

Feintuch, Burt [interviews], and Gary Samson [photographs]. *Talking New Orleans Music: Crescent City Musicians Talk about Their Lives, Their Music, and Their City*. Jackson: University Press of Mississippi, 2015.

Fernández, Loyola, J. *La Charanga y sus Maravillas Orquesta Aragón*. Havana: Ediciones Museo de la Música, 2015.
Fernández, R. *Latin Jazz: The Perfect Combination*. San Francisco: Chronicle Books, 2002.
Fiehrer, Thomas. "From Quadrille to Stomp: The Creole Origins of Jazz." *Popular Music* 10, no. 1, "The 1890s" (January 1991): 21–38.
Figueroa, Frank M. "New York's Latin Music Landmarks." In Claudio Ivan Remeseira (ed.), *Hispanic New York: A Sourcebook*. New York: Columbia University Press, 2010, 361–36.
Flores, Juan. *Salsa Rising: New York Latin Music of the Sixties Generation*. New York: Oxford University Press, 2016.
Floyd Jr., Samuel A. *The Power of Black Music: Interpreting Its History from Africa to the United States*. New York: Oxford University Press, 1995.
Floyd Jr., Samuel A. "'Ring Shout!' Literary Studies, Historical Studies, and Black Music Inquiry." *Black Music Research Journal* 22 (Supplement: Best of *BMRJ* 2002): 49–70.
Forsdick, Charles, and Christian Høgsbjerg. *Toussaint Louverture: A Black Jacobin in the Age of Revolutions*. London: Pluto Press, 2017.
Gammond, Peter. *Scott Joplin and the Ragtime Era*. London: Abacus, 1975.
Garcia, David. F. "Contesting That Damned Mambo: Arsenio Rodríguez, Authenticity, and the People of El Barrio and the Bronx in the 1950s." *Centro Journal* XI, No. 1 (Spring 2004):155–75.
Garcia, David F. *Arsenio Rodríguez and the Transnational Flows of Latin Popular Music*. Philadelphia: Temple University Press, 2006.
Garriga, Silvana, ed. *Mamá yo Quiero Saber . . . Entrevistas a Músicos Cubanos*. Havana: Editorial Letras Cubanas, 1999.
Gates, Henry Louis, Jr. *The Signifying Monkey: A Theory of African-American Literary Criticism*. New York: Oxford University Press, 1989.
Gerard, Charley, and Marty Sheller. *Salsa: The Rhythm of Latin Music*. Tempe, AZ: White Cliffs Media, 1989.
German, Héctor Agustín Ulloque. *Orquesta Aragón*. Havana: Editorial Unión de Periodistas de Cuba, 2004.
Ginell, Cary. *The Evolution of Mann: Herbie Mann and the Flute in Jazz*. Milwaukee, WI: Hal Leonard Books, 2014.
Gioia, Ted. *The Imperfect Art: Reflections on Jazz and Modern Culture*. New York and Oxford: Oxford University Press, 1988.
Giro, Radamés (ed.). *Panorama de la Música Popular Cubana*. Havana: Editorial Letras Cubanas, 1995.
Giro, Radamés (ed.). *Música Popular Cubana*. Havana: Editorial José Martí, 2007.
Glasser, Ruth. *My Music Is My Flag: Puerto Rican Musicians and Their New York Communities 1917–1940*. Berkeley and Los Angeles: University of California Press, 1995.
Gómez Cairo, Jesús (ed.). *Ernesto Lecuona*. Havana: Letras Cubanas, 2005.
Gushee, Lawrence. "The Nineteenth-Century Origins of Jazz." *Black Music Research Journal* 22 (Supplement: Best of *BMRJ* 2002): 151–74.
Hentoff, Nat, and Nat Shapiro. *Hear Me Talkin' to Ya: The Story of Jazz as Told by the Men Who Made It*. New York: Dover, 1955.

Hobson, Vic. *Creating Jazz Counterpoint: New Orleans, Barbershop Harmony, and the Blues*. Jackson: University Press of Mississippi, 2014.

Horn, D., Heidi Feldman, et al. *The Continuum Encyclopedia of Popular Music of the World (EPMOW): Part 3, Genres (Caribbean and Latin American Genres)*. London: Bloomsbury, 2014.

Hurston, Zora Neale. *The Sanctified Church*. Berkeley: Turtle Island, 1981.

Hutchinson, Sydney (ed.). *Salsa World: A Global Dance in Local Contexts*. Philadelphia: Temple University Press, 2014.

Hutchinson, Sydney (ed.). "Mambo on 2: The Birth of a New Form of Dance in New York City." *Centro Journal* XVI, no. 2 (Fall 2004): 109–37.

Jones, Will. *How to Read New York: A Crash Course in Big Apple Architecture*. Brighton: Ivy Press, 2016.

Jottar, Berta. "From Central Park—Rumba with Love." *Voices: Journal of New York Folklore* (New York Folklore Society) 37, no. 1/2 (Spring–Summer 2011): 24–31.

Keil, C., and Steven Feld. *Music Grooves: Essays and Dialogues*. London and Chicago: University of Chicago Press, 1994.

Kent, Mary. *Salsa Talks: A Musical Heritage Uncovered*. Altamonte Springs, FL: Digital Domain, 2005, 260.

Kernfeld, Barry. *What to Listen For in Jazz*. New Haven and London: Yale University Press, 1995.

Kmen, Henry A. "The Roots of Jazz and the Dance in Place Congo: A Re-Appraisal." *Anuario Interamericano de Investigacion Musical* 8 (1972): 5–16.

Lapidus, Benjamin. *Origins of Cuban Music and Dance: Changüí*. Lanham, MD: Scarecrow Press, 2008.

Lechner, Ernesto. Sleeve notes to *Pacheco y su Charanga*. Fania Records 773 130 219-2 CD, reissue Emusica Records, 2007.

Legg, Andrew, and Carolyn Philpott. "An Analysis of Performance Practices in African American Gospel Music: Rhythm, Lyric Treatment and Structures in Improvisation and Accompaniment." *Popular Music* 34, no. 2 (May 2015): 197–225.

Léon, Javier F., and Helena Simonett (eds.). *Views from the South: A Latin American Music Reader*. Urbana and Chicago: University of Illinois Press, 2016.

López-Cano, Rubén. "Mambo." In *The Continuum Encyclopedia of Popular Music of the World (EPMOW): Part 3, Genres (Caribbean and Latin American Genres)*. London: Bloomsbury, 2014.

López-Cano, Rubén. "Notes for a Prehistory of Mambo." In Léon, Javier F., and Helena Simonett (eds.), *Views from the South: A Latin American Music Reader*. Urbana and Chicago: University of Illinois Press, 2016.

Lozano, D. "The Charanga Tradition in Cuba: History, Style, and Ideology." MA thesis. Los Angeles: University of California at Los Angeles, 1990.

Malcomson, Hettie. "The 'Routes' and 'Roots' of *Danzón*: A Critique of the History of a Genre." *Popular Music* 30, no. 2 (2011): 263–78.

Manuel, Peter (ed.). *Essays on Cuban Music: North American and Cuban Perspectives*. Lanham, MD, New York, and London: University Press of America, 1991.

Manuel, Peter. "Puerto Rican Music and Cultural Identity: Creative Appropriation of Cuban Sources from Danza to Salsa." *Ethnomusicology* 38, no. 2, Music and Politics (Spring-Summer 1994): 249–80.

Manuel, Peter. *Caribbean Currents: Caribbean Music from Rumba to Reggae*. London: Latin America Bureau, 1995.

Manuel, Peter. "Representations of New York City in Latin Music." In Ray Allen and Lois Wilcken (eds.), *Island Sounds in the Global City: Caribbean Popular Music and Identity in New York*, 23–43. New York: New York Folklore Society, 1998.

Manuel, Peter. "Improvisation in Latin Dance Music." In Bruno Nettl and Melinda Russell (eds.), *In the Course of Performance: Studies in the World of Musical Improvisation*. Chicago: University of Chicago Press, 1998, 127–47.

Manuel, Peter (ed.). *Creolizing Contradance in the Caribbean*. Philadelphia: Temple University Press, 2009.

Marrero, Gaspar. "José Antonio Fajardo: Evocación." Paper given at the conference Encuentro Nacional de Orquestas Charangas Rafael Lay in Memoriam. *Palma Soriano* no. XIV (1998).

Marrero, Gaspar. *La Orquesta Aragón*. 2nd ed. Havana: Editorial José Martí, 2008.

Martín, Mimi Ortiz. "La Clave del Rey: En Casa de Johnny Pacheco—Patriarca de la Música Latina." *El Nuevo Día* (Puerto Rico), April 15, 2007. Available from the Herencia Latina website.

Martínez Rodríguez, Raúl. *Benny Moré*. Havana: Editorial Letras Cubanas, 1993.

Martínez Rodríguez, Raúl. *Para El Alma Divertir*. Havana: Editorial Letras Cubanas, 2004.

Matthews, Bunny. "Fredy Omar: The Latin King of Frenchmen Street." *OffBeat*, December 1, 2002.

Mauléon, Rebeca. *Salsa Guidebook for Piano and Ensemble*. Petaluma, CA: Sher Music, 1993.

Metzer, David. "Shadow Play: The Spiritual in Duke Ellington's Black and Tan Fantasy." *Black Music Research Journal* 17, no. 2 (Autumn 1997): 137–58.

Miller, Sue. "Interview with Richard Egües, Flautist from Orquesta Aragón and Cuban Flute Legend." *Pan: Journal of the British Flute Society* 19, no. 4 (December 2000): 51–53.

Miller, Sue. "Interview between Melquiades Fundora and Sue Miller, Havana 2001." *Pan: Journal of the British Flute Society* 22, no. 1 (March 2003): 27.

Miller, Sue. CD review. "*Out of Cuba: Latin American Music Takes Africa by Storm.*" *World of Music* 48, no. 1 (2006): 151–52.

Miller, Sue. Book review. "*Music and Revolution: Cultural Change in Socialist Cuba* by Robin D. Moore." *Cultural Politics* 3, no. 2 (2007): 265–68.

Miller, Sue. "Flute Improvisation in Cuban Charanga Performance: with a specific focus on the work of Richard Egües and Orquesta Aragón." PhD thesis, University of Leeds, 2010.

Miller, Sue. "Perceptions of Authenticity in the Performance of Cuban Popular Music in the UK: 'globalised incuriosity' in the promotion and reception of UK-based Charanga del Norte's music since 1998." *Journal of European Popular Culture* 4, no. 1 (2013): 99–116.

Miller, Sue. "Cuban Son." In *The Continuum Encyclopedia of Popular Music of the World (EPMOW): Part 3, Genres (Caribbean and Latin American Genres)*. London: Bloomsbury, 2014.

Miller, Sue. "Música Guajira." In *The Continuum Encyclopedia of Popular Music of the World (EPMOW): Part 3, Genres (Caribbean and Latin American Genres).* London: Bloomsbury, 2014.

Miller, Sue. *Cuban Flute Style: Interpretation and Improvisation.* Lanham, MD: Scarecrow Press, 2014.

Miller, Sue. "Activating Improvisational Creativity in the Performance of 'World' and 'Popular' Music." In Pam Burnard and Elisabeth Haddon (eds.), *Activating Diverse Creativities for Changing Higher Music Education: Contemporary Research and Practices.* London: Bloomsbury, 2015, 99–122.

Monson, Ingrid. "Doubleness and Jazz Improvisation: Irony, Parody, and Ethnomusicology." *Critical Inquiry* 20, no. 2 (Winter 1994): 283–313.

Monson, Ingrid. *Saying Something: Jazz Improvisation and Interaction.* Chicago: University of Chicago Press, 1996.

Moore, Robin D. "The Decline of Improvisation in Western Art Music: An Interpretation of Change." *International Review of the Aesthetics and Sociology of Music* 23, no. 1 (Croatian Musicological Society HMD) (June 1992): 61–84.

Moore, Robin D. "Representations of Afrocuban Expressive Culture in the Writings of Fernando Ortiz." *Latin American Music Review/Revista de Música Latinoamericana* 15, no.1 (Spring–Summer 1994): 32–54.

Moore, Robin D. *Nationalizing Blackness: Afrocubanismo and Artistic Revolution in Havana, 1920–1940.* Pittsburgh, PA: University of Pittsburgh Press, 1997.

Moore, Robin D. *Music and Revolution: Cultural Change in Socialist Cuba.* Berkeley and Los Angeles: University of California Press, 2006.

Moore, Robin D. *Music in the Hispanic Caribbean: Experiencing Music, Expressing Culture.* New York and Oxford: Oxford University Press, 2010.

Moore, Robin D., general ed., and Walter Aaron Clark, contributing ed. *Musics of Latin America.* New York: W. W. Norton, 2012.

Moore, Robin D., and Alejandro Madrid. *Danzón: Circum-Caribbean Dialogues in Music and Dance.* New York: University of Oxford Press, 2013.

Moore, Robin D. (ed.). *Fernando Ortiz on Music: Selected Writing on Afro-Cuban Culture.* Philadelphia: Temple University Press, 2018.Morales, Ed. *The Latin Beat: The Rhythms and Roots of Latin Music from Bossa Nova to Salsa and Beyond.* Cambridge, MA: Da Capo Press, 2003.

Morales, Ed. "The Story of Nuyorican Salsa." In Claudio Ivan Remeseira (ed.), *Hispanic New York: A Sourcebook.* New York: Columbia University Press, 2010, 367–92.

Murphy, John P. "Jazz Improvisation: The Joy of Influence." *Black Perspective in Music* 18, no. 1–2 (1990): 7–19.

Murphy, John P. "The Charanga in New York and the Persistence of the Típico Style." In Peter Manuel (ed.), *Essays on Cuban Music: North American and Cuban Perspectives.* Lanham, MD, New York, and London: University Press of America, 1991, 115–36.

Nettl, Bruno, and Melinda Russell (eds.). *In the Course of Performance: Studies in the World of Musical Improvisation.* London and Chicago: University of Chicago Press, 1998.

Nooshin, Laudan. "Improvisation as 'Other': Creativity, Knowledge and Power—The Case of Iranian Classical Music." *Journal of the Royal Music Association* 128, no. 2 (2003): 242–96.

Orovio, Helio. *Diccionario de la Música Cubana, Biografico y Técnico*. Havana: Letras Cubanas, 1981.

Ospina, Hernando Calvo. *¡Salsa! Havana Heat, Bronx Beat*. Trans. Nick Caistor. London: Latin American Bureau, 1995.

Owens, Thomas. *Charlie Parker: Techniques of Improvisation*. 2 vols. PhD diss., University of California at Los Angeles. 1974.

Owens, Thomas. *BeBop: The Music and Its Players*. New York and Oxford: Oxford University Press, 1995.

Pérez, David A. "The Five Key Charanga Flute." 2009. Article on the Descarga.com website (now defunct). http://www.descarga.com/cgi-bin/db/archives/Article15, accessed September 24, 2018.

Pérez Firmat, Gustavo. *Life on the Hyphen: The Cuban American Way*. Austin: University of Texas Press, 1994.

Powell, Josephine. *Tito Puente: When the Drums Are Dreaming*. Bloomington, IN: AuthorHouse, 2007.

Pugh, Megan. *America Dancing: From the Cakewalk to the Moonwalk*. New Haven and London: Yale University Press, 2015.

Quintana, Jorge. "Humara y Lastra: 100 Años al Servicio Comercial de Cuba." [Humara and Lastra: 100 years of Commercial Service in Cuba.] *Bohemia* 46, no. 23 (June 6, 1954): 64–65.

Raeburn, Bruce Boyd. "Beyond the 'Spanish Tinge': Hispanics and Latinos in Early New Orleans Jazz." In Luca Cerchiari, Laurent Cugny, and Franz Kerschbaumer (eds.), *Eurojazzland: Jazz and European Sources, Dynamics, and Contexts*. Boston: Northeastern University Press, 2012, 21–46.

Ran, Amalia, and Moshe Morad (eds.). *Mazal Tov, Amigos! Jews and Popular Music in the Americas*. Leiden and Boston: Brill, 2016.

Remeseira, Claudio Ivan. *Hispanic New York: A Sourcebook*. New York: Columbia University Press, 2010.

Robbins, James. "The Cuban Son as Form, Genre, and Symbol." *Latin American Music Review* 11, no. 2 (1990): 182–200.

Roberts, John Storm. *Black Music of Two Worlds*. London: Allen Lane, 1973.

Roberts, John Storm. *The Latin Tinge: The Impact of Latin American Music on the United States*. New York: Original Music, 1985 [originally published by Oxford University Press, 1979].

Roberts, John Storm. *Latin Jazz: The First of the Fusions, 1880s to Today*. New York: Schirmer Books, 1999.

Rodríguez de Tió, Lola. "A Cuba." In *Mi Libro de Cuba: Poesías*. Habana: Imprenta La Moderna, 1893, 3–6.

Rodríguez Domínguez, Ezequiel. *Iconografía del Danzón*. Havana: Sub-Dirección Provincial de Música 14, 1967.

Rodríguez, Olavo Alen. Sleeve notes to Fajardo y sus Estrellas, *Esto Sólo Se Da En Cuba*. BIS music CD-109, reissue, 1995.

Rondón, César Miguel. *El Libro de La Salsa: Crónico de la Música del Caribe Urbano*. Trans. Frances R. Aparicio with Jackie White. Caracas: Editorial Arte, 1980.

Rondón, César Miguel. *The Book of Salsa: A Chronicle of Urban Music from the Caribbean to New York City*. Trans. Frances R. Aparicio with Jackie White. Chapel Hill: University of North Carolina Press, 2008.

Salazar, Max. *Mambo Kingdom: Latin Music in New York*. New York: Schirmer Trade Books, 2002.

Salazar, Max. "Listo Arcaño? Antonio Arcaño, Músico Pionero de Cuba [Ready Arcaño? Antonio Arcaño, Pioneering Cuban Musician]." *Latin Beat* (June 2001). http://find articles.com/p/articles/mi_m0FXV/is_5_11/ai_76963693/?tag=content;col1, accessed August 22, 2010.

Sánchez-Coll, Israel. "Belisario López Rossi (1903–1969): El Rey del Danzón Puro." Herencia Latina, n.d. www.herencialatina.com/Belisario_Lopez/Belisario.htm, accessed August 9, 2012.

Sánchez-Coll, Israel. "Tributo a Lou Pérez." Herencia Latina, n.d. http://www.herenciala tina.com/Lou_Perez/Lou_Perez%20I.htm, accessed December 9, 2016.

Schuller, Gunther. *Early Jazz: Its Roots and Musical Development*. New York: Oxford University Press, 1968.

Singer, Roberta L., and Elena Martínez. "Tradition and Innovation in Contemporary Latin Popular Music in New York City." *Latin American Music Review/Revista de Música Latinoamericana* 4, no. 2 (Autumn–Winter 1983): 183–202.

Singer, Roberta L., and Elena Martínez. "A South Bronx Latin Music Tale." *Centro Journal* XVI, no. 1 (Spring 2004): 176–200. http://www.herencialatina.com/South_Bronx_Latin/ Latin_Music_Bronx.htm, accessed October 24, 2016.

Small, Christopher. *Music of the Common Tongue*. London: Calder, 1987.

Small, Christopher. *Musicking: The Meanings of Performing and Listening*. Hanover, NH: University Press of New England, 1998.

Solis, Gabriel, and Bruno Nettl (eds.). *Musical Improvisation: Art, Education, and Society*. Urbana and Chicago: University of Illinois Press, 2009.

Solis, Gabriel. "Thoughts on an Interdiscipline: Music Theory, Analysis, and Social Theory in Ethnomusicology." *Ethnomusicology* 56, no. 3 (Fall 2012): 530–54.

Southern, Eileen. *The Music of Black Americans: A History*. 3rd ed. New York: W. W. Norton, 1997.

Stearns, Marshall, and Jean Stearns. *Jazz Dance: The Story of American Vernacular Dance*. New York: Macmillan, 1968.

Stewart, Alexander. "'Funky Drummer': New Orleans, James Brown and the Rhythmic Transformation of American Popular Music." *Popular Music* 19, no. 3 (2000): 293–318.

Stokes, Martin (ed.). *Ethnicity, Identity and Music: The Musical Construction of Place*. Oxford and New York: Berg, 1994.

Sublette, Ned. *Cuba and Its Music: From the First Drums to the Mambo*. Chicago: Chicago Review Press, 2004.

Sublette, Ned. *The World That Made New Orleans: From Spanish Silver to Congo Square*. Chicago: Lawrence Hill Books, 2009.

Szwed, John F., and Morton Marks. "The Afro-American Transformation of European Set Dances and Dance Suites." *Dance Research Journal* 20, no. 1 (Summer 1998): 29–36.

Tagg, P. *Music's Meanings: A Modern Musicology for Non-Musos.* New York and Huddersfield: Mass Media Music Scholar's Press, 2012.

Tagg, P. *Everyday Tonality II—Towards a Tonal Theory of What Most People Hear.* New York and Huddersfield: Mass Media Music Scholar's Press, 2018.

Tagg, P. "Guantanamera Endings." Etymophony channel, YouTube. https://www.youtube.com/watch?v=7CStNSlNGfo, accessed August 9, 2018.

Tamargo, Luis. "Desarrollo y Evolución de la Charanga en Los Estados Unidos." *Latin Beat* (1996). http://www.herencialatina.com/Desarrollo_de_la_Charanga/Desarrollo_de_la_Charanga.htm, accessed December 9, 2016.

Torres, D. I. "Del Danzón Cantado al Chachachá." In *Panorama de la Música.* Havana: Letras Cubanas, 1998, 173–97.

Torres, Willie. *"Here I Is . . . Willie T!": The Willie Torres Discography—A Career Timeline and LP Discography.* Compiled by Edwin Garcia with Willie Torres and Louis Laffitte. Self-published [USA], copyright Edwin Garcia, 2013. https://ia902600.us.archive.org/2/items/WillieTorresDiscography/WillieTorresDiscography.pdf, accessed December 28, 2016.

Toulou, Jean-Louis. *A Method for the Flute.* Trans. Janice Dockendorf Boland and Martha F. Cannon. Indianapolis: Indiana University Press, 1995. First pub. 1835.

Uribe, Andres Campo. "Discografía de Charlie Palmieri." Herencia Latina, n.d. http://www.herencialatina.com/Aniversario_Charlie_Palmieri/Charlie_Palmieri_Andres/Charlie_Palmieri_Andres.htm, accessed January 10, 2019.

Uribe, Andres Campo. "Ray Barretto. Que Viva La Música!" Herencia Latina, May 2006. http://www.herencialatina.com/Ray_Baretto_campo/Ray_Barretto.htm, accessed January 10, 2019.

Valdés, Alicia. *Con Música, Textos y Presencia de Mujer: Diccionario de Mujeres Notables en la Música Cubana.* Havana: Ediciones Unión, 2005.

Valiente, Jessica. "Siento una Flauta: Improvisational Idiom, Style, and Performance Practice of Charanga Flutists in New York from 1960 to 2000." DMA thesis, City University of New York, 2015.

Wade, Peter. *Music Race and Nation: Música Tropical in Colombia.* Chicago and London: University of Chicago Press, 2000.

Washburne, Christopher. "The Clave of Jazz: A Caribbean Contribution to the Rhythmic Foundation of an African-American Music." *Black Music Research Journal* 17, no.1 (1997): 59–80.

Washburne, Christopher. *Sounding Salsa: Performing Latin Music in New York City.* Philadelphia: Temple University Press, 2008.

Waxer, Lise. "Of Mambo Kings and Songs of Love: Dance Music in Havana and New York from the 1930s to the 1950s." *Latin American Music Review/Revista de Música Latinoamericana* 15, no. 2 (Autumn–Winter 1994): 139–76.

Waxer, Lise (ed.). *Situating Salsa: Global Markets and Local Meaning in Latin Popular Music.* New York and London: Routledge, 2002.

Weaver, Christian. "The Voice of the Drum in the Vision of the Dispossessed: Social Context, Musical Language and Participation in Cuban Rumba." PhD thesis, University of Salford, 2009.

Wells, Christopher J. "'And I Make My Own': Class Performance, Black Urban Identity, and Depression-Era Harlem's Physical Culture." In Anthony Shay and Barbara Sellers-Young (eds.), *The Oxford Handbook of Dance and Ethnicity*. Oxford: Oxford University Press, 2016, 17–40.

Wells, Christopher J. "'*You* Can't Dance to It': Jazz Music and Its Choreographies of Listening." *Dædalus: Journal of the American Academy of Arts and Sciences* 148, no. 2 (Spring 2019): 36–51.

Westbrook, Peter. *The Flute in Jazz: Window on World Music*. Rockville, MD: Harmonia Books, 2009.

Witmer, Ruth "Sunni." "Cuban Charanga: Class, Popular Music, and the Creation of National Identity." PhD diss., University of Florida, Gainesville, 2011.

Witmer, Sunni. "Review of *Cuban Flute Style: Interpretation and Improvisation* by Sue Miller." *Latin American Music Review* 37, no. 1 (Spring/Summer 2016): 125–27.

Yanow, Scott. *Afro-Cuban Jazz*. San Francisco: Miller Freeman Books, 2000.

Interviews by the Author

Aguirre, Eduardo, Miami, July 1, 2016.
Angeloro, Al, New York, June 21, 2016.
Berdeguer, John, Brooklyn, New York, June 15, 2016.
Brachfeld, Andrea, New Jersey, June 17, 2016.
Barrios, Felo, Miami, July 3, 2016.
Cruz, Gustavo, Miami, July 2, 2016.
De Jesus, Joe, New York, June 27, 2016.
Depestre, Arsenio, Havana, December 17, 2011.
Fundora, Melquiades, Havana, April 2001 and March 28, 2007.
Grossman, Connie, Tarrytown, New York, June 18, 2016.
Herrero, Jesse (telephone), New York, June 22, 2016.
Joseph, Karen, Brooklyn, June 24, 2016.
Lorente, René, Miami, July 2, 2016.
Nestor Torres (Skype), October 18, 2016.
Oliveros, Joaquín, Havana, April 3, 2009, and December 29, 2011.
Oviedo, Ernesto, Havana, February 24, 2006, and April 2007.
Pérez, David, Brooklyn, June 11, 2016.
Rivera, Manny (telephone), New York, June 27, 2016.
Rodríguez, Willie, Lehman College, New York, June 21, 2016.
Tamayo, Policarpo, Havana, February 19, 2006, March 3, 2006, and March 25, 2007.
Valdés, Amadito, Harrogate, UK, August 13, 2008.
Weinstein, Mark, New Jersey, June 22, 2016.
Zervigón, Eddy, New York, 2006 (telephone), July 14, 2007, 2012, 2015, and June 18, 2016.

Interviews by Others

Barretto, Ray. Interview with Aurora Flores at the Boy's Harbor Conservatory in 2003. https://www.youtube.com/watch?v=Br53oh67IQE, accessed November 27, 2017.

Flores, Luis "Máquina." Interview by David Carp, Riverdale, New York, October 22, 1993.
Pacheco, Johnny. Interview with Aurora Flores at the Boy's Harbor Conservatory in 2003. https://www.youtube.com/watch?v=Bq2wmKk2fwE, accessed November 27, 2017.
Pacheco, Johnny. Interview by Mimi Ortiz Martín. "La Clave del Rey: En Casa de Johnny Pacheco—Patriarca de la Música Latina." *El Nuevo Día* (Puerto Rico), April 15, 2007. Available from the Herencia Latina website.
Palmieri, Eddie. Interview with Patricia Rengel for the University of Wisconsin–Madison Department of Spanish and Portuguese, as part of their series "Personalidades de la Cultura Hispánica." n.d., possibly 2006 (the interview broadcast is no longer available online).
Pérez, Lou. Israel Sánchez-Coll, "Tributo a Lou Pérez: Una Entrevista." Herencia Latina, January 6, 2004. http://www.herencialatina.com/Lou_Perez/Lou_Perez%20I.htm, accessed November, 4, 2016.
Zervigón, Eddy. Israel Sánchez-Coll and Nestor Emiro Gómez, "En Casa de Eddy Zervigón, Director de la Orquesta Broadway." Herencia Latina, January 2003. http://www.herencialatina.com/Zervigon/Zervigon.htm, accessed October 14, 2010.
Zervigón, Eddy. "Rene López interviews Eddy Zervigón." Salsa-101. https://www.youtube.com/watch?v=H-egoIlBeHk, accessed August 8, 2018.

Websites

City Lore and the Municipal Arts Society, New York. http://www.placematters.net/mission, accessed October 20, 2016.
Revista Musical Latinoamericana. http://www.herencialatina.com/, accessed October 26, 2016.
Donald Clark's Encyclopedia of Popular Music. http://www.donaldclarkemusicbox.com/encyclopedia/index.php, accessed October 20, 2016.
Charanga del Norte. www.charangadelnorte.co.uk, accessed June 19, 2020.
Dr. Sue Miller, personal website. www.charangasue.com, accessed June 19, 2020.
City Limits. http://citylimits.org/2015/04/17/requiem-for-a-demolished-harlem-shrine/, accessed October 28, 2016.
NYC AGO. http://www.nycago.org/Organs/Brx/html/LoewsSpoonerTheatre.html, accessed October 28, 2016.

Film

Cachao ¡Ahora Sí!. Dir. Andy Garcia (Univision Records, Cineson 0883 10075 0, 2004).
Cachao, Como Su Ritmo No Hay Dos. Dir. Andy Garcia, 1993, USA.
Cuban Love Song. Dir. W. S. Van Dyke, 1931 (USA, Warner Brothers).
From Mambo to Hip-Hop: A South Bronx Tale. Dir. Henry Chalfant (MVD Visual MVDV4785, 2006 and 2008, DVD).
Jazz. Dir. Ken Burns, 2000 [DVD 2009] (USA, PBS/Simply Home Entertainment).
Latin Music USA, vols. 1 & 2. Dir. Daniel McCabe (PBS LMUS601, 2009).
Metropolis. Dir. Fritz Lang, 1927 (Germany, UFA).

Our Latin Thing. Dir. Leon Gast, (Fania, 1971).
Routes of Rhythm with Harry Belafonte. Vols. 1–3. Dir. Eugene Roscow and Howard Dratch (Cultural Research and Communication, Docurama DVD NVG-9476, 1989 and 1991).
The Mambo Kings. Dir. Arne Glimcher, 1992 (USA).
The Palladium: Where Mambo Was King. Dir. Kevin Kaufman, 2002. USA.

Personal Copies of Non-Commercial Archive Videos

From Eddy Zervigón's personal collection in New York, directors unknown:
Para Bailar la Havana
Y Tenemos Sabor (Estrellas Cubanas)
Variedades: Aragón, Barbarito Diez
Orquesta Broadway 50th Anniversary, The Lincoln Center New York, June 30, 2012.

Archival Collections

Cristóbal Díaz Ayala Collection of Latin American Music, Florida International University, Miami, Florida.
John Storm Roberts Collection, Schomburg Center for Research in Black Culture, New York Public Library, New York, New York.

DISCOGRAPHY

Alegre All Stars. *Descargas*. LPA 810 Alegre Records, 1961. CD reissue LPA 8100, Alegre Records, 1996.
Almendra, Johnny, y Los Jovenes del Barrio. *Evolucionando*. RMD 82006, 1996.
Arcaño y Sus Maravillas. *Cuando Los Años Pasan*. Victor V23-0095 [78 rpm], January 10, 1944.
Arcaño y Sus Maravillas. *Mambo—Danzón Mambo* [1944–51]. Tumbao Classics TCD-029, reissue 1993.
Barretto, Ray. *Acid*. Fania Records SLP346, 1968.
Barretto, Ray. *The Big Hits Latin Style—Ray Barretto & His Orchestra*. Tico LP 1099, 1964.
Barretto, Ray. "El Watusi." *Charanga Moderna*. Tico LP 1087, 1962.
Barretto, Ray. *Indestructible*. Fania Records SLP 00456, 1973. CD reissue, Emusica Records 773 130 033-2, 2006.
Barretto, Ray. *La Moderna de Siempre*. Tico LP 1102, 1965.
Barretto, Ray. *Latino!* Riverside RM 3520 US, also RLP 93520, 1963.
Barretto, Ray. *Ray Barretto Charanga Band–Barretto Para Bailar*. Riverside RLP 93531, 1961.
Barretto, Ray. *Ray Barretto and His Charanga Orchestra–Pachanga with Barretto*. Riverside RLP 97506, 1961.
Barretto, Ray. *Ray Barretto Pachanga*. Saludos Amigos Records CD 62068, 1995.
Barretto, Ray. *Señor 007*. United Artists UAL 3478, 1966.
Barretto, Ray. *Swing La Moderna—Ray Barretto Guajira y Guaguanco*. Tico LP 1114, 1965.
Barretto, Ray. "Te Traigo Guajira." *On Fire Again—Encendido Otra Vez*. Tico LP 1096, 1963.
Barretto, Ray. *Viva Watusi!* United Artists HiFi UAL 3445, 1965. CD reissue Sonodisc CDW 4058, 1990.
Barroso, Abelardo. "Tiene Sabor." *Abelardo Barroso and Orquesta Sensación*. Puchito MLP-542, 1959, Cuba. CD reissues: *Charangas de Siempre*, Egrem CD 0846, 2006; *Abelardo Barroso With Orquesta Sensación–Cha Cha Cha*, World Circuit WCV-088, 2014.
Bauzá, Mario, and Hernandez, Rene. *Arthur Murray's Music for Dancing Pachangas*. RCA Victor LSP 2448, 1961.
Boniatillo, Eduardo. A. López. *A Boniatillo Limpio*. Envidia Records A70 7025, 2001, Spain.
Brachfeld, Andrea. *Andrea*. Latina Records LTS-102, 1978.
Bravo, Pancho, y Sus Candelas De Tira Tira. *Bótate na' ma'*. Recorded in Havana 1960–61. CD reissue, Caney Records CCD 522, 2004, Spain.
Buena Vista Social Club. *Buena Vista Social Club at Carnegie Hall*. World Circuit WCD 080, 2008.

Buena Vista Social Club. *Lost and Found.* World Circuit WCD 090, 2015.
Cachao, Israel López. *Andy Garcia Presents Cachao ¡Ahora Sí!* Univision CineSon 0883 10075 0, 2004, CD and DVD.
Cachao, Israel López. *Cachao Master Sessions, Vol. 1.* Epic CD EK 64320, 1994.
Cachao, Israel López. *Cachao y Su Descarga "77" Vol. 1.* Salsoul SAL-4111, 1976.
Cachao, Israel López. *Dos.* Salsoul 20-700-2, 1976.
Cachao, Israel López. *Maestro de Maestros: Cachao y Su Descarga '86.* Tania Records 0013, 1986.
Cachao, Israel López, Tany Gil, Walfredo de los Reyes, Francisco "Paquito" Hechavarria. *Latin Jazz Descarga!!! Part 1.* Tania 0002, 1994 [1981].
Calzado, Rudy. *Rica Charanga!* Caiman LP 9023, 1986.
Chappottín. *Asi Comenzó La Salsa.* Modiner, 2008.
Chappottín y sus Estrellas. "Mi Son, Mi Son, Mi Son." 45 RPM, Areito 7207, Cuba; and Siboney (2) 45-7371.
Charanga America. *Charanga America.* Top Hits TH-AM 2135-Stereo, 1981.
Charanga America. *Charanga America with Gustavo Cruz-Flute "Live" New York City, 1983.* DAP Collection Cassette Conversion, 2011.
Charanga America. *Charanga America with Gustavo Cruz-Flute "Live" at Corso's, 1984.* DAP Collection, Cassette Master Conversion.
Charanga America. *Charanga America—The Very Best.* Combo Records RCSLP 2042, 1985.
Charanga America. *Charanga America y Algo Mas.* Combo RCSLP 2035, 1983.
Charanga America. *"Rendevouz Sensual" Gustavo Cruz con La Charanga America.* 1986, DAP Collection Cassette Conversion, 2011.
Charanga Del Norte. *Atilana.* CDNooCD11, 2015.
Charanga del Norte. *Best of Charanga del Norte.* CDNooCD7, 2005.
Charanga Del Norte. *Charanga Time.* CDNooCD12, 2017.
Charanga Del Norte. *Our Mam in Havana.* CDNooCD09, 2008.
Charanga del Norte. "Que Suene La Charanga." *The Essential Guide to Salsa.* Union Square Records, ESGCD303, 2005, reissued 2012.
Charanga del Norte. "Que Suene La Charanga." *Everybody Salsa Volume 2.* Avid Records, BMG, AVC 677, 1999.
Charanga del Norte. "Violin Pachanguero." *Everybody Salsa Volume 1.* Avid Records, BMG, AVC 636, 1998.
Charanga Del Norte. *Pachanga Time.* CDNooLP14, 2020.
Charanga Casino. *Three.* SAR SLP 1017, 1981.
Charanga Casino. *Two.* SAR Records SLP 1007, 1980.
Charanga Casino. *Oye Me Voy Para La Luna.* SAR SLP 1028, 1982.
Charanga Casino. *Roberto Torres presenta . . . La Charanga Casino.* SAR SLP 1001, 1979.
Charanga Casino. *Soy de Azucar.* SAR SLP 1037, 1983.
Charanga Casino. "Y Que Importa." *Que Importa—El Cañonazo de la SAR.* SAR SLP 1041 (compilation, various artists), 1984.
Charanga de La 4. *Charanga de La 4.* SAR 1006, 1979.
Charanga de La 4. "El Cañonero" (as Roberto Torres). *El Cañonazo de la SAR.* SAR SLP 1041 (compilation, various artists), 1984.

Charanga de La 4. *Mas Charanga Que Nunca.* SAR 11047, 1984.
Charanga de La 4. *Recuerda a Beny Moré, Vol. 1.* SAR 1025, 1981.
Charanga de La 4. *Roberto Torres con Charanga de la 4.* SAR 1054, 1993.
Charanga de La 4. *Sarandance.* SAR LP, 1980.
Charanga Sensual. *Rompiendo Collora.* Salsa Internantal LP 721, 1980.
Chihuahua Martínez (Osvaldo). *Descarga Cubana Volume 1.* Fonseca LP, 1964; reissue 1995.
Chihuahua Martínez (Osvaldo). *Descarga Cubana Volume 2.* Fonseca LP, 1964; reissue 1995.
Cole, Nat King. *El Bodeguero—Boleros—Love Songs* vol. 1. J. L Alvarez / Open Records, CD reissue, 2008.
Cruz, Gustavo. *Interpreta A Matamoros.* SAR 1072, 1986.
Cuba, Joe, Sextet. "Bang! Bang!" 45 RPM, Tico T-475, 1966. USA.
Cugat, Xavier. *The Romantic Sound of Xavier Cugat & His Orchestra.* Charly LC 8477, ARC 326, CDHOT 635, 1998. Originally recorded 1935–45.
Cueva, Julio. *Figurina del Solar—Julio Cueva y su Orquesta.* RCA Victor 23-0128, 1944, Cuba.
Cueva, Julio. *La Rareza del Siglo—Julio Cueva y su Orquesta.* RCA Victor 23-0677, 194?, Cuba.
Curbelo, José. *Live at the China Doll: 1946–1954.* Tumbao TCD-074, 1995, Spain.
Curbelo, José, y su Orquesta. *El Rey del Mambo.* RCA Victor 23-0594, 1946, USA.
Curbelo, José, y su Orquesta. *El Rey del Mambo—Rumba Gallega: 1946–1951.* Tumbao TCD-042, 2004, Spain.
De la Fe, Alfredo, Nestro Torres, et al. *Charanga Caliente—En Descarga.* Envidia B60 6295, 2003. Recorded 1979.
Egües, Richard. *Richard Egües and Friends.* Lideres 744950 096-2 [Latin World Entertainment], 2001.
Egües, Richard. *Richard Egües Descargando con . . .* Egrem CD 0927, DVD 0067, 2007.
Egües, Richard. *Richard Egües Grandes Hits con la Orquesta Aragón.* EGREM CD0338, 1999.
Estudiantina Invasora. *70 Años y Estamos Como Ayer!* Magic Music, Universal FMD 75099, 1997.
Fajardo, José. "Batman Boogaloo." *Fajardo's Boogaloo.* Kubaney LP MT-335, USA, 1968.
Fajardo, José. *Best of José Fajardo and His Charanga.* Cache Music, 2010.
Fajardo, José. *Cuba Danzón—The National Dance.* Voyager, 2008.
Fajardo, José. *Fajardo con su Flauta y Orquesta: Danzones Completos Instrumentales Para Bailar.* Antilla CD-566, date unknown. Originally on LP Puchito Records MLP 566.
Fajardo, José. *Fajardo–Danzones Completos Instrumentales Para Bailar*, Vol. II. Antilla CD-569, date unknown.
Fajardo, José. *José Fajardo y Sus Estrellas: La Flauta de Cuba.* Big World Continental Tania 0018, 1996.
Fajardo, José. *Ritmo De Pollos.* Panart LP-3051, Cuba, 1959.
Fajardo y sus All-Stars. "La Flauta de José," "La Charanga." *Cuban Jam Session* Vol. 3. CDP-1410, reissue, 1996 of Panart LP 3102 *Cuban Jam Session* Vol. 5, recorded in 1957 in Cuba and 1964 in Miami.
Fajardo y sus Estrellas. *Chachachá by Fajardo and his All Stars.* Musart-Balboa, CD reissue, 2007. Originally recorded on the Panart label late 1950s–1964.
Fajardo y sus Estrellas. *Esto Sólo Se Da En Cuba.* BIS Music CD-109, reissue, 1995.

Fajardo y sus Estrellas. *Fajardo y sus Estrellas "Live" La Maganette Restaurant & Club*. DAP Collection CD 46, 1986.

Fajardo y sus Estrellas. *Fajardo y sus Estrellas "Live" at the New York Palladium*. Original Open Reel Dubs, recorded November 1958.

Flynn, Frank Emilio. *A Tiempo de Danzón*. Milan/Latino 74321 58407-2, 1998.

Fox, Charles. *The Best of Charles Fox*. Rareza Music, CD reissue, 2010.

Fox, Charles. *Charles Fox & His Charanga Play Just For Fun*. Lorien Production Dico DHCD 1244 1995, 1963.

Gillespie, Dizzy. "Manteca." *Afro*. Norgran MG N-1003, 1954.

González, Ruben. "Mandinga." *Introducing Ruben González*. World Circuit WCD 049, 1997.

Gonzalo, Fernandez. *Bailarin!* Musicafrique LP003, 1978.

Gonzalo, Fernandez. *Picao!* Promesa sLP 001, 1980.

Gonzalo, Fernandez. *Repicao!* Tobago TLP 607, 1982.

Gonzalo, Fernandez. *Super Típica de Estrellas*. All Art AALP 582, 1976.

Kenner, Chris. "I Like It Like That." 45 rpm, Instant Records VR-3229, 1961.

Legarreta, Felix "Pupi." *Pupi Legarreta & His Orchestra: El Fugitivo*. Vaya JMV 79, 1979.

Legarreta, Felix "Pupi." *Pupi Pa' Bailar*. Vaya JMVS-38, 1980.

Loco, Joe (José Estevez). *Loco Motion*. Fantasy FCD 24733-2, 1994. Compilation of tracks originally released on *Pachanga with Joe Loco* Fantasy 8064, 1961, as *Joe Loco/ Going Loco*, Fantasy 8042, 1960, and Pete Terrace Quintet—*Going Loco*, Fantasy 3203, 1955.

López, Belisario. "Lola Catula." *Pachangas* vol. 1. Ansonia ALP 1288, US, 1961.

López, Belisario. "Lola Catula." *Pachangas* vol. 2. Ansonia SALP 1300, 1961. CD reissue, 1998 and 2008.

López, Belisario. *Orquesta de Belisario López 1942–1948: Prueba Mi Sazón*. Tumbao Cuban Classics, TCD 069, CD reissue, 1995.

López, Belisario. "Prepárate Para Bañarte." *Orquesta de Belisario López 1951–1957 Prueba Mi Sazón*. Cariño–dbm1-5804, Coleccionista Series, 1974. Recorded in Havana, September 19, 1956.

López, Belisario, y su Charanga. *A Bailar La Pachanga*. Ansonia SALP 1288, 1961.

López, Belisario, y su Charanga. *Belisario Lopez y Su Charanga*. Ansonia ALP 1318, 1963.

López, Belisario, y su Charanga. *Tu No Estas En Na'*. Ansonia ALP 1410, 1965.

López, Orlando Cachaito. *Cachaito—Orlando Cachaito López*. World Circuit Production, WCD 061, 2001.

Machito. *Afro Cuban Jazz, Machito—Mambo in Jazz*. CD 62015, Saludos Amigos, 1992. Original recordings made in 1949 (*Okiedoke*), 1950 (*Mambo Part 1 and 2*), 1958 (*Ring-A-Levio*), and the remainder in 1957

Machito. *Chano Pozo & Arsenio Rodriguez with Machito and His Orchestra—Legendary Sessions*. Tumbao Cuban Classics–TCD-017, 1992.

Machito. *Machito with Flute to Boot*. Tico LP, 1957. Roulette Records–R 52026, 1959.

Mann, Herbie. *Flautista!* Verve Records 557 448-2, PolyGram Records 557 448-2, CD reissue, 1998. Recorded June 25, 1959, at Basin Street East, New York City.

Martínez, Mike, & the Latin Dimension. *Trackin'*. Kim KLP 708, 1980.

Miller, Sue, and her Charanga Del Norte. *Look Back in Charanga*. CDN00CD10, 2010.

Moré, Benny. *Benny Moré con la Orquesta de Pérez Prado–Época de Oro de Benny Moré 1947–1952.* 1949.
Moré, Benny. *Canto a Mi Cuba.* Egrem CD 0181, 1996.
Oliveros, J. J. *"El Jilguero" de Centro Habana y sus All Stars–De Bala* . . . Envidia A70 7008, 2000.
Orquesta América. *Sabor Profundo.* Real Rhythm RR 50102, 2001.
Orquesta América del 55. *Orquesta America del 55 con Ruben González.* Tumbao Cuban Classics TCD 103, reissue, 2000. Originally recorded 1955–57 in Havana.
Orquesta América with Richard Egües. *Las Leyendas de la Música Cubana.* 4CD set Orquesta América with Cuban All Stars. Tumi Music, TMG Box 1, 1997.
Orquesta Aragón. *Bailables de Cuba.* Egrem Areito LDA-3372, 1971.
Orquesta Aragón. "Cachita." *La Colección Cubana, Cuba Eterno,* Cuba Libre/Nascente Records NSCD 046, 1999.
Orquesta Aragón. *Cha Cha Charanga!* Tumi CD 071, 1997.
Orquesta Aragón. *Charangas y Pachangas.* Discuba DICD-555, CD reissue, 2000. Originally recorded for Radio Progreso, June 10, 1959.
Orquesta Aragón. *Cojale el Gusto a Cuba.* Discuba DICD-502, 2000.
Orquesta Aragón. *Cuba's Orquesta Aragón.* Monitor Records, 1984.
Orquesta Aragón. *Danzones de Ayer y de Hoy,* Vol. 1. RCA Victor LPD 515, 1960; CD reissue, Discuba, 1990.
Orquesta Aragón. *Danzones de Ayer y de Hoy* Vol. 2. RCA Victor LPD 532, 1961; CD reissue, Discuba DCD 515, 1990.
Orquesta Aragón. "El Agua de Clavelito." *Primeras Grabaciones 1953–1955.* Tumbao Cuban Classics TCD 110, CD reissue, 1997. Originally recorded by CMQ radio, Havana, LPDBL-1-5011, 1953.
Orquesta Aragón. *En Route.* World Village/Lusafrica, 2001.
Orquesta Aragón. "Espíritu Burlón." V 23-7313, Cuba. Recorded July 30, 1957. Also on *Orquesta Aragón Legends of Cuban Music,* Nostalgia for Cuba CD G50 5030, 2001.
Orquesta Aragón. *Grandes Exitos de Cuba.* Egrem 757, 2-CD box set reissue, 2006.
Orquesta Aragón. *The Heart of Havana* Vol. 2. BMG 82876-55069-2, BMG, US Latin Tropical Series. Originally recorded in Havana 1957–58, digitally remastered 1993.
Orquesta Aragón. *La Charanga Eterna.* Lusafrica LU 220 362112, 1999.
Orquesta Aragón. *Los Aragones en la Onda de la Alegria* Vol. 1. Discmedi Blau Fondo DM060, CD reissue, 1994. Sonoro de Archivo Instituto Cubano de Radio y Televisión (radio programs from the 1950s).
Orquesta Aragón. *Los Aragones en la Onda de la Alegria* Vol. 2. Barbaro label, B218, CD reissue, 1998. Sonido Inc Fondo Sonoro de Archivo Instituto Cubano de Radio y Televisión (radio programs from the 1960s and 70s).
Orquesta Aragón. *Los Ineditos de l'Orquesta Aragon "En Vivo" Vol. 1.* Coleccion de Diamante CD 9201, n.d.
Orquesta Aragón. *Maracas, Bongó y Conga.* RCA Victor LPM-1609, 1957 (1958 according to Cristóbal Díaz Ayala); remastered for CD, BMG France 82876525322, RCA Victor Gold Series, 2003.
Orquesta Aragón. *Quien Sabe Sabe.* Lusafrica, 1998.

Orquesta Aragón. *Richard Egües Grandes Hits con la Orquesta Aragón*. Egrem CD0338, 1999.
Orquesta Aragón. *That Cuban Cha-Cha-Cha*. RCA Tropical Series 2446-2-RL, RCA Victor, CD reissue, 1990. Recorded in Havana 1955–56; CD: 1990. This recording also appears on the CD *Orquesta Aragón: Cuban Originals*. BMG, 1999.
Orquesta Aragón, Orquesta América, Orquesta Fajardo y sus Estrellas. Orquesta Sensación, Orquesta Melodías del 40. *Charangas De Siempre*. Egrem CD 08465, CD box set, 2006.
Orquesta Arcaño y Sus Maravillas. *Danzón Mambo* [1944–51]. Tumbao Classics TCD-029, reissue 1993.
Orquesta Arcaño y Sus Maravillas. *Orquesta Radiofonica: Arcaño en Vivo*. Discmedi, CD reissue, n.d. Recorded 1947, Fondo Sonoro del Instituto Cubano de Radio y Televisión, Barbaro.
Orquesta Broadway. "Quinta Guajira," "Goza La Vida." *Como Me Gusta*! West Side WSCD-4154, CD reissue, USA, 1998. Originally recorded May 25, 1972. All-Art Records AALP-1571, USA, 1972.
Orquesta Broadway. "Al Mirar No Me Vistes." *Paraíso*. Coco CLP 159X, USA, 1981. Musical Productions, CD reissue, 1991.
Orquesta Broadway. *Arrimate Pa' Aca*. Musicor MM2070, 1965. CD reissue, West Side WSCD-4270, 2003.
Orquesta Broadway. *Broadway Orchestra*. Gema LPG 3003, 1963.
Orquesta Broadway. *Dengue*. Gema LPG 1191, 1963.
Orquesta Broadway. "Descarga de Side Street," "Pare Cochero." *Orquesta Broadway "Live" Side Street, November 8, 1986*. Cassette/CD 89.
Orquesta Broadway. "Los Cuatro Pesos." *Orquesta Broadway at the Players Club, NYC "Live."* CD 32, 1980.
Orquesta Broadway. *Orquesta Broadway Esta Pegando*. All-Art Stereo AALP 1577, 1972.
Orquesta Broadway. *Orquesta Broadway Loves New York*. B'way Records BR-82-01, 1982.
Orquesta Broadway. "Pare Cochero." *Orquesta Broadway "Live" Various Sessions*. DAP Collection 1993. Notes from David A. Pérez Sr.: sessions August 3, 1990, September 10, 1991, 1992, and 1993 New York City.
Orquesta Broadway. *Pasaporte*. Coco CLP 126, 1976.
Orquesta Broadway. *Salvaje/Savage*. Coco CLP 119, 1975.
Orquesta Broadway. *Tiqui, Tiqui*. Musicor MM2093, 1968.
Orquesta Broadway. *Yo Quiero Ser Tu Juguete*. Musicor MS 6051, 1967.
Orquesta Broadway. *40th Anniversary*. Flauta Records CDF-2003-01, 2003.
Orquesta Casino de la Playa. "Coge Pa' La Cola." *Orquesta Casino de la Playa*. RCA Victor 23-0395, 1945, Cuba.
Orquesta Melodías Del 40. "Tunas Bayamo," "El Cachin Cachumba." *Montuno Favorito*. Tumbao Cuban Classics TCD-098, reissue, 1999. Recorded in 1956 in Havana.
Orquesta Melodías Del 40. "Yo Te Lo Voy a Dar," "Y Siempre en Cuba." *Orquesta Melodías del 40*. Areito 3195, 196?.
Orquesta Novel. *A Mi Me Gusto*. Fania JM 601, 1981.
Orquesta Novel. *Canta y Encanta*. Fania JM 00539, 1979.
Orquesta Novel. "La Batalla de Los Barrios." *Orquesta Novel "Live" at The Royal Club*. DAP Collection Casette, 1979.

Orquesta Novel. *La Orquesta Novel*. Hopes LP 874, 1967.
Orquesta Novel. *New York City Sounds*. Fonseca LP 1117, 1966.
Orquesta Novel. *Nocturnando Con la Orquesta Novel "Live."* DAP OR Collection 2010, 1964.
Orquesta Novel. *Nocturnando—Violins, Flutes and Rhythm 1*. DAP Collection 2013, 1965.
Orquesta Novel. *Orquesta Novel "Live."* DAP Collection CD 161/OR 28, 1965.
Orquesta Novel. *Orquesta Novel "Live" Christmas Eve at Corso's, NYC with Johnny Pacheco.* OR Conversion 2011, 1974.
Orquesta Novel. *Orquesta Novel Live Recordings 1974 and 1975*. DAP 1974 and 1975 DAP CD35/CD70.
Orquesta Novel. "Que Viva El Son Montuno." *Orquesta Novel*. Fania JM 585, 1980.
Orquesta Novel. *Salsamania*. Fania LP JM 00487, 1976.
Orquesta Novel. *Salud, Dinero Y Amor* (with Gonzalo Fernandez). Fania LP JM 00520, 1978.
Orquesta Novel. *Se Colo La Novel*. TR TLP00600S, 1973.
Orquesta Novel. *Super Tipica*. TR Records TR-0800, 1974.
Orquesta Novel. *With a Touch of Brass* (as Novel). TR Records TR 116X, 1975.
Orquesta Nuevo Ritmo de Cuba. *The Heart of Cuba: Pachangas & Charangas*. GNP Crescendo–GNP 47, 1959.
Orquesta Sensación. *Cha Cha Cha*. Puchito MLP 504, n.d. Recorded 1954–56.
Orquesta Sensación. "En Vano." *Charangas de Siempre*. Egrem CD 0846, 2006.
Orquesta Sublime. "Don Julio." *Que Viva la Charanga*. Envidia/Musical Productions 7014/6350, 2000.
Orquesta Sublime. "Dulce Ternura." *Dulce Ternura*. Egrem CD 0512, 2002.
Orquesta Sublime. "El Peletero." Panart 1898, Cuba, 1957. LP 3018, CD Egrem 20.
Orquesta Sublime. "La Pachanga." Panart 2211, Cuba. Recorded August 5, 1959. LP 2048, CD Egrem 20.
Orquesta Sublime. "La Pachanga." *A La Pachanga con la Sublime*. Artex Canada, 1956–60 recordings, 1994, EGREM license reissue.
Orquesta Sublime. "Los Carteros." Panart 1898, Cuba, 1957. LP 2026, CD Egrem 20.
Orquesta Sublime. "Seis Perlas Cubanas." Panart 1913, Cuba, 1957. Orf 45-0051, LP 3018, LP 2026, CD Egrem 20.
Orquesta Super Estrellas de Gonzao Fernández. ¡Charangas! The Best of Super *Tipica de Estrellas*. West Side WSCD-4157, 1995. Recorded September 9, 1975.
Orquesta Super Estrellas de Gonzao Fernández. *Picao*. CD Promusa Reissue PROMUSA001, LP Discos Perla 6377111, 1980.
Orquesta Típica Novel. "La Batalla de Los Barrios." *Sabrosa Típica*. TR Records TR112Y, 1975.
Orquesta Típica Novel. "Tiene Sabor." *Tipicante*. TR Records 114X, TLP 00600X, 1973.
Pacheco, Johnny. "El Bodeguero." *Early Rhythms*. Charly Records SNAP029, CD, reissue 2001. Recorded 1960 in New York.
Pacheco, Johnny. *Pacheco, His Flute and Latin Jam*. Fania LP 328, 1965. Digital remastering 2005.
Pacheco, Johnny, y Su Charanga. *By Popular Demand/Por Demanda Popular*. Recorded 1965. Fania LP 333, USA, 1966; Fania Records Venezuela LPS 99244, 1979.
Pacheco, Johnny, y Su Charanga. "Espiritu Burlón." *Pacheco y su Charanga, Vol. 2*. Alegre LPA 805, 1961.

Pacheco, Johnny, y Su Charanga. *Pacheco y su Charanga con Elliot Romero*. Alegre LPA 801, 1961. CD reissue Fania 773; 130 219-2 Emusica Records, 2007.

Pacheco, Johnny, y Su Charanga. *Pacheco y su Charanga, Vol. 1 & 2*. CD, Malanga Music MM825, 2014.

Pacheco, Johnny, y Su Charanga. *Que Suene La Flauta*! Alegre LPA 811, 1962.

Pacheco, Johnny, y Su Charanga. "Sabroso Como el Guarapo." *Pacheco y su Charanga*. Fania Records 773 130 219-2, Emusica Records, reissue on CD, 2007.

Pacheco, Johnny, Jose A. Fajardo, Pupi Legarreta, with Javier Vazquez y su Charanga. *Las Tres Flautas*. Fania JM 561, 1980.

Pacheco, Palmieri, Fajardo. *Las Charangas*. Alegre LPA 807, 1962 (Recorded 1961).

Palmieri, Charlie, and His Charanga La Duboney. "Bronx Pachanga," "La Pachanga Se Baila Asi." *Pachanga at the Caravana Club*. Alegre LPA 804, 1961; Sonido LPA-8040, CD reissue, 1999.

Palmieri, Charlie, and His Charanga La Duboney. "Mack the Knife." *Let's Dance the Charanga*. United Artists UAL 3082, 1959.

Palmieri, Charlie and His Charanga La Duboney. "Tiene Sabor." *Salsa Na' Ma'* (Alegre LPA 821), 1962, 1963 and 1967.

Palmieri, Charlie, and His Charanga La Duboney. *Viva Palmieri*. Alegre LPA 8160, 1962. CD reissue Sonido, 1998.

Palmieri, Charlie, & His Orchestra. "Tiene Sabor." *The Heavyweight*. Alegre JMAS 6009, 1978.

Palmieri, Eddie. *The Best of Eddie Palmieri*. Fania Salsa Classics, Charly, 2007 (2CD set).

Palmieri, Eddie. *The Best of Eddie Palmieri*. Charly LC08477, WAG 326, CDGR 297, 1999.

Palmieri, Eddie. "Bilongo." *Superimposition*. Tico LP 1194, 1971.

Palmieri, Eddie. "Ritmo Caliente II." *Ritmo Caliente*. Concord Picante CCD-2180-2, USA, 2003.

Palmieri, Eddie. "Tu Tu Ta Ta." *Echando Pa'lante [Straight Ahead]*. Tico 1113, 1964.

Palmieri, Eddie. "Tu Tu Ta Ta II." *La Perfecta II*, Concord CCD-2136-2, USA, 2002.

Palmieri, Eddie. "Un Día Bonito." *The Sun Of Latin Music*. Coco CLP 109, France, 1974.

Palmieri, Eddie, and His Orchestra. "African Twist." *Champagne*. Tico LP 1165, 1968.

Palmieri, Eddie, and His Orchestra. "Bilongo." 45 rpm, Tico T-574, 1968. *Salsa Légende—Best of Salsa*, 2004.

Palmieri, Eddie, y Su Conjunto La Perfecta. *El Molestoso . . . Vol II*. Alegre LPA 824, 1963; CD reissue, Alegre LPA 8240, 1996.

Palmieri, Eddie, y Su Conjunto La Perfecta. *Lo Que Traigo Es Sabroso*. Alegre LPA 832, 1964.

Palmieri, Eddie, y Su Conjunto La Perfecta. "Ritmo Caliente." *Eddie Palmieri y Su Conjunto La Perfecta*. Alegre LPA 817, 1962.

Papaito. *Rinde Homenaje a Abelardo Barroso*. SAR 1014, 1980.

Parker, Charlie. *Charlie Parker & Machito And His Orchestra—The Latin Bird*. CD Compilation: High Definition Jazz–HDJ 4076, 2000.

Pérez, Lou. *De Todo Un Poco*. Tico JMTS 1418, 1977.

Pérez, Lou. *Lou Pérez and His New York, N.Y. Sound*. Parnaso P-LP-1091, 1971.

Pérez, Lou. *Nuestra Herencia/Our Latin Heritage*. Tico TSLP 1412, 1976.

Pérez, Lou. *Of Latin Extraction*. Chateau LPS 058, 1970.

Pérez, Lou, and His Charanga Orchestra. *Bon Bon de Chocolate!* Ajay LP 3362, 1962.
Pérez, Lou, y Su Orquesta. *Fantasia Africana*. All Arte AALP 1581, 1974.
Pérez, Lou, y Su Charanga. *Para La Fiesta Voy.* Ajay HI LP-3361, 1961; reissue, 1994.
Pérez, Lou, y Su Charanga. *Pa' Fricasé Los Pollos—Tamboleo*. Corredor CLP 780, 1964; Cobo Music CD reissue, 2009.
Perez, Mike. *Mike Perez Típica New York Orchestra*. Mas LP 3363, 1978.
Portuondo, Omara. *Flor de Amor*. World Circuit WCD 068, 2004.
Portuondo, Omara. "Tiene Sabor." *Cuba Lost and Found*. World Circuit BooSSJIAXE, 2015.
Puente, Tito. *Pachanga Con Puente*. Malanga Music MM822, CD reissue, 2013, of the original two albums *Pachanga con Puente*, Tico SLP 1083, 1961; and *Vaya Puente*, Tico SLP 1085, 1962.
Puente, Tito, and His Orchestra. *Let's Cha Cha with Tito Puente and His Orchestra*. RDM France CD286, 2010.
Puente, Tito, and His Orchestra. "Mambo Gozon." *Mambo Gozon*. RCA International 901 017, France. [1958].
Puente, Tito, and Celia Cruz. *Cuba y Puerto Rico Son . . .* Tico Records SLP-1136, 1966.
Prado, Pérez. *Mambo Number 5*—RCA Victor 23-1546.
Prado, Pérez. *Our Man in Havana*. Camden 74321 588102, reissue, 1998.
Prado, Pérez. *Pérez Prado y Su Orquesta Mambo—Absolute Best*. Proper Records Recording Arts ABCD 106, 1999.
Prado, Pérez. *"Prez"—Pérez Prado and His Orchestra*. RCA Victor LC 0316, 1957; CD, 74321 26052-2, 1995. Pupi and Pacheco. *Los Dos Mosqueteros*. Vaya MMVS 63, 1977.
Pupi con la Orquesta Renovacion. *Salsa con Boog-A-Loo*. Remo LPR 1523, 1967.
Pupi Legarreta. *Salsa Nova Con Pupi Legarreta*. Tico LP 1091, 1963.
Pupi y Su Charanga. *Gonzalo, Pacheco, y Pupi*. Vaya VS 40, 1975.
Pupi y Su Charanga. *Soy Campesino*. Remo LPR 11546, 1970.
Pupi y Su Charanga. *Pupy [sic] Y Su Charanga*. Tumi Records, CD033, 1993. Originally published by Casino Records. Under contract from Colmusica–Colombiana de Musica.
Ray, Ricardo. "Lookie Lookie." *Se Solto'/On the Loose–Introducing the Bugaloo*. Alegre Records LPA 850, 1967.
Rivera, Chollo, & Latin Soul Drives. "I Could Never Hurt You Girl"/"Black & Blues." 45 rpm, Cotique C-149, 1969.
Rivera, Hector. *The New Latin Sensation Charanga & Pachanga!* Epic LN3782; reissue, 1999.
Rivera, Hector. *Viva Rivera!* Epic LN 3804, 1961; reissue, 1999.
Rodríguez, Arsenio. "El Reloj." *El Rey Del Son Montuno*. Rice Records RRS-001, 2004. "El Reloj" recorded June 21, 1946, Havana, for RCA Victor 23-0470-B, TCD-031.
Rodríguez, Pete. "I Like It Like That." *I Like It Like That*. Alegre LPA 855, 1967.
Rodríguez, Tito. *The Best of Tito Rodríguez Vol. 2*. RCA Victor, 1955.
Rodríguez, Tito. *The Best of Tito Rodríguez Vol. 3*. RCA Victor, 1955. CD reissues: Tropical Series RCA Victor 74321-19083-2; BMG U.S. Latin 74321-19083-2, 1994.
Rodríguez, Tito. *Charanga Pachanga*. United Artists 3140, 1961.
Romeu, Antonio María. *Antonio María Romeu: Danzones*. Egrem CD 0166, CD reissue, 1996.

Romeu, Antonio María. *Antonio María Romeu: Danzones—El Mago de las Teclas Canta Barbarito Díez 1937–1940*. Tumbao Cuban Classics, TCD 067, reissue, 1995. Recorded in Havana 1937–40.

Rotterdam Conservatory Charanga Orchestra. *Angoa—Cuba the Charanga*. Nimbus CD NI 5528, 1997.

Rubalcaba, William. *El Que Sabe, Sabe*. Camajan, 2002.

Ruíz Jr., Rosendo. *Continental Cha Cha Cha*. Tico SLP 1054, 1959.

Ruíz Jr., Rosendo. *Dance La Pachanga*. Tico LP 1081, 1961.

Ruíz Jr., Rosendo. *Havana Bound*. Tico TRLP 1054, 1959.

Sacasas, Anselmo. "Mambo." *Anselmo Sacasa y Su Orquesta*. RCA Victor 269002, 1946.

Santamaría, Mongo. *Mas Sabroso*. Fantasy 2338, 1962.

Santamaría, Mongo. *Mongo Santamaría "Live" in San Francisco*. Fantasy Remaster 2004, 1962 (1959).

Santamaría, Mongo. *Mongo's Greatest Hits*. Fantasy Records FCD 24735-2, 1995 CD reissue, tracks 1–11 from *Mongo's Greatest Hits*, Fantasy 4529, 1966; track 12 from *Yambu*, Fantasy 8012, 1958; track 13 from *Sabroso*, Fantasy 8058, 1961; and track 14 from ¡Viva Mongo!, Fantasy 8087, 1962.

Santamaría, Mongo. "Olga Pachanga." *Arriba*. Fantasy 8067, 1963.

Santamaría, Mongo. *Our Man in Havana*. Fantasy 8045, 1960; CD reissue, Fantasy Records Universal AAD 00025218242929, 1993.

Santamaría, Mongo. "Que Maravilloso." *Sabroso*. Fantasy 8058, 1961.

Santamaría, Mongo. ¡Viva Mongo! Fantasy 3335, 1963.

Santana. "Oye Como Va." *Abraxas*. LP CBS KC-30130, 1970.

Seijo, Rafael. *Rafael Seijo y Su Orquesta: La Pachanga*. Somerset-Korea LD 101, 1961.

Shearing, George. *The George Shearing Quintet: Latin Rendezvous*. Capitol ST2320, 1964.

Shearing, George. *Mood Latino*. Capitol T1567, 1965.

Siglo XX. *Teléfono de Larga Distancia / La Viuda Alegre—La Bella Cubana—Danzones*, Panart, n.d.

Siglo XX. *La Viuda Alegre—Los Reyes del Danzón*. Montmartre Records SY10, reissue, 1997.

Smith, Mauricio. "Madera." *Latin Rhythm & Blues Jazz*. Wenmar J131, 1996.

Sonora Matancera. *Now and Forever*. Charly, Compilation LC 8477, CDHOT 634, 1998.

Son Primero. *Tradicion Cubana en Nueva York*. Montuno Records CD TLP-524, 1987.

SonSublime. *Bailando con SonSublime/Dancing with SonSublime*. 2006.

Terrace, Pete. *Pete Terrace & His Conjunto—Charanga: Hot & Spicy*. Colpix SCP 430, 1962.

Típica Ideal. ¡Charangas! The Best of *Típica Ideal*. West Side Latino Records WSCD 4158, 1995. Originally recorded 1974–75.

Tjader, Cal. *Black Hawk Nights*. Fantasy Records, Berkeley FCD-24755-2, CD reissue; tracks 1–6 originally released as *A Night at the Black Hawk*, Fantasy 3283, 1958; tracks 7–12 from *Live and Direct*, Fantasy 3315, 1961.

Torres, Nestor. *Colombia en Charanga*. Color-TH-Records CLP 7073, 1978.

Torres, Nestor. *No Me Provoques—Nestor Torres II*. Suave/Kim LP K711, 1981.

Valdés, Alfredito. "Charanga En New York." *Alfredito Valdés y Su Orquesta: Sabrina! (Pachanga)*. TRU-SOUND 80001, 1963.

Valdés, Alfredito. *Alfredito Valdés y Su Orquesta—Pachanga in Orbit.* Co Time/Celly CLP 0100, 1961.

Valdés, Bebo. "Cactus Mambo." *Make Mine a Mambo: 25 Outrageous Classics from the Golden Age of Cuba's Big Bands.* Nascente Records, 1999.

Valdés, Felipe. "Alza Colombia." Orquesta de Felipe Valdés, S-87, V 68022 (Havana, March 6, 1907). Track 6 on the CD compilation *The Cuban Danzón Before There Was Jazz: The First Historic Recordings of African-American Dance Music: 1906–1929.* Arhoolie CD 7032, 1999.

Various artists. *Cuba Eterno—La Colección Cubana.* Cuba Libre / Nascente Records, NSCD 046, 1999.

Various artists. *The Cuban Danzón Before There Was Jazz: The First Historic Recordings of African-American Dance Music: 1906–1929.* Arhoolie Records, CD 7032, 1999.

Various artists. *Early Cuban Danzón Orchestras (1916–1920).* Harlequin HQ CD 131, 1999.

Various artists. *Montuno Sessions Live from Studio "A."* Mr Bongo Records MRBCD004, 1995.

Various artists. *New York Salsa Explosion.* Delta Music, Laserlight 12 907, 1996.

Various artists. *Nu Yorica! Culture Clash in New York City.* Soul Jazz Records SJR CD29, 1996.

Weinstein, Mark. *Con Alma.* 2007.

Weinstein, Mark. *Cuban Roots Revisited.* Ubiquity Recordings, Cubop CBCD019, 1999.

Weinstein, Mark. *El Cumbanchero.* Jazzheads JH1187, 2011.

Weinstein, Mark. *Timbasa.* 2009.

Zervigón, Eddy. *Eddie Zervigón & Orquesta Broadway "Live" May 31, 1983 & June 29, 1984.* CD75, 1983.

INDEX

Page numbers in *italics* indicate musical examples, tables, or photographs.

Abakúa, 72, 233
abanicos, 133
Abreu, Christina, xv–xvi, 7, 10, 22, 29–30, 41, 46, 47, 75, 164
a caballo rhythm, 135, *135*, 139, 143, 233
Acciaccaturas, *14*, 15, 81, 89, 112, 116, 182, 213
Acosta, Leonardo, 63
African American audiences for Latin music, 49–50, 64, 192–93, 201, 228
African American music: *bugalú* and, 189–206; *charangueaʼo en típico* and, 188; civil rights movement and, 7; Cuban musicians' receptivity to, 228. *See also specific musicians*
African American musicians in Latin bands, 117, 147, 231
"African Twist" (Palmieri), 191, 203
afro, 254n22
Afro-Cuban Jazz Orchestras, 12
Afro-Cuban music: in Cuban context, 7; political engagement and, 248n9, 265n3; religious practices, 61, 72, 73–74; as term, 5–7
"after-hours" clubs, 36–37
"Aguardiente" (Nuevo Ritmo), 86
aguinaldo, 49, 233
Aguirre, Eduardo, 230
"Alagrimo," 225
Alegre All Stars, 37, 139, 144, 146, 198, 200, 247n11, 251n30; formation and personnel of, 147

Alegre Records, 7, 37, 86, 128, 139, 144, 146, 147, 150, 193, 198, 251n30
Alfaro, Manolo, 35–36
Alfaro, Tony, 35–36
Alfredito Valdés y su Orquesta, 22
Almacenes Hernández (New York), 31
Alma Dance Studios (New York), 46
"Al Mirar No Me Vistes" (Zervigón flute solo), 92–93, 95, *96–100*, 101–6, *105*, *107–8*, 107–9, 116, 259n41
Alpha Artists, 71, 207
"Al Vaiven De Mi Carreta," 113
Alvarado, Melba, 21
Álvarez, Aulina, 78
Álvarez, Chico, 220
Alvarez, Henry, 200
Alvarito, 34
A Mi Gente (phrase), 10–12
Amití, Mike, 109
amphibrach, *14*
Anderson, Ian, 182
Andreu, José, 145–46, 157, 207
Angeloro, Al, xiv, 210, 218, 220, 246n7
"Angoa" (*danzon*), 111, 115
Ansonia label, 79, 83, 114, 259n41
Antonio Arcaño y Sus Maravillas, 21, 45, 47, 53, 54, 71, 73, 74, 146, 157, 264n16; lineup and performance aesthetics of, 9; link with Fajardo, 84; López's affinity with, 79; "Mambo," 54, 56, 57–61, *58–60*, 63, 82, 154, 157

appoggiaturas, 15
Arcaño, Antonio, 19, 78, 145–46; flute improvisations of, 113, 162; Lozano influenced by, 86; *sabor* of, 4. *See also* Antonio Arcaño y Sus Maravillas
Armenteros, Alfredo "Chocolate": career of, 15–16, 75; *cubanía* in improvisations of, 221; *sabor* as understood by, 4; studies with Egües, 246n10; trumpet improvisations of, 15–16, *16–17*, 18, 225, 228
Arnaldo "El Mulatón," 92
Aroche, Elizardo, 85
Aroz, Rafael, 145–46, 157
arrangers, Latin, 207–8. *See also* Prado, Pérez; *specific arrangers*
Arriba! (album), 86
Arsenio Rodríguez y su Conjunto, 20, 21, 46, 54, 55, 63–64, 71
Arthur Murray's Music for Dancing Pachangas (album), 260n13
ascending sequences between dominant notes, *15*
Ateneo Cubano de Nueva York (New York social club), 7, 30
augmented fourths, 86, 89
Austerlitz, Paul, 6, 59–60
Aviles, Vitín, 145
Azpiazu, Don, 21, 44–45

Bacallao, Rafael, 127, 130, 260n5
Bachata, 8, 233
backbeat, 198
"Baila Vicente" (Orquesta Aragón), 256n2
"Baile Suavito," 203
Banda Gigante, 63
bandas municipales, 225, 233
"Bang Bang" (Cuba), 190, 201
Baró, Evaristo, 145, 262n7
Baró, Ronnie, 262n7
Barosso, Abelardo, 3
Barretto, Emilio, 249n23
Barretto, Ray, 150; Alpha Artists' representation of, 207; Charanga Moderna leadership, 22, 146, 207–20, 222, 229; de Jesus and, 29, 220; "El Bantu," 60; "El Watusi,"

60, 190, 193, 209, 267n12; Fajardo and, 247n11; Fania All Stars and, 7; fusion elements in music, 206, 218; influences on, 21, 47; performance aesthetics, 221–22, 227; Rodríguez and, 266n1; *sabor* as understood by, 5; songs of, xiv
Barrio, 233
Barrios, Felo, 94, 109, *109*
Bastar, Francisco Angel. *See* Kako
Bataan, Joe, 190, 206, 265n2
"Batman Boogaloo" (Fajardo), 193, 201, 202; flute improvisation, 203, *204–5*, 206
Batman (TV show theme), 206
Bauzá, Mario, 46, 230, 260n13; fusion music, 75; instruments played, 15; as musical director for Machito and his Afro-Cubans, 56; preference for term "Afro-Cuban," 6; Sigler and, 44; "Tanga," 59; on *típico* playing, 8–9
Beatles, the, 190
Beethoven, Ludwig van, Fifth Symphony of, 109, 113, 116
Belisario López y Su Orquesta (album), 259n41
Berdeguer, John, 49, 133, 190, 265n3
Berríos, M. Juanita, 3–4
Berrios, Tommy, 201
Berríos-Miranda, Angie, 3–4
"Bilongo" (Palmieri), 15–16, *16–17*, 18, 225
"Black Is Black" (Orquesta Broadway), 189, 203
Black Panthers, 265n3
black power, 201
"Blue Moon," 225
blue notes, Lozano's use of, 85, 90, 256n2
blues elements in US-based Latin dance bands, 226, 227
Bodenheimer, Rebecca, 113
Boehm-system metal flute, 57, 90, 267n15; Canoura's performances on, 210, 217, 267n15; disadvantages for *típico* playing, 187; Joseph's performances on, 176; Sánchez's performances on, 157, 162–63; sonority of, 217, 228; Valentín's performances on, 172, 182, 187

bolero, 41, 43, 46, 254n22
bomba, 51, 234
bombo, 58, 140, 142, 151, 162, 173, 187, 193, 198, 213, 234
bongos, 169, 227
"Boogaloo Blues" (Colón), 190
Borinquen, 234
Boys Harbor Conservatory, 12, 29, 249n26
Brachfeld, Andrea, 167, 188, 213, *213*, 218, 228, 231, 249n38, 261n15
brass section: in Fania bands, 74; performances of *guajeo* patterns, 169, 219; in Puente's big band, 65, 95; swing-styled, 70, 74, 150
Bravet, Leonel, 85, 145
Brito, Felo, 146
Broadway Casino (New York), 31, 33
Bronx Casino (New York), xvii, 32, 37
Bronx Conexión, 11, 12
"Bronx Pachanga" (Charanga La Duboney), 132, 139–43, 144, 145, 146; *coros*, 140, *140*; flute improvisations, 157, *158–63*, 162–63; *guajeos*, *140*; tutti break, 142
Bronx Tropicana Ballroom (New York), 27, 33, *35*, 35–36, 46, 52, 255n51
Buena Vista Social Club, 12
Buena Vista Social Club, 218
bugalú, 131, 189–206, 229, 231; African American influences on, 191, 192–93; dancers, 266n24; decline of, 190; defined, 234; English lyrics in, 189–90; musicians' strong opinions about, 193, 206; soul and, 265n2; style elements of, 189–90
Burton, Kim, 209
Byrne, David, 29

Cabrera, Julian, 85, 145, 146, 147, 262n5
cakewalk, *14*
call-and-response: in "Batman Boogaloo," 189; in "La Pachanga," 134, *136*; *mambo* and, 73; in "Tu Tu Ta Ta," 179
call-and-response-styled improvised *inspiraciones*: of Egües, 103–4, 118; as element of New York *sabor*, 5; of Lozano, 89; of Zervigón, 117, 118, 224
callejero style, 83–84, 89, 90, 95, 106, 118, 213, 225–26, 234
Calloway, Cab, 6
Calzado, Pedro Manuel, 146
Calzado, Rudy, 85, 146, 147, 207
Cámara brothers, 41, 43
campesina feel, 109–10, 111, 113, 238, 258n25
Canoura, Joe: in Charanga Moderna, 207; flute improvisations of, 210, 213, *214–16*, 217, 226, *227*, 228, 267n15
Caravana Club (New York), 31, 32, 33, 36, *36*, 37, 139, 143, 147, 150. *See also* Bronx Casino
Carp, David, 47
Casa Blanca Club (New York), xvii, 33–34
Casa Galicia (New York), 34
Casa Latina (New York), *xiv*
Casa Latina nightclub (Leeds, England), xiii, 246n2
cascara, *14*, 104, 106, 107
Casino de La Playa (Havana), 10, 55
Castillo, Pito, 29
Castro, George, 151, 170, 263n6; biographical information on, 264n15; flute improvisations of, 83, 95, 148, 165, 172, 174–76, *175*, 178, 179–82, *180–81*, 187, 222, 227, 228, 264n16; high dynamic of playing, 181–82; in Valdés's *charanga*, 263–64n13
Catskills resorts, 48, 52, 55, 71, 77, 147, 250n49, 258n24
Chachachá: 1950s popularity of, xv, 78; African American dislike of, 49–50; *charanga* influences on, 22; dance step for, 133; elements in *mambo*, 74; López's recordings of, 79, 113–14; "Mack is Back" arrangement, 151, *153*, 153–54; New York dislike of, 108, 117; Orquesta Sublime's performances of, 126; at Palladium, 46; pattern, 115–16, *141*, 142; pedal figure in, 60; performances by different band types, 254n22; popularity among Jewish audiences, 258n24; revitalization of, xvii; rhythmic textures in, 253n4

Index

"Chanchullo" (López), 59
Charanga 76, 218
Charanga América, xvii, 192, 218, 230
Charanga del Norte, xiv–xv, 20, 209
charanga francesa. See *charanga orquesta*
Charanga La Duboney, 22, 36, 129, 144, 167, 207, 226, 251n30; Pacheco in, 150; Pacheco's arrangements for, 266n4; performance of "Bronx Pachanga," 132, 139–43, 157, *158–63*, 162–63, 165–66; performance of "Mack is Back," 151, *152–53*, 153–57, *155–56*, 165–66; personnel, 145; style elements in, *226*
Charanga La Moderna, 222
charanga mambo, 47, 56–61, 65, 73, 89, 157, 170, 179, 203
Charanga Moderna, 22, 146, 207–20, *226*; performance aesthetics, 208, 229
charanga orquestas: 1960s popularity in New York, 22, 45, 77–90, 144–68, 250n50; *charanga-conjunto* blends, 217–20, 222; conga tuning for, 132–33; Cuban vs. New York tempos, 113–14; current blends with *conjunto*, 217–18, 222; defined, 234; elements in US-based Latin dance bands, *226*; exclusion from mainstream Latin music history, 20–21, 33, 74–75; first New York, xv, 35–36, 71, 75, 77, 150, 252n42, 255–56n51, 256n1, 262n18, 263–64n13; instrumental roles in, 132–33; lack of female or African American musicians in, 147, 231; Latin arrangers and, 207–8; led by Puerto Rican and Dominican musicians, 77–78; lineup for, 57, 127, 254n15; neo-traditional, 218–19; Palladium performances, 46; percussion sections, 15, 77–78; performance aesthetics of, 127–29, 132–33, 164–68; post-Revolution trajectories in Cuba, 259n43; precursor to, 57; preferred keys for, 264n23; racial demographics of Cuban emigrés, 268n5; rebranding as *pachanga* in 1960s New York, 125–43; rhythmic textures in, 253n4; shortage of violinists for, 219;

as term, 9; venues for, 32–53; violins in, 228; waning popularity of, 165. See also flute improvisations; *charanga*
Charanga Soleil, xiv, 218, *219*
charanga típica: in 1950s Cuba, 60; defined, 234; lineup and performance aesthetics, 9, 28; New York *sabor* in, 149; stylistic elements of *cubanía* improvisational style, 13, *14–15*, 15–16, *16–17*, 18–19; Zervigón on, 106
charangueao approach, 169, 172–88, 217, 222, 229
Charansalsa, 28–29, 218
"Charlas del Momento" (Orquesta Aragón), 258n18
Charles Fox's Charanga, 22
Chateau Madrid (New York), 33
Cheetah Club (New York), 193
Chez José (New York), 47
Chicago, Cuban music in, 78, 85, 145
Child, John, 47
China Doll (New York), 33
chromaticism, 85, 90; directional, 203
church dances in New York, 33, 48, 51, 52, 150
Church of the Lord Jesus Christ of the Apostolic Faith (New York), 40, *40*
cierres (or *efectos*): clave, 61, 65, *70*, 71, 89, 133, 148, 156, 157; defined, 235
cinquillo, *14*, 105, *105*, 148, 213, 235
Círculo Cubano (Miami social club), 7
City College of New York, 12
City Lore "Place Matters" project, 45
civicas. See social clubs, Cuban
civil rights movement, 7
clave: clave defined, 235; as unifying concept, 133, 221. See also *cierres* (or *efectos*)
clave feel, 61, 89, *227*; in Canoura's flute improvisations, 213; in Castro's flute improvisations, 181; *cubanía* and, 13, 18, 117, 225; as element of *sabor*, 4, 5, 13, *226*; in Pacheco's flute improvisations, 154–55; in Zervigón's flute improvisations, 105–6
Club Cubanacán (New York), 41

Club Cubano Interamericano (New York), 21, 29–30, 33; charanga orquesta performances at, xvii
Club La Conga (New York), 33. *See also* China Doll
Club London (New York), 33. *See also* China Doll
Coen, Augusto, 44
Colíndres, Roy, 146
Colón, Johnny, 190
Colón, Willie, 191
columbia, 248n11
Columbia Records, 77
Comité de la Fiesta de San Juan Bautista, 28
Como Me Gusta! (album), 93, 109, 117
comparsa, 127, 133, 135, 235
Concord Records, 176
Conga Club (New York), 71
conga dance, 135, 235
congas: *a caballo* pattern, 135, *135*, 139, 143, 233; in *charanga orquestas*, 132–33; in *danzón del nuevo ritmo*, 79; *marcha* pattern, 141, *141*; *merengue* pattern, 134, 134–35, *137*; solo part in "Olga Pachanga," 89, *89*
conjunto. See son conjunto
Conjunto Casino (Havana), 36, 141
Conjunto Kubavana (Havana), 141
Conjunto Libre, xvii, 22, 73, 123, 192; Zervigón's performances with, xvii
Connexión, 219
Conzo, Joe, 18–19, 37, 47, 94–95
Cooder, Ry, 12
Copacabana (New York), 33
Corea, Chick, 170
Coro: call-and-response, 103–4, 134, 155; half, 61, 69; non-Latin audiences and, 55, 57, 58
corrido, 235
Corso Club (New York), 47
Cotique Records, 190
cross-rhythm patterns. *See* "3 in a grid of 4"
Cruz, Celia, 29
Cruz, Gustavo, 230, 231

Cuba, Joe (pseud. of Gilbert Calderón), 190, 198, 200, 209, 266n26
Cuba, post-revolutionary, 208; emigrés from, xvii, 52, 77, 79, 92, 117, 124, 129, 130, 144, 247n11, 250n46, 259n41, 268n5; end of easy interchange between Cuba and US, 72; musical copyright issues, 166, 262n15; musical developments, 21, 167, 226, 247n37, 259n43
cubanía, xvii; arrangement aesthetics, 63–64; as emblematic of Latin identity, 1940s–1960s, 30; *monte adentro* and, 113; as performance aesthetic, 12–13, 77–78, 90, 178, 188, 209–10, 213, 220, 221–22, 226–27; *sabor* as related to, 94, 188, 229; stylistic features of, 13, *14–15*, 15–16, 18–19; in Zervigón's improvisational style, 109–10, 111–17
Cubanidad, 7–8
Cuban Jam Sessions, 147
Cuban Love Song (film), 44–45
Cuban musicians in New York, pre-Revolution, 10, 52, 55, 72, 74, 129. *See also specific names*
Cuban Revolution, 52, 79, 123–24, 125, 144, 166
Cubop, *172*, 173
Cuesta Abajo (film), 40
Cueva, Julio, 52, 55–56, 63, 254n13
Cugat, Xavier, 21, 44, 55, 64, 71, 253n9, 255n32
cultural appropriation, claims of, 166–68
Curbelo, José, 53, 64, 71, 207, 208, 220, 251n24

Daly, Antar, 146
dance classes, 51, 131
dance imperative as element of New York *sabor*, 4, 5, 170, 209, 223–25, 226
danzón: *charanga* improvisation elements from, 15, 18; critiques on history of, 131; defined, 236; early twentieth-century, 78, 111, 112–13, 225; *estudiantina* performances of, 254n22; importance of, 18, 106; López's innovations, 259n39;

López's performance of, 79–83; López's recordings of, 113–14
danzón baqueteo, 70, 104, *105*, 106
danzón-chá, 113, 116, 236
danzón cinquillo, 254n22
danzón del nuevo ritmo, 54, 60, 72, 73, 78, 84, 236
danzonete, 78
danzón-mambo, 53, 54, 89, 112–13, 151, 157; bass line, 57, 58–59; defined, 236
danzón otra, 14, 70, *70*, 213
danzón solo, 104, *105*
Dario, Vicente, 109
Dave Clark Five, 193
Davidson, Eduardo, "La Pachanga," 125, 126–27, 129–32, 133–37, *134–38*, 139, 141–42
Davies, Rick, 21
Delabart, Francisco, 19–20
de la Hoya, Oscar, 71
"Descarga 69" (Orquesta Nuevo Ritmo), 256n2
descarga jam sessions, 37, 54–55, 95, 101, 139, 144, 147, 157, 163, 198, 230, 236
descargar, 236
descending chromatic line, 57, 60, 63, 86, *89*
diablitos, 73, 237
diablo. See *mambo diablo* sections
diana, 18
Díaz, José Antonio, 19
Díaz Ayala, Cristóbal, 71, 256n9
"Dile a Catalina," 225
disco, 167
Dominican musicians, 8, 149–51. See also specific names
Dominican Republic, 149–50
Dreamland Dancing Academy (New York), 46
Dudley, Anna Carol, 3–4
"Dulce Cha Cha Cha" (Barretto), 267n19

Early Rhythms (album), 169
East Harlem Mack Morris Theater, 32
efectos, 18, 133, 237. See also *cierres* (or *efectos*), clave

Egües, Eduardo, xv, 15, 92, 246n10
Egües, Richard: Afro-Cuban heritage of, 268n5; author's studies with, xiv, xv, 113; *cubanía* of, 12, 95; flute improvisations of, xiv, xv, 19, 20, 83, 84, 92, 103–4, 108, 116, 118, 148, 163, 164, 210, 226, 258n18; on *guajira*-style playing, 258n25; orchestration of Davidson's "La Pachanga," 125
"El Agua de Clavelito" (Orquesta Aragón), 85
"El Baile Suavito" (Gómez), 201
"El Bantu" (Barretto), 60
El Billar de Los Músicos (New York), 31
"El Bodeguero" (Pacheco), 108, 169
El Caborrojeño (New York), xvii, 27, 31, 33, 37, *38*, 39
El Campoamor (New York), 31, 32, 33, 35, 40, *40*–41
"El Cartero" (Orquesta Sublime), 126
El Cerromar (New York), 37
El Club Cubanacán (New York), 256n1
El Club Cubano Inter-Americano (New York social club), 7
El Convento de Belen, 135
El Corso (New York), 34, 190
"El Cumbanchero" (Hernández), 49
Elegua, 237
"El Gallo Canta," 225
El Gran Combo, 146
"El Güiro de Macorina" (Pacheco), 261n13, 266n4
El Hipocampo (New York), 34
Ellington, Duke, 41, 74
"El Manicero" (Simons), 44–45, 173, 225
El Morocco (New York), 37, *38*
"El Peletero" (Orquesta Sublime), 126
"El Pito" (Flores), 200
"El Reloj de Pastora" (Rodríguez), 61, *62*, 63
"El Ritmo Caliente" (La Perfecta), *172*–74, 173–76, *175*; Castro's improvisation, 174–76, *175*, 178, 179–82, *180–81*
"El Watusi" (Barretto), 60, 190, 193, 194–95, *195*, 209, 267n12

embalao approach, 144, 145, 148, 157, 163, 166, 167, 217, 222, 226, 227, 227–29
encirclement of melody notes, 116
"Esa Es La del Solar" (Barretto), xiv
escalera, 77, 198, *199*, 237. See also *mecha*
"Espiritu Burlón" (Orquesta Aragón), 265n20
estilo blanco, 64, 237
estilo negro, 64, 132, 237
Estrellas Cubanas, 92, 93, 116
estudiantinas, 237, 254n22
"Estuve Pensando" (Palmieri), 144–45
Everybody Salsa (album), xiv

Fajardo, José, 53; "Batman Boogaloo," 193, 201, 202, 203, *204–5*, 206; *callejero* style of, 83–84, 90, 95, 106, 116, 117–18, 213, 225–26; career of, 84, 90, 250n50; *cubanía* of, 12, 221; *danzó*'s influence on, 106; emigration from Cuba, 77, 92, 250n46; flute improvisations of, xiv, xv, 15, 19, 20, 83, 84, 92, 95, 103, 108, 148, 163, 164, 180, 203, *204–5*, 206, 227, 228; influence on salsa, 47; repertoire of, 78, 84; *sabor* as understood by, 4; work in Cuba, 78
Fajardo's Boogaloo (album), 201
Fajardo y sus Estrellas, 21, 22, 92; 1950s performances in New York, 75, 129, 147; Armenteros in, 16, 75; popularization of *charanga*, 10, 77; precursors of, 22; recording of Davidson's "La Pachanga," 125, 126–27; revitalization of *chachachá* by, xvii; style elements in, *226*; success of, 78, 84, 247n11; Waldorf Astoria performance, 84, 247n11
Fania All Stars, 7, 37, 74, 147
Fania Records, 7, 20, 37, 128, 147, 150, 191, 217, 218, 219, 224
"Fatima's Dance" (Kern), 187
Ferraris, Adalgiso, 266n33
"Fever" (Lee), 198
Fiesta de San Juan Bautista (New York), *27, 28, 28*–29
Figueroa, Frank, 39, 40

five-key wooden flute (*flauto de cinco llaves*), 90, 237–38, 267n15; *altissimo* notes on, 95, *101*, 101–2, *102*, 103, 118; of Belisario López, xv; Canoura's performances on, 267n15; Castro's performances on, 172; de Jesus's performances on, 29; as emblematic of *cubanía*, 21; sound of, 217; Zervigón's performances on, 172, 174, 175, 176, *177–78*, 178–79
flauta de cinco llaves. See five-key wooden flute
florear improvisational approach, 15, 16, 18, 79–83, 226–27, *227*, 238
Floredita (New York), 219
Flores, Aurora, 208, 217
Flores, Juan, 22, 40, 45, 126–27, 149, 164, 169, 190, 191, 192–93, 200, 206, 223
Flores, Luis "Maquina," 52
Flores, Marcial, 40–41
flute improvisations, *charanga*: *altissimo* notes and high-register playing, 95, *101*, 101–2, *102*, 103, 108, 118, 180; Arcaño's style, 113, 162; broader stylistic issues and, 21; Canoura's style, 210, 213, *214–16*, 217, 226, 227, 228, 267n15; Castro's style, 83, 148, 151, 165, 172, 187, 222, 227, 228, 264n16; continued use in big bands, 74; differences between *cubano* and New York aesthetics, 228; Egües's style, xiv, xv, 19, 20, 83, 84, 92, 93, 103–4, 108, 116, 148, 157, 162, 163, 164, 210, 226, 258n18; extended techniques, 182, 187; Fajardo's style, xiv, xv, 15, 19, 20, 83, 84, 92, 93, 95, 103, 108, 116, 148, 163, 164, 180, 203, *204–5*, 206, 225–26, 227, 228; *florear* approach, 15, 16, 79–83, 238; Fundora's style, xiv; Guerrero's style, 116; high dynamic of, 118, 123, 267n22; links with trumpet style, 15–16, 18; López's style, 79–83, *80–81*, 93–94, 227, 228, 259n41; Lozano's style, 85–86, *87–88*, 89, 116, 176, 227, 228, 229; Ortiz's style, *57, 58*, 157; Pacheco's style, 83, 147–48, 150–51, 154–57, 165–66, 174, 227, 228; Sánchez's style, 151, 157, *158–63*, 162–63, 164, 165–66, 227,

228; stylistic features of *cubanía* in, 13, 14–15, 15–16, 18–19; Valentín's style, 172, 182, *183–86*, *187*, 187–88, 210, 222, 226, 227, 228, 229; "whistleblowers," 148, 156, 228; Zervigón's style, 89, 92–93, 95, *96–100*, 101–8, *107–8*, 110–12, *114–15*, 119–22, 123, 172, 176, *177–78*, 178–79, 180, 187–88, 222, 227, 228, 229, 259n41
flutes. *See* Boehm-system metal flute; five-key wooden flute (*flauto de cinco llaves*)
flutter-tonguing, 85, 86, 89, 103, 108, 118, 179, 180, 182, 187
folklórico, 238
Fundora Dina, Melquiades, xiv, 126, *126*, 133, 259n39
funk, 167
Fusion Latina radio show, 230

gallego, 44, 49, 238
Garcia, David, 7, 20–21, 39, 45, 46, 47, 48, 54, 63, 64, 73, 164, 253n4
Gardel, Carlos, 40
Gema record label, 30
generation, questioning concept of, 52
"Gígue (Bach Goes Bata)" (La Perfecta II), 176
Gillespie, Dizzy, 20, 141, 201; "Manteca," 200, 208; "Salt Peanuts," 173
Glimcher, Arne, 47
Goldner, George, 190
Gómez, María Aurora, "El Baile Suavito," 201
González, Andy, 163–64, 165
González, Daniel, 145–46, 157, 207
González, Don Fernando, 217
González, Neno, 78
González, Rubén, 266n33
"Go West, Young Man," 255n32
"Goza la Vida" (Zervigón flute solo), 89, 93, 95, 117–18, *119–22*, 123–24
"Grandpa Semi-Tone Blues" (La Perfecta II), 176
Gran Plaza (New York), 208
grassroots community networks in New York, 8, 11–12, 29, 31–32, 46, 48, 75, 218, 222–23, 224. *See also* church dances; social clubs; *specific venues*
Grillo, Frank. *See* Machito
Grossman, Connie, 31, 75, *219*, 224, 225, 228–29, 231, 261n15
guaguancó, 238, 248n11
guajeo patterns in *charanga*, 56, 86, 115, 128, 132, 136, 137, 140, 142, 154, 210, 238; brass performances of, 169, 219
guajeos mambeados, 54, 56, 57–59, *59*, 61, 63, 65, *66–70*, 71, 73
guajira, 51; *charanga* improvisation elements from, 18; chord progression, 198; "country" feel of, 258n25; defined, 238; harmonic progression, 115, 116; at Palladium, 46; performances by different band types, 254n22; tempo of, 210; Zervigón's performance of, 108–10, *110–12*, 111–17, *112*, *114*, 115
guaracha, 54, 71, 194; *charanga* improvisation elements from, 15, 18; defined, 238–39; elements in *mambo*, 74; López's "Prepárate Para Bañarte," 79–83, *80–81*; *pachanga* and, 130, 135, 137, 139, 143; at Palladium, 46; Zervigón's "Goza La Vida!," 117–18, *119–22*, 123–24
Guerra, Marcelino, 21, 53, 208
Guerrero, Julio, 93, 116
Guevara, Che, 125
güira, 135, 239; *merengue* pattern, *134*
güiro, 239; *machete* pattern, 135, *138*, 141

habanera pattern, 14, 15, 70, *70*; defined, 239
Habell-Pallán, Eva, 3–4
hand claps, 198
Hansel y Raul, 230
Happy Hill Casino (New York), 34
Harlem Renaissance, 6
Harlow, Andy, 230
Harlow, Larry, 29, 150
"Hasta Decir No Mas" (Nuevo Ritmo), 86
Havana, Cuba: Anglophone audiences in, 55; bands in, 54–56, 63–67, 92; *charanga* scene in, 78, 167
Havana Madrid (New York), 55, 71

Havana San Juan (New York), 33
Heart of Cuba (album), 85, 86, 256n2
hembra, 64, 239. See also *estilo blanco*
Heredia, Robert, 230
Herencia Latina website, 75, 78
Hermann, Florian, 266n33
Hernández, Rafael, 4, 49
Hernández, René, 53, 55–56, 63, 74, 85, 154, 254n13, 260n13
Hernández, Victoria, 31
Herrero, Jesse, 217–18, 220, 229, 258n27
Herscher, David, 94, 257n1
Herscher, Ira, 94, 257n1
Hispanidad, 7–8
Hispano Dance Hall (New York), 32
Hostos Center for the Arts and Culture (South Bronx), 218
Hot Spot (Miami), 230
Hrebinka, Yevhen, 266n33
Hunts Point Palace (New York), 33, 36, 49
Hutchinson, Sydney, "Mambo on 2," 47
Hyman, Max, 252n59

"I Could Never Hurt You Girl" (Soul Drive), 190
ida y vuelta relationships of Cuban musicians, 71–72, 230–31
"I Dig Rock and Roll" (Orquesta Broadway), 189
"I Got Plenty o' Nuttin'" (Gershwin), 267n15
"I Like It Like That" (Rodríguez), 190, 193–95, *194*, 198, 200–201; correspondence with "El Watusi," 198; percussion *escalera*, 198, *199*; structure of, *196–97*
imitation as process, 163–65
improvisation, centrality in Latin music, 225–28; stylistic ingredients, 13, *14–15*, 15–16, *16–17*, 18. See also call-and-response-styled improvised *inspiraciones*; *charanga típica*; flute improvisations, *charanga*; specific performers
inspiraciones, call-and-response-styled. See call-and-response-styled improvised *inspiraciones*

inspiración (*guía*), 239
"Isora Club" (*danzón*), 111–13, 115, 117
Italian audiences for Latin music, 48–49
Iznaga, Alberto, 44, 251n24, 256n51

jazz: Barretto's performances, 208, 222; Canoura's incorporation of, 210, 213, 217, 227; elements in US-based Latin dance bands, 226, 227; fusion, 188; Lozano's incorporation of, 85, 89, 90, 227; *orquesta típicas* and early, 9, 57; Palmieri's incorporation of, 169, *172*, 178, 188, 222; Valentín's incorporation of, 187, 188, 227
Jesus, Joe de, 28, 29, 133, 219–20, 220, 224, 250n2
Jethro Tull, 182
Jewish audiences for Latin music, 48–49, 55, 258n24
jíbaro, 239
Jiménez, Nick, 200
Johnny Colón School of Music, 12
Johnny Pacheco y su Charanga, 22, 144, 167, 207, 226; personnel, 146
Johnson, J. J., 170
Jones, Will, 35
Joseph, Karen, 131, 188, 228, 229–30, 231, 261n15, 264n15; performances with La Perfecta II, 171, 175
Jovanovic, Lubomir "Lubi," xiii, 246n2
Juventud Cubano (Miami social club), 7

Kahn, Lewis, 29, 219, *219*, 230, 257n13
Kako, 147
Katherine Dunham Dance Company, 256n1, 256n51
Kaufman, Kevin, 47
Keepnews, Orrin, 207
Kennedy, John F., 84
Kenner, Chris, "I Like It Like That," 193
key slapping, 182, 187
King Solomon's Mines (film), 195
Kortwright, Wito, 209
Krupa, Gene, 64
Kubaney Records, 30, 201

La Conga Club (New York), 55
"Lamento Borincano" (Hernández), 49
La Moderna de Siempre (album), 217
Lang, Fritz, 35
La Orquesta Ideal, 92
"La Pachanga" (Davidson), 125, 126–27, 129–32, 133–37, 139, 141–42; bass line in, 135, *135*; *a caballo* pattern in, 135, *135*, 139; call-and-response in, 134, *136*; *coro*, 136–37, *137*; melody in, 135–36; *merengue* patterns in, 134, *134*, *137*; structure of, *138*; *tresillo* in, *137*; violin *montunos* in, *136*
"La Pachanga Se Baila Así" (Palmieri and Quijano), 128
La Perfecta, 22, 73, 146, 148, 151, 218, 229; flute improvisations, 172–76, 187; high dynamic level of, 170, *171*; lineup and performance aesthetics, 169–70, 208, 222, 247n27; style elements in, 226; Weinstein in, 262n10
La Perfecta II, 123, 170–71, 173; flute improvisations, 172, 174, 176–88; style elements in, 226
La Playa Sextet, 48, 191, 207
"La Rareza del Siglo" (Valdés's arrangement), 63
La Sabrosa, 22, 85, 146; style elements in, 226
La Sonora Matancera, 64
Latin Band, 29
Latinidad, 7–8
Latin music: 1940s–1960s Cuban dance music as emblematic, 30, 53, 164, 222–23; centrality of dance in, 223–25; contributions of African American players, 231; lack of female players, 147, 231, 261n15, 266n28; New York venues for, 32–53; pickup jobs for, 219; political struggles and Latin communities and, 248n9; standard historical narrative of, 74–75, 131, 222; as term, 5–6, 7. *See also specific genres*
Latin Soul Drives, 190
"La Ultima Noche" (Orquesta Casino de La Playa), 63

Lavoe, Hector, 29
Laws, Hubert, 228
"Lázaro y su Microfono" (La Perfecta II), 176, 264n20
"Leapfrog To Harlem" (La Perfecta II), 176
Lebrón Brothers, 190, 206
Lecuona, Ernesto, 45
Lee, Peggy, 198
Legaretta, Pupi, 85
Lehman College Center (Bronx), 218
Let's Dance the Charanga (album), 145
Levy, Morris, 201
llamada calls, 18, 123, 133, 189, 225, 239
Local 802 Musicians' Union, 44–45
"Lola Catula" (López flute solo), 82, 83
Long Beach, Long Island, 48, 52
"Lookie Lookie" (Ray), 190
López, Belisario, 4; career of, 79, 90, 256n9; *cubanía* in improvisations of, 221; *danzón* style and, 106, 259n39; emigration from Cuba, 77, 79, 92, 259n41; Fajardo and, 247n11; five-key flute played by, xv; flute improvisations of, 79–83, 93–94, 113–14, 227, 228, 259n41; lack of research on, 78; repertoire of, 78; Taft Hotel performances, 41
López, Cathy, 219
López, Israel, 45, 71; "Chanchullo," 59
López, Maño, 255n32
López, Orestes, 45, 71
López, René, 64, 124
López, Tommy, 146, 170, 171
López-Cano, Rubén, 71–72, 254n12
"Lo Que Traigo Es Sabroso II" (La Perfecta II), 176
Lorente, René, 230, *231*, 268n12
Los Cachimbos de Hoy, 28
Los Hermanos Castro, 71
Los Más Valientes, 218
Los Van Van, 167
Lou Pérez Orchestra, 22
Lozano, Danilo, 78, 256n2
Lozano, Rolando, 78; career of, 90; *cubanía* in improvisations of, 221; emigration from Cuba, 77; flute improvisations

of, 78, 84–90, 95, 116, 176, 227, 228, 229, 256n2; high dynamic of playing, 267n22; *sabor* as understood by, 4

Maceda, José, 37
machete pattern, 135, *138*, 141, 239
Machín, Antonio, 44–45
Machito, 208; Alpha Artists' representation of, 71, 207; dislike of "salsa" as term, 5; legacy of, 6–7; *mambo* band of, xv, 10, 22, 41, 45, 46, 55, 147; *rhumba* band influences on, 73–74; Valdés and, 141; venues for, 48–49
Machito and his Afro-Cubans, 6–7, 16, 56, 60, 74, 260n13; Fajardo in, 247n11; lineup of, 64; Palladium performances, 12; problems with racial discrimination by promoters, 268n5; Puente and, 71; Rodríguez in, 192
macho, 133, 240. See also *estilo negro*
"Mack is Back" (Charanga La Duboney), 145, 151, 153–57, 164; *coro* section, 151, *152*, 153, 155; flute improvisations, 154–57
Mahinka, Janice, 3, 247n3, 266n24
Malcomson, Hettie, 71, 131
Maldonado, Ray, 191
mamba, 230
mambear rhythmic approach, 227
mambitos, 14, 18, 70, *70*, 133, 180, 213, 240
mambo: African American preference for, 49–50; Afro-Cuban religious practices' influence on, 72, 73–74; augmented fourths as signifier of, 86, 89; central role in New York Latin music, 53; *charanga* improvisation elements from, 15; *charanga* influences on, 22, 65, 70–71, 222; *charanga*-style, 47, 56–61, 65, 73, 89, 157, 170, 179, 203; Cuban "Big Three" bands, 1940s, 54–56, 63–64; dance step for, 133; defined, 240; diverse musical elements in, 71–72; energy needed for, 51; inflated importance of in music histories, 20–21, 74–75; origins of, 53, 72; origin of term, 73; percussion patterns, 60, 61; performances by different band types, 254n22; polyrhythms in, 56, 57; riff-based sections, 73; *son conjunto*-style, 46, 61, 62, 63, 64, 65, 70, 73, 75, 166; swing band influences on, 64–65, 70–71, 74
"Mambo" (Antonio Arcaño y Sus Maravillas), 54, 56, 57–61, *58–60*, 63, 82, 154, 157
mambo bands, New York: 1950s, xv, 11, 21–22, 45, 64–72, 147; based in educational institutions, 12; critiques on history of, 131; current groups, 218–19; elements in US-based Latin dance bands, 226; influences on, 46; Jewish and Italian audiences for, 48–49; legacy, 219; orchestration of, 56; Palladium performances, 45–53; resurgence of, 11–12; trombones in, 28
mambo batiri, 74, 240
mambo caén, 74, 240
mambo diablo sections, 47, 53, 54, 61, 62, 63, 64, 72, 73; defined, 236
"Mambo Gozón" (Puente), 59, 65, *66–70*, 70
"Mambo Inspiracíon" (Orquesta Aragón), 85
Mambo Kings, The (film), 47–48
Mambo Legends, 11, 218–19
"Mambo Sensacional" (Orquesta Aragón), 85
Mamoncillo Festival (New York area), xiv–xv, *xvi*, xvii, 29, 224, 246n9
"Mandinga" (González), 266n33
Mangual, José Luis, 29
Mangual, Luis, Jr., 29
Manhattan Center (New York), 33, 35
Mann, Herbie, 228, 264n29
"Manteca" (Gillespie), 200, 208
Manuel, Peter, 225
Maraca Valle y Otra Vision, xiii
marcha, 133, 240
Marín, Orlando, 49
Marrero, Nicky, 132
Martínez, Cuco, 86
Martínez, Elena, 31–33, 37, 46, 47, 48, 164
Martínez Baro, Sara, 21

mecha, 77, 77–78; defined, 77, 241
Melodías del 40, 54
"Mentiras Criollas" (Orquesta Aragón), 85
merengue, 8, 133–39, *134*, 241
Metropolis (film), 35
Miami: Cuban exiles' preference for, 51; *sabor* of, 230; social clubs in, 7, 22
Mil Díez radio station (Havana), 54
Miller, Sue, *xiii*
Mirabal, Nancy Raquel, 52
mixolydian harmony, 57, 180
modal jazz, 59–60
moña, 170, *173*, 174, 178, 179, 182, 222, 241
Mondejar, Ninon, 85
monte adentro, 113, 258n25
Monte Carlo/Havana San Juan (New York), 39–40, 92, 144
montuno section, 54–55, 58, 65, 72, 108–9, 201, *202*, 241
Moore, Robin, 72
Morales, Ed, 32, 36
Morales, Esy, 4, 228, 230
Morales, Noro, 4, 21, 64, 207, 230, 251n24; Alpha Artists' promotion of, 71; *mambo* band of, 147; Puente and, 71
mordents, *14*, 15, 112, 182, 213, 225
Moré, Benny, 45, 63
Mount Morris Theater (New York), 40
movement in sixths, *15*
movement in thirds, *15*
Muñoz, Rafael, 145–46, 157
Murphy, Chris "Chico Malo," xiii
Murray, Arthur, 131, 143, 260–61n13
música folklórico, 9, 248n21
música tradicional, 9

New York City, New York. See *sabor*, New York; *specific venues, musicians, and groups*
Norman, Abraham, 109, 257n1
"No Sé Que Siento" (Nuevo Ritmo), 86
nuevo ritmo, 83, 146, 241. See also *danzón del nuevo ritmo*
Nuevo Tumbao, 169
"Nunca" (Orquesta Aragón), 85

Nuyorican musicians, 241. See also Puerto Rican/Nuyorican musicians; *specific names*

octave leaps, *14*, 86, 89, 103, *103*, 112, 118, 180, 210, 213
"Ojos Negros," 266n33
"Olga Pachanga" (Santamaría), xiv; Lozano flute solo, 86, *88*, 89, *89*
Oliveros, Joaquín, 113, 258n16, 258n25
Oller, Gabriel, 31
Omar, Fredy, 210
"One Hand One Heart" (Palmieri arrangement of), 145
On Fire Again/Encendido Otra Vez (album), 210
Opera House Hotel (New York), 36, 37
ophicleide, 242
Oquendo, Manny, 133, 146, 170, 171; influences on, 21, 47; Orquesta/Conjunto Libre leadership, xvii, 22, 73; timbale playing, 74; Zervigón and, 75, 123
Orange, Joe, 264n26
Orquesta Almendra, 10
Orquesta América, 60, 85, 146
Orquesta Antonio María Romeu, 20
Orquesta Aragón, 21, 47, 78; 1950s performances in New York, 75, 129, 147; Bacallao as dancer for, 130; *chachachás* performed by, 60; Egües in, 258n18; "El Baile Suavito" performed by, 201; Fajardo and, 250n50; lineup and performance aesthetics of, 9; Lorente in, 230; Lozano in, 85, 89; popularization of *charanga*, 10, 77; as premier popular 1950s Cuban dance band, 92, 260n5, 268n5; radio broadcasts of, 246n7; revitalization of *chachachá* by, xvii; *típico* sound of, 31
Orquesta Belisario López, 22
Orquesta Broadway, 22, *91*, 218; Alpha Artists' representation of, 71, 207; author's performances with, xiv–xv; *bugalú* performances, 189; fiftieth anniversary concert, 92, *123*; founding

of, 92; lineup of, 219, 257n1, 257n13; multiethnic makeup of, 94, 116, 117; Palladium performances, 34, 50–51; performance aesthetics of, 9, 227; precursors of, 144; repertoire of, 108–9; Rodríguez in, 132, 169, 192, 257n13; *sello* of, 222; style elements in, 226; Zervigón on, 91; Zervigón's leadership of, xvii, 22, 33, 123–24; Zervigón's performances with, 92–124, 229

Orquesta Casino de La Playa, 63, 71, 263n6

Orquesta Cubaney, 63

Orquesta Havana Riverside, 71

Orquesta Ideal, 116

Orquesta Jorrín, 146

Orquesta Libre, 133

Orquesta Novel, 22

Orquesta Nuevo Ritmo de Cuba, 22, 78, 85–86, 145, 250n50, 256n2

Orquesta Riverside, 71

Orquesta Santa Cecilia, 149

Orquesta Sensación, 230

Orquesta Sublime, 47, 125–26; performance of "La Pachanga," 133–39

Orquesta Tata Pereira, 10

orquesta típica: as charanga orquestas precursor, 57, 225; Cuban nineteenth-century, 9; defined, 242

Ortíz, Eulogio, 157; flute improvisations of, 57, 58

Ortíz, Fernando, 248n21

"Oye Como Va" (Puente), 59, 200, 267n12

"Oyeme Mulata" (Pacheco), 266n4

Pabón, Tony, 193, 198

pachanga, 78; charanga influences on, 22; connotation as "party," 126–27; dance step for, 127, 128–30, 131, 133, 143, 260–61n13; defined, 242; looseness of term, 127, 133; López's recordings of, 79, 83, 90; Lozano's performances of, 85; origins of term, 125–27; Palladium performances of, 49; rebranding of *charanga* as in 1960s New York, 125–43; Zervigón on, 129–30

Pachanga (album), 128

Pachanga at the Caravana Club (album), 142–43, 146, 157

Pachangas Vol. 1 (album), 83

Pachanga with Barretto/Barretto Para Bailar (album), 207

Pacheco, Johnny, 74, 217, 251n30; Alegre All Stars and, 147; as arranger, 266n4; career of, 36; *charanga orquesta* of, xv, 22, 36–37, 78, 125, 128–31, 144, 146, 150, 167, 208, 222; *conjuntos* of, 150; earlier career of, 52; Fajardo and, 247n11; family background of, 149–50, 262n16; Fania All Stars and, 7; flute improvisations of, 83, 144, 145, 150–51, 154–57, 165–66, 174, 227, 228; influences on, 21, 47, 221–22; on lack of *charanga* violinists, 219; Nuevo Tumbao leadership, 169; *pachanga* dance step, 127, 128–30, 131, 133, 260–61n13; Palmieri and, 40, 144–45, 147, 150; performance aesthetic, 147–51, 164–65, 167–68, 228, 229; reputation of, 148–49; role in development of Latin music, 150–51; Triton Club performances, 49; in Valdés's *charanga*, 252n42, 262n18, 263–64n13

Pa' Fricarse los Pollos (Pérez album), 39

Pagani, Federico, 8, 127

Palau Brothers' Cuban Orchestra, 45

Palladium, The (film), 47–48

Palladium Ballroom (New York), 27, 33; audience demographics, 48–49; *charanga orquesta* performances at, xvii, 77, 84, 125, 147, 247n11; closing of, 50; daily differences in audience and repertoire, 50–51; dance classes at, 51; *estilo blanco* and, 64; film depictions of, 47–48; historical prominence of, 46–53; importance in Cuban dance music, 12; Latin music nights at, 252n59; loss of liquor license, 45, 50; *mambo* big bands at, 29, 45–53, 54, 64–72, 150, 208; other styles performed at, 46; payment of musicians, 50; racial inclusiveness and, 8; *sabor* in performances at, 18–19

Palm Gardens (New York), 193, 201, 206
Palmieri, Charlie, 8; Alegre All Stars and, 147; Alpha Artists' promotion of, 71; Barretto and, 208; Castillo and, 29; Charanga La Duboney leadership, 36, 129, 132, 139, 142–43, 144, 145–46, 150, 157, 162–63, 165–66, 167, 207, 251n30, 266n4; *charanga orquesta* of, 22, 36–37, 50, 78, 85, 125, 144–46; childhood of, 31; influences on, 21, 47, 221–22; "La Pachanga Se Baila Así," 128; Orquesta Nuevo Ritmo's influence on, 85; Pacheco and, 40, 144–45, 147, 150; Pacheco's arrangements for, 266n4; in Palladium *mambo* band, 75; performance aesthetic, 164–65, 167–68; performance of "Tiene Sabor," 3; performances with brother, 171; piano soloing style, 229; recordings at the Caravana Club, 37; *sabor* as understood by, 5
Palmieri, Eddie, 20, 48–49, 145; Barretto and, 208; "Bilongo," 15–16, *16–17*, 18; *bugalú* recorded by, 191, 203; childhood of, 31; on *conjunto* formation, 263n6; current performances, 218; early career, 171; influences on, 21, 47; La Perfecta leadership, 22, 73, 146, 169–88, 208, 217, 218, 222, 247n27; musicianship of, 171–72; in Palladium *mambo* band, 75; performance aesthetics, 221–22, 227; performances in England, xiii; piano soloing style, 229; preference for live recordings, 264n20; *sabor* as understood by, 5; Triton Club performances, 49; Zervigón and, xvii, 75, 123
Palomo, John, 145, 146, 262n5
Palo Monte, 7, 72, 242
Pan-African movement, 6–7, 248n9, 265n3
Panart Records, 30, 84, 125, 134, 147, 251n30
Pancho el Bravo y sus Candelas de Tira Tira, 92
Paraíso (album), 93
Parker, Charlie, 208
Park Palace (New York), 41

Park Plaza (New York), 20, 27, 33, 41, 46, 47, 52, 64, 255n31
pedal bass pattern, 58–59, 65
Peguero Vega, Gabriel Eladio. *See* Yayo el Indio
Pellot, Hector, 146
percussion section: in *charanga orquestas*, 15, 77–78, 141, 227; in *mambo* big bands, 57, 61, 65
Pereira, Tata, 19, 55, 249n23
Pérez, David A., 10–11, 12, 18–19, 31–32, 37, 47, 51, *51*, 94–95, 145, 157, 162, 167, 249n38, 255n51
Pérez, Lou, 33; *charanga orquestas* of, 22, 39, 92
Pérez, Victor David, 146
"Pete's Boogaloo" (Pabón), 198
Pete Terrace and his Orchestra, 22
piano *montuno*, 57, 59, 115, 151, 153, 173, *173*, 174–75, 210, 241
Piantini, Carlos, 146
Piñeiro, Ignacio, 3, 247n1
plena, 51, 242
ponce break, *14*, 156, 213
pool halls in New York, 31
Portuondo, Omara, 3
Powell, Josephine, 255n32
Pozo, Chano, 20
Prado, Pérez: descending mambo line of, 60, 63; Hernández and, 254n13; as major figure in *mambo* evolution, 71, 72; *mambo* arrangements, 55, 56, 57, 63, 64, 74, 154, 253n9; *mambo* band of, 45, 61, 73
pregón, 179, 242
"Pregón de la Montaña" (López flute solo), 259n41
"Prepárate Para Bañarte" (López flute solo), 79–83, *80–81*
Prueba Mi Sazón (album), 79, 80, 259n41
Puchito record label, 30
Puente, Tito, xviii, 8; Alpha Artists' representation of, 71, 207; approach to Cuban music performance, 94–95; Berdeguer influenced by, 190; *chachachás* of, 60; *charanga* influences on, 95; childhood

of, 31; as dancer, 65; de Jesus and, 29; dislike of "salsa" as term, 5; earlier career of, 52; ensemble lineup, 65; Fajardo and, 247n11; influences on, 221–22; as major figure in *mambo* evolution, 71; *mambo* arrangements, 64; *mambo* band of, xv, 10, 22, 29, 41, 45, 46, 64, 147, 150; "Mambo Gozón," 59; "Oye Como Va," 59, 200, 267n12; Pacheco and, 150; Palladium performances, 12, 64, 208; Park Plaza performances, 64; problems with racial discrimination by promoters, 268n5; *rhumba* band influences on, 73–74; *sabor* as understood by, 5; timbales placement of, 64–65; Valdés and, 141; venues for, 48–49
Puerto Rican audiences for Cuban music, 49, 51, 165
Puerto Rican/Nuyorican musicians: adoption and adaptation of Cuban music, 28, 31; *bugalú* and, 190–206; *conjuntos* and *charangas* of, 150; identity affirmation in music, 167; migration patterns in New York, 32; Pacheco's influence on, 151; preference for term "Afro-Cuban," 5–6; repertoire mix of, 8; respect for *cubanía*, 13, 223; *sabor* as understood by, 4–5. *See also specific names*
Pupy y su Charanga, 217

"Que Maravilloso" (Santamaría), xiv; Lozano flute solo, 86, 87
Quijano, Joe, 29; "La Pachanga Se Baila Así," 128
"Quinta Guajira" (Zervigón flute solo), 93, 95, 109–10, *110–12*, 111–17, *112*, *114*, *115*
Quintana, Ismael, 170
quotations, melodic, 12, 18, 111, 173, 187, 203, 213, 225–26, 266n33, 267n15

racial discrimination at venues, 7–8, 39, 44
Rafael Seijo y su Orquesta, 22
Ramírez, Louie, 208, 266n4
Ramos, Tito, 265n11
Ray, Ricardo, 190, 191, 209

Ray Barretto Charanga Moderna (album), 194
RCA Victor, 10, 30, 77, 79, 260n5
Reina, Felix, 92
Rendón, Victor, 12, 219
rhumba, 230, 251n24; as broad term, 127–28, 248n11, 255n47; critiques on history of, 131; defined, 243; differentiated from *rumba*, 248n11; orchestras, 1920s–1940s, 21, 34, 45, 64, 73–74, 147; at Palladium, 46
rising chromatic line, 86, 176
rising phrases from a 5th degree axis note, 14
Ritmo Caliente (album), 176
"Ritmo d'Azucar" (Orquesta Aragón), 85
Ritmo de Pollos (album), 84
Rivera, Chollo, 190
Rivera, Eddie, 29
Rivera, Hector, 162, 207, 208
Rivera, Manny, 74, 132, 133, 190, 218, 229, 261n20
Riverside Records, 207, 209, 218
Roberts, John Storm, 22, 45, 47, 149, 164, 166, 167, 191
Robinson, John Henry, III, 29, 231, 232
Rodrígues, José, 170, 171
Rodríguez, Arsenio, 174; Afro-Cuban heritage of, 7; Barretto and, 208; Conjunto de Estrellas leadership, 46; "El Reloj de Pastora," 61, *62*, *63*; influence on salsa, 47; innovations of, 74; as major figure in *mambo* evolution, 71; *rhumba* band influences on, 73–74; *son conjunto* of, 9–10, 39, 45, 53, 61, 63; Zervigón and, 92. *See also* Arsenio Rodríguez y su Conjunto
Rodríguez, José, 145, 146
Rodríguez, Manny, 193
Rodríguez, Pellín, 85, 146
Rodríguez, Pete "El Conde," 189, 190, 192, 209; "I Like It Like That" arrangement, 193–95, *196–97*, 198, *199*, 200–201
Rodríguez, Roberto, 132, 147, 169, 170, 227, 257n13

Rodríguez, Tito, 207, 230; Alpha Artists' representation of, 71, 207; *cubanía* of, 266n1; Fajardo and, 247n11; *mambo* band of, xv, 10, 22, 29, 41, 45, 46, 64, 147; Palladium performances, 12; Palmieri and, 171
Rodríguez, Willie, 12, 13, 166–67, 192, *192*, 206, 223
Rogers, Barry, 146, 147, 169, 170, 171, 263n6, 263n10
Rojas, Tony, 265n11
Rolón, Catalino, 50
Romero, Elliot, 146, 207
Romero, Helio, 257n1
Romeu, Antonio María, 78, 113
Rondón, César Miguel, 252n59
Roseland Ballroom (New York), 33, 44–45, 131
Rosendo Ruiz Jr. and his Latino Charanga, 22
rubatiando improvisational approach, 16, 18, 83, 113
rubato, 18, 81–82, 90, 111–12
Rubio, Carlos, 109, 132, 222
rumba, 243; Afro-Cuban as applied to, 7, 248n9, 265n3; connotation as "party," 126, 127, 248n11, 255n47; as Cuban style, 127, 248n11, 255n47; differentiated from rhumba, 248n11. *See also* rhumba

sabor, New York, xvii, 103, 220; "big city drive," 149, 150, 168, 226, 249n38; compared with *sabor cubano*, 4, 18–22, 94, 167; connotations for Puerto Ricans and Nuyoricans, 4–5; in context of Nuyorican and Dominican interpretations of Cuban *charanga*, 145; cross-fertilization and creative borrowings, 31, 74–75, 116–17, 153–54, 164, 165–68, 188, 209–10, 217, 223, 226–27, 229–30; *cubanía* and, 94, 225, 226–27, 229; defined, 243; in different instrumentation formats, 20; elements in improvisational style, 227; elements in US-based Latin dance bands, 5, 226; energy in, 116, 117, 144, 150–51, 157, 166–67, 175, 222; flute style and, 148; multiethnic mix of musicians and, 13, 29, 49, 221–22; place and community in, 31–32
sabor cubano, xvii, 90, 220; compared with New York *sabor*, 4, 18–22, 94, 167; concept of, 3–4; elements in improvisational style, 227; in flute improvisations, 187–88; nostalgia and, 117; signification to Cuban musicians, 4
Sabroso! (album), 85, 86
Sacasas, Anselmo, 10, 53, 55, 71, 72, 251n24
Salazar, Max, 4, 39–40, 44, 45, 47, 85, 127, 191, 201, 255n51, 257n13
Salsa: criticism of, 223; debates about term, 5, 7, 127–28; defined, 243; histories of, 32, 131; horn section of, 219–20; *mambo* as precursor of, 47; Pacheco's rebranding of Cuban dance music as, 149; *timba*, 28–29
salsa dura, 47, 243
salsa monga. *See salsa romántica*
salsa romántica, 243–44
"Salt Peanuts" (Gillespie), 173
Sanabria, Bobby, 12, 219
Sanabria, Juancito, 71
Sánchez, Armando, 85
Sánchez, Rod Lewis (or Luís), 141, 145, 151, 207; flute improvisations of, 157, *158–63*, *162–63*, 164, 165–66, 227, 228
Sánchez-Coll, Israel, 3–4, 47, 78, 256n9
Santamaría, Mongo, xv, 36, 52; Fajardo and, 247n11; La Sabrosa leadership, 22, 85, 86, 146; Lozano and, 78; in Palladium *mambo* band, 75, 208; songs of, xiv; in Valdés's *charanga*, 264n13
Santana, 60
Santería, 7, 72, 244
Santiago, Al, 37, 127, 128–29, 139, 144–45, 147, 148, 193, 220, 251n30
saxophone sections in *mambo* big bands, 56, 57, 63, 65, 73
"Seis Perlas Cubanas" (Orquesta Sublime), 126

sello, 208, 217, 222, 226, 227–28, 232, 244, 258n23; of Zervigón, 92, 94, 108, 124
sextuplets, 15, *15*, 103
Show Boat (Kern musical), 187
Sierra Maestra, xiii
Sigler, Vicente, 21, 43–44
"Silencio" (Hernández), 49
Silva, José "Chombo," 85, 86, 146, 147, 207
Simons, Moisés, 173
Singer, Roberta, 9, 31–33, 37, 46, 47, 48, 164
Sissle, Noble, 6
Smith, Mauricio, Jr., 230
Smith, Mauricio, Sr., 74, 230
Socarrás, Alberto, xv, 10, 21, 40–41, 44, 75, 77, 129, 251n24, 256n1
social clubs, Cuban, 147, 235; in Miami, 7, 22; in New York, 7, 10–12, 20–21, 22, 29–30, 46, 224; role in popularity of *charanga*, 77. *See also specific clubs*
Son 14, xiii
son-chá, 133, *135*, 139, 201
son clave, 63, 73, 106
son conjunto: 1960s popularity in New York, 45; bongos in, 28; *bugalú* and, 192; *charanga* improvisation elements from, 15, 18; current blends with *charanga*, 217–20, 222; defined, 235; elements in US-based Latin dance bands, *226*, 227; exclusion from mainstream Latin music history, 74–75; flute's role in, 147–48; lineup for, 244, 254n15, 263n6; *mambo* big bands influenced by, 70, 73; *mambo diablo* of, 61, 62, 63, 64; melo-rhythm patterns in, 73; Pacheco and, 166; at Palladium, 46; Palmieri's La Perfecta and, 169; performance aesthetics, 227; rhythmic textures in, 253n4; *sonora* differentiated from, 249n42; *timbale* placement, 65; timbales in, 263n2; *típico* term and, 10
Son del Monte, 218, 222
sonero, 244
son montuno, 111, *112*, 130, 153–54, 254n22; Afro-Cuban influences on, 72, 73;

charanga improvisation elements from, 15; defined, 244; *diablo*-styled, 47, 54–55, 61, *62*, 63; Orquesta Broadway's performances of, 91; at Palladium, 46
sonora, 21, 244, 249n42, 263n2
Sonora Matancera, 21, 31, 249n42
SonSublime, 31, 74, 132, 217–18, 220, 229
soul: elements in *bugalú*, 189–90, 192–94, 198, 201, 203, 206, 208, 210; elements in US-based Latin dance bands, *226*, 227; Latin, 190, 193, 198, 203–6, 265n2
South Bronx, New York, 31, 32, 33, 34, 47, 52, 130, 147–51, 164, 218. *See also specific venues and musicians*
Soyer, David, 146, 262n6
Spanish Harlem, New York, 31, 32, 47, 52. *See also specific venues and musicians*
Spanish Harlem Orchestra, 11, 219
Spooner Theater (New York), 35, 36
Suárez, Gil, 94, 109, 258n27
suavecito (smoothness), 210, 217, *226*, 229
Sublette, Ned, 56, 65, 73, 254n12
Sublime, 217
"Sugar's Delight" (Canoura flute improvisation), 267n15
swing bands, 56–57, 61, 64–65, 70–71, 74

Taft Hotel (New York), 31, 33, 41, 42, 43
Tagg, Philip, 116
Tamayo, Polo, 258n16
tambora, 134, 135, 244
tango, 14
Tara Ballroom. *See* Caravana Club
Tatay's Spanish Music Center (New York), 31
taxonomies of Latin music, 5–7
Teatro Puerto Rico (New York), 33
Terrace, Pete, 171, 207
tessitura, one-octave, *15*, 16, 89, 154, 156, 173, 225, 227
"Te Traigo Guajira" (Charanga Moderna), 210, *211–12*; flute improvisation, 213, *214–16*, 217
"3 in a grid of 4," 14, 15, 89, 107, 112, 114, *114*, 116, 156, 162–63, *163*, 176, 210, 213, 225

Tico Records, 7, 207, 209
"Tiene Sabor" (Piñeiro and Valdés), 3, 247n1
timba, 29, 167, 250n2
timbales, 15, 64–65, 104, 106, 169, 263n2; merengue pattern, 134
Típica 73, 218
Típica Novel, 3, 132, 218, 230
Típica Tropical, 230
típico playing in New York, 8–10, 47, 154–57; aesthetic, 13, 230, 232; dance forms, 21; enduring importance of, 221; meaning of term, 9–10; migrant perspective on, 9; preference for term among musicians, 224–25
Tito and Tony, 190
Tito Puente and his Orchestra, 74; "Mambo Gozón," 65, 66–70, 70
Tito Rodríguez and his Orchestra, 22
Tjader, Cal, 78
TnT, The, 190
Tom and Jerry-o, 193
tongue clicks, 182
toques de santos, 72, 245
Torres, Nestor, 165, 188, 228, 230
Torres, Roberto, 92, 94, 257n1
Torres, Willie, 45, 146, 198, 200
tresillo pattern, 15, 136–37, 137
"Tres Lindas Cubanas" (Orquesta Aragón), 85, 113
triple-tonguing, 187
Triton Club (New York), 31, 33, 36–37, 49, 127, 129, 130, 143, 147, 150, 251n30
trombangas, 73, 170, 171, 188, 222, 227; defined, 245, 247n27; flute's role in, 148
Tropicana (Havana), 36
trumpet style, Cuban: Armenteros's improvisations, 15–16, 16–17, 18, 225, 228; diablo figures, 61, 62, 63, 170, 174; difficulty of finding New York conjunto performers, 170; trajectory of, 21
Tumbao label, 259n41
tumbao pattern, 15, 57, 58, 73, 115, 173, 245
turns, 14, 15, 81–82, 116, 182, 213, 225
"Tu Tu Ta Ta" (La Perfecta), 176, 179–82, 180, 181
"Tu Tu Ta Ta II" (La Perfecta II), 182, 183–86, 187, 187, 264n16
Tyner, McCoy, 170

Una Charanga con Algo Mas (album), 223
"Un Día Bonito" (Palmieri), 188
"Union Cienfuguera" (Orquesta Sublime), 126
United Artists label, 145
Uribe, Andres Campo, 145

Valdés, Alfredito, Sr., 39, 47, 92
Valdés, Alfredo, Jr., 207, 208
Valdés, Alicia, 261n15
Valdés, Carlos "Patato," 141, 146
Valdés, Gilberto, 21, 52, 129; charanga orquesta of, xv, 36, 71, 75, 77, 150, 252n42, 255–56n51, 256n1, 262n18, 263–64n13
Valdés, Joseíto, sabor of, 4, 248n7
Valdés, Marcelino, 147
Valdés, Miguelito, 8, 53, 55
Valdés, Ramón "Bebo," 56, 63, 72, 74, 254n12
Valdés, Rolando, 3, 247n1
Valdés, Vicentico, 171, 207
Valdespí, Armando, 78
Valente, José, 257n1
Valentín, Dave, flute improvisations of, 171, 172, 176, 182, 183–86, 187, 187–88, 210, 222, 226, 227, 228, 229
Valiente, Jessica, 261n15
Valladares, Dioris, 147
Vázquez Tuero, Miguel "El Moro," 19
Velazco, Enrique "Florecita," 16
Velazco, Victor, 146
Vélez, Enrique, 109, 257n1
Venegas, Victor, 85
vibrato, 111–12, 187
"Violin Pachanguero" (Charanga del Norte), xiv
violin section in charanga orquestas, 56, 57–58, 136, 165, 188, 210, 218, 219
Viva Palmieri (album), 145
Vivar, Alejandro "El Negro," 208
Viva Watusi! (album), 194, 267n15, 267n19

"Voy Hablar Con Tu Papa" (Orquesta Aragón), 113, 117

Waldorf Astoria (New York), 33, 35, 43, 43–44, *44*, 77, 84, 247n11
"Watusi '65" (Barretto), 194–95, *195*, 198
Watusi (dance), 194–95
Waxer, Lise, 55, 64
WBAI radio station, xiv, 220, 246n7
Weaver, Christian, 248n15; on Afro-Cuban music as term, 6
Webb, Art, 188, 217, 228, 231
Webb, Chick, 6
Weill, Kurt, "Mack the Knife," 145, 151
Weinstein, Mark, *48*, 48–49, 51, 52, 54–55, 141, 147–48, 151, 157, 162, 163, 168, 170, 171, 174, 175, 182, 191, 200, 225, 228, 262n10
Westbrook, Peter, 165
West Side Story (Bernstein musical), 145
White, Barry, 8
Winding, Kai, 170
Wonder, Stevie, 191

yambú, 248n11
Yayo el Indio, 147
Yerason, 218
"Yo Soy Manuel Garcia" (López flute solo), 259n41
Young Lords, the, 248n9, 265n3

Zanzibar (New York), 71
Zervigón, Eddy, *vii, xiii, xvii, 93, 118, 221*; on 1960s performances, 33–34; *altissimo* notes, 95, *101*, 101–2, *102*, 103, 118, 123–24, 180; author's performances with, xiv–xv; on Bronx Casino ownership, 37; on *bugalú*, 190; *callejero* style of, 213; on Canoura, 210; career of, xvii, 75, 92; on Club Cubano, 29–30; *cubanía* in improvisations of, 221; on difference between *orquestas* and *conjuntos*, 254n15; on difference in *conjunto* and *charanga* playing styles for percussionists, 132, 227; on difficulty of getting *charanga* sound right, 17; on El Caborrojeño house rules, 37, 39; emigration from Cuba, xvii, 92, 117, 124, 130; flute improvisations of, 89, 92–93, 94–124, 172, 174, 175, 176, *177–78*, 178–79, 180, 187–88, 222, 227, 228, 229, 259n41; flute studies in Cuba, 92; on growth of interest in *charanga* in New York, 250n50; on *guaracha* chord progression, 141; illness of, 257n13; on importance of *danzón*, 18; on importance of Palladium, 34; on interaction between dancers and improvisations, 224; on López, 79, 83; on Lozano, 85; on *mamoncillo*, 246n9; as meteorologist, 92; on Orquesta Broadway, 91; Orquesta Broadway leadership, xvii, 22, 33, 34, 50–51, 257n1; on *pachanga*, 129–30, 136; on Pacheco, 262n16; Palladium performances, 50–51; performance at Monte Carlo Club, 39; performance on faster tempos, 259n41; performances with La Perfecta II, 171; on Roseland, 44; on *sabor*, 3–4, 248n7; on slower-tempo styles, 108–9; style evolution of, 94; style influences on, 93–94, 95, 103–4, 116; on Taft Hotel performances, 41, 43
Zervigón, Kelvin, 92, 94, 257n1
Zervigón, Rudy, 92, 94, 109, 257n1

ABOUT THE AUTHOR

Credit: Simon Sid Bartle

Dr. Sue Miller is associate professor in music at Leeds Beckett University, UK. Her work combines historical musicology with music analysis, ethnomusicological method, performance, and practice-led research. Specializing in Cuban popular music and improvisation, her first book *Cuban Flute Style: Interpretation and Improvisation* (Scarecrow Press, 2014) explored the role of influence in the development of a style in the context of Cuban charanga performance. This, her second book, *Improvising Sabor: Cuban Dance Music in New York*, looks afresh at the history of Latin music in the USA with a focus on the 1960s New York Latin music scene and the seminal charanga groups within it. Sue studied Cuban flute improvisation with Richard Egües from Orquesta Aragón in Havana and is also a professional flute player and musical director of charanga orquesta Charanga del Norte, which she founded in 1998.

www.ingramcontent.com/pod-product-compliance
Lightning Source LLC
Chambersburg PA
CBHW030334240426
43661CB00052B/1628